GENDERING EUROPEAN WORKING TIME REGIMES

The standard approach to regulating working hours rests on gendered assumptions about how paid and unpaid work ought to be divided. In this book Ania Zbyszewska takes a feminist, socio-legal approach to evaluate whether the contemporary European working-time regimes can support a more equal sharing of this work. Focusing on the legal and political developments surrounding the EU Working Time Directive and the reforms of Poland's Labour Code, Zbyszewska reveals that both regimes retain this traditional gender bias and suggests the reasons for its persistence. She employs a wide range of data sources and uses the Polish case to assess the EU influence over national policy discourse and regulation, with the broader transnational policy trends also considered. This book combines legal analysis with social and political science concepts to highlight law's constitutive role and relational dimensions, and to reflect on the relationship between discursive politics and legal action.

ANIA ZBYSZEWSKA is a Postdoctoral Research Fellow at University of Warwick Law School.

Cambridge Studies In European Law And Policy

This series aims to produce original works which contain a critical analysis of the state of the law in particular areas of European law and set out different perspectives and suggestions for its future development. It also aims to encourage a range of work on law, legal institutions and legal phenomena in Europe, including 'law in context' approaches. The titles in the series will be of interest to academics; policy-makers; policy formers who are interested in European legal, commercial and political affairs; practising lawyers, including the judiciary; and advanced law students and researchers.

A complete list of books in the series is at the back of the book.

GENDERING EUROPEAN WORKING TIME REGIMES

The Working Time Directive and the Case of Poland

ANIA ZBYSZEWSKA

CAMBRIDGE
UNIVERSITY PRESS

CAMBRIDGE
UNIVERSITY PRESS

University Printing House, Cambridge CB2 8BS, United Kingdom

Cambridge University Press is part of the University of Cambridge.

It furthers the University's mission by disseminating knowledge in the pursuit of education, learning and research at the highest international levels of excellence.

www.cambridge.org
Information on this title: www.cambridge.org/9781107121256

First published 2016

A catalogue record for this publication is available from the British Library

ISBN 978-1-107-12125-6 Hardback

To my parents, Bogumiła and Bogdan;
and to their mothers.

CONTENTS

TABLES

ACKNOWLEDGEMENTS

This book began as a PhD thesis at the University of Victoria on Canada's west coast and was completed at the Universities of Warwick in the United Kingdom and Lund in Sweden. Working on it has been both humbling and enriching, and a happy reminder that I have much to be thankful for, as many people have helped me navigate this process.

My greatest thanks go to Judy Fudge, who supervised the doctoral research on which this book builds and whose intellectual challenges and superb mentorship I cherish. Similarly, I am grateful to Oliver Schmidtke and Amy Verdun, both at the University of Victoria, for their incisive comments and helping me venture into the world of EU studies. I also wish to thank Nicole Busby and the judges of the University Association for Contemporary European Studies (UACES) 2013 Best Thesis Prize, as well as the two anonymous reviewers, for their useful feedback and comments on the earlier thesis and parts of the book manuscript, respectively.

I would like to acknowledge my colleagues at the Universities of Victoria, Warwick, and Lund, particularly Kerry Sloan, Areli Valencia, Agnieszka Doll, Anastasia Tataryn, Sharifah Sekalala, and Niklas Selberg, for intellectual stimulation, friendship, and commenting on my work at various stages. I wish to acknowledge also my political science colleagues Jill Alwood, Heather MacRae, Roberta Guerrina, and Jemima Repo for engaging with my work in various forums. In Poland, invaluable assistance in accessing the field was provided by Marek Pliszkiewicz and Michał Seweryński. I am particularly indebted to members of the Institute of Labour and Social Studies in Warsaw: Helena Strzemińska, Lucyna Machol-Zajda, and Dorota Głogosz. Also, I owe thanks to Monika Latos-Milkowska from the University of Warsaw and Magdalena Barbara Rycak from the Łazarski University. The staff of the Feminoteka Foundation in Warsaw helped me gain access to the women's advocacy groups in Poland and to contact key informants. And to the individuals whom I interviewed for this study: thank you for your time and candid accounts.

I want to also express my thanks to the University of Victoria, the Interuniversity Research Centre on Globalization and Work (CRIMT), and the Social Sciences and Humanities Research Council of Canada (SSHRC) for the financial assistance required to carry out the research for this book, and to the Warwick Law School Research Fellowship for giving me a chance to finish writing it. I owe many thanks to my editors and the staff at Cambridge University Press.

Last but not least, I would like to express my gratitude – and love – to my family and to my dear friends for pulling me away from work when necessary, while giving me the courage to go on. To Marc-Oliver, who has seen me through much of this project and who inspires me daily: thank you for everything else.

ABBREVIATIONS

AWS	Electoral Action Solidarity
CBOS	Public Opinion Research Centre
CEEP	European Centre of Employers and Enterprises Providing Public Services
CJEU	Court of Justice of the European Union
EC	European Communities
ECE	Eastern Central Europe
ECJ	European Court of Justice
EEC	European Economic Community
EES	European Employment Strategy
EESC	European Economic and Social Committee
ESF	European Social Fund
EIRO	European Industrial Relations Observatory
EIRR	European Industrial Relations Review
EMU	Economic and Monetary Union
ECSC	European Coal and Steel Community
ETUC	European Trade Union Congress
EPSU	European Federation of Public Service Unions
EU	European Union
EWL	European Women's Lobby
GDP	Gross National Product
GIP	Central Workplace Inspection
GUS	Central Statistical Office
IMF	International Monetary Fund
KKP	Polish Employers' Confederation; Employers of Poland
LPR	League of Polish Families
NSZZ	Independent Self-Governing Trade Union
OECD	Organization for Economic Cooperation and Development
OPZZ	All-Poland Alliance of Trade Unions
PiS	Law and Justice
PIP	National Workplace Inspection
PKPP	Confederation of Polish Private Employers 'Lewiatan'
PLC	Polish Labour Code

PO	Civic Platform
PRL	People's Republic of Poland
PSL	Peasant Party
RP	Republic of Poland
SER	Standard Employment Relationship
SME	Small and Medium Enterprises
SLD	Left Democratic Alliance
UNICE	Union of Industrial and Employers' Confederations of Europe
UP	Union of Labour
UW	Freedom Union

Note: Some abbreviations and acronyms have been left in Polish, with the nomenclature being translated into English.

TABLE OF CASES

Joined Cases C 281, 283, 285, 287/85 *Germany, UK and Others* v. *Commission* [1987] ECR I-3203 64

Case C-84/94 *United Kingdom* v. *Council of the EU* [1996] ECR I-5755 98–99

Case C-303/98 *Sindicato de Medicos de Asistencia Publica* v. *Consellaria de Sanidad y Consumo de la Generalidad Valenciana* [2000] ECR I-7963 103–9, 111–16, 209n61

Case C-173/99 *The Queen* v. *Secretary of State for Trade and Industry* [2001] ECR I-4881 103n24

Case C-241/99 *Confederación Intersindical Galega (C.I.G)* v. *Servicio Galego de Saude* [2001] ECR I-5141 103n25

Case C-133/00 *J.R. Bowden e.a.* v. *Tuffnells Parcels Express Ltd.* [2001] ECR I-7051 103n24

Case C-151/02 *Landeshaupstadt Kiel* v. *Norbert Jaeger* [2003] ECR I-8415 103–9, 111–16, 209n61

Case C-438/05 *International Transport Workers Federation* v. *Viking Line ABP* [2007] ECR I-10806 71n36

Case C-341/05 *Laval un Partneri Ltd* v. *Svenska Byggnadsarbetareforbundet* [2007] ECR I-11845 71n36

Introduction

The struggle over a normal working day was one of the defining conflicts in the history of industrial capitalism. Fraught with tensions and controversies, not least because of the challenge it posed to the liberal ideology and the capitalist system of production, the progressive limitation of the daily and weekly work hours through statutory means and collective bargaining was a crucial working class victory. Its pinnacle, the quintessential standard of a 40-hour workweek and an 8-hour workday, constituted a key element of the normative employment pattern that became dominant after the Second World War in most industrialized economies. While itself based on a conviction that submission to paid work must not compromise a worker's right to leisure and rest, this model nonetheless took for granted other crucial tasks required for the maintenance of lives, such as the unpaid work of care traditionally carried out by women in households. In the process, this temporal pattern of work organization reified and stabilized a particular sexual division of labour based on various incarnations of the male breadwinner/female housewife household model.

Pervasive as it was, this model was not universal. In post-war Eastern Central Europe's (ECE) socialist planned economies, women's equal participation in paid work was expected by the egalitarian worker–state ideology and presumed by policy. In countries like Poland, for example, institutional arrangements were made to accommodate and support women's traditional domestic roles within very similar patterns of employment and regimes of working time as those existing in the West, with the result that women's full-time employment became the norm. The Polish model was distinct from its western counterparts in part because it was embedded in a universe of political discourse, which, in the context of broader debates about the total organization of work in society, and the more specific ones about organization of the daily and weekly work hours, was shaped by a different range of interests and receptive to different types of claims for recognition and redistribution.

Profound shifts in the global political economy, cycles of recession, developments in the organization and the technologies of production, and the changing composition of labour markets over the course of the late twentieth century have challenged the viability of traditional working-time regulation. Calls for modernization of this model came initially from neo-liberal reformers and business lobbies eager for more deregulated and flexible markets and more adaptive, efficient, and responsive enterprises. What is more, the work–family conflict that escalated with women's mass labour market entry in the West, and following structural adjustment and dismantling of supportive state institutions over the course of the transition to free markets in former socialist countries like Poland, exposed this traditional model also as a barrier to women's labour market participation.

In combination, these critical insights have had an important impact on the policy discourse. Yet, as I will show in this book by example of the working-time models adopted at the European Union (EU) level and in the transitioning, post-1989 Poland, the goals of efficient production and business-friendly flexibility have been ultimately far more influential on regulation than the aspiration to institute a more egalitarian and family-friendly working-time regime, particularly in the context of temporal norms that regulate standard, full-time work. This happened because the traditional, historic contestation between the protection of the workers' rights to health, safety, and leisure time on the one hand, and the employers' right to efficiently organize the productive process on the other, has shaped the European discursive universe in a way that consistently subordinated other interests and goals potentially served by regulation of work hours. Helping *all* workers achieve a better balance between employment and family responsibilities and facilitating a more equal sharing of paid and unpaid work between women and men are two such objectives that, although now recognized as important for equality and for Europe's long-term social and economic sustainability, have long played a secondary and, too often, an instrumental role within the discursive universe on working time.

Working Time as a Gendered Issue at the European Union Level

To be sure, EU policy has for some time acknowledged that working time is a gendered issue, already in the 1980s recognizing that more flexible and adaptable hours and patterns of work are necessary for reconciling work and family, and thus vital to women's labour market inclusion.

For this reason, as of the 1990s, the EU has actively promoted part-time and other non-standard forms of work, and forms of parental accommodation such as temporary child-care-related leaves. While these policies have been essential to helping women in western Europe access labour markets, they have been less successful in *removing* barriers to women's standard employment, or redressing persistent gender inequalities within the labour market and society. Indeed, there is ample evidence that accommodating women workers through non-standard forms of work has, at best, left unchallenged the traditional, even if modified gender-based divisions of labour within the workplace and the home, and at worst, reinforced these divisions (Fagan 1996, 2001; Rubery et al. 1998; European Commission 2014[1]).

The European Commission recently acknowledged this unsatisfactory outcome, as its 2010–2015 *Strategy for Equality between Men and Women*[2] pointed out that achieving equality demands active steps to help women and men more equally distribute unpaid work, insisting that working-time regulation can play a role in this endeavour. This is a significant development, and one that feminist activists and scholars have long lobbied for. However, translating this policy aspiration into practice depends on the willingness to fundamentally rethink the traditional organization of work and the core working-time standards, which, like the *Directive concerning certain aspects of the organization of working time* (the *Working Time Directive*),[3] the EU's first instrument addressing work hours, have been up to now only marginally concerned with balancing work and family, or fostering gender equality. This book is a critical and contextual study of how and why that very Directive came to be framed in a characteristically gender-neutral manner; it also assesses whether the EU working-time regime[4] for which the Directive sets a foundation can support the egalitarian goals the European Commission now deems essential to the longevity of the European project. While I argue that the

[1] Commission Staff Working Document. Report on Progress on Equality Between Women and Men in 2013. COM(2014) 224 final, SWD(2014) 141 final (14 April 2014). http://ec.europa.eu/justice/gender-equality/files/swd_2014_142_en.pdf

[2] Communication on the *Strategy for Equality between Men and Women 2010–2015* COM(2010) 491 final.

[3] *Council Directive 93/104 EC concerning certain aspects of the organization of working time*, [1993] O.J. L 307/18 (repealed); *Council Directive 2003/88 EC of the European Parliament and of the Council of 4 November 2003 concerning certain aspects of the organization of working time*, [2003] O.J. L 299/9.

[4] For the definition and elaboration on the concept working-time regime, see Chapter 1, Section 1.4.3.

'writing out' of gender from this key EU instrument was not inevitable, but rather a result of a particular universe of political discourse within which the original Directive developed, I also show that this universe has continued to prevent emergence of a more gender-sensitive approach to working-time standards. The constraining effect and the problematic nature of the EU discursive universe becomes even more evident in light of how the European debates on working time and the transposition of EU regulations and policy proscriptions have influenced the national working-time regime in Poland. What this latter case reveals is that the gendered assumptions underlying the *Working Time Directive*'s norms, particularly the forms of flexibility that it prescribes, have practical and problematic, if unintended, gender consequences.

This introductory chapter more precisely defines the aims and scope of this book and elaborates how the socio-legal, feminist approach adopted here helps to illuminate the role of law in the process of constituting and reproducing gender relations, as well as to assess and reveal the shortfalls between policy aspiration and practice. The first section specifies how the book goes about exposing the gendered character of standard working-time norms in general, and the gendered dynamic of the regulatory regimes established at the EU level and in Poland specifically. Next, I explain the book's approach, and how it contributes to academic debates on working-time regulation, Europeanization of policy debates and legislation in EU Member States, and the ongoing feminist scholarly project of *gendering* labour law norms (Conaghan and Rittich 2005; Fudge and Owens 2006; Busby and James 2011; Busby 2011; Fudge 2013; Conaghan 2014; Fudge and Grabham 2014). After a discussion on my sources of data, I conclude with a description of the chapters that follow.

Aims and Scope of the Study

As just suggested, my key aim in this book is to critically scrutinize the working-time model currently legislated and promoted at the EU level, and to evaluate whether it indeed can facilitate a more egalitarian redistribution of responsibilities for paid and unpaid work between women and men, which is a key condition of equality. For this purpose, I use a detailed case study of the *Working Time Directive* in order to trouble the EU's current approach, while the case of Poland is used to analyse how this approach interacts with and influences working-time regulation in particular Member States. Poland joined the EU in 2004, alongside several other ECE countries, following a 15-year process of transition from socialism to democracy and planned economy to one based on free-market principles. What in my view makes Poland especially interesting for this study is the fact that it has had an enduring and pervasive long-hours culture for women and men alike, which both were (more or less) able to manage during socialism because of significant state support. However, the fairly long statutory working-time norms and the widespread tendency to work long hours[5] have contributed to an elevated level of work–family conflict and significant labour market inequality following the drastic structural adjustment the country experienced after 1989 (Balcerzak-Paradowska 2008; Borkowska 2011). In the run-up to the 2004 'Eastern enlargement' of the EU it was generally presumed that the ECE candidates such as Poland offered their citizens inferior conditions of work and boasted less protective labour standards than those set in the Community's older members. Widespread fears about what the potential effects of this disparity in standards may have on work conditions in western and northern Europe aside, one might have expected that adoption of EU Directives and social policy will have some positive impact on legal developments in countries like Poland. In this book, I reflect on whether or not this has been indeed the case, and on what being 'brought up' to EU standards has meant for Poland, at least in the context of working-time regulation. Beyond working time, the Polish case also speaks to broader issues related to law's constitutive role in reproduction of gender relations, its role in political-economic change, and its potential to transform society.

As I will elaborate below, the book's perspective and approach are socio-legal, interdisciplinary, and feminist,[6] and this orientation very much informs the three-fold way in which I go about evaluating the EU working-time regime's compatibility with work–family reconciliation and a more egalitarian distribution of responsibilities for unpaid work. To begin, the book sets out to expose the gendered normative assumptions about model workers and their lives that have informed traditional

[5] Poland is among EU members with the longest work hours: see Eurostat database, Carley (2005), Parent-Thirion et al. (2007), and Czarnasty (2009).

[6] As legal scholar Jo Shaw explains (Shaw 2000: 411), a feminist perspective is characterized by a focus on gender as a central organizing principle of social life and 'a concern to challenge the perceived gender neutrality of legal theories, practices or institutions', so as to 'acknowledge[e] and destabiliz[e] the power of law, brin[g] politics of law to the fore, and address questions of reform'. In the words of another legal scholar, Nicole Busby, such a perspective is also guided by the 'commitment to include the hitherto excluded voices of women in accounts and explanations of the past with a view to advocating suitable political and legal reform for the future' (Busby 2011: 32).

Fordist-style forms of work organization and associated working-time standards. I achieve this by tracing the historical development trajectory of standard working-time norms to highlight how they have been institutionalized in Europe's industrialized economies, including in state-socialist planned economies. This historical exposition is augmented with a critical perspective grounded in the feminist conceptualization of the relationship between production and social reproduction; particularly the latter's subordination under conditions of capitalism. I do this in order to show that even those labour law norms that appear neutral have been based upon, and have been constitutive of, particular gender relations. This insight is then used as an interpretative frame in the rest of the book and to analyse critically whether the current EU and Polish working-time regimes and the legal norms within them perpetuate or challenge traditional assumptions about men and women's respective roles and about how labour should be divided within the family, labour markets, and society more broadly.

Second, I consider the development and the content of the EU working-time regime to reveal how and why this regime is gendered. As already noted, particular attention is given to the *Working Time Directive* as the Community's first binding instrument in this field. Interestingly, unlike subsequent EU instruments regulating other aspects of working time (i.e. part-time work) and temporal forms of parental accommodation (i.e. parental leave), the *Working Time Directive* was on its adoption framed neutrally or, in other words, in a manner not explicit about the fact that the norms it set and the forms of flexibility it prescribed may interfere with balancing paid work with family life or result in reifying a particular gender-based division of labour. On the contrary, the limits on work hours that the Directive imposed were subsequently deemed as supportive of work–family reconciliation, albeit this latter rationale was never translated into a binding provision. I explore the 'writing out' of gender from this instrument by critically examining the structural and discursive reasons for the asymmetric treatment of different aspects of working-time regulation at the EU level. A contextualized analysis of the European debates on regulation of work hours reveals the key rationales that have been invoked, when, and by whom, which helps to distil why some regulatory rationales dominated over others. I inevitably address a range of rationales not explicitly connected to gender equality because elucidating why some of them were deemed more appropriate in the context of working-time regulation suggests why and how gender concerns were marginalized, compartmentalized, or completely written out of the original Directive. This exposition also helps me explain why the Directive, or the proposals and discussions on its revision, have remained mostly neutrally framed, or, at the least, not explicitly gendered, despite the growing awareness of the link between working-time organization and gender inequality, a more gender-aware approach adopted in relation to other forms of temporal regulation, and the prominence of gender mainstreaming in the broader EU policy.

Examination of the Directive's practical influence on national working-time regulation and its gendered consequences is a third way in which I accomplish the aim of gendering the Community working-time regime. I consider this 'Europeanization' effect in the final part of the book, through the case of Poland's gradual adjustment of national working-time norms to those set at the Community level over the course of Poland's EU accession and in the first decade of its membership. This process is historically contextualized, as I also use the Polish case to examine the unique, if also gendered co-organization of production and social reproduction processes, its institutionalization under conditions of economic planning and state socialism before 1989, and the way in which both rendered Poland's socialist-era working-time regime distinctive yet still inherently unequal. In tracing that regime's subsequent development and change, I also reveal the gendered consequences of its disembedding from state support during political-economic transition. Because Poland's EU accession formed an integral part of that latter process (Shields 2008), the Polish case is also used here to examine the role of EU discourses and norms in shaping regulatory actions at the national level, including those related to labour law reform more broadly and working time reform specifically, as well as the promotion of gender equality. I show that the Polish reforms, the progressive deregulation and flexibilization of the country's working-time regime (and its effective weakening) in particular, were, apart from endogenous pressures and politics, also facilitated through the incremental adoption of the *Working Time Directive*'s minimum standards and exceptions, and propelled by the focus on growth, creation of conditions for a viable market economy, and unemployment reduction, all partially stemming from EU policy discourse and the conditionalities of EU accession. What I reveal is the paradoxical effect of Europeanization, wherein protective (but minimum) EU labour standards served to undermine the more extensive national ones in a context where the opposite may have been expected. I then comment on the gender consequences of the resulting working-time regime, as well as its long-term social and economic sustainability.

The Book's Approach and Contribution

Since its 1993 adoption, the *Working Time Directive* has been the subject of nearly constant political and legal controversy – the failure of its revision process in 2009 being one of the more recent sources of tension. Despite this, with the notable exception of the United Kingdom,[7] there has not been a lot of English language legal and socio-legal writing on this instrument. There are no monographs dedicated to this particular Directive, nor legal studies of the EU working-time regime as a whole.[8] Likewise, while the gendered aspects of working-time regulation have been well researched by scholars in a range of academic disciplines, particularly from the perspective of comparative institutionalism and social policy,[9] the EU working-time regime and its interaction with the supranational and domestic gender regimes has received only limited treatment in law literature. Crucially, most legal scholars writing on the gendered aspects of the regulation of work hours have tended to focus on non-standard patterns of work – part-time and temporary work – or special temporal accommodations that exist for the purpose of the provision of care, mostly of children, and facilitation of work and family reconciliation generally.[10] Important exceptions include Alain Supiot's report on the future of EU labour law, *Beyond Employment* (2001), and the work of Joanne Conaghan (2005, 2006). Both provided important early commentaries on the gendered legacy of standard norms inherent in the Directive and, in the case of Conaghan, on the gendered implications of the model the Directive promotes, particularly its model of flexibility, for working-time

[7] See Hepple (1990, 1997), Barnard (1997b), Barnard et al. (1997), Moffat (1997), Barnard et al. (2002, 2003a, 2003b), Kenner (2004), and Hardy (2006).

[8] However, EU working-time regulations have been considered in the context of broader comparative studies on working time: Messenger (2004), Boulin et al. (2006), and Lee et al. (2007).

[9] See, for example, research on working-time regimes (Figart and Mutari 1998, 2000, 2001; Rubery et al. 1998, 1999), working-time trends (Golden and Figart 2000; Rubery et al. 2006; Tang and Cousins 2005; Strzemińska 2008a, 2008b; Plantenga and Remery 2009), the working-time aspect of work–family reconciliation policies (Perrons 1999, 2000), and non-standard work (Fudge and Vosko 2001a; Fudge 2005; Vosko 2007, 2010; Fudge and Strauss 2013).

[10] Within the EU regulation and policy context, legal scholars have addressed specific aspects of working time and accommodation such as night work (Kilpatrick 1998), part-time work (Jeffery 1998), temporary work (Murray 1999), parental leave (McGlynn 2005, 2006), work–family reconciliation (McGlynn 2001; Rittich 2005; Conaghan 2006; Masselot and Caracciolo Di Torella 2010), and work–life balance (Grabham 2014).

regulation in the UK context.[11] Another notable exception is the 2010 volume by lawyers Annick Masselot and Eugenia Caracciolo Di Torella, *Reconciling Work and Family Life in EU Law and Policy*, which examines EU working-time regulations in tandem with leave provisions and care strategies as essential aspects of EU work–family reconciliation policies. However, given that book's broader focus, Masselot and Caracciolo Di Torella's treatment of the *Working Time Directive* is fairly limited, and the authors ultimately do not problematize the instrument's gender neutrality or examine its 'unintended' gender consequences.

The approach I adopt here is different because it builds on the premise that since the Directive is the foundation of the EU working-time regime, revealing its gendered assumptions and the inherent limitations of its approach is crucial to understanding the overall shape of that regime and its egalitarian potential or lack thereof. In this sense, the book takes up the challenge of gendering labour law norms that feminist labour lawyers have been urging for some time in response to the broader calls for this law's modernization, and which they have proposed to do by expanding and rethinking the scope of labour law beyond the territorial boundaries of the state, and by folding into its scope the unpaid care and other essential but undervalued work usually performed by women within families and communities (Conaghan and Rittich 2005; Fudge and Owens 2006; Busby 2011; Busby and James 2011; Fudge 2013; Conaghan 2014; Fudge and Grabham 2014). My study of the relationship between working-time standards and gender equality in the multilevel EU space, as conceptualized through the feminist lens of social reproduction, seeks to also contribute to this process of '(re)viewing' and '(re)considering' (Conaghan 2005: 19), or gendering, labour law and employment regulation, and moving gender analysis 'from the margin to the mainstream of labour law debate' (Conaghan and Rittich 2005: 2). Only in this manner can we embolden labour law to develop in a way that meaningfully responds to and supports the needs of a greater range of people and facilitates social justice.

Consistently with my socio-legal orientation and feminist commitments, this book combines a number of disciplinary perspectives and uses

[11] See also Fredman (2005) and Fudge (2005, 2008) for a similar articulation of this approach in context of the Canadian jurisdiction. See also McCann's (2005) discussion of the gendered assumptions underlying the European Court of Justice (ECJ) interpretation in on-call work cases; also discussed in Chapter 3 of this book.

a methodological 'tool-kit' that extends beyond traditional analysis of the law. A socio-legal approach analyses the nature, operation, and impact of law in the broader context. Beyond studying law as a self-referential system, socio-legal scholars are interested in its relationship to society and the state, and view it as a force constitutive of social relations.[12] As such, a socio-legal approach is particularly compatible with feminist legal scholarship, because the latter also seeks to destabilize the view of law as an autonomous, objective, and politically neutral structure (Lacey 1998: 186), and to expose the gendering process which underlies it and which law tends to reproduce (Shaw 2000). Examination of legal norms in their historical context to reveal how they reproduce inequality is one element of the particular approach I adopt here, and the book also blends detailed critical legal and policy analysis with examination of the structural and discursive context of their adoption, and attention to the role of key actors.

This contextualized, critical study of legal and policy developments is supported by an interdisciplinary conceptual framework, which, as I elaborate in Chapter 1, integrates theoretical insights from a range of non-legal literatures. The concepts I use to gender working-time regimes and assess their 'unintended' gender consequences are taken from, among others, feminist political economy (i.e. social reproduction, unpaid work), gender studies (i.e. gender, care), comparative social policy, and comparative institutionalism (i.e. gender regimes and contracts, and working-time regimes) literatures. Moreover, the book's key framing device – the universe of political discourse – which I use to highlight the dynamic manner in which ideational (discursive) and material (structural) forces interact with each other, and to emphasize the roles of various actors (interests) in the process of shaping policy and legal regulation, is derived from historical and sociological institutionalism literatures, mostly the work of a French sociologist Pierre Bourdieu and a Canadian political scientist, Jane Jenson. Likewise, in evaluating the degree to which EU discourses, policies and norms, and interests have interacted with and influenced those present in the Polish context, I draw on political

[12] Combining empirical and theoretical approaches, socio-legal scholarship is by nature inter-disciplinary, and studies of EU law are particularly well suited to such an approach. According to Francis Snyder (1987, cited in Shaw 1996: 234), EU law 'represents, more evidently perhaps than most other subjects an intricate web of politics, economics and law' and 'virtually calls out to be understood by means of a political economy of law or an inter-disciplinary, contextual or critical approach'. Likewise, 'the conceptualization of European labour law is . . . influenced by the interaction of law and context' (Bercusson 1995: 9).

science literature on Europeanization, particularly perspectives that combine rationalist and constructivist insights.[13]

My focus on Poland as an illustrative as well as a stand-alone case study is another distinctive aspect of this book, which enables me to contribute to a number of scholarly debates. The process of EU enlargement, its impact on, or consequences for, the European social model and national welfare states, and the effects of Europeanization, have been of interest and explored by a range of scholars, particularly in fields of political science and social policy. Labour lawyers have also examined the relationship between EU regulation and regulation in domestic contexts,[14] including in relation to particular aspects of working time,[15] while gender scholars have studied how the processes of accession and implementation of EU policies affect national gender relations.[16] Nonetheless, detailed investigations of more recent accession states are still rare in this literature, as most contributions take the form of edited collections with a wide range of country studies. And while such comparative perspectives are extremely rich, the individual cases within them often remain limited in terms of depth or longer-term, historical perspective. Combination of the single national case study approach with a detailed examination of the EU working-time regime makes this book distinctive yet complementary to the developing literature in a number of already noted fields. Such an approach allows a contextualized, thorough, and critical examination of how a particular country's regulatory regime interfaces with gender relations, while permitting an account that is attentive to the historical legacy of socialism and trajectory of Poland's political-economic transition. I present Poland's EU accession as a phase of the latter process, while law and policy – both national and supranational – are highlighted as key elements or drivers of continuity and change in Poland's approach to working-time regulation and gender equality. Given Poland's

[13] As I elaborate in Chapter 1, 'rationalist' approaches to Europeanization focus on more top-down cost-benefit analysis of adopting or disregarding EU rules, while the more bottom-up 'social constructivist' ones focus on the independent incentives of local actors to adopt EU rules (see Radaelli 2001; Schimmelfennig and Sedelmeier 2005b for a useful review). Although conceptually distinct these approaches are not mutually exclusive (Sedelmeier 2011).

[14] See, for example, Kenner (2003), Ashiagbor (2004), Ahlberg et al. (2008), Rönnmar (2008), Barnard (2012), and Syrpis and Novitz (2015), as well as various contributions in the *European Labour Law Journal* and *Industrial Law Journal*, among others.

[15] See Sciarra et al. (2004) for an excellent example.

[16] See, for example, Hervey and O'Keffe (1996), Beveridge and Velutti (2008), Locker and Prügl (2008), Roth (2008), Velluti (2010, 2014), and Bego (2015).

increasingly important role within the EU, a study that engages in a deeper, more contextualized understanding of these processes provides an important complementary counterpoint to the already existing literature on this topic.

Finally, echoing my earlier comments about research on the interface between working time and gender regimes, particularly by lawyers, it should be pointed out that many contributions that directly tackle the gender aspects of Europeanization also focus on policy areas that are already more explicitly gendered. Regulation of non-standard work and leaves, gender equality and work–family reconciliation policies, or the strategy of gender mainstreaming, have been the archetypal areas of feminist engagement, although the developing literature on unintended gender consequences of EU policies has certainly broadened the scope of gender research.[17] The present book provides a key contribution to this latter scholarship.

As I hope the forgoing discussion articulates, in examining the highly topical yet relatively underexplored issues surrounding the *Working Time Directive*'s gendered character, and thereby the gender consequences of standard working-time norms, from a distinctive socio-legal, interdisciplinary, and feminist perspective, the book hopes to engage with and contribute to a number of scholarly debates. While the book is mainly addressed to those interested in labour law and EU social and employment policy, I also wish to engage researchers in the law and society or the law and politics traditions and those interested in the processes of political-economic change or Europeanization. Quite obviously, given this book's feminist and interdisciplinary orientation, I seek to enter into a dialogue with other feminist lawyers, particularly, but not only, those interested in the interface between paid and unpaid work, as well as other researchers working in areas of feminist political economy, policy studies, gender and politics, or European and post-socialist women's studies. Finally, given that working time, and its relationship with work–family reconciliation or work–life balance, and gender equality, continue to be a matter of considerable policy importance given the ongoing dispute over how to regulate work hours, and, more generally, the demographic and care-related challenges faced by European countries, I hope the book will be of interest for policymakers.

[17] See the July–August 2013 special issue of *Women's Studies International Forum* on the 'Unintended Consequences of EU Policies'.

Sources of Data

The key sources of data used in the book are textual. They include various EU legal instruments, including the major Treaties, Directives (on working time, part-time work, parental leave), preparatory documents, Recommendations and drafts, and the framework agreements between social partners. In addition, I have consulted White and Green policy papers issued by the European Commission, other strategic documents including its *Roadmaps to Equality*, and the reports prepared by various groups of experts constituted by the Commission. Communications of the European Commission, the Council of the European Union, and the European Parliament pertinent to the *Working Time Directive* and its ongoing revisions were also analysed, as were the position papers and official consultation submissions of major social partner organizations, European Trade Union Congress (ETUC), BusinessEurope (formerly Union of Industrial and Employers' Confederations of Europe, UNICE), and European Centre of Employers and Enterprises Providing Public Services (CEEP). Finally, the European Commission's reports on Poland's progress during the process of accession were also reviewed.

In the Polish context, the key sources of evidence are the statutes amending the *Labour Code*, drafts of legislative bills and amendment proposals that were unsuccessful or subject to further amendments, published opinions of various parliamentary committees, the European Integration Committee and the Office of the President, and transcripts of pertinent parliamentary proceedings. In addition, reports of the National Workplace Inspection (Państwowa Inspekcja Pracy, PIP), and the published proposals of the Labour Law Reform Commission have also been reviewed. The book also draws on data from websites of the major organizations representing Polish enterprise and trade unions, as well as women's organizations (Foundation Feminoteka, Women's Rights Centre (Centrum Praw Kobiet), Karat Coalition), the survey reports of the Public Opinion Research Centre (CBOS), and the archives of two major Polish daily newspapers, *Gazeta Wyborcza* and *Rzeczpospolita*.

In addition, the portraits of the historic and contemporary working-time regimes in Poland have been supplemented with statistical data on working hours, men and women's employment rates, unemployment, and economic performance (among others). I have drawn on the statistical information gathered by the International Monetary Fund (IMF), Organization for Economic Cooperation and Development (OECD), Eurostat, and the Central Statistical Office of Poland (Główny Urząd Statystyczny, GUS), although mostly on secondary synthesis of the available statistics.

Uniquely, in addition to textual sources, the book also incorporates data from nineteen in-depth interviews conducted with key informants representing the main actors involved in policy and regulation of working time and the process of negotiations and revision of the *Working Time Directive* as well as its Polish transposition. I carried out these interviews in Brussels and Warsaw in the spring 2010, shortly after the prolonged and controversial revision negotiations that culminated in the collapse of the conciliation procedure and before the commencement of the fresh and currently ongoing review of the Directive. In Brussels, I interviewed three members of the European Commission, two members of the European Parliament, as well as representatives of the ETUC, the European Federation of Public Service Unions (EPSU) and BusinessEurope (formerly UNICE). In Warsaw, interviews were conducted with three officials from the Ministry of Labour and Social Policy, (two from the Labour Law Department and one from the Department of Family Policy), one member of Sejm (the Parliament's lower house) and a former Minister of Labour and Social Policy, representatives of two major Polish trade union confederations, the Independent Self-Governing Trade Union 'Solidarity' (Niezależny Samorządny Związek Zawadowy, NSZZ 'Solidarność') and the All-Poland Alliance of Trade Unions (Ogólnopolskie Związki Zawodowe, OPZZ), as well as representatives of two of the major national employers' organizations, the Confederation of Polish Private Employer's 'Lewiatan' (Lewiatan) and Employers of Poland (previously the Polish Employers' Confederation (Krajowa Konfederacja Pracodawców, KKP)). I also interviewed one former Polish Member of the European Parliament and representatives of two different women's advocacy groups. I use these interviews in a supplementary way. Specifically, the data derived from them helps me better illustrate and triangulate my findings on the rationales for regulatory action on working time, and particularly on the extent to which gender equality objectives were considered, which themselves stem from a careful critical analysis of the dominant discourses and legal regulations that forms the core of the book.

Book Organization and Chapter Summaries

Following this introduction are five substantive chapters and a conclusion. The first, conceptual chapter is followed by four detailed, contextualized studies of the EU (Chapters 2 and 3) and Polish working-time regimes (Chapters 4 and 5). The separate treatment of EU and Poland, and the division of each 'case' into two chapters reflects the aim of examining regulations within their discursive and political context and helps to deal with the substantial time period covered. However, as what is also examined here is the interaction between the two sites of regulation, the book also strives to weave together the EU and Polish cases by considering the supranational influence in the discussion of the national context, while the process of Eastern enlargement is noted as a factor in the analysis of the developments at the EU level. Both are also examined with the view to broader international and transnational developments, discourses, and influences.

The book's first substantive chapter is theoretical and its key task is to elaborate an interdisciplinary conceptual framework for thinking through the gendered politics of working-time regulation (and, to some extent, labour law and employment regulation more broadly) in multi-level contexts. This framework combines three complementary lenses – the universe of political discourse, multi-level regulation, and critical gender perspective grounded in the concept of social reproduction – which, respectively, help to capture (1) the complex and dynamic process by which legal norms and policies are made and remade, (2) the operation and interaction of these norms and policies (and discourses) at many levels, and (3) the gendered character and consequences of these norms. To elaborate, while the first of these lenses or framework components provides a distinctive approach that both appreciates and helps to systematically account for the complex relationships between the structural and the discursive forces and the roles of various, differently situated actors in the process of law and policy making, the second highlights the multi-scalar or multi-level nature of the regulatory space in which these processes and interactions take place. Finally, given this book's primary interest, another component of this chapter elaborates why and how a feminist perspective that centres on the relationship between production and social reproduction as a key site and source of gender inequality is useful, if not essential, to thinking about and rethinking labour law norms. Because the gender perspective adopted here builds on much western scholarship, and hence might invite a charge of its western bias, the discussion here also explains why this approach is appropriate in a post-socialist context and why a study of that very context helps to better illuminate the inherent gender bias and consequences of standard labour law norms.

In Chapter 2, I shift to examine the development of the Community-level discursive universe related to the use and regulation of working time. The chapter opens with a critical discussion of flexibility, with the view to clarify it and expose its political dimension. Flexibility is a dominant concept in contemporary labour regulation and in EU social, employment, and economic policies, yet its heterogeneity, its contradictory uses, and its political embeddedness in the discourse of deregulation are not always apparent in policy discussions. This treatment of flexibility relates to the second chapter's key aim, which is to contextualize EU working-time regulation (itself considered in more detail in Chapter 3) through mapping it against the evolving discursive universe that elevated it, as well as the shifts in institutional architecture of the EU that made it possible and gave it content. Thus, I begin this chapter by retracing changes in the Community's institutional architecture, allocation of power between the different EU bodies and actors, and the gradual expansion of EU regulatory competences over social policy, including regulation of employment and its temporal aspects. I complement this structural background with a detailed study of the distinct discourses related to hours of work regulation operating at the EU level to explain why the *Working Time Directive* constituted a watershed in EU regulation in this area, and why the subsequent instruments were rationalized so differently. Tracing the development of the Community discursive universe also makes apparent the rise of flexibility as the hegemonic discourse in the context of working time, and shows a gradual change in its deployment in the policy context: namely, a shift from flexibility as the key driver of economic efficiency and competitiveness towards flexibility as (also) the enabler of equal opportunities through facilitating women's employment activation and work–family reconciliation. In the last part of this chapter, I assess and evaluate the egalitarian potential of this policy shift by drawing on feminist critiques of gender mainstreaming.

Chapter 3 continues with the EU, but here I turn more directly to the analysis of specific working-time instruments, with the primary focus being the *Working Time Directive*. Drawing on the insights from Chapter 2, the Directive's development and revision are closely analysed, and the way in which the tensions between flexibility and security/health and safety rationales have shaped this particular instrument is illuminated, as is their continued impact on confining the Directive's scope despite the more recent broadening of the discourse on working time. While the historical rationales for hours of work regulation have always been related to protection of health and safety, this chapter shows that through the 1980s, the European Commission pursued a broader approach to working time; one that was more consistent with gender equality objectives. However, I also show that this approach was reframed in a more traditional manner following the broadening of the Community's competences in the field of health and safety, with the result of constricting the range of regulatory objectives this instrument could serve and leaving gender equality concerns out of the Directive's ambit. Subsequent efforts to incorporate the language and goals of work–family reconciliation and gender equality into the Directive's scope have not been successful, partly due to the legal constraints but also because they tended to be overshadowed by and subordinated to other concerns, mainly those related to the contentious derogations and exceptions from the Directive's norms, such as the controversial individual opt-out provision. In discussing what makes the *Working Time Directive*'s key norms and flexibility mechanisms problematic, I juxtapose its approach with that taken by the instruments regulating other aspects of working time in order to highlight the particular gender dynamic, or bias, of the EU working-time regime as a whole. This chapter's conclusion provides a transition into the discussion of Poland, which is divided between Chapters 4 and 5.

The historic developments in Poland's discursive universe and regulation of working time are the subject of Chapter 4, which opens with an overview and examination of the temporal norms enacted since the end of the Second World War. As the chapter points out, the Ministerial Acts, and later the *Labour Code* and subsidiary regulations enacted in People's Republic of Poland (People's Republic)[18] between 1945 and 1989 contained many provisions that were also found in western European countries. I elaborate the key distinctions of the Polish model related to the more limited role of collective bargaining in socialist enterprises and, crucially, to the fact that all adults, both women and men, were required to subject themselves to the pattern of work the Polish regime prescribed. I highlight both the political discourses rationalizing these norms and the institutional arrangements that during state socialism made possible the reconciliation of full engagement in paid work with the tasks of

[18] Officially, Poland changed its name from Republic of Poland (Rzeczpospolita Polska, or RP) to People's Republic of Poland (Polska Rzeczpospolita Ludowa, or PRL) in the *Constitution of the Polish People's Republic of 22 July 1952*, (1952) Journal of Laws, No. 33, item 232 [all statute names translated from Polish by author]. However, for my purposes here, I use the term 'People's Republic' to refer to the period after the Second World War and up to 1989, and 'Poland' in general reference to the country, and particularly to the post-1989 period.

social reproduction. Drawing on Polish and non-Polish studies on gender relations under socialism, I also examine the tension between the official discourse of egalitarianism and the latent inequality of Poland's pre-1989 working-time regime. The pervasive long-hours culture, insufficiency of state provision, as well as the country's cultural specificity and its unique gender contract, are identified as some factors explaining this inequality. In the second part of the chapter, I shift to examine the impact of Poland's political-economic transition and structural adjustment on the country's broader discursive universe, as well as organization of working time and related legal reforms. The chapter brings attention to the remarkable continuities – both discursive and regulatory (at least with respect to work hours) – despite the otherwise profound changes in the country's political economy and social relations. Finally, I consider the negative effects of the structural adjustment programme adopted by Poland in the early 1990s; particularly, I note the impact on workers' ability to balance long hours of work with care-giving obligations, and effects on labour market access, equality, and viability of Poland's social reproduction. I wrap up this chapter with a look at the key discourses of the transition era – neo-liberalism and social conservatism – which have been crucial in shaping Polish working-time and work–family reconciliation policies, respectively, and against which further changes in the Polish working-time regime will be assessed.

Chapter 5 picks up the narrative at the turn of the new millennium and carries it through its first decade. This period saw the most legislative activity on the working time front, partially due to Poland's impending EU accession and the requirement of adopting the *acquis communautaire*. Both the impact of EU discourses and EU policy and legal norms, as well as the more general impact of the accession conditionality, are explored with reference to the successive amendments of the *Labour Code*'s working-time rules. I examine the importance of the key discourses and objectives of flexibility and economic efficiency and, later, work–family reconciliation and gender equality – as articulated at the EU level – and their respective influence on Polish working-time regulation is assessed. At the same time, I also consider the importance of home-grown discourses and local pressures for more employer/business-friendly flexibility, and reflect on the extent to which the process of EU accession merely exacerbated existing tendencies and provided rationales for Polish lobbyists and politicians to push for a more flexible legal framework. Finally, I explore the 'promise' of the EU discourses and policies on work–family reconciliation and gender equality by reflecting on Polish *de facto* labour market realities, women's labour market positions, and the state of work–family reconciliation that average Poles are able to achieve.

In the concluding chapter, I take stock of the key findings and reflect on my research questions. The book's conclusions might inevitably be read as a critique of the *Working Time Directive*, and as such the book might invite a charge of undermining an important instrument that has a highly symbolic value as one of the milestones of 'Social Europe', particularly as its future is so uncertain at the time of writing. Yet maintaining *status quo* is rarely a good reason to shy away from critique. Indeed, the key premise of this book, in line with other feminist scholarship in labour and employment law and policy to which this book seeks to contribute, is that exposing the Directive's gender bias and the bias that is inherent in the EU's working-time approach or, indeed, in the standard approach to working-time regulation, is essential to the process of gendering, and improving, labour law norms. Without such critical perspectives, more adaptive working-time regimes and forms of workplace regulation that better respond to the living and working realities of women and men are unlikely to emerge. Nor can gender equality be achieved unless these regimes are truly egalitarian in that they encourage, enable, and support men in engaging in home-based unpaid care work alongside women. For that too, exposing and addressing the gender bias in the EU working-time approach is crucial. I conclude the book by emphasizing the political importance of lobbying for such a more adaptive and transformative approach to regulation of work hours.

1

Theorizing the Gendered Politics of Working-time Regulation in Multi-level Contexts

1.1 Introduction

In this chapter, I propose a conceptual framework for analysing the European Union (EU) and Polish working-time regimes and the regulations that comprise them from the perspective that is attentive to their multifaceted, relational, and embedded quality and their gendered character. A key point of departure is that such a study requires a broader conceptual toolkit than that offered by traditional legal analysis. While the latter is also crucial to this project, it alone cannot capture the way in which the law and policy or legislative processes are conceptualized here, or the types of legal norms and regulatory interactions that I examine; nor can orthodox legal analysis alone support the task of gendering labour law. For these reasons, the particular socio-legal approach I adopt draws on conceptual tools and insights from a range of disciplines, such as gender theory, feminist political economy, comparative institutionalism and policy studies, political science, labour law, and labour history. Here, I show how these various concepts assembled together form a theoretical lens through which regulatory choices and their gender consequences can be revealed, critically analysed, and assessed.

The chapter proceeds in three sections. I argue that the task of uncovering the shared meanings and normative assumptions underlying legal norms, and the law's constitutive role or transformative potential, requires that these norms be examined as embedded within a particular context, and with the view to the complex interactions and struggles that (re)produce them. Hence, in examining the EU and Polish working-time regimes – their emergence, institutionalization, and ways in which they have at once persisted and changed – I will be attentive to their political, discursive, and institutional context, and the roles of various actors involved in their development. In this chapter's first section I conceptualize these processes at the broadest level of abstraction by drawing on the concept of the 'universe of political discourse' developed in the work of Jane Jenson (1986, 1989) and Pierre Bourdieu (1991). This conceptualization of the political and policy-formation processes, with its focus on the role of social actors – their agency and its limits – in shaping dominant societal paradigms and, through them, the associated legal norms, will provide a continuous thread linking my analysis of the historic and contemporary working-time regimes operating at the EU and the national levels, as these are discussed in the book's subsequent chapters.

The second section shifts to consider the multi-level character of labour regulation and employment policy in EU context, capturing the dynamic nature of which also requires going beyond legal orthodoxy, and indeed, reaching beyond the EU space itself. As I explain, this is accomplished in two ways. First, I complement insights from EU (and broader) labour law scholarship, some of which is itself informed by other disciplinary perspectives, with key insights from political science studies on conditionality and Europeanization of national politics and policies. Second, in analysing how working-time regulation and gender equality in the EU and Polish contexts have been framed and how they influence each other, I also draw on the premise articulated by labour lawyers like Diamond Ashiagbor (2004) or Kerry Rittich (2002b, 2006a, 2010a), that to grasp these complex discursive and regulatory interactions we must also attend to the broader context of transnational governance within which national and supranational debates occur.

Finally, the third section, which comprises the most substantial portion of this chapter, explains and draws on the concepts of 'social reproduction', 'gender order', 'gender regime', and 'gender contact', 'working-time regime', and the 'standard employment relationship' (SER) to frame a gender-focused analysis of working-time standards and regulations based upon them. Building on and extending the work of several feminist legal scholars, the goal here is not only to unpack the gendered nature of labour and employment standards, including those governing working time, but also to provide the tools needed to analyse the contemporary working-time regimes from the perspective of equality and social and economic sustainability more broadly. In doing so, my work responds to the call for legal scholarship that genders the existing labour law standards, which, from a strategic perspective, constitutes an important step towards making the space for new visions of labour law to emerge (Conaghan 2005: 19) that better respond to the living and working realities of women and men.

1.2 Contextualizing Legal Norms in the Universe of Political Discourse

My focus in this book is on particular legal standards concerning working time: their operation, interaction, and impact. However, I am equally interested in the historicity of these standards, how they have evolved, changed, or persisted, and how they embody and help to reproduce particular gender relations or, alternatively, whether they can help to transform these relations by taking account of the differences between workers and responding to their varying needs. At a conceptual level, a very useful framework for capturing the relational and constitutive role of politics and law, and their transformative potential, is that offered by Jane Jenson (1986, 1989) in her work on political discourses and historic social policy developments. Particularly appealing is the manner in which Jenson conceptualizes the roles of social actors and their competing claims in shaping the political discourses and, in turn, the process of social policy (and law) formation. In this view, all norms and institutional arrangements emerge out of complex struggles over meaning, representation, power, and legitimacy in which social actors engage, with the context for these struggles being the 'universe of political discourse' (Jenson 1986, 1989), or the universe of thinkable political possibilities delineated by the 'political field' (Bourdieu 1991).

While both the social relations and the 'thinkable possibilities' are dynamic and always in the state of flux, they can nonetheless take on stabilized forms during certain historical periods and can be reproduced over time (Jenson 1986, 1989: 236). Jenson explains that such stabilization occurs when a compromise within the universe of political discourse renders an emergent 'societal paradigm', or a set of inter-connected premises or meaning systems, so widely shared by social actors that it becomes *hegemonic* (Jenson 1989: 238–239). However, since all struggles over meaning and representation are fraught with inequalities in access to power and influence over the discursive universe, those hegemonic paradigms necessarily subordinate or exclude some identities and alternative competing meanings that too are present within the universe of political discourse. This subordination occurs in part because participation in the political field or the political process requires knowledge (of this field), which, along with social position and access to resources, affects one's ability to participate and have their interests represented (Bourdieu 1991). Absent this knowledge, some meanings and interests get filtered out because the political field 'produces the effect of censorship by limiting the universe of political discourse, and thus of what is politically thinkable, to the finite space of discourses capable of being produced or reproduced within the limits of the political problematic' (Bourdieu 1991: 172).

As Jenson posits, however, the dynamism of the process of political participation means that opportunities do arise for the temporarily subordinated identities to extend their representational reach and strength. Such opportunities surface particularly during periods of 'crisis', which occur when the dominant or hegemonic paradigm's ability to absorb its internal contradictions becomes compromised. Moments of crisis, therefore, are the 'moments of efflorescence in the universe of political discourse'; they can lead to a shift in the hegemonic paradigm and enrich it with contributions from the actors who gained 'new representational strength' during crisis (Jenson 1989: 239).

The concept of the universe of political discourse, then, is useful for understanding the historical processes through which certain rationales, such as those that justify policy choices and legislative activities, become dominant or hegemonic, and why others remain subordinated. It is particularly compelling because without ignoring the role and materiality of institutional structures, norms, and legal rules, it attends to human agency by showing that these very structures (and social and legal norms) can be challenged and transformed given the right historical circumstances and strategic alliances. From this perspective, the key discourses on the role of law, organization of production activities, and regulation of working time that dominate the EU and Polish debates can be viewed as negotiated settlements that reflect historically and contextually specific power dynamics; dynamics which can nonetheless be destabilized over time. In the same way, the extent to which the EU and Polish discursive universes have recognized, represented, and have been open to claims for gender equality, a particular division of responsibilities for production and social reproduction (at the state, society, market, and family levels), or the need to better support women and men in balancing their participation in employment with unpaid family obligations, reflects such power dynamics, yet it too is subject to change.

Who are the actors most pertinent to shaping the working-time discourse? At the EU level, the discursive universe is first and foremost established by the Member States of the EU and the major EU institutions – the European Commission, the Council, the European Parliament, the European Council, and the Court of Justice of the European Union[1] –

[1] However, in this book, I will mostly use the term European Court of Justice (ECJ), because that was the name of the EU's highest court's prior to the coming into force of the Treaty of Lisbon on 1 December 2009, a period to which most of the book's content refers.

that are responsible for setting the EU agenda, proposing and overseeing EU law and policy, the legislative process, and the Treaty interpretation and application. The European 'social partners' are the second set of actors. At the EU level they consist of key organizations representing employers and business on the one hand (i.e. umbrella organizations such as BusinessEurope, formerly Union of Industrial and Employers' Confederations of Europe (UNICE), and the European Centre of Employers and Enterprises Providing Public Services (CEEP)), and the labour movement and employees on the other hand (i.e. European Trade Union Congress (ETUC), the European Federation of Public Sector Unions (EPSU), and others representing interests of organized labour). In addition to these more formal social partner organizations whose role in shaping the political discourse is particularly important in matters of employment and social policy, various lobby groups operating at the Community level (such as the European Women's Lobby (EWL)) may also be pertinent to shaping the discursive universe. Even when not officially consulted, these latter actors can have influence through issuing of opinions on EU policy and legislative initiatives and lobbying other 'friendly' actors who may have a more direct influence. Similarly, in the Polish national context, the state, different political factions, institutional entities (i.e. various Ministerial authorities and Reform Commissions), the national social partners acting through the Tripartite Commission (the cross-sectorial employers' organizations and trade unions), as well as other special interest groups (such as the business lobby and associated policy think-tanks, women's groups, and the Church), all coexist and interact within a shared discursive universe.

Given that the extent to which particular actors are able to exert influence over the discursive universe and influence concrete policies and institutional forms at either the domestic or supranational level varies over the course of time, the framework I adopt here seeks to capture major shifts in institutional architecture and political economy as significant historic moments during which shared or hegemonic meanings are disrupted and potentially renegotiated with concrete implications for institutions, legal rules, and social (gender) relations. I pay particular attention to key developments at the European level, the process of transition that began in Poland at the end of the 1980s, and the processes of further structural adjustment leading up to Poland's EU accession. As Chapter 2 elaborates, EU enlargement, successive constitutional amendments, and changes to the EU's institutional structures, voting rules, and legislative procedures, have led to two major and related shifts, both of which have shaped the

EU discursive universe. First, successive legal and institutional changes have precipitated the progressive expansion of the Community competences over various policy areas originally reserved for the Member States, thereby increasing supranational influence over the (increasing number of) national universes of political discourse (and action) in a growing number of fields, including that of working time. Second, the roles and relative influence of particular European institutions vis-à-vis each other have also changed. As will be discussed in more detail in Chapters 2 and 3, the influence of specific Member States within the Council, and later, the growing role of the European Parliament and the social partners have been crucial to the development trajectory of the Community working-time discourse and regime. Similarly, the path of the Polish political-economic transition, the associated process of institutional change or structural adjustment, and the process of EU accession have also had a significant impact on the power relations between different actors shaping the local discursive universe, privileging certain discourses on working time over others, and thus shaping the Polish working-time regime.

1.3 Political Discourses and Labour Law in Multi-level Contexts

While societal paradigms, with their complementary clusters of institutions, gender relations, norms, and legal rules are historically and contextually specific, the processes of globalization and regional integration, or 'transition', provide excellent case studies for examining the impact of supranational standards on domestic regulatory regimes. As these processes also occur in the sphere of discourse, they broaden and complicate the discursive universe or contribute to overlaps and interactions between multiple such universes operating at different levels. In political science, these types of interactions have been examined through various theories of European integration and Europeanization.[2] Comparative policy

[2] The process of European integration has been explained by various intergovernmental (Moravcsik 1993), neofunctionalist (Haas 1964), historical institutionalist (Pierson 1996), multilevel governance (MLG) theories (Hooghe and Marks 2001), and social constructivist theories (Kauppi 2003; Rosamond 2002), with the role that the law and the courts play explored by Burley and Mattli (1993), Mattli and Slaughter (1995, 1998), Garrett (1995), Alter (2000), Alter and Vargas (2000), Cichowski (2004), and Beach (2005). Also, rationalist and constructivist theories of Europeanization examine the impact of EU policies and institutions on domestic 'polities, politics, and policy' (see Radaelli 2001 and Schimmelfennig and Sedelmeier 2005a for a useful review), with recent literature on implementation combining both approaches (i.e. Falkner et al. 2005; Leiber 2005, 2007; Falkner et al. 2008; Trieb 2008; Toshkov 2008; Sedelmeier 2009 for implementation studies relating to

and institutionalism scholars, for example, have paid particular attention to the impact of EU integration and enlargement, focusing on the extent to which various policy fields and institutional clusters or regimes (be they welfare regimes, gender regimes, employment regimes, industrial relations systems) remain distinct or converge under the influence these processes engender.[3] Legal scholars also have been exploring these plural and multi-level governance dynamics. In labour law scholarship, interaction between different types of legal orders and regulations operating at many levels or scales has been long a source of investigation, most prominently addressed through legal pluralism and reflexive law theories,[4] with the relationship between the EU and domestic labour law regimes becoming one key area of interest.

In an early comment on the nature and content of EU labour law itself, Brian Bercusson (1995) suggested that this body of law is a symbiosis between national labour law systems and the law of the Community, with actors at the supranational, national, and subnational levels having important roles in its development, and the Community and national laws mutually influencing each other. Studies on this co-constitutive influence have become even more prevalent and pressing with employment policy and regulation becoming one of the most established areas of EU social policy following the adoption of the European Employment Strategy (EES) in 1997 (Kenner 2003; Ashiagbor 2004; Barnard 2006). As the corpus, reach, and mechanisms of EU labour law and employment policy expanded, more recent studies have examined supranational impact on domestic labour law regimes, seeking to understand whether the pressures exerted by EU norms, policy discourses, or by EU institutions have contributed to Europeanization or some degree of convergence between these national regimes, and some ultimately pointing a more complex reflexive relationship, or dialogue between the two levels.[5]

Already complex, the EU-Member State interaction is further complicated by the fact that it itself takes place within a broader discursive and regulatory context that also encompasses the trans- and international

social *acquis* and ECE Member States). On Europeanization of gender equality policies see Sedelmeier (2009), Kantola (2010), and Velluti (2014).

[3] See, for instance: Rubery et al. (1998, 1999), Esping-Andersen (1992, 1999), Perrons (1999), Figart and Mutari (2000, 2001), Walby (2004), and Lewis et al. (2008).

[4] On legal pluralism, in relation to European labour law, see Flanders (1968), Fox and Flanders (1969), Fox (1973), Clegg (1975) (as cited in La Faro 2000). On reflexive law or reflexivity, see Teubner (1983) and Rogowski (2013).

[5] See Bercusson (1995), Deakin and Reed (2000), La Faro (2000), Kilpatrick (1998, 2003, 2012), Ashiagbor (2004), Sciarra et al. (2004), Rogowski and Deakin (2011), and Rogowski (2013).

levels. While the norms and discourses promoted by the International Labour Organization (ILO) are one such source of influence that labour lawyers have long engaged with, some have been increasingly attuned to the influence of international economic and financial institutions. Thus, in her study of the EES, for instance, Ashiagbor (2004) goes beyond the relationship between the EU and domestic labour-law regimes (the Netherlands and the UK), to also take account of other policy-shaping transnational institutions. Specifically, she argues that developments in EU policy and governance have been strongly influenced by the Organization for Economic Cooperation and Development (OECD), through OECD's promotion over the last several decades of regulatory discourses based on neo-liberal principles and neoclassical economics. Rittich (2002a, 2002b, 2006a, 2006b, 2010a), another legal scholar, develops a similar argument in relation to key financial institutions such as the World Bank, the influence of which, she maintains, contributed to the progressive re-regulation of labour markets through reforms of national labour and employment regimes. These institutions, Rittich argues, exert their influence by mainstreaming the discourse of deregulation, or the consensus around non-desirability of 'excessive' labour laws and institutions of the labour market, and thus shaping how particular labour market concerns are being presented and solved (i.e. in terms of competitiveness, efficiency, and flexibility) at more localized levels of governance. Rittich has also shown the distinctly gendered impacts of these processes, particularly in the context of post-socialist political economic transition and restructuring (Rittich 2002b), and more recently in the context of policies regarding the nexus between work and family (Rittich 2006a; 2010a).

I find such broader conceptualization of these multi-level interactions compelling and useful for gaining a more complex understanding of both, why EU working-time policy discourse and regulatory regime developed in a way that it has, and in the case of debates on Poland's own working-time regime's development and reform before and after EU accession. Existing research suggests that as in the EU context, in Poland, the pressures and/or incentives to comply with international standards, conditions, and benchmarks – whether those required for 'successful' market transition, membership in the OECD, accession to the EU, or most recently, the goal of EMU-membership – have prompted much policy (Leiber 2005, 2007; Stenning et al. 2010; Shields 2011) and legal change since 1989, including change in labour law (Leiber 2005, 2007; see Chapters 4 and 5 of this study). Indeed, as I show here building on available research and my own findings, the process of political-economic transition in Poland has been also a process of legal transition; it has been facilitated by legal norms while simultaneously shaping these norms to reflect the dominant neo-liberal ideology and political discourse of the time. What must be pointed out is that while the processes of globalization and 'systemic' change have broadened (or changed) the range of discursive and regulatory influence, the impact of multi-level hegemonic discourses and governance structures is certainly not only a post-transition phenomenon in Poland. The ideology of socialism and the political and economic influence of the Soviet Union had also been facilitated by legal norms and political discourses during the People's Republic of Poland (People's Republic) period,[6] which lasted from shortly after the Second World War up to 1989. In Chapters 4 and 5, I will examine the implications of these interactions, both prior to and since the onset of transition, and assess how they have influenced the regulation of working time, gender equality, and the broader process of social reproduction in the Polish context.

Crucial as it is, attention to the influence of broader discourses and governance regimes in shaping EU policies and those of its Member States should not overshadow the fact that such influence requires local translation and may be either rejected or welcomed depending on how consistent it is with local institutional structures, interests, and the discursive universe. There is evidence that some national systems of labour and employment law have been remarkably resistant to change, while others have more or less readily complied with EU policy directions. The Austrian political scientist Gerda Falkner's (et al.) research on the domestic implementation of EU labour law Directives in the 'old' (Falkner et al. 2004, 2005) and 'new' Member States (Falkner and Trieb 2008; Trieb and Falkner 2008), for example, identifies at least three different 'worlds of compliance', with the political elites receptive to EU norms in some national settings yet resistant to some aspects of Europeanization in others, either by active opposition to specific measures, or by, what Falkner and her colleagues term 'opposition through the back door' (Falkner et al. 2004: 452; 2005: 278). The fact that such 'back door' opposition is necessary, however, suggests that domestic actors nonetheless feel *some* compulsion or obligation to comply, even if this compliance remains merely formal or on the surface.

The degree to which EU policies and regulations are consistent with the local interests tends to be decisive. Or indeed, the supranational policies themselves may be a reflection (or reflexion) of shifting preferences in some national contexts, as the contributors to the edited volume by Silvana

[6] See fn. 18 of the Introduction for explanation of this nomenclature.

Sciarra et al. (2004) demonstrate in relation to the EU regulation of part-time work. Of course, not all Member States will be in the position to participate equally in this reflexive process, as the ability to inform supranational policy or resist it will depend on a state's relative power and political sway within the EU. Newer members, such as Poland, or countries in the process of accession certainly lack such ability, since EU membership depends on adoption of pre-existing policies and laws these states had no role in developing. Unsurprisingly, political science research on the impact of accession conditionality points to high compliance in ECE in general (Schimmelfennig and Sedelmeier 2005b), and in Poland in particular (Leiber 2005, 2007; Toshkov 2008).

Nonetheless, as a study on Czech Republic, Hungary, Slovakia, and Slovenia shows (Falkner et al. 2008), *prompt* adoption of the *acquis* does not necessarily translate into *effective* adoption. The study revealed a 'gulf between law and action', showing poor record of subsequent enforcement of the Europeanized policy in those four countries (Trieb and Falkner 2008: 165). At the same time, these results were not necessarily inconsistent with the compliance patterns of the 'old' EU members, as they fit into the 'world of dead letters', a subset of one of the three worlds of compliance characterized by highly politicized transposition process and also identified in Ireland and Italy. While Poland's example does not precisely fit into this 'world of dead letters' (162), Simone Leiber (2005, 2007) also shows that Poland's often at-the-last-minute and minimal compliance was not always followed with proper administrative and enforcement support either.

Thus in addition to external pressures and influences coming from the EU or the broader transnational governance space, domestic or endogenous conditions are also significant to whether compliance with or assimilation of EU policies is achieved, and whether it is meaningful. The presence of local actors who are motivated to facilitate this process is one variable highlighted in institutionalist literature on Europeanization, both by scholars employing rationalist and constructivist models (Radaelli 2001: 127–128; Schimmelfennig and Sedelmeier 2005a; Sedelmeier 2011 for a useful review). Indeed, actors are seen as conduits of the process of Europeanization, whether, as rationalists contend, their decisions to comply and adopt EU rules, or defy them, are seen to be made on the basis of a politically motivated, rational cost-benefit analysis[7] (Schimmelfennig

[7] According to this model, actors will be guided by the logic of consequence and will consider factors such as the clarity of the rules, power imbalance, and the size and proximity of potential rewards (Schimmelfennig and Sedelmeier 2005a: 10–17). Actors who see the

and Sedelmeier 2005a), or because they are thought to recognize these norms and deem them appropriate and resonant in the local context, as a constructivist model suggests[8] (Sedelmeier 2011). While obviously distinct, these two ways of conceptualizing the role of actors are not necessarily mutually exclusive, although as Ulrich Sedelmeier points out a rationalist explanation tends to better account for this process in the ECE members prior to 2004 given that meeting conditionality requirements was necessary for EU membership (Sedelmeier 2011).

Since the concept universe of political discourse already presumes that actors are influential, and it has been suggested that the adoption of transnational agendas in Poland was indeed facilitated by particular local actors whose own projects and preferences either aligned with those promoted at other levels (Shields 2001, 2008, 2011) or who were influenced by exogenous elites (Zeniewski 2011), these insights from political science are helpful in ascertaining the relative roles and relationships between the EU discourses (and institutions promoting them), conditionality, and working-time laws and policies on the one hand, and the role of the local actors, including political, social, and lobby groups on the other. The extent to which Polish labour law, particularly the rules on working time, have been affected by European law and policy discourse, and the discourses operating at the level of international financial institutions, and how this influence has changed over time, will be evaluated in Chapters 4 and 5.

1.4 Towards a Gendered Labour Law Analysis – Social Reproduction, Gender, and the Regulation of Working Time

The first two sections of this chapter sought to conceptualize the context for the analysis of legal rules and policies more generally and to capture the multi-level character of regulation in EU space. In this last, most

EU rules and policies in question as useful to their own policy agenda are more likely to push for compliance, meaning that 'conditionality may change the domestic opportunity structure in favour of those domestic actors and strengthen their bargaining power vis-à-vis their opponents in society and government' (Schimmelfennig and Sedelmeier 2005a: 12). Factors that will facilitate this are the quality of political opposition, the presence of 'veto players', administrative capacities, and other supportive local institutions.

8 A constructivist perspective suggests also that adoption of EU rules depends on social learning, so it is not 'hard' conditionality that achieves Europeanization but rather socialization and persuasion, with the logic of appropriateness and transnational networks and experts having a significant role in facilitating this process (Schimmelfennig and Sedelmeier 2005a: 18–20).

substantial section, I set out a framework for the critical gender analysis and assessment of the EU and Polish working-time regimes, and the legal standards that are associated with them. As I argue, the political discourses and negotiations within which policies and norms are embedded and which help to reproduce them are inherently gendered. Yet, whether gender is explicit or not within these discourses, and what assumptions policy makers and other involved actors make about gender relations, gender roles, and the meaning of gender equality depends on the dominant understandings and social settlements that are reached within the multilevel discursive universe. One of my goals is to understand what sorts of rationales underlie working-time policies of the EU and those operating in the Polish context, and to question how they came to dominate and to what extent they embody specific gendered notions that impede their more transformative recasting.

Because I wish to highlight the gender dimension of working-time organization and regulation, the approach that I develop here draws on theories which place gender and the essential processes of maintaining lives, or social reproduction, within a broader political economy and at the core of policy and labour law analysis. Following the work of other feminist scholars, this approach demonstrates that the manner in which the demarcation between production and social reproduction is made and the way in which responsibilities for the latter are distributed between the state, the enterprises, and individual households, as well as between women and men, has consequences for gender equality in the labour market and society as a whole. This relationship is particularly evident when we consider the historic development of the organization and regulation of 'normal' working time and ask *what sort of work* and *whose working hours* it standardized.

As I show in the remaining pages of this chapter, managing time has been a decisive factor in reproducing gendered forms of work organization. In industrialized European economies, work patterns and hours historically evolved in a manner that made the work of care increasingly incompatible with employment participation. Differences in the dominant political discourse translated into different institutional arrangements to support social reproduction. In Europe's market economies, for example, taking an unencumbered male worker as the baseline meant that regulation of work hours largely ignored reproduction. Assuming that men would not be burdened by unpaid domestic duties, and so entrenching the notion of exclusive engagement, this regulatory model put women at a disadvantage in terms of their access to *standard* jobs.

By contrast, in planned economies, such as pre-1989 Poland, there was a more explicit acknowledgement that social reproduction should be supported by the state and the (state-run) enterprises because the focus was not on male employment, but rather on *all adult* workers. Even if the rationale underlying this latter model was only formally that of equality or worker–state egalitarianism, but practically often that of securing a larger workforce (see Chapter 4), it nonetheless did enable women's mass participation in standard employment.

To draw the crucial link between standard norms of time and work organization and the unequal and gendered division of responsibilities for paid and unpaid work, I will rely on a number of key concepts developed in feminist political economy and used in feminist analyses of the labour market. I begin with social reproduction, a key concept that helps to identify some of the main assumptions underpinning the role of the family within the capitalist mode of production and explain the consequent social marginalization of women and the limitation of their labour market opportunities. To explain how gender figures in the institutionalization of social reproduction in various societies, I then refer to concepts of 'gender order', 'gender regime', and 'gender contract'. Turning my focus to working time, first, I recount the historical processes by which the organization of work under industrial capitalism set the stage for temporal standards that were increasingly incompatible with unpaid tasks of social reproduction, particularly the care of children. Next, I address the concept of working-time regime and argue that since gender equality in a given society depends on the temporal arrangements that are available to labour market participants (Fagan 1996, 2001; Rubery et al. 1998, 1999; Figart and Mutari 2000, 2001), unpacking the gendered assumptions on which standard temporal arrangements have been based is crucial to developing a more equitable concept of working time. Accordingly, I then go on to consider the so-called 'standard employment relationship' (SER) and its associated temporal norms, and demonstrate how these norms are gendered by what they assume about work and workers.

A final note before I turn to the concepts themselves concerns the question of their appropriateness for a study of Poland, particularly its socialist phase, since most have been developed in reference to advanced capitalist economies. As I hope will become evident, the conceptual framework I propose quite usefully captures and explains how the approach to the organization and institutionalization of social reproductive activities in state-socialist countries like Poland enabled the emergence (albeit incomplete and imperfect) of more egalitarian employment patterns than those in western Europe. As such, the Polish case illustrates very well that how production and social reproduction are co-organized and how the latter is valued and accommodated within a given society is not simply a reflection of some natural order but rather stems from the interplay between normative assumptions, legal rules, and concrete institutional arrangements negotiated by social actors within the universe of political discourse. Indeed, the Polish case – both the historical and the contemporary findings – enriches the framework proposed here because it powerfully reveals that employment norms, particularly those that govern the temporal organization of work, can only facilitate sustainable social reproduction and gender equality if significant measures and institutional arrangements are made to support carers and to encourage redistribution of paid and unpaid work between women and men. Failure to ensure either has concrete gender consequences. As I show here drawing on this case, this is not the sort of model that currently exists at the EU level or in Poland.

1.4.1 *Theorizing Social Reproduction*

A key concept in feminist political economy, social reproduction – the process of the daily and generational maintenance of the working population – is also one of the crucial mechanisms necessary for the maintenance of economy, culture, society, and humanity (Laslett and Brenner 1989; Fudge and Cossman 2002; Bakker and Gill 2003a, 2003b; Bezanson and Luxton 2006; Luxton 2006; Bakker and Silvey 2008). It refers to both a process and specific tasks (Bezanson 2006: 25), which although mostly carried out by households, operate simultaneously at the levels of the market, the state, and the family (Lewis 1992). Crucially, social reproduction reflects and involves negotiations of imbalances in gender and other social relations, such as class, race, and citizenship, and is affected by structural inequalities in those relations (Acker 1988; Fudge and Cossman 2002; Bakker and Gill 2003a, 2003b; Luxton 2006; Bakker and Silvey 2008). These inequalities play out in the way that responsibilities for unpaid and paid work – the fulfillment of which is necessary for social reproduction – are unequally distributed.

Social reproduction has been variously theorized in feminist literature, with most definitions, nonetheless, relating to its three aspects: (1) biological reproduction; (2) reproduction of labour power; and (3) social practices connected to care, socialization, and the fulfillment of human needs (Bakker and Gill 2003a: 23; Bakker 2007: 541).[9] Earlier discussions

[9] This last element includes public policy and social provision associated with health, education, welfare, and socialization of risk, as well as institutions, norms, and relations that

of social reproduction focused on the first two aspects identified above to make apparent the essential contribution of unpaid reproductive and domestic work to the capitalist economy (Seccombe 1973; Humphries and Rubery 1984; Laslett and Brenner 1989). Later accounts, most notably that proposed by Antonella Picchio (1992), sought also to explain the interdependence between production and social reproduction by defining the particular relationship that links them and identifying the structures and institutions that help to mediate the tensions between them. Beyond its economic aspects, feminists extended the scope of social reproduction to incorporate the elements of care and social provisioning, including the provision of sexual, emotional, and affective services (such as are required to maintain family and intimate relationships), voluntary work directed at meeting needs in the community, and the reproduction of culture, ideology, and 'human constitution' generally (Bakker and Gill 2003a; Hoskyns and Rai 2007). Some accounts, for instance, focus on the role of care in building effective functionings and capabilities (Picchio 2003) or on its relational and affective, thus not readily commodifiable, dimensions (Himmelweit 2000; Lewis and Giullari 2005). Feminist political economists have also examined the transformations in organization of social reproduction in the context of developed liberal economies, although increasingly with the view to the global effects of these processes and consequent transformations in social reproduction everywhere (Fudge and Cossman 2002; Rittich 2002b; Bakker and Gill 2003b; Spike Peterson 2003a, 2003b; Bezanson 2006; Bakker and Silvey 2008; Stewart 2011; Kofman and Raghuram 2015).[10]

In the following, I review in more detail a number of key analytical contributions to the conceptualization of social reproduction. I begin with those that demonstrate the links between the processes of capitalist production and accumulation and the usually unpaid social reproductive work carried out within households. Specifically, I refer to Picchio's (1992) articulation of the political economy of social reproduction in early capitalism. Next, following Isabella Bakker's (2007) suggestion that we distinguish between *work* and *labour* to expand the concept of social reproduction beyond its role in the economy (while nonetheless affirming

shape how the social, political, and moral orders are understood, evolved, and perpetuated (Bakker 2007: 541).

[10] See also Pearson (1997, 1998) on re-articulation of the relationship between production and social reproduction in Cuba during the 1990s as a result of post-Soviet Union dissolution economic crisis.

its vital importance and contribution to it), I consider select literature on the affective and relational dimension of care work. Finally, I briefly note recent developments in the analysis of social reproduction that address the impact of the global political, social, and economic transitions on its organization in different contexts. This latter literature makes apparent the linkages between social reproduction in the developed market economies, transition economies such as Poland, and those in the process of development, and brings inequalities based on race, nationality, and citizenship into sharper focus. It also underscores that although the framework of social reproduction has been developed in relation to its operation and institutionalization in capitalist economies, it continues to be of considerable analytical value, particularly given the worldwide reach of the market economy, prominence of neo-liberal discourses, and the increasing permeation of capitalism into the 'structures of everyday life'.[11] As this book shows, examining changes in social reproduction in transition economies such as Poland, and the role of legal norms in facilitating these changes, also provides insights that strengthen this theoretical framework.

Social Reproduction as a Corrective to Orthodox Political Economy

Contrary to dominant neoclassical approaches which regard the family or labour supply more generally as exogenous to the economy, feminist political economists locate social reproduction within basic economic processes including production, distribution, and circulation (Seccombe 1973; Humphries and Rubery 1984; Picchio 1992). They do so by demonstrating that the work involved in it, the bulk of which is carried out within the household on an unpaid basis and mainly by women is, by its very nature, *productive* – it produces and maintains the labouring population without which the economy could not be sustained. As Picchio (1992: 97) explains, 'housework is the *production* of labour as a commodity, while waged work is the *exchange* of labour. To be exchanged, labour must be produced; and to be used in the production of other commodities, labour must be produced and exchanged'. However, both this functional dependence and the productive nature of domestic work remain largely unacknowledged in the capitalist system, and the unpaid work of social

[11] Bakker (2007: 542) makes reference to historian Fernard Braudel's term to reinforce that the spread of capitalism has material and structural effects on life at all levels of organization, including people's ability to meet their daily needs.

reproduction is not subject to the same logic or organization that governs productive activity. In fact, what makes the capitalist mode of production unique is its tendency to *separate* the site of procreation from the site of production (Picchio 1992; Fudge and Cossman 2002) and divest itself of the responsibility for the costs associated with the former. This separation is arbitrary as the processes that are involved in the two are in fact 'inextricably intertwined' (Picchio 1992; Rittich 2002b: 185). Picchio notes that although familial work is linked to the productive process through wages (supporting the subsistence of the homeworker) or social transfers, wages are regarded as costs of production, but housework, as unpaid labour, is a deduction from the costs; it is not compensated with a wage of its own and when it is (e.g., indirectly, through the family wage or social transfers), the relationship is still such as to guarantee a high surplus/profit (Picchio 1992). Thus, Picchio (121) observes that 'the more labour is embodied in its reproduction the less it costs the employer' – an increase in housework leads to an increased standard of living and better quality labour without necessarily costing the employer any more. This paradox, she maintains, can only be explained by the separation of the processes of production from reproduction and the transfer of responsibility for the latter from the employer to the worker, or, more precisely, by shifting the burden onto the household and especially women family members. According to Picchio (121) then, the 'subordination of social reproduction to the needs of capital accumulation' illuminates the essential contradiction within the capitalist society – the conflict between the standard of living of the workers and the drive for accumulation by those who own the means of production.

Picchio and other feminist political economists have pointed out that, aside from the family, state institutions play a key role in mediating this contradiction (see also Fudge and Cossman 2002; Rittich 2002a, 2002b). The state assumes its mediation role of a 'regulator' by enacting social policies and laws that often take for granted women's domestic labour (Picchio 1992: 112). Thus, as Picchio points out, although the state has historically assumed some responsibilities connected to social reproduction (such as health services, education, some income security, etc.) in most developed market economies, it has always done so in a supplemental way and on the presumption that the basic needs will be met at the household level.[12] Consequently, women's work within the

12 The vast literature on different forms of welfare state sketches out the array of institutional arrangements that developed in an effort to socialize some of the risks and costs of social

household acts as an 'alternator', with women constantly adjusting its level to the changing demands and conditions under which social reproduction is carried out, including the expansions or contractions in the state's involvement, impact of the market forces, and changing family circumstances (Picchio 1992; Bezanson 2006: 27; Luxton 2006: 38). But there is a limit to the family's (and women's) ability to mediate these tensions. As Luxton (2006) points out: "without sufficient support, standards of living drop, the most vulnerable households typically collapse, and a crisis in social reproduction is produced" (Luxton 2006: 38), meaning that there is a general breakdown in the ability of individuals, families, and communities to sustain themselves, care for and educate one another and, in turn, to sustain and reproduce society as a whole.

Social Reproduction and the Labour of Love

The conceptual incorporation of social reproduction (and women's unpaid work) into political-economic theory and explanation of the process by which it is subordinated within capitalism provides an important corrective to more mainstream theories, mainly those offered by the neoclassical tradition.[13] Through focus on unpaid household work it also draws the attention to the unequal gender relations that characterize its organization and to the role of the state in institutionalizing this inequality.[14] Yet regardless of its economic significance not all work involved in social reproduction can be explained through productive and economic relationships, and this has been one source of criticism of the early articulations of the social reproduction framework. Aspects of social reproduction, such as the care of dependents, are not only hard to commodify fully, they are also valuable beyond the economic contribution they make.

In a review essay surveying the development of the social reproduction concept, Bakker (2007) suggests one way of rearticulating it in a manner that responds to the above critique, namely, to broaden our understanding of the concept 'work'. Drawing on Antonio Gramsci, she (2007: 548)

reproduction but also to 'organize' the work involved in it. For discussion on the state's role in organization of social reproduction through stabilizing a specific gender order see the following section. Also, on the role of the socialist state in organizing social reproduction in Poland, see Chapter 4.

[13] Although it also corrects classical Marxist approaches which tended to downplay social reproduction.

[14] I discuss the process by which these unequal gender relations that characterize social reproduction under capitalism are institutionalized in Section 1.4.2 of this chapter.

suggests that a clearer distinction between *work* and *labour*, the latter being a specific aspect of work that in capitalism is characterized by alienation of the labourer and appropriation of surplus labour, allows for a conceptualization of social reproduction that is not entirely mediated by capitalism and thus better accounts for those forms of social reproductive *work* that cannot be completely commodified.[15]

A similarly expanded conception of 'work', which defies the dichotomy between paid and unpaid work, production and reproduction, employment and domestic work is that offered by the British sociologist Miriam Glucksmann. Glucksmann (1995, 2000, 2005) conceptualizes work as a relational process that occurs in many different spheres and is embedded in and defined by particular social relations or expressed through kinship connections. 'Total social organization of labour', the conceptual device that Glucksmann proposes, illuminates 'the manner by which all the labour in a particular society is divided up between and allocated to different structures, institutions and activities' (Glucksmann 2000: 67). These divisions and allocations are historically contingent and change over time and across space. Whether specific activity is considered 'work' depends not on whether it is paid for, but rather on the particular relations or circumstances within which it is carried out. Accordingly, Glucksmann suggests that the dichotomy between *paid* work (or employment) and *unpaid* (household) work is unhelpful since the former can occur outside of the formal employment sphere and the latter can be carried out in other contexts than the household (such as voluntary work: Glucksmann 2005: 29; see also Taylor 2004). This reconceptualization of work highlights the interdependencies between different types of work in society (and economy) and challenges the classical dichotomy between productive and reproductive work, paid and unpaid work, thereby highlighting the importance of all types of work to the sustainability of the economy and society as a whole.

The expanded conception of work that includes but is not limited to labour, finds further support, as Bakker points out, in the literature on the economy of care and, more recently, literature on social policy of care. From the economy of care perspective, Susan Himmelweit revisits early

[15] See also Bakker and Gill (2003a: 20–23). Both Bakker (2007) and Bakker and Gill (2003a) draw on Gramsci's broad conception of work as encompassing both the social relations defined by capital (labour) and the creative process that could exist outside of labour relations. Bakker and Gill see this distinction as crucial to explaining the crisis in social reproduction as primarily occurring when capitalist market forces penetrate into basic human and social institutions that were previously shielded from commodification.

writing on domestic work and considers the analytical implications of the manner in which feminist economists attempted to include domestic activity into the realm of 'work'.[16] She notes that these analyses often likened domestic activities to all other work types by showing that they are: (1) extrinsic/purposeful; (2) part of the division of labour; and (3) separable from who performs them (Himmelweit 2000: 104–105). The problem with this definition, she notes, is that it abstracts the essence of 'work' from its dominant characterization as wage *labour* producing manufactured products for the capital thereby assuming the dominant definition as the baseline. She also suggests that rather than dichotomize or try to show that all work is alike, a more useful approach is one, which recognizes that different types of work exhibit different degrees of commodification because of their particular characteristics. The abstracted definition of 'work' may be suitable for domestic tasks such as cleaning and cooking, but it does not apply to those forms of work in which it matters who performs it (both to the effective execution of the work and to the person carrying it out). Caring work, she notes, provides one such example because it is often 'an activity which is inseparable from the person doing it [and] in which the relationship between a carer and her work is crucial' (110). As such, caring (both paid and unpaid) is distinct and Himmelweit urges that rather than attempt to valorize it through showing that it is like all other work, we need to recognize its unique relational and affective dimension. Much like Glucksmann's, her goal is to challenge the artificial dualism between work and home, production and reproduction in order 'to make care be a part of paid labour and work to be recognized in the caring activities that go on in the home' (Bakker 2007: 548 referring to Himmelweit). This characterization of work, Bakker notes and I agree, has crucial implications for policy, particularly in the area of working time.

Another strand of feminist writing on care, which picks up on this theme, comes from the social policy literature on the provisioning role of the state. Drawing on concepts of care as a universal human need (involving the rights of both the person receiving care and also the person providing it) (Nussbaum 2003) and the recognition that aside from the labour that goes into its provision, care often involves love and is integral to identity formation (Graham 1983; Lewis and Giullari 2005; Lewis 2006b: 107), scholars writing from this vantage point are also underscoring that

[16] Note that this reference to 'work' is not that in Gramscian sense specified at note 15 but the more narrow conception that Bakker attempts to distinguish by referring to it as 'labour'.

among the types of work that are involved in social reproduction, the work of care is unique. Jane Lewis (2006a, 2007; with Giullari 2005), for instance, argues that given its crucial importance to human flourishing, care work must be regarded as inherently valuable and accommodated in a manner that provides meaningful opportunities to individuals (both women and men) to be able to carry it out should they choose to do so, and whether they do it within their own families or as part of paid employment. In part, this means that they must have *the time* to do it without having to absorb the costs and suffer from negative consequences in the labour market.

In a similar vein, other scholars have pointed out that social reproduction, particularly its care aspects, is important for those who perform it and, more significantly, is essential to building effective functionings and capabilities for the future generations (Picchio 2003; Chiappero-Marinetti 2008). These insights are important because they highlight that beyond its economic contribution, social reproduction has significant relational dimensions that make it an integral part of maintaining the overall well-being and health of the society. Accommodating (and this includes making the *time* for) social reproduction, then, is much more than a matter of accommodating individuals and their families (and their choices or preferences (Hakim 1996, 2000)); it is a matter of recognizing that this process is indispensable for social cohesion and human sustainability. Failure to attend to its inherent complexities will inevitably lead to a crisis; indeed, high levels of stress (particularly among women), and low fertility rates in many capitalist economies, including Poland, are some of the warning signs that such a crisis is already present.[17]

Social Reproduction – the Global Perspective

The crisis tendencies in the organization of social reproduction under capitalism are also the focus of a substantial literature that considers how the processes of change in social reproduction in the countries of the North/West articulate with those in the developing world. For the purposes of this chapter, I only wish to point to the recognition that the

[17] The crisis in social reproduction occurs when the gender contracts existing in a given context can no longer contain the inherent contradictions (Fudge 2005). Phenomena such as women's double burden, time poverty and stress, and decreasing rates of fertility indicate that there are serious discrepancies in how productive and socially reproductive activities are distributed and organized between different institutions and among men and women. This in turn compromises the ability of individuals, families, communities, and society as a whole to sustain themselves.

economic, political, and social transformations, including the transnationalization of capitalism and market principles, are not only contributing to the reorganization and the crisis of social reproduction in developed economies but also to destabilizing these processes everywhere else, leading to increasing human insecurity on a global scale (Bakker and Gill 2003b; Bakker and Silvey 2008), and to depletion of social reproductive capacities (Rai et al. 2014). As the already artificial boundary separating production from social reproduction (both paid and unpaid) is being redrawn, the division of labour is increasingly occurring not just along gender and class lines but also along those of race, ethnicity, nationality, and geographical location (Bakker and Gill 2003b; Bakker and Silvey 2008; Stewart 2011). The work of care and the maintenance of lives – key aspects of social reproduction – is central to many of these transformations, as is demonstrated for example by studies on restructuring in the ECE, or the literature on migration and particularly the global migration of carers.

For example, in her study on the political, economic, and legal transition in the former planned economies, Rittich (2002b) notes that one of the key impacts of market restructuring on social reproduction is that it sharpens the boundary between productive and reproductive spheres in a context where the articulation between them was once far more acknowledged by economic planning and public policy than it is under capitalism (see also True 2003). The extent to which the underlying gender relations are equal, means that this shift towards the more pronounced separation in the organization of social reproduction, will have more or less disparate impact on men and women in different transition states.

A similar process of redrawing the lines between production and reproduction and the division of responsibilities for either is also taking place in other parts of the World, since the market logic underlying restructuring in ECE has also been informing development efforts more generally. Given this chapter's other focus, I cannot possibly do justice to the vast literature that examines the impacts of this process. What I do wish to note, however, is that political economists and other feminist scholars are urging that many of these impacts are related to disruptions in social reproduction and human security that are a direct result of capitalist expansion and the expansion of neo-liberal discourses (Bakker and Gill 2003a, 2003b; Bakker and Silvey 2008; Stenning et al. 2010). As people's and entire communities' means of survival and daily maintenance become circumscribed across the world by capitalism's reach, the global dimension of the processes of social reproduction is becoming more apparent.

Migration for work, for instance, exemplifies the transnationalization of social reproduction, whether it involves migrant care provision (Bakker and Gill 2003a, 2003b; Arat-Koc 2006; Stewart 2011), or other forms of labour (both licit and illicit) including sex services, or production of necessities such as food, building, or home repairs (Wolkowitz 2002; Perrons et al. 2010; Stewart 2011), it starkly illustrates that the division of labour between production and social reproduction is increasingly drawn along geographical lines, and social reproduction is increasingly commodified yet persistently undervalued and rife with inequalities (Bakker and Silvey 2008; Kofman and Raghuram 2015). In so far as its short and long-term sustainability, one problem that these developments raise is that while migrant labour from transitioning and developing economies (in itself a result of distortions in social reproduction in those contexts) may provide temporary solutions to the crisis in social reproduction in the receiving states and secure the means of existence in the sending states, it also leads to significant distortions in this process everywhere and entrenches further inequality in its organization. Importantly, it represents social reproduction's continued subordination to the needs of capitalist accumulation.

Expanding the framework of social reproduction beyond its original context, these insights provide important analytical tools for examining the historical transformation in the mechanisms and institutions by which it is carried out and mediated in developing countries, including transition economies such as Poland. Given Poland's relatively recent transition to the liberal market economy and even more recent accession to the EU, these insights also help us better grasp the relationship between political-economic forms and the organization of social reproduction, as well as the impact of transnational policies and regulations on national political discourses and normative and legal orders.

In the next section, I consider the manner in which social reproduction is institutionalized, with particular focus on how it is gendered and what accounts for the diversity that exists among specific contexts.

1.4.2 Institutionalization of Social Reproduction – Gender Orders, Regimes, Contracts

As discussed above, the process of social reproduction is characterized by tensions and asymmetries. It is inherently gendered, because biological propagation of the species constitutes one of its key elements, with men and women assigned different roles, also in part due to biology.

Moreover, depending on the specific context, relations of class, race, and nationality are also significant to how the process is organized and institutionalized.

As I explain in this section, these asymmetries, and particularly those based on gender difference, are stabilized in the process of institutionalizing social reproduction, and the state has an important role in this process. Specifically, while the family is the main institution that carries out the tasks involved in social reproduction, the state also partakes in its organization and mediation of the tensions that may arise between social reproductive and productive activities in order to ensure that the social reproduction continues (Fudge and Cossman 2002). One way in which the state does this is by way of social provisioning, although, unlike the family (mainly female family members), which carries the most significant burden of this process, the state's role in this, particularly in liberal market economies, has been generally residual. Although under certain political-economic conditions, such as during the Polish state-socialism, the state assumed a much more direct role in provisioning, as I will explore in Chapter 4, even during this period it was taken for granted that some work involved in social reproduction will still continue to be carried out within households. This assumption relates to a second form of state intervention in social reproduction, and that is the state's role in stabilizing a particular 'gender order', or the overarching relations of power and ideas about masculinity and femininity (Connell 1987, 2005), which too is done to ensure that social reproduction continues. To explain better the state's role in this process, I will first elaborate the concept 'gender' and then discuss the significance of 'gender regimes' and 'gender contracts' in the organization of social reproduction.

To begin, although gender is often mapped onto biological differences between the sexes, it is not in fact a predetermined category that is reducible to sex or to the body, but rather refers to a process whereby the socially and culturally produced ideas about male-female difference, power, and inequality structure the reproduction of these differences in the institutionalized practices of society (Connell 1987, 2005; Gal and Kilgman 2000: 5). Gendering is *reciprocal*, meaning that while cultural and social norms inform how institutions and social structures are envisioned and made, institutional and structural patterns reflect and further reinforce the normative assumptions that underlie them. This process is also *dynamic*; gender relations are constantly made and remade (Connell 1987, 2005) and a change at one level results in changes in the gender relations as a whole (Connell 1987, 2005; Walby 2004).

The state's key role in the process of gendering is to stabilize the overarching gender order in various social sites, among them, the legal system, the labour market, the family, and the school. Each of these sites itself contains a specific set of gender relations, which Raewyn Connell refers to as its gender regime (Connell 2005: 120). Alternatively, Sylvia Walby (2004) conceptualizes the gender regime more broadly and essentially as parallel (although not identical) to Connell's gender order. Walby's (10) gender regime is then composed of other subordinate gender regimes (which are more institutionally specific, although she does not limit them to singular institutions), 'domains', (economic, polity, and civil) and 'social practices'. In her conceptualization, much like in Connell's, gender relations are constituted by all of these levels and changes at any level affect changes in the overall gender relations. Thus in the context of the EU, for example, Walby has noted the emergence of an overarching EU gender regime that is evolving as a result of regulation and policy enacted at the supranational level, and which, in turn transforms more localized gender regimes in various EU member states.[18] Although the relationship between these gender regimes is inherently dynamic, the stability of a society's gender order can be achieved when at particular historical moments the gender regimes of interacting institutions (or spheres) are 'harmonized' and there is 'some fit, however temporary, fragile, and incomplete, between the processes of reproduction and production' (Fudge 2005: 265). Judy Fudge (2005) suggests that this fit is achieved if a gender contract is institutionalized in key sites including families, firms, schools, state policies, and the market (see also Vosko 2010: 6–9).

Defined as 'a socio-cultural consensus about the respective organisation of interaction between the sexes which affects the orientations and actions of men and women in a social system' (Pfau-Effinger 1994: 1359, citing Hirdman 1988), the gender contract includes unspoken rules about how men and women should distribute and prioritize their time between reproductive and productive work. The concept gender contract was developed partially as a critique of previous typologies, such as Lewis' degrees of breadwinning model (1992), which tended to emphasize institutional and economic factors and were unable to account for diversity existing within specific regime types. Brigit Pfau-Effinger (1994, 1998), for example, suggested that one way to explain such *intra*-regime variations is to account for the importance of cultural norms and that the concept gender contract better accounts for variations because it

[18] See also Heather MacRae (2006) on the role of EU in shaping the national gender regime in West Germany.

emphasizes that the state of gender relations is a reflection of historically (and thus contextually and culturally) specific relations and negotiations.

Gender contracts develop historically and as such their content is contextually specific (Pfau-Effinger 1994, 1998).[19] Much like gender relations in general, gender contracts are typically marked by asymmetrical relations of power, but they are also dynamic and *consensual*, meaning that there is some degree of resistance and agency involved in their negotiation, which helps to account for change in their content over time, however slow or whatever the nature of this change may be. This dynamism and consensual nature of gender contracts explains why some of them are more egalitarian than others. Thus, while the unequal division of labour between production and reproduction is a common feature of all gender orders, the degree to which responsibilities for reproduction are shared (between the state, the enterprise, and the families, as well as between men and women) can vary – from place to place and over time – depending on the particular gender contracts that exist and the institutional arrangements that are made to support them. As I further elaborate in the following section, the extent to which these gender contracts have also presumed specific allocation of time between paid and unpaid work among men and women relates to the specific working-time regimes that exist in a given society. It in turn has a bearing on the degree of inequality in the labour market.

1.4.3 Time, Working-time Regimes, and the Standard Employment Relationship

> The traditional concept of working time arranges the world around two poles. On the one hand, there is the pole of measured time, comprising recognised and paid work, workers, and occupational solidarities; this is male time *par excellence*, to which women must conform if they intend to partake of it on an equal footing. On the other hand, there is unlimited time, female time, a space populated primarily by retired workers, women and children, their poorly understood and unpaid work, non-occupational solidarities, rest, consumption . . .
>
> Alain Supiot (2001: 68)

[19] The cultural or contextual intra-regime variation, however, does not mean that culture is the determining factor in the overall gender relations, but rather that it is a significant factor in the reciprocal and constitutive interplay between norms and structures which shapes the overall gender order of a particular society, much as class and race, or regional differences do (Duncan 1995; Warren 2000).

The gendered separation between productive and socially reproductive spheres, which is particularly marked and institutionalized in advanced market economies, is, at least in part, a product of the historical peculiarities of nascent capitalism and industrialization. It is generally agreed that the organization of modern work was forged in the gradual transition from household to market production; a process that was accompanied and aided by changing social values, conceptions of time, and specific technological and organizational innovations.[20] In this section, I provide a brief overview of this process with specific emphasis on the development of industrial time discipline and division of labour, and note how this relates to social reproduction. Specifically, I show that because industrial work and the organization of time developed in a way that made it increasingly incompatible with labour-intensive tasks such as the care of dependents, it has had particular labour market consequences for those whose primary responsibility is to carry them out. I then explain the concept of working-time regime to show that how working time is organized in a given society has, depending on the context, profound implications for access to paid employment and serves to reproduce gendered forms of work organization, and contributes to phenomena such as overwork and double-shift. I conclude this section by considering the relationship between working-time regimes, the SER, and social reproduction.

Time and Industrial Discipline in Historical Perspective

As already noted, it is widely believed that the advent of industrial capitalism was accompanied by the emergence of the modern concept of time and a significant increase in working hours (Thompson 2001, originally 1967; Schor 1991). In his seminal essay entitled 'Time, Work Discipline and Industrial Capitalism', British historian Edward P. Thompson traces the rise of modern time discipline through a process of transition from the pre-industrial 'task-orientation' to the clock-dependent 'timed work' of industrial production (Thompson 2001). While the former was characterized by uneven rhythms and governed by completion of specific tasks and routines, the latter was measured by the standard of the clock, with time becoming increasingly regarded as currency to be spent and accounted for, not something to be idly passed and wasted: '. . . all time

[20] The development of the organization of industrial work has received considerable attention in social, political, and economic sciences literature, with Benjamin Franklin, Karl Marx, Max Weber, Edward P. Thompson and numerous prominent theorists having written about this process. For review and references see Adam (1995).

must be consumed, marketed, put to use; it is offensive for the labour force to "pass the time"' (Thompson 2001: 91). Thompson associates this transition not only with technological innovations but also with influence of Puritanism and increased popularity of capitalist principles, including the impulse to exploit workers maximally in the interest of the production process. Combined with increased reliance on the clock, Thompson suggests, these new attitudes of 'time thrift' gave rise to a more disciplined tempo of work (what he refers to as 'time discipline') and marked increases in working hours, eventually contributing to clearer demarcation between work and leisure and commodification of time and work more generally (Thompson 2001: 83–84, 93). Although Thompson's analysis does not make explicit reference to the impact of this transition on the processes of social reproduction he notes that women's task-oriented activities such as rearing of children and household maintenance would have made their submission to industrial time discipline more difficult.[21]

Thompson's depiction of the new tempo of life and work set by industrialization is still commonly cited; however, more recent social science theories and empirical research have questioned his stark binary between clock time and task orientation (Adam 1995; Glennie and Thrift 1996). As Barbara Adam (1995) notes, such dualism by implication fails to recognize that task orientation and clock-time/industrial time can be, and have been, simultaneously experienced. Even those people whose work is not completely structured by the clock economy, she argues, are nonetheless under the pressure of it since they are embedded in a market economy organized by its principles (Adam 1995: 87). To exemplify, Adam points to the feminist research on women's work time, which shows that this time cannot be easily placed within a perspective that separates work from leisure, or clocks from tasks, and as such, renders women's work times invisible by the assumptions and categories of classical social science analysis (Adam 1995, citing Davies 1989, 1994).

[21] As is evident from the quote cited at this section's outset, Supiot (2001) also draws on this polarized conception of work time and notes that women had to conform to the 'measured time' of men's work if they wanted to participate in paid employment. As Conaghan (2006: 109) points out, however, this characterization does not adequately capture the process of gendering: 'for workers to be free to engage in "timed-work", arrangements must be in place to ensure that other essential activities – particularly tasks associated with reproduction and rearing of children – continue to be carried out'. Thus, Conaghan argues, and I agree, that beyond the difficulties that the industrial tempo and presumption of exclusive engagement caused for women's ability to participate in industrial work; women's caring and reproductive work within the home likely made the entrenchment of the timed-work arrangements possible in the first place and viable in the long term.

Although I agree with Adam that Thompson's cursory treatment of women's experience of industrial discipline was a missed opportunity for more elaborate exploration of the multiplicity of time in this process of transition, I do not think that this fact completely detracts from his description of the transition *per se*. Provided we bear in mind that his account tends to overdraw and dichotomize task and clock-time orientation in a way that leaves out the complexity of people's and, particularly, women's experiences of work time, it nonetheless vividly illustrates the impact of new forms of temporal and structural organization of production on people's working conditions, and the implications of these changes for social reproduction can still be deduced. It is evident that during this process of transition women were not completely excluded from paid work; most women, particularly those who were poor, had to, and did, find ways of reconciling child-care and household chores with paid work to support their family's subsistence. Since the submission to this new tempo of work was a matter of survival, women coped even if this came at an expense to their leisure and the overall standards of living. It is more likely in fact, at least in the early phases of this transition, that the negative consequence was not so much women's complete exclusion from paid work, but rather the severe costs to social reproduction as a result of their increased workloads and time commitments.[22]

Aside from the temporal and structural constraints and intensification of work, it was also the change in the *site* of production that exacerbated the tension between production and reproduction, and created further impediments for women. As Laura Leete (2000) notes, subsequent technological and organizational innovations, such as the division of labour and mechanization, led to mass industrialization, economies of scale, and significant productivity gains. Many goods and services previously produced in the home were eventually commodified, arguably 'freeing' people of some tasks previously carried out within households, but also shifting the site of production from homes and cottage industries into mills and factories. This latter shift, however, created further obstacles for women's participation given that labour-intensive nature of care makes it generally compatible only with work that can be performed on an intermittent

[22] Ample evidence exists of women's participation in paid work even at the expense of standards of care and maintenance during this period, with food scarcity and high infant mortality, particularly among the poor. When children lived, they were seen as an economic resource for families and many worked from a very early age: see Schor (1991: 58, 92–93), where she refers to such evidence in Britain and the United States.

basis (Leete 2000: 254). While spinning and weaving for pay in one's home made looking after young children and the elderly possible, it is unlikely that the factory floor afforded similar opportunities. Thus, Leete argues that it was also this shift away from home production together with the time-intensive nature of childrearing and care that progressively created the structural barriers for women's engagement in the labour market.[23]

Working-time Regimes and Standard Employment Norms

Women's exclusion or marginalization was further cemented through the dominant working-time regimes that emerged across Europe after the Second World War, and the associated standard employment relationship (SER) (Fudge and Vosko 2001b: 271; Supiot 2001: 59; Fudge 2005: 226). According to Deborah Figart and Ellen Mutari (1998, 2000), working-time regimes are composed of particular standards or regulations of work hours and patterns, *and* the normative assumptions about the appropriate organization of the unpaid work of social reproduction. Specifically, literature concerning these regimes demonstrates that how working time is organized in a particular context is shaped by and simultaneously reinforces specific institutional arrangements and associated normative assumptions about the organization of productive and reproductive work and the distribution of responsibilities for either at various societal levels and between men and women (Figart and Mutari 1998, 2000; Rubery et al. 1998, 1999). As such, these regimes are crucial predictors of equality in the labour market because they have a significant impact on how men and women allocate their time between paid and unpaid work and among each other, which in turn determines their availability for paid work.

The dominant working-time regime that emerged across Europe in the post-war years was based on the standard of 8 daily hours and 48, and later 40 weekly hours and ensured other benefits such as paid annual leave and public holiday entitlements (Lee et al. 2007). A product of bargaining and legislation aimed at protecting workers and ensuring efficient and predictable organization of production in the manufacturing sector, this standard simultaneously reflected and further entrenched the division between paid labour and unpaid work of social reproduction (albeit to a different extent in specific contexts) that widened with the shift

[23] However, Leete (2000: 258) argues that it was not just a women's issue: 'Rather, it is century long changes in production technology and the basic economic forces of capitalist market economies that have removed production from the home and changed the nature of work. All parents, men and women alike, face these issues'.

from home to industrial production, and institutionalized the underlying expectations about the appropriate distribution of women's and men's respective responsibilities for either sphere. In many advanced market economies, for example, the standard working-time regime ignored reproductive work on the basis of gender contracts based on different incarnations of the male breadwinner/female caregiver model that, as the name suggests, generally presumed that women not men would perform most reproductive work (Rubery et al.1998: 23; Supiot 2001; Fudge 2005: 267). A key feature of the working-time regime in that context and the linchpin of the gender contract underlying it was the SER (Fudge and Vosko 2001a; Supiot 2001: 59; Fudge 2005: 226).

The SER refers to a particular model of employment contract which became dominant in industrialized economies and was characterized by full-time, full-year work, usually executed on employer's premises, under their supervision and typically lasting over the employee's life-course (Supiot 2001). Much like the working-time regime with which it was associated, the SER was constructed on presumption of exclusive engagement and therefore it best suited workers unencumbered by other responsibilities. Consequently, since women were assumed to be primary caregivers, the SER largely circumscribed their participation in paid work by failing to accommodate their unique schedules. Job stability, access to a family wage, and a full range of social protections and benefits – all key aspects of the SER – were meant to provide stability and efficiency in the Fordist-style enterprises of the post-war era along with ensuring protection for workers (Bosch 2004). These same features of the SER, however, were also the means of indirectly subsidizing and thus stabilizing social reproduction.

As I discuss in Chapter 4, the SER model of work was not just unique to liberal market economies. Parallel models of work and time organization, which shared some of the SER's features (although also had important differences) and those of the working-time regimes built on its basis, also developed in industrialized planned economies of the state-socialist ECE countries, including Poland. The extent to which these latter models differed among themselves and from those adopted in western Europe reflected differences in ideology and social settlements, and, crucially, differences in the distribution of responsibilities for the process of social reproduction between the state, the state-run enterprise, and the family, and in the specific gender contracts in place in each country. Even then, however, the presumption that residual work of care will be carried out within the home contributed to women's subordinate status. These inherent tensions became particularly visible when these models began to be disembedded from the institutional frameworks that made them possible in the first place.

1.5 Conclusion

The above unpacking of the SER and the working-time norms that have been associated with it was the first step to achieving this book's objective of critically analysing the EU and Polish working-time regimes and assessing the extent to which they accommodate gender difference and promote or impede equality and social sustainability. Understanding how these norms are gendered and what they assume about workers also required a closer scrutiny of the relationship between the processes of production and social reproduction, since the legal rules and institutional arrangements that structure employment relations and working-time regimes tend to presume and simultaneously reproduce a particular, inherently gendered, relationship between these processes. The extent to which this relationship is also unequal (or the processes of social reproduction are subordinated, insufficiently supported, or undervalued) shapes the relative opportunities and access for women and men, and has an impact on the long-term sustainability of a particular political economy.

As will be apparent from Chapters 2 to 5, gender equality or issues of work–family reconciliation were not significant rationales for regulation of *standard* working time and, thus, did not feature predominantly in the European discursive universe until the mid-1990, nor until recently in the Polish context. For this reason, the discussion of working-time discourse and regulation that follows examines a range of other objectives, which were ultimately more influential in setting up the foundation for the EU and Polish working-time regimes. Nonetheless, the framework set out in this chapter is important for understanding why this apparent absence of attention to gender may also be a reflection of specific presumptions about the subjects of regulation. When we analyse legal norms and policies, including those regulating working time, we must remember that *all* policies are in fact gendered, whether they make gender or concerns of equality explicit or appear to be gender-neutral. This gendering occurs because, as I have argued here, policy rationales and justifications tend to reflect the hegemonic paradigms, which in turn are reflections of the social settlements that are reached through struggles among collective actors. As these (gendered) actors are variously and unequally situated within the universe of political discourse, assumptions about gender will always have direct bearing on the social paradigms that emerge and, in turn, on the dominant ideologies or discourses that inform concrete policies, laws, and institutional structures. In the multi-level context such as that of the EU, the universe of political discourse is significantly expanded, or different discourses interact with each other, thereby multiplying the number of actors and collective identities that vie for attention. While this multi-level 'reality' significantly complicates the process, it may nonetheless create openings for actors on one level, which may not have existed on another, or, as the case of Poland will show, it can at times reinforce existing tendencies and furnish additional rationales for certain policy directions. Periods of transition, such as that which has been occurring in Poland for a couple of decades, are particularly interesting for examining and evaluating these multi-level processes and their consequences.

To set the foundation for the analysis of the Polish working-time regime, I begin by looking at the supranational level. In the following chapters, Chapters 2 and 3, I consider the evolution of working-time political discourse and regulation at the EU level, keeping in mind the broader political-economic context, the national developments, the influence of other transnational actors, such as the OECD, and, most crucially, the stance taken by EU institutional actors and the social partners, namely, the representatives of industry and organized labour acting at the EU level.

2

The European Union Universe of Political Discourse on Working Time – from Security to Flexibility and Beyond

2.1 Introduction

> The regulation of working hours is fundamental to society. It was one of the original trade union demands, and now lies at the heart of Social Europe. It is a key aspect of health and safety in the workplace, and recognizes that allowing working people time to raise their families ('the short-term and long-term reproduction of the labour force') is vital to the interests of workers, societies and economies. *And it is crucial to achieving gender equality at work.*
>
> European Trade Union Congress (2006a)

The acknowledgement of the relationship between working time, social reproduction, and gender equality that is so explicitly articulated in the European Trade Union Congress (ETUC) position statement cited above, has, until fairly recently, been largely absent in most European Union (EU)-level documents dealing with working-time regulation. In fact, European trade unions themselves paid scant attention to the relationship between working time and gender equality, as this was not historically the focus of working-time regulation (Lehndorff 2007). Instead, the traditional rationales for regulation of hours have been protective and organizational, with the most prominent ones being security and flexibility: the first, related to maintaining existing standards or further limiting work hours to protect workers' health and safety and their right to leisure time; and, the second, being concerned with the right to manipulate work hours in a manner that suits the production process, meets business needs, and enables firms to remain efficient and competitive. As this chapter explains, the tensions existing between these competing objectives – and between their social and political proponents – have, through the 1980s and early 1990s, defined the Community discursive universe on working time in a way that significantly subordinated other rationales for regulation in this area. Although other social motivations, including better reconciliation of employment and family obligations, have been present in the working-time political discourse since the 1970s, paradoxically, it was the rise of flexibility as a hegemonic component of this universe at the end of the 1980s and through the 1990s that coincided with the resurgence of interest in work–family reconciliation in the new millennium. However, the historical embeddedness of flexibility in the discourses of deregulation and 'labour market rigidities' has made it a conflicted and unstable universe for the discussion of the interface between working time and gender.

The chapter proceeds as follows. To begin, the concept of flexibility is examined. Although flexibility has figured in the European debates on labour market and employment regulation since the 1970s and became hegemonic through the 1990s, what flexibility means is in fact highly ambiguous. Defining this concept more precisely in part requires locating its ideological origins and its political and economic dimensions, particularly its place within the broader discourses of deregulation and neo-liberalism.[1] Building on this discussion, the chapter then shifts to a more detailed consideration of EU policy discourses concerning flexibility and, particularly, how they have influenced the development of the EU working-time regime, which itself is discussed in detail in Chapter 3. I first map out how particular changes in the institutional arrangements and the allocation of power between the different actors who influence the Community-level discursive universe have created the space for development of EU social and employment policy, of which working-time regulation is a component. I then consider the evolution of EU working-time discourses, focusing on the already alluded to contest between security or health and safety, and flexibility, as well as the more recent recasting of the latter as the potential facilitator of a range of social and economic

[1] Drawing on work of others, Leah Vosko (2010) conceptualizes neo-liberalism as (1) a theory of political and economic practice, and (2) based Frederick Von Hayek's ideas on the one hand, and a series of projects emerging in the 1980s typically associated with Thatcherism, Reaganomics, and monetarism, on the other hand. In the first sense, neo-liberalism proposes that well-being is best advanced by maximization of entrepreneurial freedoms within the institutional framework formed by the rights to private property, individual liberty, free markets, and free trade (Vosko 2010: 90, note 2, referring to Harvey 2006). In the second sense, Vosko identifies three 'projects' of neo-liberalism: (a) the *economic* project, which is associated with liberalization, deregulation, and privatization of public/state services, (b) the *political* one that substitutes certain forms of state intervention with new forms of governance aimed at supporting the markets, and (c) the *social*, which consists of withdrawing collective responsibility and its reconfiguration, i.e. as in the process of dismantling the Keynesian welfare state. See also, Fudge and Cossman (2002) for an earlier and similar conceptualization of neo-liberalism, with emphasis on elaborating the project of privatization and its many strategies, including the legal ones.

goals. The question of whether flexibility can indeed provide 'win-win' solutions to employers and employees and, more fundamentally, challenge working-time standards that take for granted unpaid work relating to the care of family members and the running of households is considered next. The chapter concludes with the reflection on the content of the Community policy discourse related to regulation of working time.

2.2 From Security to Flexibility – Defining the Terms of the Working-time Debate

2.2.1 Shifting the Priorities in the Debate on Working Time

Through much of the twentieth century, particularly its latter part, the goal of reducing hours of work dominated the political discourse on working time in most developed economies of Europe (Bosch et al.1993; Supiot 2001). Largely driven by the trade union movement and workers' demands, and guided by social rationales such as the promotion of a better balance between work and leisure, or protection of health and safety, working-time reductions were also an important source of productivity gains and economic growth (Bosch 1999: 135). Significantly, because the labour movement focused on the preservation or improvement of what was the established working time *status quo*, the interests represented and protected by labour unions were often those of typical (male) workers in standard (male) jobs (Supiot 2001). However, with changes in work organization, composition of the labour force, and the broader political-economic developments, this long-standing focus on reducing working hours began gradually giving way to the emphasis on flexibility (Bosch 1999; Anxo et al. 2004a). Gaining in importance through the 1980s (Pollert 1988: 281), flexibility became the dominant component of the political discourse on work and work-time organization by the mid-1990s, with transnational and supranational organizations like the Organization for Economic Cooperation and Development (OECD), the EU, and even the International Labour Organization (ILO) actively promoting it.

The consensus around flexibility suggests it has been accepted as a key principle of working-time organization and, more broadly, that it has become a hallmark of our times (Bauman 2000). Yet, despite the widespread reference to this concept, what is actually meant by flexibility has been highly ambiguous in the mainstream discourse. To begin with, the term flexibility is rarely defined in the numerous policy prescriptions and strategic papers that refer to it, and the relationship between its various dimensions, forms, and strategies is often unspecified. This, as legal scholar Sandra Fredman (1997b: 301) points out, renders 'flexibility itself a flexible term' (see also Perrons 1999: 392); or a vague catch-all or abstract phrase (Pollert 1988) that, in the policy discourse, often carries either neutral or explicitly positive connotations by its association with other positively tinged keywords like efficiency, growth, or competitiveness (Standing 1986). This overall vagueness obliterates the fact that flexibility is a heterogeneous phenomenon; there are not only different types of flexibility and flexibility strategies, but as Gerhard Bosch (1995: 17) reminds us, flexible working-time arrangements differ across national labour relations contexts and employment models. This neutrality also glosses over the fact that flexibility's various forms have distinct and often opposing impacts on different stakeholders, be they parties to the employment relationship, firms, different labour market participants (Goudswaard and de Nanteuil 2000; Strzemińska 2008a, see Chapters 4 and 5 of this study), or society in general (Bauman 2000; Sennett 1998). Finally, such a characterization obscures the fact of flexibility's historic embeddedness in the broader discourse of deregulation and its promotion by neo-liberal reform agendas in most Western industrialized countries (Ashiagbor 2004; Fudge 2005) and in the former socialist states undergoing political-economic transition to liberal market economies (see Chapters 4 and 5 of this study).

Contrary to these neutral depictions of flexibility practices, as the American sociologist Richard Sennett (1998: 74) convincingly argued in an early and influential study on workplace flexibility, flexibility has concrete, and often negative, personal consequences. These, in turn, extend beyond the realm of work, and tend to affect people's everyday lives, as well as their relationships and the communities to which they belong (Sennett 1998; Bauman 2000).[2] But flexibility may also carry a transformative potential because in posing a challenge to the traditional (and gendered) conceptions of 'work' and 'worker' (Conaghan 2005; Collins 2005), it could potentially facilitate more egalitarian work organization and distribution of tasks in society (Plantenga and Remery 2010). Given these complexities and diverse takes on flexibility's conceivable consequences, it

[2] The recognition that flexibility has some negative consequences prompted the shift towards promoting 'flexicurity' at the EU-level as an optimal balance between flexibility and security. See *Employment in Europe Report – 2006* (not published in the Official Journal) and Viebrock and Clasen (2009) for a comprehensive review of the concept. Nonetheless, flexibility continues to be an important element in the flexicurity discourse and some still deem it hegemonic (Fredman 2004; Monks 2007; Lewis and Płomień 2009).

is necessary to unpack this ubiquitous yet ambiguous concept by defining it more precisely and uncovering its origins. This elaboration will allow us to assess how flexibility has been used in the context of working-time regulation at the EU level and in Poland, to decide whether it indeed can contribute to development of more socially sustainable organization of work activities.

2.2.2 *Defining Flexibility and its Three Dimensions*

According to the OECD, flexibility is the ability of systems, organizations, and individuals to adapt successfully to changed conditions by adopting new structures and patterns of behaviour (OECD 1986). This definition has been a common frame of reference in the debate on flexibility, and illustrates well the largely positive and politically neutral connotations of flexibility in the dominant discourse. Although the latter has been very influential in the context of policymaking, the more recent elaboration of the concept by the European Foundation for the Improvement of Living and Working Conditions (the European Foundation) tends to be more incisive because it better reveals the political and economic aspects of flexibility. Specifically, the European Foundation's definition disaggregates flexibility's three key dimensions: (1) the employer, or business efficiency flexibility; (2) employee, or work–family balance flexibility; and (3) flexibility as the policy response to 'labour market rigidities' (Chung et al. 2007; *Eurofound Industrial Relations Dictionary* 2007). While contemporary policy discourse frequently refers to the first two, the last dimension is usually less explicit. I begin with this political dimension because making it apparent helps to historicize the concept of flexibility; it also provides the crucial foundation for understanding how the other two have been employed in the official discourse and practice.

Flexibility as the Policy Response to Structural Rigidities

The concept of flexibility initially arose in the 1970s to address the needs of firms dealing with increasing competition and the growing pressures to improve economic efficiency and productivity (Bosch et al. 1993; Goudswaard and de Nanteuil 2000). These changing conditions, sometimes referred to as the 'new economy', emerged from the interplay between ongoing processes and new phenomena, including the globalization of markets, internationalization of finance, introduction of new production techniques and modes, demand for just-in-time delivery, and the information technology revolution (Perrons et al. 2005; Fudge and

Owens 2006; Albo 2010; Clement et al. 2010). In response, an economic and organizational consensus began to develop, according to which business survival and success in this altered environment required a new kind of firm, one that was nimble, adaptive, and flexible (Atkinson 1984; Pollert 1988).

Through the 1980s, the notion of flexibility, one of the key elements of this new consensus, became progressively mainstreamed in the political and economic discourse and actively promoted at most levels of governance as the essential strategy for regaining and maintaining economic competitiveness (Pollert 1988; Fredman 1997b; Ojeda Avilés and Garcia Viña 2009: 79). But this shift to flexibility did not occur in a political vacuum: rather, it was highly politicized because flexibility was closely tied to deregulation. As Diamond Ashiagbor (2004: 33–71) explains, both were essential elements of neo-liberal reforms that were carried out in the 1980s and 1990s in most industrialized countries on the advice of key financial and economic institutions, the International Monetary Fund (IMF), and the OECD. Informed by neoclassical economic theory and the 'law and economics' school of regulation, these reforms targeted and sought to dismantle or 'trim down' various forms of government interference and regulation of markets, such as those that developed in many Keynesian-style welfare states in the post-Second World War period. This intervention was based on the thesis that regulation is a source of rigidities and impedes the functioning of markets (10–22). As Ashiagbor shows (40–43), application of this perspective to the labour markets meant that employment protection systems, or institutional arrangements that include labour and employment laws and collective agreements, were deemed to weaken the demand for labour by making hiring less attractive and limiting the capacity of firms to respond to changes in external markets by adopting flexible patterns of workplace management.

In Europe, this focus on the removal of rigidities became particularly prominent in the 1980s, amid growing concerns about weak economic performance and high unemployment (Bruun and Hepple 2009: 47–48; Ojeda Avilés and Garcia Viña 2009: 79). According to the OECD's *Jobs Study*, the continent's economic downturn did not compare favourably to the 'robust' American economy and the vibrancy of the emerging and highly competitive markets in East Asia (OECD 1994). As unemployment became regarded the key source, and the symptom, of this decline, systems of labour market regulation that existed in most EU Member States came under attack of the neo-liberal reformers (Ashiagbor 2004: 38).

In accordance with the prevailing economic orthodoxy, the IMF and the OECD advised the European governments and the European Community to deregulate their labour markets and restructure their welfare regimes (Ashiagbor 2004: 38–43). Soon after, as Ashiagbor (2004) shows, combating unemployment and increasing employment rates became key EU policy objectives, and the flexibilization of labour markets was prominently adopted as one of the main strategies for their achievement. As I show later (Section 2.3), this focus on flexibilization and deregulation was a significant force in shaping the EU's discursive universe on working time. I will also suggest that the embeddedness of flexibility in the discourse of deregulation privileged certain types of flexibility over others.

Reconciling Business Efficiency with Employee Needs?

Official endorsement and promotion of flexibility in the political discourse contributed to an increased reliance on flexibility strategies and practices that many European firms have experimented with already since the 1970s (Machol 1980; Bosch et al. 1993; Strzemińska 1984, 2008a, 2008b). In the context of the overall push for competitiveness, productivity, and efficiency that characterized the 1980s, however, firms tended to favour forms of flexibility they deemed most likely to promote these objectives.

From the business standpoint, flexibility can be driven by the 'employers' desire for variable (flexible) labour inputs, in terms of numbers employed or hours worked, to match changes in demand for products and services' and can be achieved by a range of employer-led strategies designed to meet these objectives (*Eurofound Industrial Relations Dictionary* 2007). Increased productivity can be achieved also through workforce reskilling or changing the tasks that employees are required to carry out (*Eurofound Industrial Relations Dictionary* 2007). Overall, firms have at their disposal a range of strategies that are qualitative or quantitative, external or internal and can choose from numerical, productive, organizational, or temporal flexibility practices (Atkinson 1984; Goudswaard and de Nanteuil 2000; Vielle and Walthery 2003; Strzemińska 2008b, see Table 2.1).[3]

[3] In practice, these various types of flexibility often overlap, i.e. part-time work can be situated on the border between internal and external flexibility (Goudswaard and de Nanteuil 2000; Vielle and Walthery 2003: 8).

Table 2.1 Forms and practices of business efficiency flexibility

	Quantitative flexibility (volume of work)	Qualitative flexibility
External flexibility	*Employment status* Types of contract (fixed duration, temporary, on-call work, etc.)	*Production systems* Outsourcing (subcontracting, freelance labour)
	Numerical/contractual flexibility	*Productive/geographical flexibility*
Internal flexibility	*Working hours* (overtime, part-time, weekend working, irregular/variable hours)	*Work organization* (job rotation, multitasking, making workers responsible for planning, the budget, etc.)
	Temporal/financial flexibility	*Functional/organizational flexibility*

Based on Goudswaard and de Nanteuil (2000: 19–20) and Vielle and Walthery (2003: 8).

Since all these strategies are ultimately employer-driven, many will tend to interfere with employee interests in one way or another, although not all of them will be equally intrusive. Those forms of flexibility practice that do interfere have been sometimes referred to as 'negative' flexibility (European Foundation 2007: 10–11; Strzemińska 2008b: 106–107). By contrast, if utilized in a way that also coincides with the 'employees' desire for variable (flexible) contractual arrangements and working conditions to match changing private and domestic needs', flexibility strategies can have a 'positive' or employee-friendly effect (*Eurofound Industrial Relations Dictionary* 2007; European Foundation 2007: 10–11).

Indeed, there is a broad recognition that, provided they are predictable and secure, flexible work arrangements can be a key component of 'decent working time', because they support individual preferences related to work–life articulation in a way that standard forms of work organization may not be able to (Anxo et al. 2004b: 202–203; McCann 2004; Lee and McCann 2006). Importantly, in addition to helping people cope with balancing of work with leisure or non-paid work responsibilities, more flexible work arrangement can also support various life transitions, including enabling workers to continue education or engage in retraining, or to remain active in later life, even beyond pensionable age (Goudswaard and de Nanteuil 2000; Supiot 2001; Vielle and Walthery 2003; Anxo et al. 2004b; Plantenga and Remery 2010), all of which are key to the success of active labour market policies that are currently promoted throughout Europe. This last point alludes to the potential broader, also economic, benefits of positive flexibility. Indeed, firms utilizing such flexibility are also likely to benefit in the long term since it has been shown that adaptable and predictable work schedules with positive forms of flexibility tend to decrease staff absenteeism and tardiness, as well as boost morale and decrease staff turnover (e.g. facilitating the retention of women), with the plausible effect of actually increasing productivity and saving costs (OECD 2001b; Anxo et al. 2004b: 202–206).

Yet evidence suggests that most firms either do not recognize the mutually beneficial character of positive flexibility, or do, but many chose not to adopt it anyway. For example, European Foundation's past research shows that firms have a clear preference for deployment of external or quantitative forms of flexibility (Goudswaard and de Nanteuil 2000: 4), a preference that is also evidenced by the continuing spread of temporary work, outsourcing, part-time and asocial hours, and excessive overtime. As these forms of flexibility tend to diminish job stability, increase insecurity, and guarantee little predictability in the scheduling of work, their potential role in improving working conditions or helping workers with reconciling work and other obligations is very low (Perrons 1999, 2000; Goudswaard and de Nanteuil 2000; Strzemińska 2008b; Rittich 2010). Indeed, research suggests that even functional flexibility, which is somewhat more worker-friendly, does little to improve working conditions. One European Foundation study, for instance, concluded that such flexibility is still unlikely to compensate for the persistence of job monotony and job intensification in the workplace, concluding that '[i]n a more flexible environment, the improvement of working conditions increasingly becomes an issue in its own right' (Goudswaard and de Nanteuil 2000: 4). Similarly, a 2007 study on the impact of flexibility on work–life balance found that it was 'lack of flexibility [that] actually improves work-life satisfaction of parents employed full time', since many parents who have some flexibility in their work arrangement tend to also work longer hours (European Foundation 2007: 25–27).

The fact that enterprises have utilized mostly those flexibility practices and strategies that may have negative consequences for workers' well-being is ultimately unsurprising given the broader discourse of and drive for deregulation with which flexibility has been so closely associated and which has always prioritized the markets, efficiency, and competitiveness. Indeed, transnational and supranational institutions have until recently encouraged flexibility primarily by way of promoting part-time work, temporary work, and other types of atypical and precarious labour arrangements (Fredman 1997a, 1997b; Jeffery 1998; Ashiagbor 2004, 2006; Rittich 2006a; Vosko 2010), and choices of flexibility at the firm-level are very much a reflection of this policy menu. More recently, an effort has been made to recast atypical, flexible work in a more favourable light by connecting, at the policy level, flexibility and 'adaptability' of work with the reconciliation of work and family life or work and other non-work activities (Perrons 1999; Lewis and Giullari 2005; Lewis 2006b, 2006c; Jenson 2009; Plantenga and Remery 2009). The OECD's *Babies and Bosses*[4] series and the emphasis on activation of women or better reconciliation of work and family in many EU policy documents, including the EES and employment guidelines, the Green Paper on the *Partnership for a New Organization of Work*,[5] and the 2006–2010 *Roadmap to Equality*,[6] are some examples of this tendency. Nonetheless, as elaborated in the following section (which focuses on how the concept of flexibility has been employed in the EU universe of political discourse on working time), there are good reasons to be wary of this more recent shift.

2.3 European Working-time Regulation – the Terrain of Competing Discourses

Regulation of working time has been a long-standing issue on the EU agenda, as it has been at the national level. However, the extent to which the Community could regulate in this area, and the types of regulatory actions it could adopt, have depended on its competences and the availability of legal instruments and processes by which to assert it. As was the case with much of the Community's social *acquis*, the adoption of hours of

[4] *Babies and Bosses* is OECD's series on work–family reconciliation policies and family outcomes in Australia, Denmark, and the Netherlands (2002); Austria, Ireland, and Japan (2003); New Zealand, Portugal, and Switzerland (2004a); and Canada, Finland, Sweden, and the United Kingdom (2005).

[5] COM (97) 128 final.

[6] COM (2006) 92 final (hereinafter *Roadmap to Equality between Women and Men 2006–2010*).

work standards was enabled by a series of constitutional changes that expanded the Community's regulatory reach and the allocation of power between the different political and institutional actors with the influence over the universe of political discourse (i.e. the particular Member States, the Commission, the Council, the Parliament, and the social partners). The following section briefly traces the key historical shifts in the EU's institutional architecture in order to set the frames of reference for a closer examination of the discursive universe that gave rise to the Community's working-time regime.

2.3.1 *The Institutional Framework of Social Europe*

As it is well known, the contemporary EU has its genesis in the 1950s, when it was established as a steel and coal community[7] and later expanded into a broader European Economic Community (EEC) of six neighbouring states.[8] The 1957 *Treaty of Rome*,[9] which founded the EEC, had a relatively narrow and mainly economic thrust, as its primary purpose was to establish a common market between the signatory states. This task was to be accomplished through the removal of barriers to movement (of goods, persons, services, and capital) and the impediments to competition. Thus, while the *EEC Treaty* conferred significant regulatory powers on the Community institutions for the purpose of market building, it envisaged only a limited role for them in the field of social policy,[10] reserving this area for the regulatory action of the individual Member States (Barnard 2006). Specifically, the Treaty's Social Policy Title committed the Member States to 'agree upon the need to promote improved working conditions and an improved standard of living for workers' (*EEC Treaty*, Article 117), while its Article 118[11] charged the Commission – an institution responsible for

[7] *Treaty Establishing the European Coal and Steel Community*, 18 April 1951, 261 U.N.T.S. 140 (expired 23 July 2002) (*ECSC* or *Treaty of Paris*).

[8] Germany, France, Italy and the three Benelux countries (Belgium, Luxembourg, and the Netherlands). The communities together, the ECSC, the EEC, and the Atomic Energy Community are often referred to as the European Communities (EC) or European Community for short.

[9] *Treaty Establishing the European Economic Community*, 25 March 1957, 298 U.N.T.S. 3 (hereinafter *EEC Treaty* or *Treaty of Rome*).

[10] The Treaty included binding social provisions on freedom of movement of workers (Article 48–49) and establishment (Articles 52–58), and equal pay (as necessary to minimize distortions in competition, Article 119).

[11] These articles were subsequently renumbered in 1997; however, I will use the previous numbering where I refer to them in their historical context.

co-legislating (with the Council) and for 'guarding' the Treaties – with the limited procedural/consultative task of promoting 'close coordination' and 'facilitation' of Member State actions in the field of social policy.[12] As Catherine Barnard (2006: 4–5) observes, neither of these articles were binding on the Member States and thus neither conferred enforceable rights on European citizens or significant regulatory competency in the social field to the EEC institutions.

The asymmetry between the social and economic components of the *EEC Treaty* was not necessarily an indication that the Member States saw the former as unimportant (Rogowski and Deakin 2011: 7). Rather, it stemmed from the consensus that economic integration did not require harmonization of social standards, which instead should remain within the scope of national competence (Barnard 2006: 5–7). First, the EEC (EC as of 1967) structure was superimposed on the existing national social protection models and standards, which the majority of the Member States and expert opinion at the time deemed not sufficiently discrepant to cause distortions in competition (Moffat 1997: 48). Second, it was believed that the development of the social dimension was not necessary because the benefits of market integration would eventually lead to the overall improvement in social standards across the Community (Barnard 2006: 5–6). Indeed, through the 1960s and early 1970s, the policies of Keynesianism and the steady economic growth and prosperity among the Member States made for a political climate that was fairly receptive to improvements in national social standards, including labour standards (Kenner 2003; Bruun and Hepple 2009: 34–40).

The EC's first enlargement in 1973,[13] however, provided the impetus for the expansion of the Common Market's social dimension to counteract potential distortions of competition that might have ensued following accession of states with different social standards[14] (Kenner 2003: 24). Moreover, with the human costs of the uneven growth across the Community becoming increasingly evident, the Community's architects realized that further market integration would require 'a human face' to retain popular support (Kenner 2003: 24; Barnard 2006: 9). Hence,

[12] Barnard (2006: 4) cites *Germany, UK, and Others* v. *Commission* (Joined Cases 281, 283, 285, 287/85) [1987] E.C.R. 3203, as the case affirming the limited, procedural scope of this article. According to Barnard, the article could not be used to impose on Member States results to be achieved, nor prevent them from adopting measures at the national level.

[13] The accession of Denmark, Ireland, and the United Kingdom.

[14] As Kenner (2003: 24, note 8) points out, the need to secure the high level of social protection in Denmark after its accession was a significant factor.

in 1974, the Council passed a Resolution adopting the Community's *First Social Action Programme* (SAP)[15] and proclaiming commitment to social progress alongside the Community's further economic and political expansion. Specifically, the 1974 SAP referenced the attainment of full and better employment, the improvement of living and working conditions, and the increased role for social partners – the representatives of labour and business – for decisions taken at the Community-level and for workers at the enterprise-level, as the key social policy goals. Nonetheless, as Jeffrey Kenner (2003: 27–42) shows, with the 1974 Council Resolution setting out the programme being a form of non-binding soft law the application of which required political will, and with Europe's economic stability having been shaken by the twin oil shocks of the 1970s, the legislative programme and the subsequent actions adopted under it fell short of expectations. Consequently, although some areas of social policy experienced rapid expansion during this period,[16] with the area of equality between men and women being perhaps most prominent,[17] the Commission's ability to take further and broader action on social policy was largely constrained by the limited Treaty bases and the requirement of unanimity in the Council.

Just how limiting this latter requirement was became particularly evident with the 1979 election of the Margaret Thatcher Conservatives in the United Kingdom (UK). While not opposed to continuing the process of market integration, the UK Conservatives were fully averse to developing the EC's social dimension (Hepple 1987: 80–83, 1990). Instead, through the 1980s, the Thatcher administration became Europe's key promoter of the neo-liberal policies of deregulation, opposing harmonization of standards and the expansion of social dialogue and worker consultation as primary sources of rigidities and market constraints (Hepple 1990; Bruun and Hepple 2009: 46–47). Accordingly, through much of the 1980s, the UK vetoed all proposals for common social standards, making this period one of particular 'stagnation' in the development of the Community social *acquis* (Bercusson 1995; Kenner 2003; Barnard 2006: 10).

[15] *Council Resolution of 21 January 1974 Concerning a Social Action Programme* [1974] O.J. C 013/1 (hereinafter *Social Action Programme* or *SAP*).

[16] Bruun and Hepple (2009: 44) explain that the EEC labour Directives adopted during this period reflected the context of recession brought on by the OPEC crisis, with the main issues tackled being collective dismissals, transfers, and insolvencies to equalize costs and thus improve economic competition.

[17] The provisions of the EC Treaty on equal treatment were implemented by Directives on equal pay (1975) and equal treatment (1976), and several landmark ECJ decisions.

A major breakthrough for Social Europe came with the adoption of the *Single European Act*[18] in 1986, which, in Barnard's words (2006: 11), 'breathed new life' into the integration project and at least partially alleviated the UK-imposed stalemate. In reality, despite the Delors Commission's stated commitment to developing the Community's social dimension, or the 'European social space', the driving force behind the *SEA* was to complete the single market (Kenner 2003: 71–72). However, to legitimize further market integration and the entrance of new Member States (Greece, Portugal, and Spain) whose GDPs and labour costs were significantly lower than in older EC members, the Act also introduced several changes to the Social Policy Title of the *EC Treaty*. According to Kenner (2003: 79), the *SEA* was 'a pale shadow' of the earlier institutional reform proposals drafted by the European Parliament. Nonetheless, the Act introduced some important innovations, the long-term effects of which were probably unforeseen by its drafters, especially the UK. Of particular significance was the inclusion of Article 118a into the Social Title, which gave the Community new regulatory competences to adopt minimum standards Directives in the areas of working environment and health and safety at work. To ease the passage of binding instruments, the *SEA* changed the voting rules, extending qualified majority vote (QMV) rule to matters falling under Article 118a. Further, one of the Act's most important innovations was to provide for the 'co-operation' between the European Parliament and the Council in the adoption of legislation falling under Article 118a, thus partially addressing the critiques about the Community's democratic deficit by giving the Parliament a far greater role and influence over the content of the Community legislation than it previously had (Craig and de Búrca 2011: 11).[19] Along similar lines, Article 118b was added to emphasize the importance of social dialogue at the EC level, and the Commission was charged with the role of promoting talks between the representatives of management and labour (Kenner 2003: 79–80).

[18] *Single European Act*, [1987] O. J. L 169/1, 25 I.L.M. 506 (an act modifying the basic treaties) (hereinafter *SEA*).

[19] In the QMV procedure votes in Council are weighted in accordance with the size of population, though adjusted; it applies to matters listed in Article 153(1) and Article 153(2) of the Treaty on the Functioning of the European Union (TFEU). Under the cooperation procedure, the Council could, with the support of Parliament and acting on a proposal from the Commission, adopt legislation by qualified majority. The Council could also overrule the Parliament's rejection of the proposed law, when acting unanimously. Cooperation procedure was limited by the Treaty of Nice and eliminated entirely by Treaty of Lisbon (Craig and de Búrca 2011).

This expansion of the Community's social competences in 1986 was followed by the proclamation of the *Community Charter of Fundamental Social Rights of Workers*[20] (*Social Charter*) at the 1989 Strasbourg Summit, which, building on the *Treaty of Rome*'s objectives of improving living and working conditions and the Social Title of the *SEA*, established twelve basic categories of workers' rights.[21] As a symbolic declaration of political intent, the *Social Charter* was not legally binding. However, the *Action Programme*[22] that accompanied the Charter outlined the Commission's legislative plans for giving effect to the rights the latter contained. Specifically, the programme included forty-seven different measures, ten of which were to be adopted as Directives.[23] While the UK opted-out of the *Social Charter*, it was well known that any actions proposed by the Commission and adopted by the Council under the 1989 *Action Programme* would be taken under the EC Treaty (post the *SEA* amendments), and thus bind all Member States, the UK included. Significantly, since unanimity was no longer required for Article 118a actions, the sole UK veto would not be capable of blocking social legislation proposals. In effect, after the 1980s inertia, the early 1990s constituted a period of some expansion for the Community's social *acquis*, with several labour and employment law Directives, including the Directive on working time, adopted under the new legal basis provided by Article 118a.[24]

The scope of the Community's competence in the social field continued to expand through the 1990s, although initially without application to the

[20] *Community Charter of Fundamental Social Rights of Workers*, Luxembourg: Commission of the European Communities (hereinafter *Social Charter*).

[21] The twelve categories of workers' basic social rights included the freedom of movement (Articles 1 to 3), employment and remuneration (Articles 4 to 6), improvement of living and working conditions (Articles 7 to 9), social protection (Articles 10), freedom of association and collective bargaining (Articles 11 to 14), vocational training (Articles 15), equal treatment of men and women (Article 16), information, consultation, and participation for workers (Articles 17 to 18), health protection and safety at the workplace (Article 19), protection of children and adolescents (Articles 20 to 23), protection of elderly persons (Articles 24 and 25), and protection of disabled persons (Article 26). The *Social Charter* also included provisions on Member States' action (Articles 27 to 30).

[22] *Action Programme relating to the Implementation of the Community Charter of Basic Social Rights of Workers*. Communication from the Commission, COM (89) 568 final (29 November 1989) (hereinafter 1989 *Action Programme*).

[23] Mainly in areas where the *SEA* established competence.

[24] Nonetheless, as Barnard (2006: 14) points out, even at this highpoint of Community activity in the social field, these actions remained modest vis-à-vis the far-reaching economic measures simultaneously proposed and adopted to achieve the single market goals by 1992.

UK, which, maintaining its earlier stance, opted-out of the Social Chapter (Social Policy Protocol and Social Policy Agreement) appended to the 1992 *Treaty on European Union*.[25] Binding on the remaining eleven Member States, the agreement listed additional fields to which QMV and the co-operation procedure applied, and identified new areas of social policy in which the Council could adopt measures by unanimous vote. Moreover, the agreement envisaged greater policy-making involvement for the social partners, whose opinions on the direction of the Community policy and action would from now on be sought by way of formal consultation process. Going even further, the agreement also provided that the Council would give legal (and binding) effect to collective agreements reached by the representative social partners acting at the Community level. Contrary to the expectation, however, this expansion of EU competences in the social field and the new power given to the Parliament and the social partners in the legislative and policy-making processes failed to yield significant policy developments in the years following the Social Chapter's adoption. While the Commission's 1993 Green and 1994 White papers on social policy,[26] issued shortly after Maastricht, continued to profess the EU's commitment to the dynamic development of its social dimension, the stringent Economic and Monetary Union (EMU) convergence criteria and the budgetary constraints associated with them on the one hand,[27] and the ongoing UK Social Chapter opt-out on the other, significantly tempered the enthusiasm of the remaining eleven Member States (Barnard 2006). In effect, in the five years between the 1992 Maastricht and 1997 Amsterdam Treaties the Council adopted only four social Directives under the Social Chapter.

Following the electoral victory of the British Labour Party in May 1997, the UK ended its opt-out, which enabled the Social Chapter's amendment

[25] *Treaty on European Union* (EU), 7 February 1992, [1992] O.J. C 191/1, 31 I.L.M. 253 (hereinafter *Treaty of Maastricht*). Importantly, the *Treaty of Maastricht* also introduced the co-decision procedure which further strengthened the role of the Parliament because it gave it the power to block legislation of which it disapproved, if it was subjected to this procedure (Craig and de Búrca 2011: 14).

[26] *European Social Policy: Options for the Union*. Green Paper, COM (93) 551 (17 November 1993) and *European Social Policy: A Way Forward for the Union*. White Paper. Part A. COM (94) 333 final (27 July 1994).

[27] Article 121(1) of the *EC Treaty* lists four main criteria of convergence. This tension between the social and economic policy goals was also reflected by the 1993 White Paper on *Growth, Competitiveness, Employment: The Challenges and Ways Forward into the 21st Century*, COM (93) 700 final (5 December 1993).

and its insertion into the EC Treaty on occasion of the 1997 Amsterdam intergovernmental conference.[28] The substantive changes to the Chapter entailed: (1) the amendment of Article 117 to include an express reference to 'fundamental social rights' set out in the 1961 *European Charter* and the 1989 *Social Charter*; (2) the replacement of the co-operation procedure with co-decision under Article 137, thereby further strengthening the role of the European Parliament; and (3) particular attention to the principle of equality (of opportunity and treatment in matters of employment and occupation) between men and women to which the co-decision procedure was also extended. Moreover, special emphasis on employment was reflected by the insertion of a new Title on Employment into the Treaty and a more general mainstreaming of the objective of attaining high levels of employment.

Significantly, in addition to the expansion of the Social Chapter, the Amsterdam Treaty also ushered in a new regulatory mechanism for its governance. By contrast with the 'hard' and rights-based approach taken at the end of the 1980s and in the early 1990s, the approach adopted in Amsterdam focused instead on the 'soft' coordination of the national employment policies.[29] Specifically, while individual Member States remained in charge of their own policy development, the Amsterdam Employment Title required them to do so by taking into account the Council's annual broad economic guidelines, additional guidelines drawn up by the European Council, as well as the non-binding employment guidelines proposed by the Commission on an annual basis. The European Employment Strategy (EES) – as this yearly cycle of policy making became referred to after the 1997 Luxembourg summit – marked the official shift away from the Community's emphasis on measures securing workers' rights to those addressing the rates of European unemployment, particularly the promotion of active labour markets and the development of a skilled, trained, and adaptable workforce (Ashiagbor 2004, 2006). As Ashiagbor points out, the EES also marked the shift away from social policy to employment policy at the European level (Ashiagbor 2004).

[28] *Treaty of Amsterdam*, a result of this IGC, was signed on 2 October 1997, [1997] O.J C 340/1, 37 I.L.M. 56.

[29] 'Soft' methods of governance involve legal and policy processes that move away from harmonization by hard law Directives, and instead focus on monitoring of policy implementation through coordination, reporting, peer review, name and shame mechanisms, etc. See, for example, Mosher and Trubek (2003) and Trubek and Trubek (2005).

The soft regulatory mechanism adopted in Amsterdam was further developed by the 2000 Lisbon Strategy,[30] which labelled it the open method of coordination (the OMC).[31] Although Lisbon shifted even further away from the traditional method of harmonization (through Directives, for instance) to coordination of Member State action (through the activities of the Council, the European Council, and the European Commission), this shift was also accompanied by greater expansion into areas over which the Community had some competence but where the Member States continued to exercise significant control. Barnard (2006: 27) notes that this shift was especially significant with respect to areas where 'law has proven to be a rather blunt instrument to bring about social change' (such as equality), and in the context of the prospective fifth, Eastern enlargement, which would bring in new Member States with distinct legal and industrial relations traditions. The Lisbon Strategy's ambitious goal of making the EU 'the most competitive and dynamic knowledge-based economy that would be capable of sustainable economic growth with more and better jobs and greater social cohesion'[32] was reinforced by emphasis on employment activation and promotion of equal opportunities (to enhance that end). Lisbon set specific targets for employment rates at 70 per cent for men and 60 per cent for women (to be met by 2010). Finally, to improve the legitimacy of its action, Lisbon extended the realm of social actors whose input would be sought beyond the industrial social partners to actors in the broader civil society.

While Lisbon was not the last instance of Treaty change, for the purposes of the present chapter the most significant developments in the Community institutional architecture had taken place by that point. What should be mentioned is that the non-binding commitments to workers' basic rights contained in the 1989 *Social Charter* and the 1961 *Charter of Rights* found a more robust expression in the *Charter of Fundamental Rights of the European Union*,[33] which was signed and proclaimed on 7 December 2000 at the European Council meeting in Nice, and became legally binding on 1 December 2009, with the coming into force of the *Treaty of*

[30] Presidency Conclusions, Lisbon European Council, 23 and 24 March 2000, Bull EU-3/2000, 7–17.

[31] However, similar mechanisms of governance have been used in coordinating Economic and Monetary Union policies (the Broad Economic Policy Guidelines), and thus date back to the Masstricht Treaty (Szyszczak 2006).

[32] Note 30 above, para 5.

[33] *Charter of Fundamental Rights of the European Union*, [2010] O.J. C 83/389 (hereinafter *Charter of Fundamental Rights*).

Lisbon.[34] Among others, the *Charter of Fundamental Rights* recognizes the rights 'to limitation of maximum working hours, to daily and weekly rest periods and to an annual period of paid leave' (Article 31(2)), the right to 'reconcile family and professional life' including protections against dismissal for reasons connected to maternity or parental leaves (Article 33(2)), and the right to equality between men and women (Article 23). Although the Charter presents an important development and has been greeted with enthusiasm, both the UK and Poland negotiated a special protocol (Protocol No 30), which limits the Charter's application in both countries by restricting its interpretation by the Court of Justice of the European Union and British and Polish national courts, specifically with regard to the 'solidarity' rights contained in Title IV of the Charter.[35] Both the right to work–family reconciliation and the limitation of working time are contained in that Title.

This brings me to another issue which has not been mentioned up to this point, and that is the role and influence of the European Court of Justice (ECJ, now Court of Justice of the European Union) in the process of advancing and broadening the scope of the European social policy, and particularly the competences over working time. While opinions on the Court's role in advancing social and equality rights are divided,[36] for my purposes here it is worth to recount Barnard's (2006: 36) observation that one of the key issues related to the Court's role is the way in which its decisions have challenged the national systems of labour law and social protection. Claire Kilpatrick has more recently added that the Court, even

[34] *Treaty of Lisbon, Amending the Treaty on European Union and the Treaty Establishing the European Community,* Signed at Lisbon, 13 December 2007, O.J. C 306/01.

[35] However, as commentators noted, much as the Charter itself does not guarantee new rights but rather recognizes those already inherent in Community law and identifies 'objectives for action', the special protocol does not constitute an opt-out but rather clarifies how the national courts should interpret the Charter's provisions. See: Hepple (2001), Barnard (2006). See also Guerrina (2005), who is skeptical on the Charter's contribution to substantive equality.

[36] While the ECJ played a key role in expanding the early Community equality jurisprudence, feminist scholars have since critiqued the Court's approach, pointing out that its 'ideology' on motherhood and parenting remains gendered and conservative. See i.e: Ward (1996), Hervey and Shaw (1998), Shaw (2001), McGlynn (2001, 2005), Busby (2011), and Koldinská (2011). More recently, the ECJ also came under attack of labour lawyers for imposing stringent limits on attempts to use collective bargaining and the right to strike as measures against social dumping in the *Laval un Partneri Ltd* v. *Svenska Byggnadsarbetareforbundet,* C-341/05, [2007] E.C.R. I-11845 [*Laval*] and *International Transport Workers Federation* v. *Viking Line ABP,* C-438/05, [2007] E.C.R. I-10806 [*Viking*] cases, which have been subject to a lively scholarly debate.

if not directly involved in the process of legislating, nonetheless provides important input into the content of secondary legislation and can have a significant influence in the context of institutional struggles among the EU institutions or between the Member States within the Council (Kilpatrick 2011). As Chapter 3 shows, this has indeed been the case in the context of working time.

Ultimately, what the foregoing summary demonstrates, and as a number of European law specialists have already observed, the process of Treaty amendment and Community's geographical expansion had significantly reconfigured the balance of power between the key institutional and social actors, extended the Community's competence vis-à-vis Member States (indeed, the Member States had ceded power via the very process of Treaty change), and diversified the legal instruments and techniques by which to exercise these powers (Barnard 2006; Craig and de Búrca 2011). This process of rearrangement and growth has had a particular effect on the universe of political discourse on working time, to which I will turn next.

2.3.2 Between Security and Flexibility – Fostering Economic Efficiency and Combating Unemployment as Rationales for Community Working-time Regulation

Given the limited regulatory competences in the social realm just discussed, the issues of working time were not very prominent in the EEC discourse before the 1970s as the matter remained within the competence of the Member States, whose economic prosperity and stability in the preceding two decades made for a political climate that was receptive to progressive working-time reductions (Bosch et al.1993; Moffat 1997).[37] Although specific regulations differed between countries, by the early 1970s most EEC Member States had individually legislated the 40-hour (or 48-hour) workweek (Bosch et al. 1993: 1), which became the 'fixed reference poin[t] around which enterprises developed their work organization paradigm' (Bosch 1999: 135).

From that point on, flexibilization of working time began to attract attention within national debates. Alongside concerns for productivity, discussions on working-time flexibility during the early 1970s also

[37] Bosch et al. (1993: 1, citing Blanpain and Köhler 1988) point out this tendency towards harmonization was reinforced by the establishment of the international framework of working-time standards by, among others, the ILO.

focused on its potential to enable the achievement of various *social* objectives. Specifically, matters of worker's choice of working time (Bosch et al. 1993: 26), concerns about leisure, consumption, and work–life balance (Moffat 1997) all figured in these discussions. Indeed, in the early 1970s, even the official discourse of transnational institutions like the OECD (that have since then most eagerly promoted the flexibility-for-competitiveness agenda) acknowledged the social dimension of working-time regulation, commenting on its potential role in the improvement of living and working conditions and better adaptation of working time to workers' needs at different life stages (OECD 1973a, 1973b, 1976).[38]

The objectives of improving the living and working conditions also prompted some discussion on working time at the EC-level, particularly in light of the interest in expanding the Community's social dimension and the Council's adoption of the 1974 *Social Action Programme.* Lacking the competence to propose binding Community legislation in this field, however, the Commission drafted a non-binding Recommendation affirming the 40-hour workweek and a 4-week annual leave as social standards. While the Council adopted this Recommendation in July 1975, with Europe's economic outlook drastically altered by the OPEC crisis that began in October of the previous year, no concrete follow-up measures were taken to implement it (Moffat 1997). In fact, along with the economic downturn, the tone of the debate surrounding working time began to change once again. Rationales for regulation based on desire to improve working conditions gave way to those of the need to respond to economic change (Bosch et al. 1993), stimulate job growth, and increase efficiency and competitiveness of firms (Moffat 1997). Working-time reductions were not completely off the agenda as the creation of new workspaces was initially explored through job sharing and work redistribution, with further working-time reduction measures being proposed by the governments in France, Belgium, and Luxembourg into the early 1980s.[39] However, there was a growing consensus that more flexibility was required to

[38] According to Bosch et al. (1993: 26), however, this shift to focus on individual choice was also prompted by the early 1970s labour shortage, and they cite the 1973 Rehn Report, which proposed that policy should promote solutions that align individual choice as much as possible with manpower requirements, to support this argument.

[39] This was clear from the European Commission's 1982 *Memorandum on the Reduction and Reorganization of Working Time*, Information Memo, P-77/82 (December 1982), and the draft Council Recommendation prepared by reference to it: *Draft Council Recommendation of 23 September 1983 on the Reduction and Reorganization of Working Time*, COM (83) 543 final, [1983] O.J. C 290/4.

better respond to the changed economic circumstances, and concessions on working-time organization were being obtained through social dialogue and collective bargaining in some national contexts (Bosch et al. 1993).

Consensus around flexibility continued to strengthen through the 1980s, along with the deepening recession. Introduction of new modes or production, information technologies, and the globalization of markets exacerbated the tensions already felt after the oil shocks, spreading the general mood of pessimism across Europe (Kenner 2003: 72). Loss of manufacturing jobs due to the dropping demand and migration of firms to developing countries on the one hand, and the privatization of publicly-run enterprises and sectors on the other (Standing 2009), meant losses in union membership in most EC Member States (Ebbinghaus and Visser 1998[40]) which, in turn, gave employers more influence over the working-time agenda. Moreover, changes in staffing and organizational demands were required due to the shift towards a service-based, 24-hour economy and the influx of women into the labour markets (Supiot 1999, 2001; Anxo et al. 2004a). Consequently, through the 1980s, further concessions on hours of work were made in various national contexts,[41] which were reflected in new working-time laws that included 'longer daily and weekly maximum hours, longer periods of variability, widened possibilities for Sunday work and night work for women and greater derogation from legal minimum standards through collective agreements' (Bosch et al. 1993: 26–27). According to Gerhard Bosch, Peter Dawkins, and François Michon (1993: 27), these national developments were being 'coordinated' by the Member States, 'probably [. . .] to generate a new and more flexible regulatory framework for employers in the more competitive EEC internal market'. With major economic institutions such as the OECD urging deregulation and flexibility of Europe's labour markets as the cures for

[40] Ebbinghaus and Visser (1998: 3) identify the period from 1975 to 1995 as a period of 'crisis' during which the rates of union density fell rapidly across western Europe, from 40 per cent at the start of the 1980s to 34 per cent by 1990, albeit with national variations in attrition.

[41] Bosch et al. (1993: 26) cite Belgium, France, and Sweden as having made legislative changes by that time, and similar laws being on the agenda in Austria, Germany, and the Netherlands. Also, Tergeist (1995), refers to a 1986 European Trade Union Institute (ETUI) document noting that organized labour does not oppose flexibility per se, provided that it can retain a right to examine and evaluate different forms of flexibility from the standpoint of their likelihood to lead to the improvement of working conditions and the ability of employees to have some control over their working time (Tergeist 1995: 12, citing ETUI 1986).

'eurosclerosis' (Grahl and Teague 1989: 91–92), high unemployment, and lagging performance (Ashiagbor 2004), along with similar urgings by the European business, a further shift to flexibility was inevitable.

While the EC Member States generally agreed on the need for more flexibility, there was no similar consensus on how flexibility should be accomplished, or whether there was any role for the Community in this field. Niklas Bruun and Bob Hepple (2009: 48) suggest that most continental Member States did not see minimum standards and social dialogue as incompatible with flexibility. Working time had long been regulated through state-level legal intervention in continental Europe (Blanpain and Köhler 1988: 18; Blainpain et al. 1997), and despite growing concerns over labour market flexibility and economic efficiency, most of these states' governments maintained that social and economic standards could coexist and, indeed, bolster each other (Ojeda Avilés and Garcia Viña 2009: 79). Similarly, as Simon Deakin and Frank Wilkinson (1994) have pointed out, continental EC members viewed transnational social standards as actually capable of raising productivity along with positive social and economic outcomes, provided that these standards retained some room for collective negotiations and derogations to reflect local circumstances. In this view, a *regulated* approach to flexibility was not only compatible with efficiency – it could even lead to more equity (Deakin and Wilkinson 1994).

By contrast, apart from select protective regulations (such as protections of vulnerable groups, children, young persons, and women, adopted in the nineteenth century), the UK had developed a *collective laissez-faire* approach to regulation of working time, wherein the matter was left almost entirely to collective bargaining and employer regulation (Hepple 1990; Rubery et al. 1994: 274; Barnard 1997b: 9). While the working-time norms obtained as a result were in fact similar to those adopted in continental Europe, these norms were significantly undermined in the 1980s, through Thatcher government policies which aimed to weaken trade unions and dispense with other forms of labour regulation on the basis that they were sources of rigidity inhibiting labour market flexibility, undermining job creation, and economic growth (Hepple 1987: 80–83; Ashiagbor 2004; Bruun and Hepple 2009: 45–49). From the UK's perspective, any harmonized transnational approach to regulation was undesirable, regardless of the amount of flexibility it was said to enable. Instead, the UK believed that only full deregulation could provide the flexibility and efficiency that was necessary for economic success (Deakin and Wilkinson 1994), with the bottom line being that since the UK had avoided setting minimum working-time standards of its own, it was not prepared to accept any from the EC (Bruun and Hepple 2009: 48).

Thus, although both the continental and the UK approaches ultimately aimed to facilitate efficiency and flexibility, the ideological and regulatory differences between them were fundamental and produced significant tensions at the EC level through the 1980s. Given that the existing institutional framework provided limited legal basis for the Community action in the social field and made any such action dependent on the political will of all Member States, these differences made futile most of the Commission's efforts to secure a Community-wide approach to regulation of working time during this period.

In the early 1980s, for instance, the Commission proposed a series of working-time measures, partially in response to the regulatory developments already taking place in many of the Member States, and as a result of the business lobby's pressures for more flexible and diversified work arrangements (Hepple 1990). Reflecting the existing competences, these measures included draft Directives on part-time (1982)[42] and temporary work (1982),[43] both of which were proposed under the equal treatment provisions of the *EC Treaty*, as well as a non-binding *Council Recommendation on Reduction of Working Time* (1983) in light of the fact that the Community lacked competence to regulate on working time per se. While all three proposals reflected the growing emphasis on flexibility, when considered together they suggested an overall approach that had the potential to challenge and breach the tensions between security and flexibility and the social and economic rationales present in the working-time discourse of the late 1970s and the early 1980s.

In a 1980 Commission Communication on Voluntary Part-time Work,[44] for instance, the Commission urged Member States to diversify working-time arrangements, but also to promote 'voluntary' undertaking of part-time work, ensure that such work is not only promoted for women, and 'upgrade' its quality, so as to encourage a broader range of workers into part-time jobs[45] (Voluntary Part-time Work Communication 1980: 6). This goal was to be accomplished through extending part-time opportunities to a variety of occupations and positions, including

[42] *Proposal for a Council Directive on Voluntary Part-Time Work*, [1982] O.J. C 62/7.

[43] *Proposal for a Directive of the Council on Temporary Work*, [1982] O.J. C 128/2.

[44] Voluntary Part-time Work. Communication from the Commission. COM (80) 405 final (17 July 1980) (hereinafter Voluntary Part-time Work Communication).

[45] The Commission developed this approach on the basis of the *Council Resolution of 18 December 1979 on the adaptation of working time*, [1980] O.J. C2/1.

those requiring 'higher qualifications' and 'more responsibility', and ensuring that a wide range of part-time or reduced work schedules (on a daily, weekly, or monthly basis) be explored to best meet the varying needs of workers at different stages of their lives (Voluntary Part-time Work Communication 1980: 15). One of the overarching objectives, or the 'ideal solution' that the wide promotion of part-time work would help facilitate, was '. . . without restricting each worker's freedom of choice, to seek a gradual reduction and redistribution of working time and at the same time to encourage greater sharing of non paid family and occupational responsibilities between marriage partners' (Voluntary Part-time Work Communication 1980: 1).

Similarly, the 1982 *Memorandum on the Reduction and Reorganization of Working Time* and the *Draft Council Recommendation* of 1983 appear to have sought to balance the diverse needs of (different types of) workers and employers. While more flexibility in work organization was to enable the latter to take full advantage of production facilities and, hence, maximize productivity gains,[46] reduced hours of work were to create new jobs and serve a range of social objectives. Among others, reorganization and adjustment of daily hours was to promote also women's employment opportunities, create the conditions 'which would allow a greater sharing of family responsibilities', as well as enable flexible retirement and life-long training (*Draft Council Recommendation* 1983: 4). So as not to interfere with the creation of jobs and the other social benefits created by shorter work times, the Commission's 1982 *Memorandum* and the 1983 *Draft Council Recommendation* urged against excessive reliance on overtime (as a particular form of flexibility) and, to that effect, suggested introducing overtime restrictions in the national legislation.

Thus, along with the potential to balance security and flexibility and ease the tensions between their proponents (management and labour, as well as the different Member States), and reconcile the social and economic objectives that working-time regulation could serve, the Commission's approach in the early 1980s also seemed to promote some degree of convergence in everyone's working hours. Crucially, with references to issues such as the reconciliation of paid work with the obligations involved in the care of children and dependent adults, training, or flexible

[46] Economic benefit was also to be realized by simultaneous reduction in compensation (to reflect the reduced hours) and removal of labour market rigidities through, for instance, relaxing mobility laws to ensure that workers were free to move to take advantage of job gains achieved in different areas.

retirement the 1983 *Draft Council Recommendation* had the potential to also expand the working time political discourse. Nonetheless, since the Commission's proposals in the early 1980s fell within the regulated flexibility approach, all ultimately met with the UK's opposition as the country exercised its Council veto power to block any Community action in this area (Hepple 1990; Moffat 1997). Indeed, it was not until the passage of the 1986 *SEA* and the subsequent adoption of the *Social Charter* and the *Action Programme* in 1989 that new opportunities opened for regulatory action on working time. As will be shown below, however, the necessity to reframe the working-time issue to 'fit' the new legal basis for action and to overcome the UK opposition had specific and limiting consequences for the political discourse on working time.

2.3.3 *Limiting Flexibility, or Embedding Flexibility? – Health and Safety and the 1993* Working Time Directive

The passage of the *SEA* in 1986 enabled further development of the Community social dimension. One of the Act's most significant innovations in the realm of social policy, and one that had a particular impact on the evolution of working-time discourse and regulation, was the expansion of the EEC's regulatory competences to include matters related to the working environment and health and safety at work (Article 118a), and the application of the QMV rule to these matters. The Act also gave the European Parliament a greater role in shaping the Community policy discourse and legislation by extending the cooperation procedure[47] to matters falling under Article 118a, which was an important innovation given the Parliament's more pro-labour tendencies vis-à-vis the Council and the Commission.

Another development that was significant in elevating the issue of work hours in the context of Community policy was the adoption of the 1989 *Social Charter*, which referred to working time in two of its articles. Specifically, the Charter's Article 7 envisaged measures on 'the duration and organization of working time and forms of employment other than open-ended contracts', while Article 8 declared the right of every worker to a weekly rest period and annual paid leave. Although these provisions were not themselves binding on the Member States, given that the Charter was merely a 'solemn declaration', the Commission's accompanying *Action Programme* of 29 November 1989 called for adoption of more concrete

[47] See n. 19 above.

and binding Community legislation. With respect to working time, this Programme called for a Directive on the 'adaptation of working time' to be adopted under the new Article 118a competences of health and safety (*Action Programme* 1989: 17–18). In 1990, the Commission presented a draft Directive precisely on these grounds.[48]

As Graham Moffat (1997) observed, this shift in the framing of working time from an organizational matter related to reduction of unemployment and more efficient use of production facilities (but also other social objectives), to a more narrowly construed matter of health and safety was clearly tailored by the Commission to take full advantage of the new competences, and thus be able to propose a Directive binding on all Member States where it had previously been able to only propose Recommendations. Perhaps more importantly, given that unanimity was no longer required for matters under Article 118a, reframing working time in terms of health and safety would also increase the likelihood of the proposal's adoption by the Council, because it would effectively neutralize the UK veto (Moffat 1997).

While this strategy made some sense, particularly since working time had historically been a health and safety matter, re-characterizing working time as such was not without controversy because the approach was vehemently resisted by the UK, which saw it as the Commission's opportunistic way of sidestepping its opposition. As a result, the Commission had to be careful in making a very clear case for health and safety, and this had particular consequences for the conceptualization of working time. Specifically, since the broad notion of working time that lay at the heart of the 1983 *Draft Council Recommendation* was no longer fully congruent with the Commission's health and safety case, most references to the broad range of social objectives that could be achieved through working-time reductions were left out of the Directive's 1990 draft. Thus, while the Treaty did enable the Commission to propose a binding instrument, it also limited the scope of such document to one prescribing only minimum standards, hence harmonizing national regulations at the lowest common denominator.

Furthermore, while the British support was ultimately unnecessary for the Directive's adoption, the country continued to play a key role in shaping the working-time discourse, with the effect that when the *Working Time Directive* was eventually adopted by the Social Affairs Council in

[48] *Proposal for a Council Directive on the Organization of Working Time*, O.J. C 254/4 (9 December 1990).

1993 (over the UK's abstention), the instrument's protective value was more symbolic than real. Over the course of the Council negotiations and the legislative process, a long list of derogations and exclusions from the rules the Directive prescribed was added, thereby significantly circumscribing the Directive's protective functions (Kenner 2003, 2004). Indeed, as Moffat (1997: 63) suggested, the key driving force behind the instrument, 'perhaps even its raison d'être', was labour market flexibility, not the protection of health and safety. The fact that the Directive officially sanctioned significant working-time flexibility, particularly the flexibility to extend hours of work for certain sectors and categories of workers and in certain specified circumstances, tends to support this interpretation.

Ultimately, whether the motive behind its adoption was to prescribe flexibility or not, the Directive did appear to run counter to its own aims or those more broadly espoused by the *Action Programme* with which it was associated, namely to improve living and working conditions. It is important to note that in narrowing down the discussion of working-time reductions to matters of health and safety, the Directive omitted references to promotion of other social goals, including the commitment to work–family reconciliation and the link between work hours, sharing of domestic responsibilities, and the promotion of equal opportunities. As the future discussions on the Directive and working time in general would elucidate, and as will be discussed in Chapter 3, the framing and legal choices made with regard to the *Working Time Directive* in the years preceding its adoption would prove to be a source of ongoing tensions. More importantly, these choices had crucial consequences for the shape of the emerging working-time regime for which the Directive provided the foundation.

Although the economic climate continued to be unfavourable in the period between the 1992 Maastricht and 1997 Amsterdam Treaties, the EU appeared to be moving away from neo-liberalism (Kenner 2003). This shift, according to Kenner (2003: 310), reflected political developments in the UK and the US, where more moderate political parties were already in or about to come into office. While flexibility continued to be seen as the primary antidote to unemployment and inefficiency, Kenner suggests that the focus shifted from labour market flexibility to workplace flexibility (Kenner 2003: 229–30). Flexibility and diversification of work and working-time arrangements were to play key roles in making work more adaptable for a broader range of workers, so as to support the employability and adaptability objectives that eventually formed the central pillars of the EES, Title VIII of the Amsterdam Treaty, and the post-Amsterdam Employment Guidelines. Both the European Commission's 1996 *Action for Employment in Europe* paper,[49] and the 1997 Green Paper on the *Partnership for a New Organization of Work* reflected this shift by claiming security in this new context would have to come at the cost of flexibility. Much like the 1983 *Draft Recommendation*, the Green Paper identified issues like mainstreaming equal opportunities, integration of people with disabilities, and lifelong learning, which were important elements of the new debate on workplace organization, including reorganization of working time.

Although this new attention to the impact of work hours on other aspects of life remained firmly tied to the rationales of economic efficiency and competitiveness, the broader conceptualization of working time, and the recasting of flexibility as capable of promoting various social objectives, appeared to recall the approach taken by the Commission in the 1980s and, as such, opened doors to a new engagement with gender and gender equality.

2.3.4 Working-time Flexibility Beyond Economic Efficiency – Reconciliation of Work and Family, and Gender Equality

To say the shift towards a more social dimension of working-time policy did not come until the late 1990s is not to deny, of course, that working-time regulation has always had an important social dimension. Indeed, the key historical rationales for regulation in this area, the protection of health and safety and leisure time, have always been social in nature, and for a brief period in the 1970s and the 1980s the goals of facilitating better balance between work and life and/or family through regulation of work hours were already on the Community's agenda. Having been left out of the *Working Time Directive* in the early mid-1990s for the reasons just elaborated, however, the objective of work–family reconciliation, and to a lesser extent the pursuit of equal opportunities, once again became notable social variants of the working-time flexibility discourse. To be sure, the recognition that standard organization of working time had a negative impact on women's access to employment and that measures enabling better work–family reconciliation should be promoted was also related to the perennial goal of increasing overall employment rates by encouraging active employment participation among groups with traditionally lower

[49] *Action for Employment in Europe. A Confidence Pact*, CSE (96) 1 final (5 June 1996).

activity rates. Policymakers realized that to get more women into labour markets they had to pay closer attention to ensuring that at least some temporal aspects of work organization are congruent with care roles. At the international level, the OECD and the World Bank, for instance, signalled they were putting reconciliation issues on their respective agendas through the OECD's *Babies and Bosses* report series and the World Bank's *Engendering Development: Through Gender Equality in Rights, Resources, and Voice*[50] (Rittich 2006a: 43). Both sets of publications featured flexible working-time arrangements as crucial to achieving women's inclusion in the labour force through fostering better balance between their private and public lives (Rittich 2006a: 52).

As for the EU, various non-binding commitments to reconciliation of work and family had been espoused by Member States since the *Treaty of Rome* (Lewis 2006c; Masselot and Caracciolo Di Torella 2010), and the 1989 *Social Charter* made a clear, although also non-binding commitment to this principle in the context of its equal treatment provision (Article 16).[51] Subsequent inclusion of work–family reconciliation within the equal opportunities pillar of the 1997 EES and the post-Amsterdam Employment Guidelines more firmly embedded this principle within EU employment policy and discourse, albeit it did so by way of soft governance modes. Likewise, the goal of increasing women's employment was central to the Lisbon and Barcelona Strategies and the *Roadmap to Equality 2006–2010*, all of which strengthened further the EU commitment to work–family reconciliation and promotion of equal opportunities, not least because of the increasing need to address the EU's impending demographic crisis (Duncan 2002; Stratigaki 2004: 44–46; Guerrina 2005).

In terms of their more specific nexus with working-time policy and regulation, work–family reconciliation and promotion of equal opportunities were used as key rationales for several instruments addressing various aspects of working time, parental accommodations, or new forms of work at the EU level. The *Parental Leave Directive* and the *Part-Time*

50 A 2001 World Bank policy research report, co-published by the World Bank and Oxford University Press.

51 The Article 16 principle of reconciliation in the 1989 *Social Charter* was quite broad, providing that measures should be developed to enable men and women to reconcile their professional and family obligations. The 2007 *Charter of Fundamental Rights* (in force since 2009) limited the now binding Article 33 right to reconciliation of family and professional life to discrete periods following birth of the child, including protection against dismissal during maternity and parental leaves and the right to paid maternity leave.

Work Directive provide two key examples. Also years in the making and also subject to disputes during the 1980s, these Directives eventually pursued a different path from the *Working Time Directive*.[52] Unlike the latter, the issues of part-time work and parental leave were successfully negotiated by the social partners during the mid-1990s, leading to framework agreements later adopted by the Council as Directives in 1996 and 1997, respectively. These Directives echoed the enthusiasm of the 1993 White Paper on *Growth, Competitiveness, Employment*, the 1996 *Action for Employment in Europe*, and the 1997 Green Paper on the *Partnership for the New Organization of Work* for working-time flexibility and work–family reconciliation strategies as ways of achieving women's activation and equal access to the labour market.

Although absent from the original *Working Time Directive*, the objective of work–family reconciliation reappeared in the context of discussions about the Directive's scheduled revision. The Commission's 2004 consultation documents,[53] and its subsequent proposal for a new Directive,[54] referred to the issue of work–family reconciliation as a significant consideration in rethinking the approach that the Directive adopted a decade earlier. Less emphasis was placed on the objective of equal opportunities, despite the links that have been made between equality and work–family reconciliation in broader policy discourse and research the Commission had at its disposal (see e.g. Kravaritou 1999). In consultations over the Directive, the social partner organizations also took up the agenda of flexibility as work–family reconciliation, even if with a different focus and varying degrees of commitment. The European Trade Union Congress's (ETUC) historically protective stance on traditional working-time standards,[55] gave way to a more open support of flexibility in light of workforce diversification and the need to address the critique that the

[52] For the discussion of all three Directives, see Chapter 3.

[53] Re-examination of *Directive 93/104/EC Concerning Certain Aspects of the Organization of Working Time*. Communication from the Commission to the Council, the European Parliament, the European Economic and Social Committee, and the Committee of Regions and the Social Partners at Community level, COM (2003) 843 final/2 (15 January 2004); Second Phase of Consultation of the Social Partners at Community Level concerning the Revision of *Directive 93/104/EC Concerning Certain Aspects of the Organization of Working Time* (hereinafter *Second Phase Consultation*).

[54] Proposal for a Directive of the European Parliament and of the Council amending *Directive 2003/88/EC Concerning Certain Aspects of the Organization of Working Time*. COM (2004) 0607 final, COD (2004) 0209.

[55] Although, as was noted above, some openness to flexibility was expressed by the ETUI as early as in its 1986 Report. Above, n. 41.

Congress had not sufficiently represented or been concerned with the lot of non-standard workers (Passchier Interview, 16 February 2010, Brussels). Yet, while the ETUC accepted that achieving better work–family reconciliation and gender equality might indeed require more flexible organization of standard work, it has insisted that for these objectives to be fulfilled, flexibility should be promoted for *all* workers, not just some, and that flexibility should be introduced within a protective framework to ensure that workers can really benefit from flexibility practices (Pillinger 2006; ETUC 2006a, 2006b; Passchier Interview, 16 February 2010, Brussels).[56] The EU-level employer organizations, such as BusinessEurope (formerly UNICE), which have been long promoting flexible organization of work hours but urging fewer protective regulations at the EU level, have also agreed that work–family reconciliation agenda is important (Second Phase Consultation 2004; Rønnest Interview, 16 February 2010, Brussels). Yet, in contrast with ETUC, the organization has opposed discussing work–family reconciliation in the context of the *Working Time Directive* (Second Phase Consultation 2004; UNICE 2004a, 2004b), instead, focusing on the role that part-time work, temporary work, and parental leave can play in its promotion. Focus on reconciling work and family was also missing from the organization's *Go for Growth: An Agenda for the European Union in 2010–2014* (BusinessEurope 2009a). Although the report identified the demographic crisis as one of the five key challenges facing Europe and listed the need to increase the supply of skilled workers as one of the two key ingredients in its strategy to boost growth (BusinessEurope 2009a), it did not mention flexibility or assistance to working caregivers who presumably are also in that skilled workers' pool. How the pool of workers is to be increased without meaningful strategies for work–family reconciliation and redistribution of tasks between paid work and unpaid caring duties is unclear.

The particular way in which social partners have engaged with the flexibility's work–family reconciliation potential, especially in the context of standard work hours, has had an impact on the discourse surrounding the Directive. As I will elaborate in the next chapter, the discussion of the Directive's most controversial provisions – those that promote negative forms of flexibility – has continued to be debated in largely the same terms

[56] The ETUC's official position and its more nuanced gender perspective on working time was not necessarily uniformly accepted among national and European labour movement leadership (Passchier Interview, 16 February 2010, Brussels), for many of whom gender sensitivity remained a marginal concern.

as before and without much consideration to gender impacts of these flexibility forms. The rationales of health and safety on the one hand, and those related to the necessity to provide sufficient flexibility for the most efficient operation of firms on the other, continued to constitute the key positions in the dispute over the Directive's future and the Directive's 2004–2009 revision negotiations failed precisely because no agreement could be reached on these grounds. Once again, the issue of work–family reconciliation was subordinated to the objectives on the basis of which a safer legal and political argument could be made.

2.4 Taking Gender Seriously?

While working-time flexibility and work–family reconciliation are now frequently featured side by side in EU policy discourse, as I have discussed in the first section of this chapter, not all forms of flexibility are in fact compatible with the objectives of work and family reconciliation. Nor are all forms of flexibility, including those that do help with reconciling family and employment obligations, necessarily compatible with the goals of gender equality. It is evident, and confirmed by the Commission itself, that although diverse working-time arrangements have indeed flourished in some national and industry contexts, these arrangements have not always provided workers with permanent and adequate solutions, or effectively redistributed how women and men allocate their time and share their paid and unpaid work responsibilities.

A key problem, as already discussed earlier, has to do with the forms of flexibility that have been available and most often used, and to whom they have been directed. Until recently, part-time and temporary contracts, as well as other forms of non-standard work, have been primarily targeted at women workers, and these types of flexible contracts have been packaged as convenient forms of family accommodation. Shorter work hours or irregular periods of work such contracts provide can be indeed helpful to workers unable to submit to a standard, full-time work schedule, however, the limitations of these forms of flexibility have been well documented, with the attendant insecurity, low wages, and lack of career advancement opportunities being key among them. By contrast, flexibility within the context of standard work has generally entailed increased, if periodic, reliance on extended working hours and overtime, balanced out with periods of rest or reduced work hours. Periods of intensified work, compromised predictability, and low worker control over the scheduling of work are some features that render such forms of flexibility less compatible with balancing work and family obligations. Indeed, the prospect of having one's hours extended or being expected to work overtime can have particularly dire consequences for, or outright exclude, those workers who maintain the primary responsibility for the provision of care within the family, a task that is still more often than not carried out by women. Thus, what constitutes flexibility for whom is not inconsequential from the perspective of work–family reconciliation, and different forms of flexibility will compromise or enhance one's ability to more equally engage in paid and unpaid work. Unsurprisingly, researchers have found that national contexts where long-hours persist also evidence a significant degree of polarization in working times, with the long hours of work on one end of the spectrum being 'balanced' by below-average, short, part-time hours on the other. This polarization retained a clearly gendered pattern – a hallmark of an unequal labour market (Fagan 1996; Anxo 2004).

The fact that the disproportionate numbers of workers relegated to the low end of the working-time spectrum still tend to be women highlights the important relationship between working-time organization, its regulation, and equal opportunities. Thus, it is also crucial to remember that even where working-time flexibility measures are promoted as 'family friendly', these measures do not necessarily foster gender equality. As Dominique Anxo and colleagues (2004b: 203) urge, promoting equality requires going beyond measures that enable women to be on an equal footing with men in employment (the level or status of jobs, promotion prospects, etc.), to encourage a more equal sharing of the time-consuming aspects of family responsibilities between men and women. For that objective to be facilitated, it is men who must be encouraged to adjust their working time at different stages in the life course, such as when they have young children (Anxo et al 2004b, Anxo 2004), and this is something that the EU policies have not been that effective at achieving (Morgan 2009).

Granted, the emphasis on the very redistribution of responsibilities for care time as a necessary step to gender equality has now become more prominent in the EU policy discourse. However, I argue that such redistribution is unlikely to occur if the current tendency to promote part-time work and other forms of reduced work times continues alongside the tendency to achieve flexibility by way of significant working-time extensions, especially in light of the obviously gendered relationship between the two flexibility types. This inconsistency in approach – between rhetoric and actual practice – is highly problematic and illustrates that something is amiss in the sudden turn to promote flexibility as not only a work–family reconciliation but also an equality-enhancing strategy. Why has the emphasis on gender been so selective and uneven in the EU discourse on working time and why has the focus on gender equality been almost entirely absent in the context of the *Working Time Directive*? One of the explanations for this trend is offered in the feminist literature on gender mainstreaming, or a transversal strategy of incorporating gender concepts beyond their more traditional deployment in social policy and into the realms of economic, fiscal, and monetary policy. Adopted by most major transnational and regional institutions in the aftermath of the 1995 Beijing UN conference on women (True and Mintrom 2001; Mazey 2001, 2002; Rittich 2006a; Jenson 2009; Knijn and Smit 2009), it has been driven partially by feminist research and recommendations, activism, and policy networks (True and Mintrom 2001). In the EU context, gender mainstreaming was codified as a primary policy tool for achieving gender equality in the 1997 Amsterdam Treaty (Walby 2003; Abels and Mushaben 2012).

The fact that this strategy places attention to gender difference and the specificity of women and men's experiences on the policy agenda is without a doubt a positive development. However, the practical application of this strategy has been contested (Walby 2005), and feminist policy scholars like Jane Jenson (2009), Jane Lewis (2006c), and Maria Stratigaki (2004), among others, have questioned whether its adoption has been a genuine step in the right direction, or an instrumental move intended to serve other objectives. As Trudie Knijn and Arnoud Smit (2009: 486) ask with respect to incorporation of the gender perspective into the mainstream policy agenda: '[. . .] what happened with all these insights, and how are they reflected in current policy discourse?' Unfortunately, it appears that importing the gender language has not necessarily translated into transformative policy and lawmaking, or gender egalitarianism. Instead, in various policies, including those on reconciliation of work and family, gender concepts have been often deployed in ways that suggest their appropriation, subordination, 'cooptation', and general diluting (Stratigaki 2004: 30; Lewis 2006c; Jenson 2009; Knijn and Smit 2009: 486). The gender equality agenda, while omnipresent, has been at best weakened and lacking in coherence, and, at worst, subordinated to other policy goals.

The use of gender equality as a means to an end distinct from equality itself, and its subordination to other policy objectives, has also been noted in critical analyses of EU employment policy beyond the specific context of work–family reconciliation policies (although these policies are part and parcel of various employment strategies promoted by the EU). Collette Fagan and colleagues (2006), for instance, have detected instrumentalism in the broader EU employment policy's focus on women and the apparent commitment to advancing gender equality. They suggest that this policy appears to be motivated primarily by the perennial objective of increasing the overall employment rate, which is evidenced by an approach that favours supply-side labour market policies but pays insufficient attention to the promotion of quality of work, and pays more attention to reducing the employment gender gap rather than the gender gap in wages (Fagan et al. 2006: 577). This is consistent with what Ashiagbor (2006) has suggested in relation to the EU promotion of non-standard – precarious – forms of work in general, which are apparently more adaptable for a broader range of workers, but in reality are an integral part of re-regulating labour markets for economic reasons.

This sort of instrumentalism has led some feminists to question what precisely is being mainstreamed by way of this mechanism, with some scholars concluding that gender mainstreaming lacks transformative potential as it actually diffuses a rather narrow, neo-liberal conception of equality based on market citizenship and thus institutionalizes hegemonic masculinity (Kronsell 2005; Perrons 2005; Rubery 2005; Woehl 2008). Indeed, the more recent decreased visibility of gender in EU coordination processes, its lower prominence in the *Europe 2020 Strategy*,[57] and its underplaying or complete absence in the EU's post-2008 crisis response tends to confirm gender and gender equality's secondary status and their subordination to other policy objectives (Smith 2009; Smith and Villa 2010; Leschke and Jepsen 2011).

The analysis of EU working-time discourse suggests that the shift to work–family reconciliation rationales for reorganization of working time may have also been driven by an instrumental agenda. The relative absence of gender equality goals in the *Working Time Directive* can be partially attributed to the fact that the working-time debate has always been dominated by other considerations and tensions, such as those between security and flexibility, with the security at stake being mainly that of standard (male) workers. As the working-time discourse shifted towards flexibility, this shift was deeply linked with the goals of labour market activation and economic efficiency, making references to gender and equal

[57] *Europe 2020. A Strategy for Smart, Sustainable, and Inclusive Growth.* Communication from the Commission. COM (2010) 2020 final, 3 March 2010 (hereinafter *Europe 2020 Strategy*).

opportunities, when featured, largely instrumental and subordinate to achieving economic goals. In light of this, while increased emphasis on the promotion of flexibility as an aid to more effective work–family reconciliation and facilitating redistribution of care between women and men are no doubt significant developments, it is hard not to see them too as tied to other policy goals, including (still) increasing employment rates, meeting the care needs of the young and the elderly, and the concern about decreasing fertility rates in an ageing society.

An alternative, albeit related explanation for lack of more meaningful and coherent gendering of working-time policy has to do with the key actors involved in the shaping of the universe of political discourse on issues of working time. Organization of working time has been in many Member States traditionally the purview of collective bargaining and social partners' negotiations. In this context, the debate too has been framed by considerations of security versus efficiency; standard employment was addressed separately from non-standard or 'atypical' employment. Bifurcated in this way, the two have been treated as separate subsets of the working-time regulation agenda, not unlike at the European level. Although the trade unions, as represented by ETUC, have certainly come to recognize the connection between gender equality and working time more generally, this is a recent development and as such has not been incorporated meaningfully into the debate on working time until the 2004–2009 failed round of negotiations on the *Working Time Directive* (see Chapter 3 for more discussion). At the same time, according to a former officer of the European Federation of Public Service Unions, Brian Synnott, women's umbrella organizations, like the European Women's Lobby (EWL), were absent from negotiations on the initial Directive and only more recently became involved with the issue of working time (Synnott Interview, 18 February 2010, Brussels). Lack of EWL's or other women's organizations' input also meant that gender equality has been, until recently, largely marginalized in the political discourse on working time.

2.5 Conclusion

The goal of this chapter was to examine the role of the flexibility discourse in shaping the broader universe of political discourse on working time in the European context. As I explained, although flexibility has gradually become the dominant component of the regulatory discourse, alternative rationales for regulation were present in the European Commission's approach through the 1980s. Given the institutional arrangements, lack of Community competence, the significant differences of opinion between Member States on how flexibility should be achieved, especially the UK's push for deregulation, it was not until the passage of the *SEA* in 1986 and the adoption of the *Social Charter* and the *Action Programme* in 1989 that opportunities for regulation on working-time materialized. The adoption of the 1993 *Working Time Directive* was enabled by the new Article 118a and QMV voting rule. However, the prominence of the flexibility discourse, the tensions between the different Member States (the UK opposition), and between the EU institutions (the Council and the European Parliament, and the social partners), culminated in a choice of a fairly traditional but in the EU context legally narrow health and safety framing, as well as the inclusion of significant negative flexibility within the scope of this protective measure.

Subsequent changes in EU policy have given rise to a new social deployment of the working-time flexibility discourse. This new direction offers the promise of a transformative approach to labour market regulation; one, which is more attentive to different workers' needs, the process of social reproduction, and takes into account the total social organization of work. At the same time, however, the extent to which it is possible to construct a more egalitarian working-time regime in Europe depends on the manner in which the most fundamental, 'core' working-time standards have been conceptualized and handled. As the next chapter will show, although the rise of work–family reconciliation has had an impact on the overall approach to working-time regulation at the EU level, it has been far more important in shaping the periphery of the EU working-time regime, but not nearly as successful in transforming its 'core'. In the next chapter, I consider the EU's first and key instrument regulating working-time, the *Working Time Directive*. As the story of this Directive illustrates, the foundation of the EU working-time regime remains embedded in standard conceptions of work and worker, and this has specific gendered consequences.

3

The European Union Working Time Directive – Laying the Gender-neutral Foundation for a Flexible Working-time Regime

3.1 Introduction

As Chapter 2 elaborated, the pursuit of more flexible labour markets and workplaces was crucial in defining the European Community (EC) discursive universe on working time, with the adoption of the *Working Time Directive*[1] in 1993 being in a number of ways a watershed event in the development of the Community's regulatory approach in this area. For one, the Directive was enacted by way of a 'hard' instrument, while most subsequent measures addressing aspects of working time or special leaves (i.e. part-time work and parental leave) would be adopted as social partner negotiated framework agreements, only subsequently formalized into EC Directives. Moreover, while the Directive invoked traditional rationales for regulation of work hours and constituted a symbolic nod to security and protection of workers' interests in health and safety, it also clearly signalled that flexibility had become the dominant regulatory discourse and objective at the EC level. Indeed, the inclusion of wide-ranging derogations and exceptions from the Directive's protective standards (a number of which were highly controversial) – all in the interest of flexibility – had some suggest that the key impetus behind the measure was deregulatory (Moffat 1997). As I will show here, the fact that several Member States subsequently re-regulated their national working-time regimes by drawing on the Directive's flexibility provisions tends to support such a claim, albeit the fallout of the European Court of Justice (ECJ) rulings on the scope of 'working time' certainly contributed to this process (Düvel 2003; Hardy 2006). Finally, in contrast to measures on part-time work and parental leave enacted some years later, and given its distinct legal basis, the 1993 Directive made no reference to either equal opportunities or the principle

[1] *Council Directive 93/104 EC concerning certain aspects of the organization of working time*, [1993] O.J. L 307/18 (repealed); *Council Directive 2003/88 EC of the European Parliament and of the Council of 4 November 2003 concerning certain aspects of the organization of working time*, [2003] O.J. L 299/9.

of work–family reconciliation, thereby setting an entirely gender-neutral tone for the EC's 'core' working-time standards. The question of how such standards would potentially impact those workers charged with unpaid care obligations remained outside of the debate surrounding the Directive, at least until the start of its revision process in 2003. However, as will become evident, even with growing profile of work–family reconciliation in the Community's broader social policy discourse, efforts to incorporate gender concerns into the discussion surrounding this key instrument have been only partially successful.

This chapter looks in more detail at the *Working Time Directive* to explain how the Directive's narrow framing and the uneasy balance between security and flexibility that was originally struck within this Community instrument has continued to pose problems for the Directive's more progressive recasting. First, more background is provided on the Directive itself and the challenges that it faced in the aftermath of its adoption. Next, I consider the consultation and revision process that began in 2003 and lasted until 2009, and through which the issue of work–family reconciliation re-emerged as a rationale in regulation of working-time standards.

3.2 The 1993 *Working Time Directive*

The Council of the European Union (the Council) adopted the *Working Time Directive* in November 1993, pursuant to Article 118a (now Articles 137 and 138) of the *Treaty of Rome*.[2] Justified on the basis of health and safety, the Directive established basic working-time standards at the EC-level, including maximum permissible weekly hours of work, daily and weekly rest periods, and annual leave, though setting them at a level lower than that legislated or collectively agreed to in many Member States (Fajertag 1998, cited in Adnett and Hardy 2001: 116; Fajertag 1999), with, at the time, the exception of United Kingdom (UK).[3]

As noted in Chapter 2, what made this Directive remarkable and controversial, was the fact that the European Commission (the Commission)

[2] *Treaty Establishing the European Economic Community*, 25 March 1957, 298 U.N.T.S. 3 (hereinafter *Treaty of Rome* or *EEC Treaty*).

[3] Prior to the 1998 *Working Time Regulations* transposing the Directive, the UK had no statutory rules on working hours, rest, and vacation periods, which were instead left to collective bargaining (Rubery et al. 1994: 274–75; Barnard 1997b). In practice, low union density resulting from Thatcher-era industrial policy meant that collective agreements covered very few employees (Bruun and Hepple 2009: 47).

and a Council majority decided to take it on without there being the usual consensus in the Council.[4] While the Directive's adoption resulted from a confluence of several factors, politically speaking, the majority of the Council was able to pass the Directive over explicit protest of the UK government because the Commission's reframing of working time as a health and safety issue meant that a qualified majority (QMV) was sufficient to pass it in a Council vote. The measure was an outcome of the post-*Single European Act*[5] commitment to a more balanced social and economic policy, expressed in the Commission's 1989 *Social Charter*[6] and the accompanying *Action Programme*.[7] However, with the UK long opposed to EC-wide social standards and having opted-out of the *Social Charter*, this new social commitment was hardly universal. The UK's dedication to the notion that more flexibility could only be achieved through less regulation meant that it was opposed to harmonization of working-time standards. This stance contrasted sharply with that of other Member States which neither equated flexibility with deregulation *per se* nor regarded basic working-time standards as sources of rigidity (Hepple 1990; Ojeda Avilés and Garcia Viña 2009: 79). In fact, various forms of flexibility had already been made integral to the more regulated continental working-time regimes (Bosch et al. 1993). These differences in practice and policy outlook, particularly as of the late 1970s, produced significant regulatory divergence between the UK and continental Europe. In light of progressing market integration, the UK's lack of centrally legislated or bargained working-time standards, with the exception of a few sectors (Hepple 1990; Rubery et al. 1994: 274–75; Barnard 1997b: 9), raised concerns about the country's unfair competitive advantage (Mills 1996: 137).

Thus, the establishment of a basic floor of working-time rights by way of the 1993 Directive was not only a way to follow-through on the commitment to a more Social Europe but also to even-out the playing field. The choice of health and safety basis meant that this objective could be

[4] The Directive was opposed by the UK's Conservative government, which abstained from voting on this instrument and later challenged the Directive's legality. See Sections 3.2.1 and 3.2.3.

[5] [1987] O.J. L 169/1 (29 June 1987) (hereinafter *SEA*).

[6] Commission of the European Communities, *Community Charter of the Fundamental Social Rights of Workers*. Luxembourg: Office of the Official Publications of the European Communities, 1990 (hereinafter *Social Charter*).

[7] *Action Programme relating to the Implementation of the Community Charter of Basic Social Rights for Workers. Communication from the Commission.* COM (89) 568 final (29 November 1989) (hereinafter *Action Programme*).

achieved without having to rely on the UK's approval or, indeed, without having to foreclose flexibility within the overall protective framework. That the latter was a consideration was already evident from the Commission's 1990 proposal,[8] which despite framing the Directive as a health and safety instrument was in fact fairly sparse on protective provisions, proposing only to set minimum rest periods (daily, weekly, annual), minimum conditions for shift and night work, and provided that health and safety principles be observed in 'the event of changes in working patterns resulting from adjustments in working time' (Commission Proposal 1990: 2). Issues of systemic overtime, maximum duration of working time, and weekend work were to be left to national collective bargaining or legislation, which in accordance with the principle of subsidiarity were deemed the more appropriate levels for their regulation (Commission Proposal 1990). The 48-hour weekly maximum standard was only added at the European Parliament's insistence (Moffat 1997: 56), though even this provision was eventually matched with longer reference periods and the infamous individual opt-out from that maximum negotiated at the insistence of the UK (Von Prondzynski 1994: 93). Effectively, after two years of supranational and inter-governmental bargaining, there was so much flexibility in the version of the Directive that was actually adopted that its health and safety purpose was significantly circumscribed. Some observers deemed it to be a 'bizarre' and a 'most unsatisfactory' compromise (Kenner 2004: 589, 600), and even the British Secretary of State for Employment was reported to have had declared the Directive 'toothless' (Barnard 1997b: 11).

3.2.1 Minimum Standards and Maximum Flexibility

In terms of its objectives of protecting health and safety at work and 'encouraging improvements . . . in the working environment' (preamble), the 1993 Directive set limits on the maximum hours of work (Article 6[9]), established minimum entitlements to daily (Article 4, Article 5), weekly (Article 5), and annual rest periods (Article 7) for most workers, and made special provisions on hours' regulations for night workers (Article 8–11). To complement the overarching health and safety rationale the Directive

[8] *Proposal for a Council Directive on the Organization of Working Time*, [1990] O.J. C 254/4 (9 December 1990) (hereinafter Commission Proposal 1990).

[9] The numbering used here is that which appeared in the original 1993 instrument, not as subsequently revised.

also invoked the principle of 'adapting work to workers', requiring that any changes in the patterns and organization of work at the enterprise level take account of this principle, particularly where work is monotonous or carried out at a predetermined rate (Article 13).

In addition to its core provisions (see Table 3.1), the Directive included a series of derogations and exceptions making for significant flexibility within its overarching protective framework. Specifically, although the 1993 Directive applied to 'all sectors of activity, both public and private', it outright excluded a number of sectors, including air, rail, road, sea, inland waterway and lake transport, sea fishing, other work at sea, and the activities of doctors in training.[10] Moreover, all of the Directive's key provisions, save for the annual leave and the principle of adaptability, were subject to some sort of a limitation, including: (1) complete derogations for specific categories of workers and in cases where the specific characteristics of an activity mean that working time is not measured and/or predetermined, or can be determined by the workers themselves; (2) legislated or negotiated derogations from provisions on rest breaks, night work, and reference periods in certain specified circumstances; (3) derogations from the basic 4-month reference period for the calculation of the weekly hours by legislation or collective agreement; and (4) derogation from the 48-hour maximum via the optional individual opt-out provision.

Article 17(1), for instance, provided that the 48-hour maximum calculated over the basic period of 4 months did not apply to managerial staff or workers with 'autonomous decision-making power', 'family workers', and workers 'officiating at religious ceremonies in churches and religious communities'. Derogations from breaks, night work, and reference periods were also made for workers residing far away from their place of employment (Article 17(3a)), those employed in 'security and surveillance activities' (Article 17(3b)), where continuity of service or production was required (Article 17(3c)), where there was a foreseeable surge of activity (such as in agriculture, tourism, or postal services, Article 17(3d)), railway transport workers (Article 17(3f)), and in case of accident or its imminent risk (Article 17(3g)).

[10] These sectors were eventually included into the Directive's ambit by the so-called 'horizontal' Directive (2000/24/EC, O.J. L195), and the *Council Directive on the organization of the working time of persons performing mobile road transport activities* (2002/15 EC, [2002] O.J. L 080/35) adopted on 12 March 2002. In 1998, the social partners reached another agreement, which provided for either a maximum number of working hours or a minimum rest regime for seafarers (see Hardy 2006; see note 21).

Table 3.1 *1993* Working Time Directive, *key protective provisions*

Key entitlement	Articles and provisions
Weekly working-time limits	**Article 6(a)**: all Member States required to adopt measures necessary to ensure that weekly working time is limited, whether via national legislation, collective agreements or agreements between two sides of the industry. **Article 6(b)**: the maximum weekly working time set at 48 hours, including overtime, to be averaged over a 7-day period.
Daily and weekly rest	**Article 4**: mandatory break, required when daily work-time equals or exceeds 6 hours. **Article 5**: minimum daily and weekly periods of uninterrupted rest. Eleven hours in each 24 hours, and 35 hours in each 7-day period. Detailed provisions to be set by national legislation, collective agreement, or by another agreement between social partners.
Annual leave	**Article 7**: all Member States to take measures necessary to ensure that every worker is entitled to paid leave of at least 3 weeks, rising to 4 by 23 November 1999. **Article 7(2)**: the annual leave cannot be derogated from or replaced by an allowance in lieu, except in the event that the employment relationship is terminated.
Night-work provisions	**Article 8: (a)** night workers are not to work more than the *average* of 8 hours in any 24-hour period, and **(b)** those workers whose work involves particularly hazardous conditions or heavy physical or mental strain, not to work more than 8 hours in the 24-hour period in which they perform night work. **Article 9**: entitlement to a free and confidential health assessments for night workers. **Article 10**: employers who utilize night work on a regular basis to report this to the competent authorities on request. **Article 11**: employers to ensure that worker's special health and safety needs that are necessitated by night-work environment are met.
Adapting work to worker	**Article 13**: Member States to take necessary measures to ensure that any changes in the patterns and organization of work at the enterprise level take account of the general principle of adapting work to the worker, with the particular view to alleviating monotonous work and work at the predetermined work-rate.

The calculation of the maximum 48-hour limit could also be varied in accordance with the *derogations via extended reference periods.* Specifically, the Directive enabled Member States to extend the basic reference period for calculation of weekly maximums, provided that the period did not exceed 6 months (Article 17(4)). Indeed, the reference period for averaging working time could always be extended to 6 months by collective agreement or workplace agreement, and where 'objective or technical reasons or reasons concerning the organization of work' required further extensions, it could be extended up to even 12 months (Article 17(4)).

In addition to the specific derogations and exceptions listed above, one of the most controversial provisions that allowed for exceeding the weekly maximum was the *individual 'opt-out'* provision included in Article 18(1)(b)(i) of the Directive, at the insistence of the UK government. This provision gave Member States the option to not apply Article 6 (48-hour maximum) provided that certain requirements are met. In practice, the opt-out enabled Member States to adopt legislative provisions in the national working-time regulations that would allow individual workers essentially to waive their right to the maximum weekly working-time limit, with the provisos being that the worker does so without detriment, that employers keep records of working time, and that such records be made available to appropriate agency for the purpose of monitoring.[11]

Finally, to allow the Member States to comply and to adjust their national laws and workplace practices without significant economic detriment, the Directive stipulated relatively lengthy phasing-in periods (Article 18(1)(a)). This last stipulation also included the annual leave provision (Article 18(1)(b)(ii)), which had to be extended to all workers and could not be derogated from. Overall, the Member States had three years, until 23 November 1996, to transpose the Directive's provisions into national law, by which date many had indeed passed new legislation, amended existing laws, or were in the process of discussing how best to comply with the Community law (EIRR 1997). The exception was the UK: the only Member State without existing working-time legislation that also happened to have a well-established long-hours culture (EIRR 1997;

[11] Neither the 12-month reference period nor the opt-out appeared in the 1990 Commission Proposal (O.J. C 254/4, 9 December 1990), as only a 6-month reference period was contemplated. Clearly, the process of the Directive's negotiation cut both ways – the weekly maximums, not previously contemplated by the proposal, were set, but longer reference periods and the opt-out were included to provide more overall flexibility.

Barnard 1997b; Barnard et al. 2003b). As it turned out, the UK stalled in transposing the Directive not only because its implementation would require significant adjustment in national practice (Mills 1996; Barnard 1997b) but also because its Conservative government was set on challenging the Directive's legality.

3.2.2 The UK's European Court of Justice Challenge

With the transposition deadline looming, in 1996 the British government formally asked the ECJ to annul the Directive, claiming that its legal basis was inappropriate.[12] The UK argued that the Directive should have been enacted either under Articles 100 and 235 EC (now, 94 or 308 EC), which required unanimity, or the Social Policy Agreement in the Treaty of the European Union, which excluded the UK, and not under Article 118a (now 137), which required qualified majority (QMV) only. Moreover, the UK disputed the link to health and safety as tenuous, maintaining that working time was in fact an employment issue. In a related manner, the UK submitted that the concept of 'working environment' in Article 118a of the EU Treaty should be restricted only to concerns about physical conditions and safety risks in the workplace and not to matters of working time, which should be dealt with by broader social policy measures. Rejecting these arguments, the ECJ held that while the Directive might indeed affect employment, its primary objective was nonetheless to lay down measures related to the 'working environment' which were motivated by the concern for the health and safety of workers and so properly within the ambit of Article 118a (now Article 137).

Defeated on the key issue, the UK was legally obliged to transpose the Directive into domestic legislation by the set deadline of 23 November 1996.[13] It was not immediately clear whether the government would comply as the cabinet's Ministerial Committee on Defence and Overseas Policy considered a range of options, including public defiance, in anticipation of the ECJ decision (Beach 2005: 131–32). A decision to comply with the ruling was taken in the end, even if the Conservative government's subsequent steps towards the Directive's transposition confirmed

[12] *United Kingdom v. Council of the EU*, C-84/94, [1996] E.C.R. I-5755 (hereinafter *Working Time Case*).

[13] *Ibid.* The UK government was only successful on the issue of Sunday trading. The original Directive, on German insistence, provided that Sunday should in principle be designated as the weekly rest-day. The Court upheld the UK's challenge to this provision.

a remarkable lack of enthusiasm for the endeavour. A case in point was the Consultation Paper (URN 96/1126) issued in December 1996, which emphasized the need not to 'over-implement' the Directive or impose unnecessary burdens on business. As Barnard (1999: 61) later observed, the proposals included in this government paper, 'fell short of the minimum requirements of the Directive'.

Ultimately, it was not the Conservatives but the incoming Labour government that transposed the Directive by way of the 1998 *Working Time Regulations.*[14] Ironically, the government did so in a manner that was not inconsistent with its predecessor's stance on the need to not restrain business, and that was ultimately somewhat at odds with the support for the Directive and EU social standards in general that New Labour voiced while in opposition.

3.2.3 Diluting the Standards, Narrowing the Political Discourse

The Directive's adoption and the UK's failed challenge to its legality were symbolic milestones for the social dimension of Europe's growing internal market (Hepple 1997). Yet, the Directive's actual content left much to desire and only in principle challenged the UK's preferred approach to labour regulation. The instrument was sufficiently deregulatory to not only leave the UK's own long-hours culture unchallenged (Barnard et al. 2003b) but also to open doors to future deregulation in other Member States (Hardy 2006: 595) through various exclusions, possibilities of longer reference periods and, particularly, the ability to derogate through the opt-out. Disagreements over whether these forms of negative flexibility should be retained in the Directive would continue to define the discursive space surrounding it over the years.

While the Commission's ability to exploit the broad scope of Article 118a and to take advantage of the change in voting rules made the Directive possible, the approach also had significant consequences. Framing the Directive as a health and safety instrument was no doubt consistent with a long-standing tradition in labour law and was affirmed by the ECJ as such. The key limitation of that legal basis, however, was that it precluded, for legal and political reasons, a more expansive vision of working time; one that incorporated some focus on the social (and gender) impact of standard working-time norms beyond the health and safety

[14] SI 1998/1833.

considerations. Unsurprisingly, references to broader social goals that reorganization of working time could promote, such as those that the Commission advanced a decade earlier (*Draft Council Recommendation* 1983), were absent from the 1993 Directive (Moffat 1997). Instead, the Directive's approach was sparse and traditional as it assumed a clear distinction between 'free time' and 'work time', which, as Alain Supiot noted (1999, 2001: 53), was the hallmark of standard (Fordist-style) work organization. As such, the Directive was also built around and reified a particular conception of 'work' and 'worker' – one that presupposed availability and reflected the very same assumptions about the subjects of regulation that have formed the basis of the standard employment relationship (SER). The Directive's SER-centrism was further reflected by the fact that its key derogations provided for only one form of flexibility, namely, the flexibility to *extend* work hours, either on a temporary basis (through longer reference periods) or a more permanent basis (in case of excluded workers or the opt-out), without regard of how this would impact different types of workers. At the same time, apart from the overarching principle of adaptability provided for in Article 13, the instrument contained no flexibility to *adapt* or *reduce* work hours for individual reasons. The goals of work–family reconciliation and more gender equal distribution of work, although present in the 1983 *Draft Council Recommendation* and symbolically acknowledged by most Member States in the *Social Charter*, were completely absent.

Thus, with the Directive preserving the *status quo* and, indeed, enabling considerable negative flexibility, other goals working-time regulation could serve appeared to move to the far periphery of the discursive universe surrounding this instrument. As the next section will elaborate, subsequent changes in how the Community defined its policy priorities and the development of new regulatory mechanisms for coordination of Member State strategies broadened once again the debate surrounding working time and the *Working Time Directive.*

3.3 *Working Time Directive* Review and Failed Revision Attempt

In the decade following the Directive's adoption, several developments had an impact on its scope and on the broader policy discourse surrounding working time. Promotion of employment, economic growth, and competitiveness continued to be key priorities at the EC-level. Already in 1993, the Commission's White Paper on *Growth, Competitiveness,*

Employment[15] called for a more integrated unemployment strategy, with early formulation of such a strategy being devised during the Essen European Council in 1994 (Ashiagbor 2004). The Commission reiterated this concern in the 1996 *Action for Employment in Europe*,[16] which called for a strategy 'engendering the climate propitious to growth' through closer macroeconomic and internal market coordination, and the creation of new jobs with the aid of 'revitalized' (reformed) national employment systems and active employment policy (1996: 2). While the Commission's reformist agenda had previously met with the UK Conservative government's opposition, change of power in Westminster meant that new possibilities for EC-level social initiatives were now open. Indeed, the active employment policy approach the Commission advocated was quite congruent with the vision of the newly elected UK Labour government, headed by Prime Minister Tony Blair, which sought to deploy social and employment policy to enhance the markets (Blair 2010: 15–16; Kenner 2003; Vaughan-Whitehead 2003: 27–28).

Thus, with the UK more cooperative, employment policy became integrated into the Amsterdam Treaty[17] (Title VIII), and the subsequent launch of the European Employment Strategy (EES) in 1997 was designed to facilitate the EC-level coordination of national policies through the open method of coordination (OMC), a new regulatory mechanism utilizing 'soft' measures, including guidelines and benchmarks (Ashiagbor 2004). With an overall focus on activation of the labour market, the Strategy identified four pillars – entrepreneurship, employability, adaptability, and promotion of equal opportunities – as key priorities for European employment. Likewise, the strategy revealed an emphasis on promoting more flexible, diversified forms of working time in the interest of meeting the needs of diverse groups of workers and enabling their labour market participation. This focus was in line with the 1993 White Paper on *Growth, Competitiveness and Employment* and the 1997 Green Paper on *the Partnership for a New Organization of Work*,[18] both of which suggested new forms of work and more working-time flexibility could achieve a range of objectives, including job creation and adaptability for firms and

15 *Growth, Competitiveness, Employment: The Challenges and Ways Forward into the 21st Century*. White Paper, COM (93) 700 final (05 December 1993).

16 *Action for Employment in Europe. A Confidence Pact*, CSE (96) 1 final (05 June 1996).

17 *Treaty of Amsterdam*, October 1997, [1997] O.J. C 340/1, 25 I.L.M. 506 (10 November 1997).

18 *Partnership for a New Organization of Work. Green Paper*, COM (97) 128 final (16 April 1997). Bulletin of the European Union, Supplement 4/97.

workers, but could also serve to enhance equal opportunities and better employment inclusion.

Promotion of this broader conceptualization of working time and an approach to flexibility that was somewhat more balanced and focused on creating 'win-win' solutions found their expression in social partner-negotiated Framework Agreements on parental leave (1995) and part-time work (1997), which were then adopted as Directives in 1996 and 1997, respectively.[19] Unlike the *Working Time Directive*, both of these instruments made a more obvious link between work–family reconciliation and regulation of work hours. With the EC's overall policy emphasising the need to rethink organization of work and working time, this new attention to work–family reconciliation would also have an impact, albeit, as will be seen, a more limited one, on the discussions surrounding the *Working Time Directive.*

3.3.1 *Developments Related to the* Working Time Directive

In the context of this overarching focus on working-time flexibility, in 1997 the European Commission, somewhat paradoxically, issued its White Paper on *Sectors and Activities excluded from the Working Time Directive.*[20] Perhaps aware of the tension between the more traditional approach taken in the 1993 Directive and the approach to working time that it was now pursuing, the Commission made its case for extending the Directive's coverage to new groups of workers on the basis that its minimum standards would prevent '[the] direct risk to the welfare and safety of others' (Sectors and Activities White Paper 1997: 3). In Commission's view, long hours of work, particularly among doctors-in-training or in road transport, were not only harmful to these workers' own health and safety, but more importantly, also interfered with the broader public interest. The tactic proved successful, and the sectors of air, rail, road, sea, inland waterway and lake transport, sea fishing, other work at sea, and the activities of doctors in training came under the scope of minimum working-time standards by

[19] *Council Directive 96/34/EC of 3 June 1996 on the Framework Agreement on Parental Leave Concluded by UNICE, CEEP and the ETUC,* [1996] O.J. L145/4 (19 June 1996), amended by *Council Directive 97/75/EC of 15 December 1997,* [1998] O.J. L 10/24 (16 January 1998); *Council Directive 97/81/EC of 15 December 1997 on the Framework Agreement on Part-time Working* [1998] O.J. L14/9 (20 January 1998), amended by *Council Directive 98/23/EC of 7 April 1998,* [1998] O.J. L 131/10 (05 May 1998).

[20] COM (97) 334 final (15 July 1997) (hereinafter Sectors and Activities White Paper).

way of the 2000 *Horizontal Directive*,[21] while the 2002 Council Directive regulated working time in the sector of road transport.[22]

Another significant and related development involved a series of legal challenges stemming from the Directive's national transpositions. By 2000, most Member States, apart from France and Italy, had implemented the Directive,[23] and several court cases seeking clarifications of its various provisions had been referred to the ECJ for preliminary ruling.[24] The references from the Spanish and German courts in the 2000 *SIMAP v. Conselleria de Sanidad y Consumo de la Generalidad Valenciana*[25] and the 2003 *Landeshaupstadt Kiel v. Norbert Jaeger* cases,[26] respectively, proved to have the most far-reaching legal and political implications as far as the Directive's prospective revision. The key issue in both cases concerned the definition of working time (Article 2 of the Directive), and, specifically, whether on-call work, or its inactive portions, could be excluded from the scope of this definition for the purpose of calculating weekly working

21 *Directive 2000/34/EC of the European Parliament and of the Council of 22 June 2000 amending Council Directive 93/104/EC concerning certain aspects of the organization of working time to cover sectors and activities excluded from that directive*, [2000] O.J. L195/41 (1 August 2000) (hereinafter *Horizontal Directive*). Additional regulations and amendments to original Directives were subsequently adopted for sectors of civil aviation (Regulation (EC) No 1899/2006), seafarers (Directive 2009/13/EC), and cross-border rail transport (Directive 2005/47/EC).

22 *Directive 2002/15/ECof the European Parliament and of the Council of 1 March 2002 on the organization of the working time of persons performing mobile road transport activities*, [2002] O.J. L 080/35 (23 March 2002). Additional regulation subsequently added: (Regulation (EC) No 561/2006).

23 However, as the Commission's 2000 state of implementation report indicated, only Finland, Germany, the Netherlands, Spain, and Sweden had transposed the Directive by the 23 November 1996 deadline. France and Italy had been 'condemned' by the ECJ for failure to transpose but had not at the time of the Report informed the Commission of any measures they planned, while the UK had adopted the *Working Time Regulations* in 1998, following its failed ECJ challenge: State of Implementation of *Directive 93/104/EC of 23 November 1993 concerning certain aspects of the organization of working time*. COM (2000) 787 final (1 December 2000) (hereinafter State of Implementation 2000).

24 *J.R. Bowden e.a. v. Tuffnells Parcels Express Ltd.*, C-133/00, [2001] E.C.R. I-7051, considered the scope of exclusions in the Directive's Article 1(3); while *The Queen v. Secretary of State for Trade and Industry*, C-173/99, [2001] E.C.R. I-4881, considered the possibility of laying down qualifying periods for the Article 7 annual leave entitlement.

25 *Sindicato de Medicios de Asistencia Publica v. Consellaria de Sanidad y Consumo de la Generalidad Valenciana*, C-303/98, [2000] E.C.R. I-7963 [*SIMAP*]. This case was considered together with another case that concerned the definition of 'working time' under the Directive in the context of 'on-call' activities of medical emergency personnel, *Confederación Intersindical Galega (C.I.G) v. Servicio Galego de Saude*, C-241/99, [2001] E.C.R. I-5141 [*SERGAS*].

26 *Landeshaupstadt Kiel v. Norbert Jaeger*, C-151/02, [2003] E.C.R. I-8415 [*Jaeger*].

hours. The 1993 Directive and its 2000 amendment defined working time as 'any period during which the worker is working, at the employer's disposal and carrying out his activity or duties in accordance with national laws and/or practice' (Article 2); while rest, constituted 'any period which is not working time' (Article 2). This dual construction classified 'working time' and 'rest' as mutually exclusive, providing no intermediate category. By contrast, legislative provisions or national practice in several Member States specifically differentiated between'active' and 'inactive' parts of working time, particularly in the context of on-call work. Importantly, periods of inactivity during the on-call duty were typically excluded from the scope of working time, and thus from the calculation of the average 48-hour weekly norm.

Whether this type of exclusion was appropriate and consistent with the 1993 Directive was first considered in the 2000 Spanish reference case, *SIMAP*. Under Spanish regulations, medical on-call staff were required to be either present at their health establishment or to be otherwise contactable. In either case, only those on-call periods during which doctors were actively engaged in the performance of their duties were regarded as working time, and the Spanish regulations classified the inactive portion of on-call as falling within the category of rest. In ruling on whether these regulations complied with the 1993 Directive, the ECJ had to first clarify the meaning of working time, as defined by the Directive's Article 2.

One of the key legal issues the Court considered was whether the particular elements of the definition in Article 2– '. . . working . . . at the employer's disposal . . . carrying out duties . . . ' – ought to be interpreted in a cumulative or independent manner. Seeking to support the distinction between active and inactive parts of working time, the Spanish authorities urged a cumulative interpretation that required the fulfilment of all three elements, including the actual performance of duties. By contrast, pointing to the imprecise nature of the definition in Article 2, the Advocate General put forth that the elements should be interpreted independently, nonetheless making a distinction between doctors who were required to remain on and off-premises. In the Advocate General's opinion, the definition of working time encompassed periods of inactivity for doctors required to be physically present at the health establishment, but not for those able to be on-call while off-premises. In the latter case, designation of on-call's inactive parts as rest periods was not inconsistent with the Directive.

Contrary to the Advocate General's submissions, the Court decided that the appropriate interpretation of the wording in Article 2 was indeed cumulative. However, in opposition to what the Spanish authorities argued, the Court found that this interpretation did not preclude the inclusion of inactive periods of on-call into the scope of working time for those doctors who had to remain on the premises. According to the Court, if doctors were obliged to be 'present' and 'available with a view to providing their professional services' they were automatically 'carrying out their duties in that instance'. Crucially, the Court justified its interpretation by reference to the Directive's health and safety aims, which, in the Court's view, would be 'seriously' undermined if the on-call duty were excluded from working time, particularly where a worker's physical presence was required.[27] Thus, in emphasizing the worker's physical presence at the health-care establishment, the Court followed the Advocate General's distinction between doctors required to remain at the health-care establishment and those allowed to be off-site.[28] The Court explained that the latter group experienced fewer constraints on time and could 'pursue their own interests' while inactive during on-call duty,[29] hence, their periods of inactivity were properly designated as rest.

The Court's clarification of the definition of working time and its affirmation (and generous interpretation) of the Directive's health and safety objectives was a significant development with potentially far-reaching consequences for work organization in health-care establishments and other sectors heavily reliant on on-call work. As the European Commission's report on the implementation of the Directive pointed out, several other Member States had also implemented intermediate categories not explicitly defined by the Directive – similar to those at issue in *SIMAP* – and those provisions would likely be caught by the ECJ's ruling (State of Implementation 2000: 7). Indeed, the on-call issue came up again in the 2003 *Jaeger* reference from the German court, which sought to clarify the *SIMAP* ruling, particularly in so far as its application to the on-call in German law.

Unlike the Spanish rules at issue in *SIMAP*, which permitted on-call staff to be either on or off-site, German labour law explicitly defined on-call as the period during which an employee was required to be present at a place determined by the employer and had to be available to answer the employer's call. However, the staff members on on-call duty were

[27] Above, n. 25 *SIMAP*, para. 49. [28] *Ibid.*, para. 50. [29] *Ibid.*

authorized to rest so long as their services were not required and, as was the case in *Jaeger*, accommodations were made for them to do so when they were not actively discharging their duties.[30] *Inter alia*, the referring German court asked the ECJ to clarify whether the Court's previous *SIMAP* ruling – that entire period of on-call duty was working time where a worker's physical presence was required – still applied under these distinct circumstances, or whether periods of inactivity could properly be designated as rest periods in the German case. Alongside the reference, Germany (supported by four other Member States) also submitted evidence of the major economic and budgetary impact that a positive ECJ finding on the first issue would have in the context of health-care administration. Specifically, the German government contended that such a ruling might lead to a 24 per cent increase in staffing requirements, meaning that an additional 15,000 to 27,000 doctors would be needed (with only 7,000 doctors being out of work in the country), with the extra costs involved being estimated at EUR 1.75 billion (Kenner 2004: 596).

Given this political and economic context, there was some expectation that the Court might see the case as an opportunity to 'rein back' on its earlier expansive interpretation of the Directive (Kenner 2004: 595). However, the Court's 9 September 2003 ruling not only followed the *SIMAP* judgment, it further strengthened and expanded its interpretation of both working time and the health and safety rationale. In affirming the overarching importance of health and safety as a fundamental right embedded in the Community's commitment to the improvement of living and working conditions, the Court drew on the 1989 *Social Charter* and the *EC Treaty* (its Article 118a). Moreover, in rejecting the German suggestion that the Directive should be interpreted by reference to national law and practice, the Court urged the Directive's primacy over national regulations as necessary for securing its 'full efficacy and uniform application' by Member States.[31] Any other interpretation, the Court held, frustrated the objective of harmonizing the protection of health and safety by means of minimum requirements.[32] Turning to the specific issue of the German on-call regulations, the Court followed *SIMAP* in finding that the necessity to remain at the workplace and ready to carry out one's employment duties meant that the doctors were in fact working. Even where an employer provides a designated rest room, such as was the case in *Jaeger*, 'an employee available at the place determined by the employer cannot be regarded as being at rest during the periods of his on-call duty when he is not actually

[30] Above, n. 6 *Jaeger*, para 15. [31] *Ibid.*, para 58. [32] *Ibid.*, para 59.

carrying on any professional activity', particularly since 'periods during which their services are not required . . . may be of short duration and/or subject to frequent interruptions'.[33] Significantly, reaffirming *SIMAP*'s broad conceptualization of health and safety, the Court emphasized that the necessity to remain at the workplace and the lack of effective control over one's time due to the intermittent and unpredictable nature of on-call work had a negative effect beyond one's ability to rest, as crucially it also interfered with her or his ability to participate in family life and/or engage in social activities.[34] Indeed, the Court held, *contra* Germany's economic arguments, that the Directive's protective health and safety objectives, as broadly construed to include one's ability to engage in the life of the community and family, were so important that they could not be 'called in question by the objections based on economic and organizational consequences',[35] or be 'subordinated to purely economic considerations'.[36]

Thus, although the different facts in the *Jaeger* reference provided the Court with an opportunity to distinguish its earlier ruling in *SIMAP*, the Court not only affirmed its earlier interpretation of working time, it strengthened and expanded its reach. The effect of these rulings was mixed. On the one hand, the affirmation that the Directive's health and safety objectives are of fundamental importance, and the observation that long and intermittent on-call work hours have a deleterious impact on the worker's ability to partake in family life and social activities, were important steps towards broadening the discursive universe surrounding this more traditionally construed working-time instrument. The Court's more expansive vision of what was at stake in protecting a worker's health was in line with how health has been defined by the World Health Organization (Kenner 2004: 594–95), and crucially, this vision recognized that the maintenance of social and affective bonds was just as significant to a worker's well-being as adequate sleep and adequate rest. Particularly, in raising the issue of family life, which had been absent from discussions on regulation of standard work hours as set by the Directive, but already a prominent component of the broader EC policy discourse, the Court was also opening doors to potential future recasting of traditional working-time norms in terms of their impact on the ability to balance work and family obligations. As Deirdre McCann (2005) observed, the Court's analysis revealed an awareness of the complexities and value of workers' lives beyond paid employment, and the fact that long hours not

[33] *Ibid.*, para 70. [34] *Ibid.*, para. 65. [35] *Ibid.*, para 66. [36] *Ibid.*, para 67.

only posed danger from the health and safety perspective but also because they removed workers from the rest of their lives (McCann 2005: 136). Somewhat paradoxically, however, the Court's interpretation and reasoning still reaffirmed the binary, mutually exclusive construction of work and rest time inherent in the Directive, which was based, after all, on the traditional conceptualization of 'work' and 'leisure' or 'work' and 'home' as discrete spheres of (productive and reproductive) activity (McCann 2005). Thus, despite the fact that the Court's reading of the Directive's key terms and objectives was more holistic and its rulings in *SIMAP* and *Jaeger* generally beneficial to workers' well-being and interests, both judgments ultimately reified standard conceptions of work as an activity that takes place at the employer's premises, and that the opposite of work time is the 'non-work' time of leisure and family engagement (Supiot 2001: 53).

Beyond these conceptual issues, the most immediate and practically problematic consequence of the *SIMAP* and *Jaeger* rulings was the challenge they posed to the national systems of law. The Court's interpretation of working time compelled a number of Member States to apply the Directive's Article 18 derogations in their health-care sectors or other sectors, using on-call work as a way to deal with the resulting budgetary and staffing problems (Re-Exam Communication 2003). By 2003, Germany, the Netherlands, and Spain were all preparing to adopt legislation permitting the opt-out's application in the health-care sector, while similar provisions were already partially adopted in France and Luxembourg[37] (Re-Exam Communication 2003). The potential for a more widespread application of the opt-out took on a particular meaning in light of the upcoming EC enlargement, which was to grant Community membership to several post-socialist states and former planned economies in Eastern Central Europe (ECE).[38] Structural adjustment and the political-economic transition process left those economically weaker ECE states with significantly deregulated labour markets and diminished collective bargaining coverage, raising concerns, particularly among organized labour in the West that the unfair competitive advantage of these countries

[37] Although, in France, the opt-out was adopted within a framework of national working-time standards that were more protective than those offered by the *Working Time Directive*, and in Luxembourg, it was applied in a single sector only (hotels and catering) and with fairly strict and short reference periods.

[38] On 31 March 1998, accession negotiations began with six applicant countries – Cyprus, the Czech Republic, Estonia, Hungary, Poland, and Slovenia. A year and a half later, on 13 October 1999, the Commission recommended opening negotiations with Bulgaria, Latvia, Lithuania, Malta, the Slovak Republic, and Romania.

vis-à-vis old EU members would lead to capital flight and trade redirection (Vaughan-Whitehead 2003). 'Social dumping' concerns had already been raised when the UK applied the opt-out in its national working-time regulations (Mills 1996).[39] Now, it was feared that the potential application of the opt-out by new accession states whose national standards were already deemed weaker could unleash a regulatory 'race-to-the-bottom'. This development significantly altered the context for the discussion on the opt-out, which was now no longer a UK-only issue.

3.3.2 Working Time Directive *2004 to 2009 Revision Process*

The legally mandated review of the Directive took place against the backdrop of these new developments. In accordance with the Commission's Communication on the Directive's Re-examination,[40] issued on 15 January 2004, the review was to take the form of a Community-wide consultation with the European Parliament (EP), the Council, the European Economic and Social Committee (EESC), the Committee of Regions, and the social partners. Aside from reviewing and assessing the impact of the Article 18 opt-out and the extended reference period provisions (Article 16), as required by the Directive itself, the other major issue on the Commission's agenda was to address the Court of Justice's redefinition of working time in the context of on-call work in the *SIMAP* and *Jaeger* cases. As already noted, this latter issue was closely related to the opt-out because several Member States had already or planned on legislating the use of this provision in sectors relying on on-call work. Finally, the Commission also flagged that it wished to explore how the Directive's revision could take better account of work and family reconciliation (Re-exam Communication 2004: 20–21).

[39] When the American-owned Hoover moved from France to Scotland in 1993, 600 French staff were replaced by 400 fixed-term contract workers (Mills 1996: 137). In 1998, the transfer of the Swedish-owned Ericsson from Sweden to Scotland was attributed to the fact that the UK's opt-out implementation led to a more flexible and cheaper regulatory environment. The Commission was asked to investigate and consider revising the opt-out prior to its scheduled re-examination. See: Official Journal of the European Communities, 21.02.1999, 1999/C 142/197, 1999/C 142/198.

[40] *Communication from the Commission to the Council, the European Parliament, the European Economic and Social Committee and the Committee of the Region and the Social Partners at Community Level concerning the Re-examination of Directive 93/104/EC concerning certain aspects of the organization of working time*, [2004] COM 843 final/2 (15 January 2004) (hereinafter Re-exam Communication 2004).

The other issues notwithstanding, it was the discussion around the use of the individual opt-out provision (Article 18(1)(b)(i)) that dominated the 2004 Communication, with the UK being its central focus because, at this point, it was the only Member State to have *generally* applied the provision. Crucially, the UK implementation data suggested that the opt-out had been applied there in a way that jeopardized the Directive's health and safety objectives (Re-exam Communication 2004: 7, citing Barnard et al. 2002). As the UK data showed as many as 33 per cent of UK workers had already signed the opt-out, of whom nearly half had reported working in excess of 48 hours.[41] There was also evidence that all remaining employees who had opted-out had worked in excess of the prescribed maximum as a matter of practice, suggesting that the opt-out was being used on a largely precautionary basis in organizational contexts where long hours were already the norm (Daniel et al. 2003). However, many UK workers who signed the opt-out expressed a clear preference for having a choice to work longer hours – a finding that was cited in support of the opt-out's retention. Employees' motivations to work long hours varied from extra pay, the prospect of promotion and higher rewards in future, or a sense of autonomy (Barnard et al. 2002). There was a concern, nonetheless, that the UK transposed some of the opt-out related provisions in a manner that would likely lead to reporting and monitoring problems (Re-exam Communication 2004).[42] There was also evidence suggesting that employees were sometimes pressured into signing the provision. Finally, as the UK legal experts' Report to the Commission pointed out, the opt-out's widespread, precautionary application by employers in the UK was an indication that the provision diluted the regulatory stimulus for employers to implement actual changes in organization of work practices (Barnard et al. 2003b; see also Blair et al. 2001).

[41] According to figures cited by the Commission, half of that 33 per cent, or 16 per cent, represented the portion of *all* UK workers, including those working part-time. In addition, the report cited that 20 per cent of full-time UK workers exceeded the 48-hour maximum, with 8 per cent working over 55 hours, 3.2 per cent over 60 hours, and 1 per cent spending 70 hours at work (Re-exam Communication 2004: 10).

[42] The 1998 *Working Time Regulations* (SI 1998/1833) implementing the Directive in the UK were revised in 1999 to reduce the administrative requirements and costs (in response to British industry and employers' complaints). First, the UK government proposed to extend the 'unmeasured working hours' derogation to include hours worked voluntarily, typically by managers and senior executives whose working hours may have been set by contract. The other key change concerned relaxation of the record-keeping requirements so that keeping a names list of those who have opted out was sufficient (Barnard 1999, 2000; Hall 1999).

In reviewing the use of reference periods and the fallout from the *Jaeger* and *SIMAP* cases, the Commission focused on rationales of business flexibility and broader economic considerations. On the issue of the Article 16 derogations, the Commission cited examples of national practice as confirmation that collectively agreed extensions of basic reference periods were already widespread in Europe and, indeed, necessary to provide enterprises with organizational flexibility (Re-exam Communication 2004: 5–6). With respect to the ECJ case law, the Communication pointed out the considerable financial costs of compliance with the Court's rulings on the definition of working time in the context of national healthcare sectors (Re-exam Communication 2004: 17–20);[43] an issue further exacerbated by the fact that the 2000 *Horizontal Directive* extended the *Working Time Directive*'s coverage to previously exempt sectors, including doctors-in-training.

A new item on the agenda was the Commission's suggestion that 'the revision of the Directive could be exploited in such a way as to encourage the Member States to take steps to improve the compatibility of work and family life' (Re-exam Communication 2004: 21). Here, the Commission took the 'long-term view' of the 1993 and 1997 White and Green papers,[44] citing a range of sociological changes – 'the mass influx of women into the labour market, increase in divorce rates, instability and heterogeneity of household structures and demographic phenomena' – requiring closer attention be paid to the relationship between organization of working time and family life (Re-exam Communication 2004: 21). Adopting the logic of the EES and post-Amsterdam guidelines, the Commission urged that measures enabling better work–family reconciliation and those enhancing equal opportunities are not only of benefit to workers; they are also needed to develop high quality labour force that is productive, motivated, and available, and to create better opportunities for training and professional development (Re-exam Communication 2004: 21).

Thus, in setting the overall tone for the re-examination and revision of the Directive, the Commission continued to emphasize the need to balance health and safety interests and economic needs of employers, but its inclusion of work–family reconciliation as an additional variable to consider potentially broadened the discussion on working time or,

[43] The UK estimated that maintaining current care levels would cost between GBP 380 and 780 mln, while Germany's estimate was EUR 1.75 billion, and the Netherlands', EUR 400 mln. Lack of qualified personnel was a related problem.

[44] Above n. 15 and 18.

perhaps, was a way to justify further flexibilization in the organization of standard work hours on the basis that it would enhance also other social objectives. Regardless of its motivating reasons, the Commission's attempt to expand the scope of discussion surrounding the Directive did not meet with widespread approval of the consulted parties, with particular resistance coming from the social partners representing both European labour and employers.

The responses to the first phase of consultation made it apparent that save for the uniform consensus on the necessity of the revision itself, there was disagreement on many of its aspects. Organized labour, for instance, accused the Commission of inconsistency. While supportive of revising the Directive with the view to improve work–family reconciliation, the European Trade Union Congress (ETUC or the Congress) chastised the Commission for not having provided any concrete propositions on how this could be achieved, particularly given that the Commission's review document did not openly reject the opt-out. Characterizing work–family reconciliation as a 'health and safety' issue in itself, the ETUC urged that the only form of flexibility that could truly benefit workers was one that would be exercised within an overarching protective framework of working time limits. As in this view the opt-out was not compatible with a focus on work–family reconciliation, the Congress accused the Commission of creating the false illusion of employers and employees having joint interests in flexibility (ETUC Position Paper 2004a). Similarly, the European Federation of Public Sector Unions (EPSU) called for the abolition of the opt-out, which it too characterized as a barrier to effective work–family reconciliation (Second Phase Consultation 2004: 6). Organizations representing employers also took issue with that aspect of the Commission's document. However, in contrast with the labour representatives, the Union of Industrial and Employers' Confederations of Europe (UNICE, currently BusinessEurope), the European Centre of Employers and Enterprises providing Public Services (CEEP) and many other employer or business organizations outright rejected the idea that work–family reconciliation be incorporated into the Directive (Second Phase Consultation 2004: 4). While neither UNICE or CEEP disputed the importance of work–family reconciliation measures *per se*, both disagreed that a 'health and safety' Directive was the appropriate context for regulation on these issues (UNICE Position Paper 2004a: 6).

Predictably, the social partners also disagreed on the opt-out, the reference periods, and the issue of redefining working time. Employer and business organizations (UNICE, CEEP) strongly advocated for retaining the opt-out. The UNICE, for instance, called on the Commission to do so and to 'resist any calls to introduce new rigidities' (UNICE Position Paper 2004a, Executive Summary). In its view, the opt-out was 'crucial' for flexibility and competitiveness in all, but particularly new, Member States, where the opt-out helped companies 'to absorb the shock of compliance with the legal *acquis* on working time' (UNICE Position Paper 2004a: 5). Moving beyond their support for the legal *status quo* in relation to the opt-out, the employers' organizations also requested the Directive's reference period provision to be amended to permit legislative extensions of the reference periods for averaging working time to 12 months with the option of negotiating even longer reference periods by way of collective agreement. Finally, both UNICE and CEEP called on the Commission to neutralize the ECJ's pronouncements in *SIMAP* and *Jaeger* through introduction of the concept 'inactive time' into the Directive and a declaration that on-call work ought not be considered for the purpose of calculating the 48-hour weekly average (UNICE Position Paper 2004a: 5–6). Essentially all of these proposals were countered by the ETUC and other major labour-side organizations acting at the Community level (Second Phase Consultation 2004: 3–4, 6; ETUC Position Paper 2004a). Commenting on the profound disagreement between social partners, Phillipe de Buck, the UNICE's Secretary General, remarked that he saw no prospects of negotiations (UNICE Press Release 2004c).

Whereas labour and management could not agree on a common position, the former found support in the Parliament, whose resolution adopted on 11 February 2004 presented a majority view largely in line with ETUC's own.[45] The Parliament also embraced the Commission's broadened focus on health and safety and work–family objectives and sought the gradual phasing out of the opt-out provision,[46] while proposing temporary measures to curb abuses and strengthen the voluntary nature of the opt-out in the interim. The European Parliament tempered its own opinions on the key consultation issues, however, by urging

[45] Resolution on the Organization of Working Time (amendment of *Directive 93/104/EC*), 2003/2165 INI, (11 February 2004) (hereinafter European Parliament Resolution 2004), adopted on the basis of a Report prepared by Alejandro Cercas (PES).

[46] Parliament voted on the report from Alejandro Cercas (PES), which was adopted by 370 votes, with 116 against and twenty-one abstentions. On the particular issue of the opt-out, 275 votes were cast in favour of removing the opt-out, with 229 votes against and nine abstentions.

the Commission to encourage more vigorous negotiation between the social partners as the preferred manner in which the revision should be achieved.[47]

In its follow-up Second Phase Consultation (2004), the Commission summarized the positions and opinions and reiterated that it was prepared to work with the social partners on crafting a 'global and consistent approach' to the issues subject to review, with the view to finding a 'solution that takes account of totality of the amendments' (Second Phase Consultation 2004: 8). Underscoring that the review should be guided by the overarching health and safety objective of the Directive, the Commission also impressed that the revision should take account of the broader context and goals set out by the Lisbon Strategy and the Wim Kok report[48] regarding the need to increase and promote competitiveness (Second Phase Consultation 2004: 8). In requesting social partners input, the Commission flagged that in absence of negotiations and/or final agreement, it would go ahead with its own proposal for a revised Directive.

Indeed, based on the rather divergent second phase consultation responses and the subsequent failure of social partners to enter into negotiations, the Commission published its own proposal for amending the Directive on 22 September 2004.[49] Of the key issues flagged by the first and second phases of consultation, three remained central to the proposal: (1) the individual opt-out from the weekly 48-hour maximum; (2) the reference period over which the average maximum time is calculated; and (3) the redefinition of working time to incorporate time spent on call (Commission's Revision Proposal 2004). While compatibility between work and family obligations remained on the agenda – as one of the overarching criteria to be taken into account, alongside other goals such as 'a high standard of protections of worker's health and safety', 'greater flexibility in managing working time' for companies, and avoidance of excessive

[47] The Commission's initial lack of clarity on the inclusion of social partners in the revision process was also critiqued by the ETUC in its Position Paper (2004a).

[48] *Facing the Challenge: the Lisbon Strategy for Growth and Employment.* Report from the High-Level Group Chaired by Wim Kok, November 2004. Luxembourg: Office for the Official Publications of the European Communities (hereinafter Wim Kok Report); see also *Enlarging the European Union: Achievements and Challenges.* Report of Wim Kok to European Commission. 26 March 2003.

[49] Proposal for a Directive of the European Parliament and the Council Amending *Directive 2003/88/EC concerning certain aspects of the organization of working time*, SEC (2004) 1154, [2004] COM (2004) 0607 final - COD 2004/0209 (22 September 2004) (hereinafter Commission's Revision Proposal 2004).

restrains on small and medium enterprises (Commission's Revision Proposal 2004: point III (9)) – the Commission did not propose to introduce any concrete provisions that would give it effect. Instead, the principle and objective of work–family compatibility was noted in points five and six of the proposed preamble, with the first point broadly acknowledging its importance, and the second calling on the social partners to negotiate on establishing rules to ensure such compatibility was supported. This more cautious approach reflected the earlier critique that the Commission was not taking seriously the Directive's legal basis.

In so far as the other aspects of the proposal, despite the more tentative tone of its earlier consultation document the Commission now proposed to retain the individual opt-out (Article 22) but to make it subject to collective agreements (Commission's Revision Proposal 2004, point 52, Article 1(8)(a)). Where such agreements were not possible by reason of national practice or legislation, the Commission proposed to retain the individual opt-out by consent with the proviso of reinforced conditions (Commission's Revision Proposal 2004: point 52, Article 1(8)(b)), to give effect to the finding that some workers, particularly in the UK, expressed the preference not to have their working hours statutorily limited. In order to control against the potential instances of abuse such as those reported in the UK and to curb the default reliance on the opt-out, the Commission suggested a series of amendments that would make use of the opt-out less attractive to employers. Thus, the proposal included (1) the requirement that the opt-out be annually renewed, (2) an explicit obligation on employers to record the number of hours actually worked by those employees opting out, and (3) a provision rendering invalid those opt-out agreements that were entered into at the time of the signing of the employment contract (Commission's Revision Proposal 2004: point 52, Article 1(8)(b)). Together, these new requirements were to make the opt-out more costly to administer in order to prevent scenarios wherein employers as a matter of administrative efficiency automatically requested that employees sign the opt-out; and to ensure that employees agree to the opt-out as a matter of free choice and not implicit coercion. An additional protective mechanism the Commission suggested was a 65-hour maximum limit on the duration of the workweek in the cases where the opt-out had been applied, unless the collective agreement between the parties provided otherwise.[50] This additional limit was to curb the most

[50] Labour Force Survey data indicated that only 0.4 million UK workers exceed the 65-hour workweek, in comparison to 4 million who exceed the 48-hour week.

extreme cases of long hours, albeit there was evidence that work in excess of 65 hours in a week is very rare, even in the UK.

The Commission's Communication did not comment on the opt-out's potential interference with work–family reconciliation, instead focusing on ensuring the abuse of the provision was circumscribed enough so as not to undermine the health and safety objectives. This narrower approach was contrary to the ETUC's earlier proposals, which expressed long hours as a work–family issue (as well as a health and safety one), or the fact that the impact assessment carried out by the Commission at the outset of the review process confirmed that there was indeed an important gender dimension to the opt-out, and that the provision needed to be removed or better regulated in part for this reason (Pereira Interview, 17 February 2010, Brussels). As recounted by the Deputy Head of the Unit for Equality, Action against Discrimination and Legal Questions of DG Employment, Fernando Pereira, this finding was not particularly influential in the decision about whether or not to retain the opt-out (Pereira Interview, 17 February 2010, Brussels).

Other changes in the Commission's review proposal included the option for Member States to extend by statute the reference period from the 4 months prescribed by the original Directive to 12 months, thereby responding to UNICE's request to infuse more flexibility into the organization of work hours. This option was seen as a trade-off potentially providing the incentive for more employers to move to a system of annualized hours, and, thus, reducing reliance on the opt-out (Hobbs and Njoya 2005: 311). Significantly, the Commission's proposal provided that only one of the options – the opt-out or the reference period extension – could be utilized by the Member States, thereby only partially satisfying the business lobby's requests.

On the issue of the definition of working time and specifically that of on-call time, which has been given an expansive interpretation in the *SIMAP* and *Jaeger* decisions, the Commission proposed to include a third, intermediate definition of the inactive part of on call time (Commission's Revision Proposal 2004: points 8, 19, 22). If introduced, this definition would essentially neutralize the ECJ's decisions, which held that the time spent on call was to always count towards working time for the purpose of the weekly norms set out by the Directive and to calculate compensation, regardless of whether or not it was spent on active duty.

Finally, to strengthen negotiations between the social partners as the European Parliament had requested during the first phase of consultation, the Commission's proposal also included a number of provisions designed to 'provide a significant regulatory stimulus for collective negotiations over innovation in working-time arrangements, pay and productivity' (Hobbs and Njoya 2005: 312). Specifically, the proposal required broad consultation with the social partners on the issue of extension of the reference period to 12 months, and required their authorization in implementing the individual opt-out. While this was an important reiteration of the commitment to collective negotiations and reinforcement of the collective framework, it was not likely to have a significant impact in those contexts where collective agreement coverage was low, and where opt-outs have already been collectively negotiated (Hobbs and Njoya 2005: 312).

3.3.3 The 2009 Revision Debacle

The issuing of the 2004 Commission Revision Proposal marked the start of a prolonged period of consultations, negotiations, and amendments, during which the proposal moved between various committees (Committee of Regions, Economic and Social Committee), and the co-legislators, the European Parliament and the Council. Finally, in 2008, within 3 months of each other, both the Council and the European Parliament adopted their respective common positions. Much as the positions adopted by the social partners during the preceding consultation, the Council and the Parliament were also far apart, particularly on the key issues of the opt-out, the extension of the reference period, and the redefinition of working time. The co-legislators also disagreed over the extent to which the issue of work–family reconciliation should feature as an element of the Directive or the manner in which it should be incorporated.

The final position of the European Parliament was based on the report prepared by the Parliament's Special Rapporteur Alejandro Cercas, the Spanish MEP delegated by the Party of European Socialists (the Cercas Report).[51] In his report, Cercas insisted in very definitive terms that the revised Directive should phase out the opt-out, because its retention would not only entail 'making the regulations more flexible, but doing away with them completely' (European Parliament Cercas Report 2005: 17). In the interim, he recommended to shorten from 12 to 6 months the

[51] Report of the Proposal for a Directive of the European Parliament and of the Council amending *Directive 2003/88/EC concerning certain aspects of the organization of working time*, COM (2004) 0607 – C6-0122/2004 – 2004/0209 COD, 25.04.2005, submitted to Committee on Employment and Social Affairs by Alejandro Cercas (hereinafter European Parliament Cercas Report 2005).

Commission's recommended duration of the renewable opt-out agreements that the original Directive permitted. The Cercas Recommendation for Second Reading,[52] including proposed changes to the Council's common position, largely maintained the thrust of his original report. The Council,[53] by contrast, supported retaining the opt-out (Common Position of the Council 2008). It also largely mirrored the business lobby's requests for extending the Section 16-mandated reference period to 12 months or beyond (by legislation and/or collective agreements) and providing for the exclusion of on-call work from the scope of the working-time definition.

The two institutions were similarly divided on the issue of work–family reconciliation, albeit not as sharply as the social partners. The Parliament saw long work hours (the opt-out facilitated) and difficulties in reconciling work and family obligations as essentially connected. More so, in its Opinion attached to an earlier version of the Cercas Report,[54] the Parliament's Committee on Women's Rights and Equal Opportunities noted that the opt-out had a clearly gendered dimension because the long-hours culture it fostered was particularly harmful for workingwomen. Contrary to the common assumption that long-hours culture is something that primarily affects men, the Committee drew attention to the realities of women's 'double burden' of work and family obligations and the fact that women more often than men combine several part-time jobs to accommodate their caring obligations. Yet, while women's cumulative weekly hours of work (in different jobs and/or combined with their unpaid contributions) frequently exceed forty-eight, the Committee noted that women cannot always benefit from the protective 48-hour maximum because this limit applies only to individual jobs in which women are indeed likely to work

[52] Recommendation for Second Reading on the Council Common Position for Adopting a Directive of the European Parliament and the Council amending *Directive 2003/88/EC concerning certain aspects of the organization of working time*, 10597/2/2008, C6-0324/2008, 2004/0209 COD (11 November 2008) (hereinafter Recommendation for Second Reading 2008).

[53] Common Position of 15 September 2008 adopted by the Council of 15 September 2008, with a view to the adoption of a Directive of the European Parliament and of the Council amending *Directive 2003/88/EC concerning certain aspects of the organization of working time*, [2008] O.J. C 254 E/3/18.

[54] Opinion of the Committee on Women's Rights and Equal Opportunities, 20.01.2004 for the Committee on Employment and Social Affairs on Organization of Working Time (revision of *Directive 93/104/EC*), 2003/2166 INI, appended to Report of 29 January 2004 on the Organization of Working Time (amendment of *Directive 93/104/EC*), 2003/2165 INI (hereinafter Committee on Women's Rights Opinion 2004).

fewer hours (Committee on Women's Rights Opinion 2004). Significantly, the Committee also observed that the long-hours culture predominant in some professional circles and managerial positions constituted a serious barrier for women's upward mobility, and thus helped to sustain gender segmentation in the workplace (Committee on Women's Rights Opinion 2004).

While the Committee's specific suggestions were only partially incorporated into the Parliament's official position, the latter did retain the spirit of these recommendations. In his 2008 Recommendation for the Second Reading,[55] for instance, Cercas urged that references to work and family reconciliation, which were replete in the Commission's Proposal, must be more than 'empty rhetoric'. Giving practical effect to these objectives, he suggested, required creation of specific mechanisms within the Directive enabling employees to request changes in working hours and patterns that employers would be obliged to consider and grant but for demonstrable organizational disadvantages that would be disproportionate to workers' benefit (Recommendation for Second Reading 2008: 11). In addition, Cercas proposed that employers should be required to inform workers of 'any changes' to the working schedule 'well in advance' of any changes to hours or patterns of working time (Recommendation for Second Reading 2008: 10–11).

Although the Council agreed to the inclusion of provisions enabling work and family reconciliation, the provisions that it was willing to support differed from those the Parliament majority proposed. The Council saw the right to request and the obligation to inform, for instance, in less categorical terms than the Parliament, and it was only prepared to agree to a provision requiring information of employees in 'due time' of only 'substantial changes', while asking the Member States to 'encourage' employers to examine employee requests, subject, of course, to business needs and both the employer's and employee's need for flexibility (Common Position 2008: Article 1(2), Statement of the Council's Reasons III (2)).

The discrepancies between the Council and the Parliament's positions mirrored those between the social partners, whose opinions of the respective proposals revealed staggering and ongoing lack of consensus. BusinessEurope maintained the position that focused on employers' interests in enterprise flexibility, albeit it now also claimed that workers too had a 'right' to flexibility so as to also increase their 'purchasing power'

[55] *Supra* note 52.

(BusinessEurope 2008b, 2009b: 2). The ETUC on the other hand, while now also open to the potential benefits of flexibility, emphasized an approach that was more inclusive of individual workers' needs yet was still protective. Its approach was now also clearly attuned to the gender dimension of standard work hours, which, as the ETUC's Confederal Secretary Cathelene Passchier noted, translated into rejection of the opt-out also on the basis that it was inconsistent with work–family reconciliation as well as the objectives of health and safety (Passchier Interview, 16 February 2010, Brussels). Another reason for the ETUC's fear of the opt-out was related to the EU's Eastern enlargement. Primarily, the Congress worried that the adoption of the opt-out in the ECE countries still undergoing political–economic change could depress social and employment standards therein, and eventually lead to broader social dumping problems in Europe (Passchier Interview, 16 February 2010, Brussels).

Indeed, Jean Lambert, the British MEP and the European Greens' Rapporteur on the issue of health and safety and working hours also expressed a similar concern about social dumping. Lambert too was strongly in favour of eliminating the opt-out provision and echoed the ETUC's concern about the increase of hours and the long-hours culture that the opt-out could potentially promote in the new accession states. She commented on her own national government's efforts to ensure that these new Member States back the UK in its opt-out campaign, specifically recalling the 'ministerial road-show' that the UK New Labour Government had taken to Poland and other ECE countries (Lambert Interview, 23 February 2010, Brussels). In contrast with the views expressed by the ETUC's Confederal Secretary, however, Lambert maintained that the discussion of the opt-out had to be focused on the health and safety aspects. She deemed any discussion of gender and family consequences of long work hours as too 'politically risky' given the already delicate situation, a reality that likely explained why there was no significant discussion or negotiation on this front (Lambert Interview, 23 February 2010, Brussels).

Mirroring the earlier impasse between the social partners, the Parliament and the Council's Common Positions were also far apart, albeit, unlike the European business lobby, both did agree on the fact that attention to work–family reconciliation should be a feature of the new *Working Time Directive* with the key question being about the extent to which it is incorporated and whether it could be reconciled with the opt-out. Despite the Commission's efforts to find the middle ground between the two, their differences proved irreconcilable. First of all, even some of those Member

States previously opposed to the opt-out were now eager to retain it, as they wished to keep the possibility of applying the opt-out provision in domestic sectors that relied on on-call work. Moreover, the competitiveness focus of the 2003 and 2004 Wim Kok reports also helped to shift the mood in the Council. Thus, while Greece and Spain still championed the opt-out opposition, the UK managed to build support, with Germany, Latvia, Malta, Poland, and Slovakia joining as the 'blocking minority' (Blair 2010: 21). That a number of newly acceded Member States supported the pro opt-out faction of the Council tended to confirm what the ETUC anticipated might indeed happen.

With the Council's final proposal insisting on maintaining the opt-out provision being rejected by the Parliament in a 2008 vote, and the subsequent conciliation procedure[56] failing to bring resolution, the revision process came to a screeching halt in April 2009 – six years after the Commission issued its initial amending Proposal in 2003. This legislative debacle was the first instance under the provisions of the Amsterdam Treaty in which the Conciliation Committee was not able to reach agreement on a joint text (Codecision News 2009): certainly not the sort of a climax that the Commission had in mind.[57] And, although, at the time the Commission officers appeared willing to start from scratch and explore other possibilities, including a search for another, more timely and more politically savvy Treaty base, it was clear that another fiasco of this sort would not be acceptable.[58]

The post-conciliation mood was rather different in the offices of the members of the European Parliament where the vision of the Directive

[56] Article 294(10), (11) and (14) TFEU prescribed the conciliation procedure applied in the working-time case. According to the European Parliament's May 2009 newsletter *Codecision News*, on 28 April 2009 (hereinafter Codecision News 2009), the appointed Conciliation Committee had to concede that after several meetings taking place over a 3-month period, the positions of the Parliament and the Council remained too far apart for reconciliation. This was confirmed in the Parliament Delegation with fifteen votes against, five abstentions, and none in favour of the latest Commission compromise package. In line with Article 251(6) TEC the procedure was thus concluded at this level, and the Commission proposal for a new Directive for the organization of working time lapsed (hereinafter *Codecision* News 2009).

[57] This statement of overall impression is based on observations during my visit to the European Commission's DG Employment, Social Affairs, Inclusion in March 2010, to interview three Commission officers (Anonymous Policy Officer, Anonymous Legal Staff Member, and Fernando Pereira, all 17 February 2010).

[58] Early in 2010, the Commission issued another communication on the re-examination of the *Working Time Directive*, as part of its first phase of consultation.

prevailed, at least as far as getting the majority of the European Parliament onside and not giving in to the Council's pressure and the Commission's attempts at forging a compromise. Although the 'old' Directive remained intact, with the opt-out still firmly embedded, there was nonetheless a clear sense of victory, even if the celebratory mood concerned the assertion of the Parliament's political power, rather than the failure of the conciliation (Cercas Interview, 23 February 2010, Brussels; Lambert Interview, 23 February 2010, Brussels). In reference to the entire process and its outcome, Alejandro Cercas acknowledged that the story of the failed revision was a story of the 'EP's political victory', just as much as it was a victory for European workers (Cercas Interview, 23 February 2010, Brussels).

As for the social partners, the ETUC celebrated the fact that the Parliament sided with the European labour, since the substantive outcome was hardly a success for the ETUC given that its proposals were not actually accepted, and the most controversial of provisions, the opt-out, remained and was now being applied by an increasing number of Member States. While the ETUC staff were no doubt relieved that at the very least the old Directive was not weakened further (Passchier Interview, 16 February 2010, Brussels), they appeared to expect this rather 'qualified victory' to be the kind of calm that comes before another storm and were bracing themselves for more working-time upheaval in the future (Passchier Interview, 16 February 2010, Brussels). Moreover, the failure to incorporate gender issues more meaningfully into the discussions about the opt-out and the long hours was something that Passchier believed stemmed from the fact that no one challenged the notion of 'normal' worker. Pointing to a 1907 Dutch poster hanging on her wall that depicted the classic labour movement demand of 'Eight Hours Work, Eight Hours Sleep, Eight Hours Leisure', she observed that it completely missed the issue of care. She added: 'we need a new poster, to integrate the new vision' (Passchier Interview, 16 February 2010, Brussels).

3.4 Regulating Working Time – Missing Gender?

The story of the *Working Time Directive*'s original negotiations and unsuccessful revision recounted earlier demonstrates that what is politically possible and whose interests tend to be most politically influential in a particular context are important variables that act as 'gatekeepers' for what makes it into the dominant political discourse and what remains on the sidelines. In case of this particular Directive, the decision to embed it in traditional health and safety rationales should have been relatively uncontroversial, yet proved to be exactly the opposite. While this controversy mostly concerned the ongoing tensions between discourses of security and flexibility on the one hand, and regulation and deregulation on the other, as well as the actual reach of Community competences, its political effect was also to delineate a relatively narrow discursive universe around this particular instrument. One consequence of prioritizing the political goal of achieving working-time regulation at the EU level was that other potential and important rationales or considerations for regulation in this area were significantly marginalized. As suggested earlier, two such considerations that the 1993 Directive omitted were the impact of working-time organization on gender equality and the related goal of work–family reconciliation. Perhaps unremarkable given that these rationales have not historically informed regulation of standard hours, I maintain that this oversight was notable in light of the fact that both issues were already present in the broader EU policy discourse by the time of the Directive's adoption. Indeed, as I detailed in Chapter 2, the Commission's failed 1983 *Draft Recommendation* on working time had already factored work–family reconciliation into the scope of that proposed measure. Similarly, the gender equality-related impacts of work hours were fairly explicitly acknowledged in the Commission's supporting policy documents issued in the 1980s, yet these aspects made it onto official working-time agenda only by way of framework agreements and Directives on part-time work and parental leave, which followed within a couple of years of the 1993 Directive.

Adopted in 1996 and 1998 respectively, the *Directive on Parental Leave* and the *Part-Time Work Directive*[59] also prescribed Community-level norms in relation to particular aspects of working-time regulation. While they shared the 1993 Directive's social policy thrust, their precise objectives differed, and so did the language in which these objectives were expressed. Namely, in addition to the broad principle of improvement of living and working conditions, preambles of these two instruments invoked also the goals of eliminating all forms of discrimination and promotion of equal opportunities, citing the *Social Charter* and the conclusions of the Essen European Council supporting it.[60] The key goal of the

[59] Above n. 19.

[60] *Follow-up to the Essen European Council on Employment*. Communication from the Commission to the Council, COM (95) 74 final Brussels (08 March 1995). The Essen Council Conclusions also stressed the need to take measures to promote equal opportunities for men and women but did so within the context of 'measures with a view to increasing the employment intensiveness of growth in particular by a more flexible organization of

Part-Time Work Directive was to facilitate equal (for both men and women) access to part-time work, with the proceeding Framework Agreement referring to retirement, reconciliation of work and family life, and continuing education/retraining as the key sets of activities or life phases wherein part-time work may play a key supportive role. A related objective was to improve the quality of part-time work; hence, acknowledge and challenge its less desirable features, which include low pay, lack of advancement opportunities, and its marginalized status within the labour market. In addition to this supply-side focus, the agreement and the Directive's invocation of business-friendly logics such as 'requirements of competition' left no doubt that meeting the organizational flexibility needs of employers was the other key intention behind this instrument. This duality of purpose, also evident in the *Working Time Directive*, was not necessarily a feature of the *Parental Leave Directive*, an instrument that drew on the same principles as the Directive on part-time work to create a right of child-related leave, a key form of parental accommodation in the employment context. Crucially, the way in which this latter right was enacted was more obviously consistent with promotion of gender equality and social change as the Directive's guarantee that women and men will be able take up their leave entitlement equally was not merely rhetorical but also made concrete through the non-transferability clause that makes it impossible for the entitlement to be transferred between parents.[61]

Adoption of a more or less explicitly gender-aware and accommodating approach in the context of the instruments on part-time work and parental leave by contrast with the 1993 Directive's gender-blindness, was an important step forward in developing the EU working-time regime. Nonetheless, some feminist critics have pointed out that these two instruments do not remain without problems and certainly do not offer a complete or satisfactory solution to labour market inequality. Indeed, as I already noted in Chapter 2, it is also problematic that in adopting different rationales and approaches to non-standard and standard working-time arrangements and related forms of flexibility, the Community policymakers have ended up with a characteristically bifurcated regulatory model

work in a way that fulfills both the wishes of the employees and the requirements of the competition'.

[61] See clause 2(2), *Parental Leave Directive*. This means that leave cannot be transferred from fathers to mothers, and then parents cannot make choices about who is going to remain at home for the duration of the entire leave. This clause was inserted to motivate fathers to take up their portion of the leave.

(Figart and Mutari 2001: 53). In 'sensitizing' some instruments to gender by invoking equality principles, the need to attend to differences between women and men, and to accommodate unpaid care responsibilities, while treating other instruments neutrally through the omission of these very considerations, the resulting model tends to leave unchallenged the traditional notion of what is standard, 'normal' work, which despite being neutrally framed has always been highly gendered and biased against women.

Of course, there are concrete reasons for why the Community working-time regime developed in this distinctively bifurcated manner, and I am not suggesting here that there was a sort of conspiracy to bring this result about. Reprising the contextual factors – the structural developments in the EU's institutional architecture, policy discourse, and allocation of power between key policy actors – makes apparent that the different treatment of various aspects of working-time regulation resulted from a confluence of these factors at a particular point in time. Unlike the 1993 Directive, the part-time work and parental leave instruments came into being in environments relatively more receptive to social regulation and with a Council that was more committed to economic and social convergence in the Union.[62] By the time of their adoption, the need to make flexible work organization also of benefit for employees gained policy prominence through the Commission's Green Paper on *Partnership for the New Organization of Work*, and was subsequently mainstreamed by the EES and post-Amsterdam employment guidelines, which integrated the principles of equality, work–family reconciliation, and adaptability of work to worker into employment policy, even if the underlying rationale may have been to increase employment rates. The fact that both of these Directives were negotiated by social partners and only subsequently adopted as Community Directives also made the process of their adoption somewhat less controversial, if not less lengthy, and thus potentially more open to their broader and more socially progressive and egalitarian casting. By contrast, the different timing of the Directive on working time, its narrower legal basis and health and safety rationale, and its consequent mandate to only set minimum standards (chosen to circumvent the UK veto), rendered inclusion of other 'social' rationales outside of its scope, especially in light of the political opposition already mounted by the UK, which at the time was highly reluctant to expand

[62] *Council Resolution of 6 December 1994 on certain aspects for a European Union social policy: a contribution to economic and social convergence in the Union*, [1994] O.J. C 368/6.

the EU's social policy reach, even in this fairly traditional regulatory field. As my earlier review of the post-2003 debates over the Directive's revision suggests, both the health and safety rationale and the limitations of the Directive's legal basis, had presented an ongoing problem for those policy actors who wanted to expand its scope and broaden the range of considerations that working-time regulation should take account of.

While the contextual factors are clear contributors, the outcome is no less unsatisfactory or unproblematic in so far as its potential gender consequences. Despite the EU's rhetoric of modernization of working time, and notwithstanding the undeniable diversification of work-arrangements over the last couple of decades, the working-time regime actually established at the EU level remains fairly strongly wedded to the traditional model of employment founded on a set of outdated presumptions about 'normal' workers as exclusively engaged and unencumbered (male) employees. The *Working Time Directive* is a case in point. Regardless of its socially informed health and safety rationale, which is without a doubt important, the instrument ultimately assumes traditional conceptions of time and leisure, which through proscription of protective daily and weekly working-time limits in a context of 'normal' work stabilize a particular temporal model that may be indeed protective for some workers but is certainly not suitable or amenable for everyone. Even more problematically than the protective core norms, which are already exclusive of workers unable to submit to the temporal regime they set, the negative flexibility forms the Directive enables – as a way to balance health and safety protection with organizational needs – tend to directly interfere with workers interests in work–family reconciliation. Yet the Directive's silence regarding these potential negative consequences obscures the fact that the model it prescribes is hardly neutral, since it derives from an employment model that presupposes workers to be available and unencumbered by roles they play outside of the labour market. Juxtaposition of this approach to 'normal' work hours with the more gender-sensitive tone of instruments regulating temporal models that are already more obviously gendered (because they tend to be more feminized) only reinforces this bias. Thus, the resulting, bifurcated, regime suggests a failure to rethink or modernize working-time regulation to reflect contemporary realities and a diversified workforce, instead revealing an attempt to 'fit' or *accommodate* women into male patterns of employment and merely *adapt* legal standards originally based on these work patterns to suit women's needs (with the inherently gendered assumptions about what these needs are). Such an approach can only go so far, for while it does acknowledge the fact that some contemporary workers have responsibilities outside of the workplace, it ultimately fails to reconceptualize regulation in a way that would place those workers – and their needs – at the centre, not at the fringe of employment regulation.

As the *Working Time Directive*'s revision consultation demonstrated, attempts have been made to expand the universe of political discourse surrounding standard conceptions of working time to include these missing references to work–family reconciliation and gender equality. However, the same example shows that doing so has proved remarkably challenging for those social and institutional actors promoting (for whatever reason) such an expanded view of working time. Both the European Parliament (Employment and Social Affairs and Women's Rights and Equal Opportunities Committees) and the ETUC sought to mainstream the relationship between equal opportunities and working time, drawing on expert reports also available to the Commission staff and other actors involved in the negotiations (Pereira Interview, 17 February 2010, Brussels; Anonymous European Commission Policy Officer Interview, 17 February 2010). Indeed, the relationship between the opt-out's promotion of long hours and women's opportunities was also something that got flagged by the European Economic and Social Committee's in their consultation/re-examination opinions as a matter that should be analyzed in greater depth.[63] However, as this case shows, good intentions can be quickly abandoned in light of political pressures. Rhetoric and official submissions aside, even those parties acknowledging the link between equality and working time were prepared to drop the issue under political pressure. As the Rapporteur Alejandro Cercas and Jean Lambert, the UK MEP and a member of the EU Green Party, both outspoken supporters of the removal of the opt-out, noted, the political debate on working time – at least in the context of the *Working Time Directive* – was dominated by the balancing of the health and safety and economic

[63] Opinion of the European Economic and Social Committee on the Communication from the Commission to the Council, the European Parliament, the European Economic and Social Committee and the Committee of the Regions and the Social Partners at Community level concerning the Re-exam of *Directive 93/104/EC concerning certain aspects of the organization of working time*, [2004] O.J. C 302; *Opinion of the European Economic and Social Committee on the Proposal for a Directive of the European Parliament and of the Council amending Directive 2003/88/EC concerning certain aspects of the organization of working time*, COM (2004) 607 final – 2004/0209 COD, [2005] O.J. C 267. However, in its 2005 opinion, the EESC noted that it will not take a stance on the opt-out, choosing instead to defer to the social partners' negotiations and decision.

efficiency/flexibility rationales. The result of this was that the discussion of the opt-out completely failed to engage with and draw the link between the adverse effects of long hours on women's employment and advancement opportunities or even the fact that long hours are incompatible with balancing professional and familial responsibilities. According to one senior Commission employee, Fernando Pereira, these issues were never brought up in the Council discussions on the Directive's revision (Pereira Interview, 17 February 2010, Brussels), as the discussion quickly shifted from technical considerations to purely ideological and political ones (Pereira Interview, 17 February 2010, Brussels).

Similarly, those discussing the contentious issues of the reference period and on-call work failed to link the impact of long hours on women's equal access to employment and to the perpetuation of gendered patterns of work. Long-hours working was at the heart of both the issue of long reference periods and the redefinition of on-call work, with the on-call problem being distinctively located in heavily feminized sectors, and with long hours having clearly adverse impact on the issues of work–family reconciliation. Yet the negative effects of these provisions were not really taken into account either, with the interests of organizational efficiency and financial considerations dominating the talks. Thus, despite all the work–family reconciliation rhetoric, the ultimate dispute in the context of the *Working Time Directive* was not over employee-friendly forms of flexibility but rather over the ability to extend working hours – the classic form of negative flexibility – and about money. The promotion of gender and equal opportunities might have appeared briefly, but they were ultimately marginal within the universe of political discourse and were left off the bargaining table at the eleventh hour of negotiations. Under political pressure, even those parties such as the ETUC and the Commission, both of which attempted to broaden the debate on working time to include gender, were not quite able to do so. In Passchier's view, one of the reasons for the Commission's failure was the lack of what she referred to as 'policy coherence': 'If you talk to [the] equality departments [within the Commission] they always have a nice position, but are they able to get this position into the mainstream? That is the real issue' (Passchier Interview, 16 February 2010, Brussels).

3.5 Conclusion

The 2010 Commission Communication issued after the debacle of the revision negotiations more squarely acknowledged that there is a link between working time – as regulated in the *Working Time Directive* – and equal opportunities:

> In parallel with these business-led transformations, there is a growing awareness that working-time flexibility can help workers to reconcile their work and private life. Now that we have a more diversified EU workforce, flexible work schedules may provide workers with more opportunities to adapt working time to individual needs. Under certain circumstances, it may also enhance equal opportunities for employment and career progress, and facilitate access to employment for disadvantaged categories of job seekers.[64]

Moreover, in its 2009 *Report on Equality Between Men and Women*[65] the Commission, reflecting on the particular context of economic crisis, acknowledged that such periods, which are often used to claw back specific gains, should be instead seen as opportunities to reflect on the established, if altered, standards, and rethink them in a way that may be more socially, and ultimately economically, sustainable.[66] This reference to rethinking standards was important, even if it were more symbolic than concrete. Nonetheless, the nesting of the reconciliation, and employee-friendly flexibility in the context of competitiveness and the concern not to overburden enterprises tended to suggest that the transformative potential that crystallizes during crisis moments was probably not going to take the form of an EU-level solution. Indeed, as austerity spread through Europe and national working-time regimes became re-regulated to respond to crisis and its aftermath (Barnard 2012), how these reforms would impact equality or work–life balance was not high on the agenda, particularly given the more general underplaying of gender equality in the response to crisis (Smith and Villa 2010).

As this and the previous chapter have shown, the *Working Time Directive* was a product of an uneasy balance between the security and the flexibility rationales, the Community's limited competences, and the fragmented

[64] *Reviewing the Working Time Directive.* First-phase Consultation of the Social Partners at the European Union level under Article 154 of the TFEU. Communication from the Commission to the European Parliament, the Council, the European Economic and Social Committee, and the Committee of the Regions, COM (2010) 106 final, (24 March 2010).

[65] COM (2009) 0694 final (18 December 2009).

[66] *Ibid.* At page 17, the Commission notes: 'The political responses given to the recession represent an opportunity as well as a potential threat for women's employment and gender equality. There is a risk that the current recession will delay advances, or even reverse progress, with longer-term consequences on the sustainability of the economy and the social protection systems, social inclusion, and demography'.

consensus between the major actors shaping the universe of political discourse: the Member States, the Council and the Parliament, the social partners representing labour and management at the EU level. While the Commission's reframing of the working-time issue to fit the EU's developing health and safety competences was sufficient for the instrument's adoption in 1993, and the ECJ's subsequent interpretation of the Directive's provisions affirmed and strengthened the legitimacy of this legal basis, both nonetheless posed a series of political problems. As the Directive's 2004 to 2009 failed revision process made apparent, this legal framing also significantly narrowed down the universe of political discourse on working time and made the Directive an uneasy foundation for the wider EU working-time regime with the consequence that actors interested in broadening the discussion surrounding this instrument – particularly the European Parliament, the ETUC and, to some extent, the Commission – have been only partially successful in doing so.

While the Directive's future is uncertain and there is concern about further erosion of this already very limited instrument, the Directive is also ripe with possibilities. Given the pronounced shift towards work–family reconciliation in EU policy, the increased focus on redressing the effects of demographic shifts and preventing a demographic crisis, and the new attention to gender equality and promotion of equal opportunities, the Directive could potentially be revised in a manner that extends the political discourse around working time. The enshrining of rights to reconciliation and limitation of work hours by the *Charter of Fundamental Rights* may also prove game changing. Noting the transformations in the realm of work and the broader social and economic situation in its Communication on *Reviewing the Working Time Directive*, the Commission asks (2010: 5): 'has regulation of working time kept pace with [the] developments? Or are reforms needed to adapt the current rules to the needs of companies, workers and consumers in the 21st century?' This question opens the doors to possibilities, but the extent to which the proposed solutions will be transformative remains to be seen. The fact that the Commission's recently adopted Roadmap on work-life balance (2015)[67] makes no reference to the *Working Time Directive*, nor is the Directive listed among the instruments identified as relevant for developing a 'comprehensive' policy approach to work-life balance in thc

[67] Roadmap for the initiative "New start to address the challenges of work-life balance faced by working families. (August 2015) http://ec.europa.eu/smart-regulation/roadmaps/docs/2015_just_xxx_maternity_leave.en.pdf.

Commission's follow-up consultation document,[68] is certainly a cause for concern. Yet, perhaps with more vigilance or the possibility of finding another treaty base, or redefinition of health and safety, the *Working Time Directive* can become part of a more coherent approach to working time at the EU level, one which would fully acknowledge the essentially gendered nature of working time and the necessity of refashioning working-time standards to achieve gender equality in the workplace, in society generally, and more sustainable working-time arrangements from the perspective of social reproduction. As the next two chapters will elaborate, such a more comprehensive vision of working time is particularly crucial for Poland, where social reproduction has been significantly undermined as a result of broader political–economic changes, and where EU regulation has had particular impact on labour law reform.

[68] First Phase Consultation of Social Partners Under Article 154 TFEU on *Possible Action Addressing the Challenges of Work-Life Balance Faced by Working Parents and Caregivers*, C(2015) 7754 final (11 November 2015).

4

Polish Working-time Regime from Socialism to the Liberal Democracy – Long Hours, Women's Double Burden, and Social Reproduction

4.1 Introduction

Despite the sea change that Polish workers have experienced in the last several decades, two things have been remarkably persistent: long hours of work and the double burden for women. Compared to western Europe and even other Eastern Central European (ECE) countries, working-time reductions proceeded at a slower pace in Poland, particularly since the Second World War. Although legislation introduced in 1918 and 1919 placed Poland among the leading group of countries that adopted the 46-hour weekly norm, this progressive trend was reversed several years later by legislation reinstating the 48-hour week.[1] The 46-hour norm, legislated once again in the late 1940s, remained the standard for nearly four decades, making long work hours the key feature of the working-time regime that developed in the People's Republic of Poland (People's Republic). Working time was finally reduced to 42 hours in 1986, but the 40-hour workweek – one of the key demands of the general strikes that swept the country in August of 1980[2] and, by then, a long-time

[1] In a seminal text on Polish labour law, Wacław Szubert (1976) notes that the 8-hour day was introduced by decree on 23 November 1918, which a year later, on the 18 December 1919, was replaced by a statute introducing the 46-hour workweek, with an 'English' 6-hour Saturday, and increasing overtime premiums from 25 per cent to 50 per cent for the first 2 hours and from 50 per cent to 100 per cent for all additional hours, night work, and holiday hours. Between 1918 and 1924, other progressive regulations were introduced, including the annual leave, provisions on leaves for pregnant workers, and the creation of factory crèches and kindergartens (Szubert 1976: 24–25, 209), but the trend reversed following the economic crisis of the 1930s (Szubert 1976: 27).

[2] In August 1980, the Independent Self-Governing Trade Union 'Solidarity', the first independent and, at the time, unsanctioned, trade union in Poland, organized a series of workers' strikes and non violent demonstrations that beyond traditional worker demands also demanded political and economic liberalization, and the improvement of general living conditions. The imposition of the Martial Law in 1981 quashed the strikes and Solidarity was forced underground, but its ongoing activism and social mobilization contributed to the political–economic reforms that initiated Poland's transition to market economy at the end of 1980s/early 1990s.

reality in most industrialized countries – was never achieved in the People's Republic. In fact, it was not until 2003, well over a decade after Poland's transition to a liberal market economy, that this standard was legislated. By that time, however, cycles of recession and the economic pressures of European Union (EU) conditionality contributed to significant flexibilization of the Polish working-time regime.

The second persistent and related feature of the Polish post-war reality, and, in part, the product of the working-time regime that developed there, has been the double burden carried by women. Its presence, although mediated by the provisioning role of the state and nationalized enterprises during the People's Republic era, was nonetheless a clear indication that the existing provisions were not sufficient, and that the traditional gender contract that had historically existed in Poland was substantially untransformed by socialist egalitarianism and women's employment activation (see Section 4.2.3). The double burden also attested to the fact that the local version of the standard employment relationship (SER) and the key norms associated with it – standard hours of work being one set – were not fully compatible with the essential yet unpaid work of social reproduction because these norms took this work for granted. Instead, these norms penalized women who were traditionally charged with carrying the bulk of unpaid work. In the People's Republic, standard norms of working time penalized women not by excluding them from the labour market, because some provisions for their full and life-long participation were made, but by substantially adding to their workloads.

Remarkably slow progress on such a key labour issue as reduction of working time demands some consideration, particularly given the ideological foundation of the People's Republic and the fact that both long working hours and women's double burden continue to be endemic in contemporary Poland. This chapter begins with an overview of the key developments in the discursive universe and working-time regulation in the People's Republic, encompassing the period between the end of the Second World War and the start of Poland's political–economic transition in 1989. I highlight the key discourses, rationales, and institutional constraints that influenced the organization and regulation of work hours during this period and describe the key features of the working-time regime, the ways in which it was supported by the state, and show how it contributed to women's double burden. Next, I examine the impact of Poland's transition to market economy on the country's universe of political discourse; I also consider how the changes in the country's institutional architecture affected the terms and conditions of women and men's labour market engagement and the process of social reproduction. This discussion sets the context for the analysis of the post-transition changes in working-time regulation, particularly in light of Poland's 2004 EU accession, which I undertake in Chapter 5 along with assessing Poland's 'new' working-time regime from the perspective of its gendered impacts. I conclude by considering the logics employed to justify long work hours during the course of Polish post-war history, focusing on the patterns of continuity and change, and assessing their comparative outcomes from the perspective of gender equality and social reproduction.

4.2 'What Have You Done to Achieve the Plan?' – the Discourse of Civic Duty and the Structural Causes of Long-hours Work in the People's Republic

4.2.1 Introduction

Reconstruction, industrialization, and economic growth – the key goals of the post-war period – had a crucial impact on shaping Poland's universe of political discourse and the development of labour regulations, including working-time standards. The primacy of 'the Plan' meant that social objectives, such as working-time reductions, became temporarily subordinated to economic rationales and growth indicators. Encouraged by the success of the *Three-Year Economic Reconstruction Plan (1947–1949)*,[3] which went a long way towards rebuilding Poland's economy and infrastructure from its wartime damage and substantially improved the living conditions in the country,[4] the *Six-Year Plan of Economic Development and Construction of the Socialist System* of 1950–1955[5] aimed to expand significantly Poland's industrial base, further increase production, and establish the foundations for socialism. These ambitious goals required enormous human effort, particularly given the low technological

[3] *Three-Year Economic Reconstruction Plan (1947–1949), Act of 2 July 1947,* Journal of Laws 1947, No. 53, item 285 (hereinafter *Three-Year Plan*).

[4] At the end of 1949, the GDP increased by 43 per cent, exceeding the 1938 figures, and the per capita GDP was 2.5 times higher than in 1937. Total employment increased from 3.4 mln to 4.4 mln in the same period. The plan also raised living standards and was generally regarded as the most successful plan in the People's Republic history (Gajos 2009, http://Historia.org.pl/).

[5] *Six-Year Plan of Economic Development and Construction of Socialist System 1950–1955* was adopted by the People's Republic Parliament on 21 July 1950: Journal of Laws 1950 No. 37 item 344 (hereinafter *Six-Year Plan*).

capacity at the People's Republic's disposal. Hence, the authorities engaged various methods to ensure that there were plenty of hands to do the job. To contribute to rebuilding the country, building socialism, and assisting the rapidly growing industrial economy came to be regarded as matters of civic duty, nestled in and supported by a powerful ideological discourse best summed up by the slogan 'What have *you* done to achieve the Plan?' – a common feature of socialist propaganda posters. These posters typically depicted young, eager workers who embodied the sense of civic duty and the level of commitment that was expected from citizens. Importantly, this call to engagement was directed at women also, as the discursive universe of this period valorized women's contribution to the productive process above their more traditional domestic roles. In her study of women workers in People's Republic, Małgorzata Fidelis (2010: 74) points out that women were not only to play a key role in the expanding textile industry and other feminized sectors but also in those previously considered the domain of men. Accordingly, pre-war protective legislation that excluded women from certain occupations or from work under specific conditions, such as truck transport or underground mining, was repealed in 1951 (Szubert 1976: 36).[6]

Besides being ideational, however, the duty to work was a concrete legal obligation[7] that took on particularly coercive dimensions during this period. Save for a few,[8] many of the regulations introduced in the 1950s were specifically designed to achieve high levels of labour market participation, maintain industrial discipline, and subordinate workers' demands to the economic goals set by the Plan. To that effect, statutes and decrees curbing the disruptive potential of trade unions by limiting their functions to more administrative and organizational ones (Zieliński 1997: 13), provisions limiting the movement of workers in some occupational

[6] This legislation was reinstated in 1959.

[7] The right to work, enshrined in the *Constitution of the Polish People's Republic of 22 July 1952*, (1952) Journal of Laws, No. 33, item 232, obligated the state to provide all citizens with full and life-long employment but also imposed duty on citizens to participate in the labour process, thus embedding the ethos of work into the official discourse. Practically, most social entitlements, provisions, and benefits stemmed from employment and were organized at the enterprise level.

[8] Two statutes legislated in the 1950s introduced protective working-time provisions. The first extended the length of annual leave for blue-collar workers and provided for potential additional leaves (20 March 1950). The second, introduced on 19 April 1950, created the basis for reductions of working time where work was being carried out in conditions particularly harmful to health.

categories, and punitive disciplinary penalties for absenteeism (Szubert 1976; Seweryński 1999) were legislated at the outset of the *Six-Year Plan* period.[9] Polish labour law scholar Tadeusz Zieliński (1997) maintains that the coercive nature of these regulations reflected the Stalinist influence in most areas of Polish social and economic policy at the time.[10] Under this totalitarian work-rule, Zieliński observes, the labour process became no less exploitative and alienating than that of the nineteenth century capitalist enterprises (Zieliński 1997).

While many of the restrictive provisions and statutes enacted between 1950 and 1955 were repealed after 1956[11] (Szubert 1976), no significant developments in the area of working time would take place for nearly two decades. In the early 1970s the legislature finally passed the long overdue working-time reform, partially phasing in the 5-day workweek by eliminating Saturday work on several days of the year, beginning with two in 1972,[12] six in 1974 and increasing to twelve in 1975 and 1976.[13] This very limited reduction was accompanied by a number of other developments related to aspects of working time, reflecting a shift in employment policy towards a greater balancing of social and economic goals, and a renewed commitment to the improvement of living standards. The focus on maternity-leave extensions and granting mothers the right to a 60-day paid leave to care for a child[14] (Szubert 1976) also marked the shift in the official family policy during this period. Nonetheless, the economic growth motives continued to play a key role in employment regulation and the organization of the nationalized enterprises.

[9] *Act of 19 April 1950 concerning Protection of Socialist Work Discipline*, Journal of Laws 1950 No. 20, item 168, aimed to limit absenteeism by prescribing severe monetary penalties for missing work. A court could order a 10–35 per cent earnings cut for a period of up to 3 months, with the employee's right to unilaterally terminate the employment relationship being suspended for that time period. Incarceration was foreseen for both failure to submit to the penalty and failure to impose the penalty by the enterprise director (Szubert 1976: 35).

[10] Industrial discipline was also maintained through installing industrial spies, informers, and special security forces (Fidelis 2010: 74–75).

[11] It is generally accepted that the period of most coercive policies and practices of the People's Republic history ended with Stalin's death in 1953. The direct Soviet influence was also diminished after 1953.

[12] *Decree of 20 July 1972 on Additional Holidays*, Journal of Laws 1972 No. 29 item 203; *Decree of 20 July 1972 on Additional Holidays*, Journal of Laws 1973 No. 29 item 160.

[13] *Act no. 41 of the Council of Ministers of 6 February 1974 concerning the Rules and Timelines for Introduction of Additional Holidays during 1974 and 1975*, Law Monitor No. 6, item 43.

[14] *Act no. 14 of the Council of Ministers of 14 January 1972 concerning Child-care Social Assistance*, Law Monitor No. 5, item 27.

'Extensive managing' – the characteristic managerial method practiced in the People's Republic state enterprises – equated productivity and efficiency with work intensification and overtime (Zieliński 1986: 222). Usually utilized to meet production goals, make up for outmoded technology, and particularly common during periods of economic crisis and shortage, these tendencies in managing the labour process were enabled by legislatively mandated weekly and daily working-time extensions in key industries.[15] These kinds of practices only served to slow down the process of working-time reduction (Zieliński 1986).

A related reason for the slow progress in this field was undoubtedly tied to the legal status and the structure of trade unions. Beginning with the early steps towards restricting union function and activity noted earlier, the People's Republic-era labour unions were controlled by the authorities and served more as extensions of the administrative and managerial apparatus than as independent representative bodies capable of collective bargaining (Seweryński 1995: 33–34; Zieliński 1997). Although the particularities of their legal status changed over the years, trade unions essentially functioned to organize productive activities rather than represent workers in negotiating conditions of work and defending their interests. One way in which union effectiveness was further impaired was through making strike activity, the fundamental tool of organized labour everywhere, illegal (Seweryński 1995).[16]

Despite the peculiar status and role of the unions, workers nonetheless managed to achieve some concessions from the state and national enterprises. In fact, according to another Polish labour law scholar, Michał Seweryński (1999), most progressive changes in employment regulation enacted by the People's Republic authorities were a result of the pressure exerted by workers' revolts and illegal strikes. Nonetheless, because they were reactionary, these concessions were partial and designed to temporarily pacify the periodic eruptions of unrest. It was not until 1982, a year after mass workers' strikes had swept the country, that the right to

[15] In the 1980s, for instance, the *Labour Code* and several other statutes mandated working-time extensions in key industries for the purpose of meeting the production objectives (1986–1990) and/or overcoming the economic crisis (1983–1986).

[16] Seweryński (1995: 44) points out that since the political and legal doctrines prevailing in Poland and other communist countries excluded the possibility of social conflicts, procedures for dealing with labour disputes were not established and the right to strike not recognized. Such procedures, and a circumscribed right to strike, were enacted in 1982 as an attempt to regulate mass workers' demonstrations similar to those that took place in 1981. Less rigorous dispute settlement and strike provisions more in line with international standards were enacted only in 1991.

strike was finally recognized,[17] the legal status of trade unions began to change, and the first independent trade union, Niezależny Samorządny Związek Zawodowy NSZZ "Solidarność" (Independent Self-Governing Trade Union "Solidarity"), was formally recognized (Seweryński 1999). While Solidarity and the social movement that rallied around it were credited with beginning the process of unravelling the Polish state-socialism and paving the way for the economic and democratic reforms that began at the end of 1980s, the extent to which Polish unions have been able to effectively secure changes in working time since then is less clear. Although the demand for the 5-day and 40-hour workweek would eventually be met in 2003, the practice of long hours continued to be prevalent during the transition period. Interestingly, despite the change in Poland's political-economic outlook, this practice of long hours was utilized for essentially the same reasons and justified in a very similar language as before.

4.2.2 The People's Republic Working-time Regime, 1945–1989

Working-time Regulations in the 1974 Labour Code

The legislatively prescribed long working-time norm of 46 hours over 6 days applied from the end of Second World War until 1986. Prior to the 1974 codification of labour and employment law, rules on working time were contained in several statutes and numerous regulations and decrees issued by the Council of Ministers (Seweryński 1999). The 1974 *Labour Code*[18] unified many of these rules. It expanded the scope of possible daily and weekly working-time extensions but also reduced some of the existing limits and included a broad provision permitting the Council of Ministers to enact further working-time reductions. To that effect, Article 150 of the 1974 *Labour Code*, for example, delegated to the Council of Ministers the phasing in of additional Saturdays as days off, a practice that had already been initiated by regulations passed earlier that year. However, apart from the six and later twelve 'free' Saturdays per year, more substantial working-time reductions would not be legislated for several more years.

[17] *Ibid.* See also: Seweryński (1999: 28–29). This legislation remained in place until it was modified by 1991 *Act concerning the Resolution of Collective Disputes*, Journal of Laws 1991, No. 55, item 236.

[18] *Act of 26 June 1974 concerning the Labour Code*, Journal of Laws 1974 No. 24, item 141 (the *Labour Code*). Articles of the *Labour Code* and other legislative acts used throughout the book reflect numbering in the original legislation and may not be consistent with the current numbering in light of subsequent revisions and consolidations.

In addition to Article 150, the 1974 Code mandated working-time *reductions* for specific categories of workers and where the conditions of work were particularly straining or harmful to human health and safety. Unlike the 1950s legislation that it replaced,[19] the Code did not provide specific reduced norms; instead, Article 130 mandated the Council of Ministers, by regulation, temporarily to reduce the existing maximum working time in the specified circumstances either by setting lower daily and weekly norms or by introducing additional breaks. Workers, whose working time was reduced pursuant to Article 130, were entitled to full compensation, since the new norm would be the maximum permissible norm in their industry or job classification.

In terms of working-time *extensions*, the 1974 Code provided that maximum daily working time could exceed 8 hours for specific occupational categories or if specific conditions or types of work organization necessitated such extensions. In these situations, permissible daily (up to 10 or 12 hours) and weekly (up to 56 hours) extensions and reference periods (2, 3, and 4 weeks) for averaging working time were specified. For workers employed in surveillance, security, and to guard property, for instance, the daily working time could be increased to 12 hours, provided that the average number of weekly hours did not exceed 56 over a 3-week reference period. The 56-hour maximum was introduced by a 1974 Council of Ministers regulation and was a significant reduction from the previous maximum limit of 72 hours (Szubert 1976). Workers employed in essential services and retail, as well as drivers in transport could work up to 10 hours per day, provided that their working time averaged to 8 hours a day and 46 hours per week over respective 4 and 2-week reference periods (Article 141). Ten-hour days (with 1-month reference periods) were also permitted for workers whose work depended on seasonal and atmospheric conditions (such as workers in agriculture and sea voyage or faring), as well as workers in sectors of hospitality and tourism, aviation, postal services, and railways (Article 141). All these workers received overtime pay for work in excess of the norm established in their particular workplace (50 per cent for the first 2 hours, and 100 per cent for additional hours or overtime night work, or Sunday or statutory holiday work, as per Article 134) or, on the worker's request, were compensated with equivalent time off (Article 143). Finally, the *Labour Code* provided special working-time rules for industries where the technological process mandated that the work be uninterrupted (Article 132). Here, daily hours could be extended to 12 and weekly to 48 over the reference period of

[19] Above n. 9.

4 weeks,[20] with overtime compensation for any hours in excess of the eight/46 statutory standard calculated at the end of the reference period of 4 weeks (Article 132(4)).

In addition to these specific exceptions and provisions for longer working-time norms, *overtime rules* also provided for extensions of the daily and weekly limits in three types of circumstances. First, the *Labour Code* permitted overtime with no maximum limits in cases of emergency, life-saving operations, or urgent repairs (Article 133(1)). Second, overtime was permitted when it was necessitated by circumstances broadly defined as the "particular needs of the employer" (Article 133(1)), with no explanation or examples provided for what such needs might comprise. The 1974 *Labour Code* also dispensed with a previously existing obligation to consult with the union or another representative workers' body on the use of overtime, leaving this determination entirely to managerial discretion (Szubert 1976: 518) subject only to the proscription that the annual overtime for each worker could not exceed 120 hours (Article 133(2)). However, the Code also permitted the Council of Ministers to adjust (i.e. increase) this annual limit for particular enterprises or sectors (Article 133(3)). Finally, overtime was also permitted in the earlier-mentioned continuous or uninterrupted mode of production or work organization.

Notwithstanding the fairly broad discretion of enterprise managers to request overtime, there was a prohibition on the overtime employment of certain categories of workers (Article 178). The provision categorically applied to pregnant women, while mothers of children under one had to agree to work over their scheduled hours. Overtime work was compensated with premiums of 50 per cent for the first 2 hours in excess of the daily norm and 100 per cent for additional hours beyond two (Article 135), albeit these premiums were not available to managerial and supervisory staff, or other workers who exercised autonomy over their work organization (Article135(1)), as well as workers engaged in project or task-based work (Article 136).

With minor amendments, the working time rules of the 1974 *Labour Code* were in effect until the re-codification of 1996.[21] One important change that occurred prior to 1996, however, was the reduction in the weekly working-time norm to 42 hours, which applied to the nationalized

[20] This was a significant change from the previous regulation, which provided that weekly working time could be increased to 56 hours without specifying any reference period for this type of work organization.

[21] *Act of 2 February 1996 concerning the Amendment of the Labour Code and certain other Acts*, Journal of Laws 1996 No. 24, item 110.

enterprises as of 1981. Subsequent Council of Ministers regulations and decrees, however, gave discretion to enterprise managers to introduce additional working-time increases.[22] Such increases could be implemented in key industries provided that they were necessitated by important production or efficiency needs. As a consequence, even after 1981, working time could be potentially extended to 46 or 48 hours per week, and from 8 to 12 hours per day, provided that it averaged to 42 hours over an extended reference period of 24 weeks (Zieliński 1986). These extensions, introduced in 1983, as part of an anti-crisis bill,[23] and then again in 1986, were examples of the 'extensive managing' philosophy that employed overtime as a way of increasing efficiency and meeting production goals.

Special Working-time Rules Related to Women and Motherhood

Aside from the prohibition on overtime work for pregnant women and its restriction for mothers of children under one (Article 178(1) and (2)), the 1974 *Labour Code* also contained other rules dealing with aspects of women's working time, which were listed in the Code's chapter addressing the 'Protection of Women's Work',[24] and which remained mostly unchanged until the 1996 re-codification. These special provisions included maternity leaves and other types of child-care leaves.

With respect to the first, Article 180 of the Code provided for an extended paid maternity leave of 16, 18, and 26 weeks depending on the number of children born.[25] Women could partially determine how to spread this entitlement between the period of before and after childbirth, with the restriction that at least 2 weeks of the leave had to be taken before the delivery date. There was less control over the total duration of the leave, however, since the Code prescribed that all but 4 weeks of the leave were obligatory. Thus, women who for some reason wished to shorten their leave were still required to take up at least 12 (of 16), 14 (of 18), 22 (of 26) weeks respectively, depending on the number of children they had given birth to (Article 180(3)). In 1974, maternity leave entitlements

[22] *Decree of the Council of Ministers, 1986, regarding Increasing Working Time in Some Enterprises during the Period of 1986–1990*, Journal of Laws, No. 6, item 34.

[23] *Act of 21 July 1983 concerning Special Legal Regulation during Social-economic Crisis and concerning the Amendment of Certain Acts*, Journal of Laws 1983 No. 39, item 176.

[24] The same *Labour Code* chapter also listed various protective provisions unrelated to working time, such as the prohibition against employing all women in specified occupations and conditions, and special rules for pregnant workers.

[25] Prior to the *Act of 6 July 1972*, Journal of Laws No. 27, item 190, the maternity leave was set at 12 weeks.

were also extended to adoptive or foster mothers, and their duration was set at 14 or 4 weeks, depending on the age of the adopted child (under 4 months or under 1 year old, respectively; Article 183(1) and (2)).

In addition to the maternity leave, the Code also provided for two other types of child-related leaves: an unpaid, job-protected leave for the care of a child, referred to as the 'child-raising leave', and additional 60 days of paid leave for the care of a sick child ('child-care leave').[26] Only mothers were entitled to the child-care leave, with a guaranteed 100 per cent income replacement for up to 60 days per year. The unpaid child-raising leave, in existence since 1968[27] and previously set at a year, was provisionally extended to 3 years in 1972,[28] and then more formally in 1974. Mothers could request this leave at any time before a child's fourth birthday and could take it either in its entirety or in part. The leave request itself had to be granted by workplace managers, but managers retained discretion over whether the leave could be broken up into parts. Besides being entitled to job protection, women who opted for this leave were also entitled to a family allowance (Article 189), and the time spent on leave counted towards seniority for the purposes of annual leave, retirement entitlements, and other benefits that were determined on the basis of employment participation.

Additional special rules related to working time that were available to women included provisions for breastfeeding breaks (twice daily, 30 minutes each, or 45 minutes if more than one child; Article 187), paid medical examination leave during pregnancy, and paid leaves for a sick child (two per year) available to all mothers of children under 14 (Article 188). With the exception of this last leave entitlement, all others were available only to mothers. The Code's Article 188(2) extended the sick child leave to fathers, but only those who were sole parents.

4.2.3 Working Time and Social Reproduction in the People's Republic – the State's Provision and Women's Double Burden

As already noted earlier, the post-war call to civic duty and to rebuilding the country was also directed at women, with their engagement in the

[26] Both leaves were initially introduced in 1958 and 1968, and then improved in 1972 following the 1970–1971 strikes in Łódz and Gdańsk, although not fully meeting the women strikers' demands for a fully paid child-raising leave. Instead, the compromise was to extend the leave to 3 years, without pay but with job protection and other entitlements (Heinen and Wator 2006). The 1974 *Labour Code* incorporated these improved provisions.

[27] *Act No. 158 of the Council of Ministers of 24 May 1968*, Law Monitor No. 24, item 154.

[28] *Act No. 14 of the Council of Ministers of 14 January 1972*, Law Monitor No. 5, item. 27.

productive process being supported by a number of rationales within the universe of political discourse. First, the egalitarian and proletarian ideology of socialism saw participation in paid work as the only route to the attainment of full emancipation, thus policies supporting women's equal opportunities had an important ideological dimension. There were also a number of pragmatic reasons that explain this phenomenon. With the size of the male population seriously diminished by the end of the Second World War, the number of woman-headed households increased sharply, and many women began to demand employment to support themselves and their families (Fidelis 2004: 309–10). While women's wage work remained a highly contested issue in the early post-War period, by the late 1940s, women's labour market participation was encouraged and actively sought after to meet the economic planners' production goals and demands of industrialization (Fidelis 2004: 312–14), which dominated the 1950s discursive universe.

Indeed, the authorities' changing approach towards protective regulations limiting women's access to certain occupations also suggests that the objectives of women's equality were likely secondary to economic goals. As already noted, such regulations were completely repealed at the outset of the *Six-Year Plan*, and from 1950 to 1955 women were welcomed and, indeed, encouraged to enter all economic sectors. However, subsequent changes in labour market composition, production needs, and lobbying efforts by men's groups led to the reinstatement of protective legislation in 1955, its further extension in 1959, and return of the discourse about the 'natural' gender differences (Fidelis 2010). As Fidelis details (2010: 319–22), reinstatement of protective legislation left many women newly skilled in 'male' professions unable to work in their chosen fields, and this change was implemented without any consultation with women's groups and without regard to their choices and preferences. The timing of this abrupt shift in gender and employment policies suggests that the principles of equal access to work and chosen occupations, which dominated during the early 1950s, had an instrumental, economic planning dimension given that shifts in national needs and interest group pressures rendered these principles easily overturned and subordinate to other considerations, particularly those of employment availability but also the need to maintain fertility rates and the residual social provision.

Despite this setback, women's activation rates continued to grow in other sectors of the economy through the 1960s, and women's full wage employment became a permanent feature of the Polish labour market (Strzemińska 1970). By the 1980s, women constituted nearly 50 per cent of the working population in the People's Republic, compared to 30 per cent three decades earlier, and the 32 per cent in contemporary western Europe (Molyneux 1990: 26–7).

Patterns of Working Time

The policy of full employment in the People's Republic meant that standard hours of work were the norm regardless of the worker's gender. Long hours were common in both feminized and masculinized sectors, and thus, the level of working-time polarization – the discrepancies in working times of different workers – remained relatively low. This was in part due to the fact that although working-time extensions mandated by the 1974 *Labour Code* applied in many male-dominated sectors, 'equivalent' system of working time permitted in essential services, retail, hospitality, and gastronomy – sectors that were feminized (Lobodzinska 1977, 1995) – diminished some of the differences that may have otherwise been caused by longer hours in heavy manufacturing and other male-dominated industries and jobs. In fact, statutory working time *reductions* were often mandated in those sectors and jobs that by 1959 were entirely off limits to women due to exposure to harmful conditions.[29]

The fact that the *Labour Code* extended special protections over women's work and working time did not translate into a gender gap in working hours either. Most of these protective provisions related to accommodating pregnancy and early periods of maternity, and thus involved only short-term leaves and absences. Although the introduction of the 3-year child-raising leave could have significantly increased women's child-related absences, in practice many women did not take full advantage of this entitlement. Barbara Lobodzinska (1978: 691) reported that between 1969 and 1970 only 90,000 women went on the child-raising leave (at that time still only of 1-year duration). Based on the number of live births during this time period, she estimated the take-up rate of this leave to be only 8.3 per cent (Lobodzinska 1978: 691, note 4). While blue-collar workers were more likely to take leave (40 per cent) than their white-collar counterparts (20 per cent), in total, only 32 per cent of women stopped working for maternity-related reasons (Lobodzinska 1978: 692).

[29] Protective legislation reinstated in 1959 listed ninety occupations (e.g. extractive industries, underground mining, and smelting) prohibited to women on the basis of health and safety, women's particular physical capabilities, and protection of women's reproductive functions.

Along with the relatively low take-up of child-related leaves, the low incidence of part-time work, even after childbirth, also kept the potential discrepancies between men and women's working hours to a minimum. Although part-time work was not prohibited, there were no regulations that governed it, and, in practice, it was unpopular and rarely utilized. Of the very few studies that looked at its incidence, one reported that in 1971 only 6 per cent of women workers were engaged in part-time work, with nearly half being women between the ages of 60–64 (Sokołowska 1978: 261–62). Another noted that, in 1970, of the 3,884,200 female public sector workers, only 103,300 worked part-time (2.7 per cent), while in 1973 these numbers were 4,648,000 and 133,800 respectively (2.9 per cent) (Wierzbińska 1978: 322). Although at the end of the 1980s, recorded rates of part-time work were somewhat higher, at 12 per cent for women and 7.6 per cent for men, they were still much lower and less polarized by gender than the equivalent rates in western Europe (Poliwczak 2003: 18). Overall, the unpopularity of part-time work (much like the relatively low take-up of the 3-year child-raising leave) was related to the low wages paid and the fact that two full incomes were necessary to maintain a decent standard of living and sustain dependents. Beyond insufficient incomes, part-time work was also perceived as limiting in terms of future career advancement (Sokołowska 1978), but women's preference for full-time work was also influenced by the legal construction of work as a right and a duty, as well as the officially espoused philosophy of socialist egalitarianism and the related belief in paid employment's emancipatory potential (Pascall and Manning 2000).

While standard, 'rigid' work organization based around a fixed schedule dominated in the People's Republic, select state-run enterprises experimented with flexible forms of work organization as early as 1973. These experiments in flexibility were motivated by social and economic considerations; though their ultimate objective was to increase productivity, they also sought to adjust the work to the workers and to the capacities of the social infrastructure. According to economists Lucyna Machol (1980) and Helena Strzemińska and Elżbieta Sobótka (1984), variable start and end times, and even arrangements which allowed individual workers or workers' teams to determine both the start and the length of their daily shifts, subject to the observance of particular timeframes and weekly averages ('own account' flexibility), were introduced as ways of decreasing absenteeism, increasing productivity and job satisfaction, and to take the pressure off the social infrastructure, including workplace canteens and public transportation. Strzemińska (2008a: 57, 2008b: 83) notes that variable start and end times were also introduced in select Polish cities to accommodate working mothers and to synchronize their work schedules with day care or kindergarten hours, as well as to accommodate late arrivals caused by transportation difficulties. Later, the recognition of the economic benefits of these and other forms of flexibility prompted their further expansion to address economic factors such as irregularities in resource and energy supply, production breaks, and the increase in paid overtime (Strzemińska 2008a: 57–58).

These experiments, although successful from the perspective of enterprise management and popular with workers (Machol 1980: 28–29; Strzemińska and Sobótka 1984), were either limited or entirely ceased by the State administration because of their apparent incompatibility with the existing statutory regulations on working time. Variable start and end times, and particularly the 'own account' working-time flexibility, could indeed be inconsistent with the definition of the working day (as a 24-hour period) under the *Labour Code*. In reality, experiments in 'own account' working-time organization were likely discontinued also because they clashed with the accepted notion that only more work and longer hours would yield better productivity, and because more flexible organization provided workers with a degree of autonomy that was inconsistent with the use of work as a form of control in the People's Republic. Ultimately, as Machol (1980: 29–31) points out, some state enterprise managers who oversaw working-time flexibility experiments, particularly those using 'own account' systems, decided to continue utilizing them, albeit unofficially, because of clear benefits for production efficiency and meeting workers' personal needs. By contrast, the practices of variable start and end times were officially sanctioned and retained, but to avoid potential inconsistencies with the Code definition of the working day, these times were pre-scheduled (Machol 1980: 30). In neither case was there a significant difference between men and women's use of these arrangements.

To sum up, although some exceptions did apply during pregnancy and after maternity, most women's working-time patterns were not significantly distinct from those of men. The discourse emphasizing productivity, existing legal framework, and actual workplace practices – particularly the practice of 'extensive managing' and reliance on overtime – contributed to relatively long standard work hours for all workers. The legislatively prescribed working-time extensions were equally likely to affect male and female workers, and, indeed, the *Labour Code*-mandated reductions often benefited workers in occupations or sectors that women could not access. The accommodations that were intended to ease transitions between work and motherhood applied during relatively short periods of women's working lives, with the result that even with career breaks caused by maternity leaves and child-care obligations, women's rates of workplace absence were, on average, lower than men's (whose rates of absenteeism were higher and their year-long mandatory military service tended to make up for any difference) (Strzemińska 1970: 229), and generally fit within the *standard* norm for the majority of their working lives.

Despite this reality, the very existence of special statutory provisions contributed to the perception that women's rates of workplace absence were significantly higher than men's because of their familial duties. Women, particularly mothers, were also regarded as less committed to their jobs, as it was assumed and, even expected (particularly after the late 1950s), that their primary commitment be to their families. In a clear contradiction to the premises of socialist egalitarianism on which the People's Republic was said to be based, these presumptions about women's commitment, together with the naturalization of gender difference in the mainstream political discourse (and the popular belief that men and women were differently predisposed), stifled women's advancement opportunities, contributed to occupational segregation, and translated into the gender pay gap. In turn, women's secondary status in the workplace tended to reinforce traditional gender contracts in the private sphere.

Institutional Supports and the 'Double Burden'

> At home, no one can replace a mother's care – regardless of the children's age; similarly, no one can replace the homemaker in managing the household and tending to the daily needs of family members. Participation of the other members of the household in these duties may assist a woman, but in most cases the main responsibility for the family rests on her. It is hard to imagine the existence of an institution that could replace women, and completely 'free' them from their domestic duties. Nor do women desire this sort of emancipation.
>
> Strzemińska (1970: 11) [translated by author]

As I explained in the previous section, beyond the periods of pregnancy and early maternity, no special working-time arrangements were available for female workers to reconcile full-time employment with family obligations. Instead, to support the existing model of employment and working time without detriment to fertility rates or the standards of living, the People's Republic authorities had to accommodate women's paid work and make additional provisions for the process of social reproduction. Beyond legislating the paid or job-protected leaves described earlier, other forms of institutional support included organizing and subsidizing child care, family allowances and family-support funds, and universal healthcare (Lobodzinska 1995: 7; Heinen and Wator 2006). Further, some subsidies were also available for food and housing, and education at all levels was publically funded. Many of these services, particularly kindergartens and crèches, canteens, and recreational facilities, were delivered at the workplace. Beyond being practical, this choice of delivery mechanism also fairly explicitly acknowledged that the processes of social reproduction and production were interrelated (Rittich 2002b).

While the public infrastructure and support undeniably took some pressure off of working parents, particularly mothers, it often fell short of being sufficient, with the effect that the households still carried out residual work of care and maintenance (Einhorn 1993; Fidelis 2004). Since the traditional gender contract assigning the performance of these activities to women was remarkably persistent in the face of the formal equality and women's high visibility in employment, the bulk of this residual work fell on women. Given the already long hours of paid work and the People's Republic economy of shortage, this was not an easy task. Busy, weighed-down, tired, yet always capable of juggling it all, the iconic image of a Polish woman widespread in the People's Republic-era TV series and the popular press – although somewhat exaggerated and ironic – did, in fact, convey the reality of the double burden most Polish women coped with on a daily basis. Scarcity of many foodstuffs and other necessities, the unavailability of household appliances, and the underdeveloped service sector made everyday tasks such as procuring and preparing food or household maintenance very time-consuming (Strzemińska 1970; Lobodzinska 1977).

Sociological research and time-budget studies attested to women's double burden and to the fact that their total work hours exceeded those of men. Lobodzinska's (1977) comprehensive survey of early Polish studies on women and men's respective involvement in domestic and child-rearing duties concluded that according to most available data, women's domestic contributions exceeded men's regardless of whether both partners were employed or the household was based on the traditional breadwinner model. While a woman's level of education and skills appeared to be a predictor of her partner's involvement in the domestic and child-rearing duties, even in households with highly educated and skilled women, men limited their involvement to the more 'technical' aspects of domestic work, some assistance with childrearing, and taking out the household waste (Lobodzinska 1977: 413).

One of the key studies that Lobodzinska cited was Strzemińska's (1964, 1970) research on the total working time of white- and blue-collar women, which found them to differ but also identified pronounced discrepancies between working times for all women and men. According to Strzemińska's figures, blue-collar women workers in the 1960s spent, on average, 5 hours and 38 minutes on daily household chores, thus just over 2 hours more than their white-collar counterparts who committed 3 hours 34 minutes to doing the same tasks (1966: 261, 1970). This additional work was carried out on top of the 10 to 11 hours spent on paid work (including commuting), leaving women, depending on their occupation, between 6 hours 30 minutes to 8 hours for sleep and between 1 and 2 hours 30 minutes for leisure activities. Strzemińska also calculated that all women had between 60 and 70 per cent less leisure time than men, due mainly to their unequal investment in domestic and caring activities. This latter estimate confirmed the trend noted by another study, which found that 60 per cent of women, compared to 40 per cent of men, reported having no leisure time at all, while on average, women reported having less than 1 hour of leisure time daily (Szkorzyński 1965, cited in Lobodzinska 1977: 412).

Aside from shrinking women's rest and leisure time, the double burden also contributed to women's lagging position in the labour market, the existence of a wage gap, and marked occupational segregation. Strzemińska (1970) noted that women's time poverty and related exhaustion were not only detrimental to productivity; both also had a negative impact on women's human capital development, and, thus, future career advancement opportunities. At the same time, she pointed out that double burdens also made it difficult for women to fulfil their traditional roles as mothers and wives; something that as the text quoted at this section's outset suggests she did not necessarily dispute as a woman's duty (Strzemińska 1970: 226). Her advice to policymakers was that providing opportunities and arrangements for better reconciliation of these roles was of great social and economic importance, recommending working-time flexibility, improved and more extensive service provision, and better public transit infrastructure as steps that could alleviate some of the pressure that women were experiencing (Strzemińska 1970: 11). In the process, she urged, these factors could also improve family well-being and make women more productive and valuable employees (Strzemińska 1970: 230–33).

The fact that the trends identified by Strzemińska and other researchers in the 1970s continued to be confirmed by subsequent time-use studies suggests that her recommendations were being ignored or that few concrete measures were taken to change this situation. According to Poland's Central Statistical Office (GUS) data, nearly a decade and a half later, in 1984, women were still committing more hours to daily household chores, spending on average 6 hours 6 minutes on domestic and caring work, compared to the 1 hour and 24 minutes that men spent on the same work (GUS 2005).

Not only was the Polish state unsuccessful in easing women's double burden by accommodating their dual duties more meaningfully; it also failed to challenge the traditional gender contract that contributed to the double burden in the first place (Heinen and Wator 2006; Matysiak and Steinmetz 2006). No parallel efforts were made to encourage some reassignment of responsibility for the unpaid care and domestic work or to challenge men's unequal involvement in either. On the contrary, the notion that women could not be fully replaced in their duties, and indeed, were unwilling to let go of domestic and care-giving responsibilities was quite prevalent in the Polish discursive universe. Some researchers have gone as far as to suggest that the People's Republic's authorities actively exploited traditional values and helped to institutionalize them to a greater or lesser extent. Jacqueline Heinen and Monika Wator (2006: 192), for instance, found that the official People's Republic discourse and policy practice promoted several different ideal-types of womanhood, including 'worker mothers', 'mother workers', and, at times, simply 'mothers',[30] depending on the needs of the state-run economy, the ebbs and flows in productivity, and staffing demands, as well as demographic changes. The earlier-mentioned extension of the child-raising leave to 3 years, and active calls for women to take advantage of this provision, for example, coincided with the 1970s economic crisis. This policy change – itself a response to the workers' demands for the compensation of the 1-year leave already available – was designed in a manner that avoided additional social spending (in the conditions of financial difficulties) and that dealt with the

[30] See also Zajicek and Calasanti (1995: 181–82) who describe the contradictory and changing policies promoted by the Polish state in terms of the productive and reproductive gender ideologies. See also Fidelis (2004).

unacknowledged job shortage[31] (Heinen and Wator 2006: 192). Of course, as was suggested earlier, the take-up rates of these leaves were fairly low, in part because the leaves were unpaid, or paid at a fairly low level, and because a single wage (men's) was insufficient to support a family. Although women were subsequently encouraged to re-enter labour markets once again, the sociologist Maxine Molyneux (1990: 43) observed that by the 1980s the official discourse of gender relations in Poland was entrenching difference, not equality, as the material effects of the gendered divisions in employment, and the home were being deplored but the divisions themselves were starting to be seen as natural and even desirable.

There is some evidence that women themselves helped to perpetuate this way of thinking, by taking certain pride in their ability to juggle numerous duties and in the control that they maintained over the domestic sphere (Dunn 2004: 155–65). This stance led one Polish sociologist famously to conclude that Polish women were 'grateful slaves' (Domański 1992), while another scholar noted that women were 'accomplices in perpetuating their own subordination through internalized stereotypes . . . compulsory patriotism, willingness to sacrifice our own good for the sake of family or nation, unquestioned acceptance of prescribed gender roles' (Karpiński 1995: 91).

Polish feminist researchers have argued that this very contradictory construction of womanhood and femininity in Poland was a result of historic circumstances, cultural norms, politics, and the influence of Catholicism (Ksieniewicz 2004). On the one hand, women occupied a very special, almost symbolic status in the Polish society. For a nation that had lost its independence on several occasions, the family was a key enduring institution, and as the keepers of the familial hearth women were historically charged with the duty to cultivate Polish culture, language, and the national identity (Titkow 1995). Inspired by the image of Maryja, the Mother of God, the mythical construction of Matka Polka (the Polish Mother) prevalent in art, literature, and the public discourse, was both powerful and oppressive (Dunn 2004: 165–167, 158; Fidelis 2004; Ksieniewicz 2004). This contradictory construction of femininity glorified women at the same time as it tied them firmly to the private sphere and their role within it. In the process, it either denied women access to public life or served to diminish their actual public involvement.

[31] See n. 26 above.

During the People's Republic era, when equality was the official policy and the levels of women's labour market participation matched those of men, these enduring gender constructions continued to inform the discursive universe and served to double women's workloads. The popular belief that women were irreplaceable in their domestic and caring roles only compounded this reality. Matka Polka went out to work but was also the one to spend her 'free time' queuing for foodstuffs, picking up the children after school, preparing the meals, and cleaning up after everyone. Titkow calls the gender-role model that developed in the People's Republic the 'managerial matrimony' model; its key features were women's lack of sleep and exhaustion, but also their sense of being the 'indispensable family manager' (Titkow 1995: 318). Along with the growing dissatisfaction with 'the system', the private sphere – the home – became increasingly regarded as the refuge and the site of quiet personal resistance (Dunn 2004: 165–67) and women's traditional, private roles as mothers and wives became even more revered and further entrenched.

The People's Republic presents an interesting case of an attempt to accommodate the processes of social reproduction within a working-time regime based on standard hours for all adult workers. On the one hand, the direct state involvement in social reproduction clearly acknowledged the importance of this process to the broader social and economic sustainability, which translated into better access to standard employment for women who were supported in their dual roles as workers and mothers. However, explicit recognition of collective responsibility for social reproduction coexisted with persistent traditional attitudes and the underlying gender contract that women were to some extent complacent in maintaining, which assumed that provision of the residual work of care and maintenance was still their duty. Most of all, however, women's heavy workloads were a result of having to combine long standard workweeks (initially 46 hours and later reduced to 42 hours) with domestic work in the context of scarce availability of goods and services. Few arrangements for the reconciliation of work and family made the balance between women's domestic and employment roles very tenuous, and this precarious balance was maintained at the cost of women's leisure time and heavy double burdens. While the situation was far from ideal in the People's Republic, it became even harder for women to balance their dual roles during the years of transition. Although the long hours of work continued, the line between social reproduction and production was being redrawn. As the state and the enterprises' roles in organizing the former began to diminish post-1989, these inconsistencies and their gendered legacy became particularly apparent.

4.3 Polish Working-time Regime in Transition – 'Catching Up' with the West

Following waves of strikes and social unrest during the 1980s, the 1989 Round Table talks officially brought together leaders of Solidarity – Poland's independent trade union and the oppositionist social movement – and the People's Republic's authorities to discuss the future of Poland's industrial, economic, and social policy, as well as the need for political reform. Partially open Parliamentary elections held later that year led to the formation of Poland's first non-Communist government in the post-war period under the leadership of Tadeusz Mazowiecki. Subsequent Presidential (1990) and Parliamentary (1991) elections brought further political victories for Lech Wałęsa, the Solidarity's spokesman and leader who was elected President, and the opposition parties affiliated with Solidarity. With democratization underway, economic restructuring was set in motion when economic and fiscal reforms aimed to liberalize the planned economy and establish the conditions for the operation of a viable and free market were adopted in 1990.

Labour law reform, including the reform of Poland's working-time regime, constituted a significant component of the transition process. While no comprehensive *Labour Code* amendments were enacted until 1996, and, indeed, the real flurry of legislative activity did not occur until the new millennium (the period between 2000 and 2004), the process of structural adjustment influenced the universe of political discourse and labour law reform from the start. In fact, the main reason for the 1996 *Labour Code* amendment, symbolically timed with Poland's Organization of Economic Cooperation and Development (OECD) membership in November of the same year, was to adapt Polish legislation to the realities of market economy and liberal democracy (Seweryński 1999). Moreover, while Poland's negotiations to join the EU did not begin until 1998, the *acquis communautaire* was also influential in the context of the 1996 amendment, since Polish legislators were inspired by the EU rules and, indeed, obligated to 'approximate' Polish law with that of the EU as of 1994 (Matey 1997: 69). Specifically, legal scholar Walerian Sanetra (2004a: 9) identifies three stages of Poland's legal adjustment to the *acquis*: (1) the period from 1989 to 1994, after the signing of the Pact between the Republic of Poland and the European Community (EC), as it was then known, on 16 December 1991 (which came into force on 1 February 1994); (2) from 1994 to 1998, when Poland officially began its accession negotiations; and (3) from 1998 to 2004, covering the period of negotiations up until Poland's official accession on 1 May 2004. While Poland had no formal obligations to comply with EC laws before 1994, Sanetra posits that Polish legislators were already 'inspired' by the *acquis*. During the second period, however, there was a more concrete obligation to 'approximate' Polish laws to those of the Community by minimizing and gradually eradicating differences between them (Sanetra 2004b: 15–19).

Accordingly, 1996 *Labour Code* Amendment, which I will discuss further, and preparatory projects that preceded it were guided by the principle of approximation, although major emphasis was also placed on the modernization of statutory norms to suit the needs of the developing market economy. Indeed, the latter contributed to providing an important rationale for the progressive liberalization of employment relations and the flexibilization of the Polish working-time regime in the subsequent years. While this shift to more flexibility had the potential to challenge the previous inefficiencies in work organization, the practices of 'extensive managing', and the long hours of work that contributed to women's double burdens, this transformative potential was largely unfulfilled. Instead, as I will elaborate next, the shift's embeddedness in the discursive universe dominated by the ideology of neo-liberalism and the notion that Poland's economy was 'on the make' ('na dorobku') and in need of catching up, meant that long hours of work continued as a matter of policy and as a matter of practice.

4.3.1 'Making' the Market Economy in Poland

Much like the plans of the People's Republic era, the economic reform plan that began the Polish transition to liberal market economy also required significant sacrifices and carried enormous human costs. Penned by the American development economist Jeffrey Sachs and the Polish economist Leszek Balcerowicz, the controversial reform plan (the Sachs–Balcerowicz Plan) adopted by Poland on 1 January 1990, was, in fact, the most drastic of the three options presented to the Polish administration by the World Bank (Kowalik 2007; Majmurek and Szumlewicz 2009: 8). Based on Chicago-school neo-liberal economic principles and the 'shock therapy' approach, the plan sought to liberalize and stabilize the Polish economy, and to facilitate the country's prompt 'return to Europe' (Sachs 1994: 269, 288). Despite critical warnings and advice that came both from within and outside Poland, the plan was approved and accepted by the Tadeusz Mazowiecki-led government with the justification that there was 'no alternative'.[32]

While no one expected the reforms to be easy, as Polish economists Tadeusz Kowalik (2007) and Grzegorz Kołodko (2009a, 2009b) observe, the economic and social costs of transition were grossly underestimated. In economic terms, instead of the projected 3 per cent drop in GDP and 5 per cent decrease in industrial production, Poland's GDP fell by nearly one-fifth[33] and industrial production declined by 25 per cent, causing deindustrialization and generating unemployment rates that exceeded expectations (Kowalik 2007: 3; see also Kołodko 2009b). While it was originally estimated that unemployment would increase by a modest 2.5 per cent (approximately four hundred thousand unemployed) (Kołodko 2009b: 326), the actual rate of unemployment reached 6.3 per cent by 1990 and more than doubled within 5 years (14.4 per cent) (GUS 2005; see Appendix A, Table 1). In addition, within 2 years of the plan's implementation, real wages fell by 36 per cent and incomes in the agricultural sector fell by half (Kowalik 2007: 3). The economic insecurity caused by loss of employment and income was compounded by cuts to social spending and dismantling of the infrastructure that once, at least partially, supported the standards of living. As a result, living standards dropped (Balcerzak-Paradowska 2004; Tarkowska 2011), and social stratification, regional disparities, and inequality became much more pronounced (Konat 2009).[34]

[32] In fact, alternatives were proposed but disregarded: Shields (2008). Polish economist Kowalik (2007, 2009) recounts that prior to the Round Table talks, a representation of Polish economists was sent to Sweden to explore the possibility of adopting a social-market economy, which was in line with the early Solidarity demands.

[33] According to IMF World Economic Outlook 2011, Poland's GDP fell sharply during the first 2 years of transition, 1990–1991 (–7.171 and –7.005). In 1992, however, it began to recover (2.033) and continued growing, reaching the highest levels (5.24, 6.7 and 6.23, 7.09) during 1994–1997 (years of the *Strategy for Poland*; see discussion on pp. 158–9 of this chapter.). As of 1998, it began to decline again, hitting the lows of 1.205 and 1.44 by 2001 and 2002, only to increase to 3.9 in 2003 and continue growing. See Appendix A, Table 1.

[34] Although Poland's GINI coefficient does not indicate significant income disparities and the IMF claimed that Poland's inequality increase was the most moderate (with the largest increase in GDP) of all transition economies (Keane and Prasad 2001), a number of researchers note progressive social stratification, including along the gender lines (Tarkowska 2002). Konat (2009: 40) notes the increase in population living below social minimum from 20 per cent at the end of 1980s to nearly 60 per cent by 2004, and those living below the 'existential minimum' representing 12 per cent of the population in 2005, from 4.3 per cent in 1996. Data also suggest that more than one in four Polish children experienced poverty (Konat 2009: 40–41); a rapid increase in child poverty having

In light of declining social and economic conditions, references to the Polish economy being 'on the make' or 'catching up with the West' became a common element of the public and political discourse, providing leaders and experts the narrative with which to convey the necessity and the rationality of reforms, but also the inevitability of the resulting hardship.[35] Likewise, the notion that people ought to 'take matters into their own hands' became popular with Poland's leaders and served to justify and normalize the country's new neo-liberal social contract, the key characteristic of which was a sudden reprivatization of responsibility for citizens' and familial well-being (Michalik 2003). As I discuss in more detail in Section 4.3.3, these shifts had particular consequences for women's ability to meet their labour market and family responsibilities, not only contributing to double burden but also casting women as undesirable employees.

The early explosion of new business ventures – evidenced mainly by the rapidly growing number of petty traders filling squares and sidewalks of most Polish cities and the establishment of small family firms – signalled that some people were indeed taking matters into their own hands. Jeffrey Sachs, in his 1994 Tanner Lecture taking stock of the 5 years of transition in Eastern Central Europe (ECE), praised this phenomenon declaring that 'Poland took to a market economy like the proverbial fish to water', pointing out that many of these petty traders were now becoming successful business owners (Sachs 1994: 276). This growth of small enterprises, although itself remarkable, could not, however, contain the rapid job loss resulting from restructuring of the public and nationalized sectors, which were the main source of employment in the People's Republic. With their progressive privatization (one of the key reform plan strategies) and the

been a characteristic phenomenon of transition, although the trend has recently reversed (Tarkowska 2011: 57–58).

[35] Balcerowicz, as the Council of Minister's Vice-President and the Minister of Finance (October 31, 1997 – June 8, 2000), used the notion of Poland 'on the make' in introducing and debating the budget (1999), new taxation statutes (1998), and to call for *'de-bureaucratization'* of Polish law to create conditions for employment, enterprise growth, and competitiveness (Parliamentary Proceedings No. 53, 02 July 1999; see also No. 32, 13 October 1998). Various Ministers of Labour and Social Policy also used it: Andrzej Bączkowski, in introducing the 1996 unemployment prevention statute (Parliamentary Proceedings, No. 91 24 October 1996); and Longin Komołowski, to stress that the government cannot shield the public sector from the consequences of privatization (Parliamentary Proceedings No. 94, 15 December 2000). Even progressive public figures and feminist scholars, like Magdalena Środa, have used this phrase in reference to Poland's post-transition environment and to explain various social phenomena (Pacewicz 2011; and personal communication).

lay-offs, bankruptcies, and closures that soon followed, unemployment soared to previously unprecedented levels[36] (see Appendix A, Table 2).

In addition to producing unemployment, the process of restructuring had a significant impact on trade union membership rates, which began rapidly shrinking. In principle, all workers in the People's Republic belonged to unions, although these unions were centrally controlled. Moreover, at the height of its popularity in the early 1980s, the Solidarity trade union boasted having a membership of ten million workers (Kowalik 2007: 6). By 1991, however, only 18 to 19 per cent of adults declared themselves trade union members; a number which continued to decline over the years reaching the low of 11 per cent by 1999 (CBOS 2002: 1–2; Stelina 2006: 200) and merely 6 per cent in 2002 (CBOS 2002: 1). According to a Polish economic sociologist Juliusz Gardawski (2002), this decline in membership was partially the result of privatization and the emergence of the home-grown private sector, where anti-union sentiments were highest and, thus, new trade unions least likely to be established. Another reason, however, was a more generalized public antipathy towards organized labour,[37] stemming from the contradictory role that trade unions played in the transition process and the loss of trust that they were invested in representing workers' interests (Gardawski 2002; Stelina 2006). After all, Solidarity's leaders, although initially proponents of a more gradual and participatory systemic change, by the early 1990s officially endorsed the technocratic and neo-liberal course of transition chosen by Poland's advisors (Ost 2000, 2005; Gardawski 2002). As Sachs (1994: 269) recalled, '[Polish] politicians and the general public understood intuitively that a "shock therapy" approach . . . was a quick route to a relatively quick target. In 1989, the quick target was Western Europe'. Not only had Wałęsa and other Solidarity leaders fully supported the Sachs–Balcerowicz plan, the union actually provided the protective umbrella for the reforms as they became instituted in the early 1990s (Gardawski 2002). Indeed, according to the Solidarity's biographer, scholar David Ost (2000, 2005: 149–58), seeing organized labour as a potential obstacle to a swift and successful economic transformation, Solidarity's top-tier leaders had the local,

36 There was no official unemployment in the People's Republic, although it is commonly observed that the full employment policy obscured 'hidden' unemployment, with many unproductive and redundant jobs.

37 According to the Public Opinion Research Center (Centrum Badań Opinii Społecznej, CBOS) (2002), 69 per cent of the polled expressed that trade unions are ineffective, compared to 15 per cent who thought otherwise.

enterprise-level stewards work to suppress the labour's militancy when the undesired effects of the reforms became apparent. Most famously, Wałęsa declared: 'We will not catch up to Europe if we build a strong union' (Ost 2000: 519).

Solidarity's failure to buffer workers against the harsh realities of economic reform and its failure to halt the erosion of its membership base had significant and enduring costs. First, it weakened organized labour vis-à-vis Poland's new, yet growing business lobby and employer organizations. Indeed, Solidarity's principled unwillingness to cooperate with the All-Poland Alliance of Trade Unions (OPZZ), Poland's other major trade union confederation, only exacerbated this problem (Ost 2000: 515, 2005). Active in the public and the newly privatized sector, the OPZZ operated since 1984, when, as was widely believed, the People's Republic authorities established it as a counterweight to Solidarity (EIRR 1999; Ost 2005). This historical legacy continued to be reflected in the two confederations' political activism and alliances after 1989, with the OPZZ being a more natural ally of the Left and Solidarity of the Right-wing and 'solidaristic' populist parties; it was also an ongoing source of tensions between them. In effect, the Polish labour movement was fragmented and its ability to counter the pressures exerted by the Polish employers compromised.

In purely political terms, the 1994 electoral victory of the social-democratic (and ex-Communist) Left Democratic Alliance (Sojusz Lewicy Demokratycznej, SLD) was a clear indication that the political wing of Solidarity had also lost public confidence. Although the incoming Left's 1994 *Strategy for Poland*, penned by another Polish economist, Grzegorz Kołodko, eschewed the non-interventionism of the Balcerowicz's 'doctrinal' neo-liberalism in favour of a more active state involvement, particularly in regulation of labour markets and social policy (Kołodko 1996, 2009a, 2009b), its approach still fit within the fiscal parameters advocated by the transnational economic organizations and was explicitly designed to gain membership in the OECD, and eventually to meet EU conditionalities of accession (Kołodko and Nuti 1997). Indeed, the Left chose to tackle Poland's unemployment by introducing what a political economist Stuart Shields (2008, 2011: 89) refers to as the 'second wave' of neo-liberal policies already promoted at the transnational level. Specifically, these policies emphasized labour market and employment flexibility, as necessary for lowering labour costs and providing a more business-friendly regulatory environment for foreign investment and the flourishing of domestic enterprise

(*Strategy for Poland* and 2002 Enterprise-Growth-Work plan).[38] Thus, despite the fact that the Left also introduced many pro-labour policies during its tenure, its acquiescence to neo-liberalism made it an easy target for Right-wing, liberal, and populist parties who drew their support from Solidarity's membership and from among anti-communist activists (Ost 2005: 82–87). Ironically, the liberals whom Solidarity supported endorsed the same or even more radical policies.

It was in this political and labour market context that the 1996 amendments to the 1974 *Labour Code* took place. In terms of working time, their combined result was moderate, but the introduction of extensions to the length of reference periods, reductions to overtime compensation, and the general liberalization of provisions regulating employment contracts laid the foundations for working-time increases and introduced considerably more flexibility into the *Labour Code*. Given the post-1989 labour market realities, however, this flexibility would mainly encompass the employer-driven forms of flexibility that were unlikely to lead to a more socially sustainable working-time regime. The powerful discourses of 'catching up' and the 'country (economy) on the make', and the goals of adjusting Polish labour law to the competitive pressures of market economy meant that long hours of work would continue in practice. In the next section, I review in more detail the 1996 *Labour Code*'s working-time provisions, their impact on the work patterns, and on women's position in the labour market.

4.3.2 Working-time Regime in Poland, 1989–1996

Working-time Regulations Under the 1996 Labour Code Amendment

Although other important labour law reforms were enacted in preparation for the 1996 re-codification, the period between 1989 and 1996 saw no major changes to working-time rules, with those set by the 1974 *Labour Code* still binding. The 1996 Amendment set out not only to reflect the systemic change by adjusting the national labour and employment law to the needs and conditions of a market economy but also to bring it in compliance with international labour and human rights standards.[39]

[38] The third document in the economic 'trilogy' developed by Kołodko was 'Euro 2006', the strategic plan for Poland's Economic and Monetary Union (EMU) membership.

[39] To that effect, the 1996 Amendment removed all references to nationalized enterprises, delegations to the Council of Ministers, and other provisions reflecting the 1974 *Labour*

To that effect, efforts were made to harmonize Polish law with the International Labour Organization (ILO) conventions, mainly in the field of health and safety, and to also begin 'approximating' Polish standards to the *acquis communautaire.*

In terms of working time, the 1996 Amendment retained the 42-hour working-time norm (Article 129) but introduced many changes that began to infuse more flexibility into work organization. For example, it increased daily working-time limits to 9 hours (Article 129.6), redefined working time by reference to the scope of employee's tasks (Article 129.8), and replaced the overtime allowance, calculated in accordance with hours worked, with a lump sum payment (Article 134(3)). The annual overtime limit was raised from 120 to 150 hours (Article 133(2)) and the reference periods for averaging weekly working time increased. For example, the basic reference period for calculations of the 42-week average was extended to 3 months. Also, a provision making it possible to collectively agree to extend the 1-month reference period applicable to essential services, retail, and road transport sectors was introduced. Moreover, the reference period for calculating the 40-hour limit applicable to work determined by seasonal and atmospheric conditions was increased to 6 months. As a form of protection against overtime abuse, the 4-hour daily overtime limit was imposed.

With respect to provisions regulating aspects of women's working time, neither the 1996 Amendment nor earlier reforms changed the maternity leave provisions. However, in 1996, the child-raising leave was extended to men, and the right to compensation was set at 80 per cent of the employee's usual income. This important change evidenced a new commitment to encouraging men to take on more responsibility for child-care. Indeed, the Leftist government's *Family Policy Program* drafted a year later, in 1997, also called for more equal sharing of responsibilities for paid work and care. However, assessment of both, that latter programme and the child-raising leave suggests that the government's commitment to equality was only half-baked. One women's advocacy organization, for example, pointed out that the way the legislation constructed the 1996 child-raising leave provisions clearly revealed the assumption that the leave would be

Code's socialist foundations. It also replaced the 'right to work' principle and the previous state obligation to pursue a full employment policy with the right to freely choose one's employment, the freedom to practice a profession (Article 10), and a state duty to pursue a policy aimed at full, *productive* employment and regulation of the minimum wage (Article 65.1). The new Code also highlighted the freedom to contract and negotiate the conditions of employment (with some exceptions and limitations) and introduced rules for mass layoffs and redundancies.

taken up by women (Centrum Praw Kobiet [Women's Rights Centre] 2000: 53–54). The main article speaking of the leave, Article 186, provided that female workers who are mothers (*not* parents) are entitled to the leave. It was only in Article 189 that the leave was *also* extended to male workers who are fathers. So, while this amendment was a positive effort on the part of the legislature, the manner in which the statute was drafted tended to reinforce the notion that the primary target and recipients of the leave would be women. Likewise, the choice of policy instruments to support equal work–family reconciliation adopted by the 1997 programme suggests that the government may have been more interested in promoting 'interchangeable breadwinning' in the context of particularly high unemployment, than in genuine promotion of gender equality (Racław-Markowska 2008).

Patterns of Working Time

The changes to working-time rules made in the 1996 *Labour Code* not only retained the 42-hour norm, they also introduced longer reference periods and provided for additional permissible overtime. Although several protective provisions were introduced (such as the 4-hour cap on daily overtime) and the child-raising leaves were extended to fathers, the main goal of the amendment was to provide for more flexibility in the deployment and organization of work, working time included. This thrust was consistent with the goals of adjusting the *Labour Code* to the needs and conditions of market economy as well as aiding the 'economy on the make' and cutting the costs of labour in order to stimulate employment and economic growth – all important conditions for the 1996 membership in the OECD and the future membership of the EU.

The massive job loss (see Appendix A, Table 2) – one of the most dramatic consequences of the radical 1990 reform plan – had an enormous effect on the Polish labour market and had a disproportionate effect on women (Pollert 2003, 2005). Struggling to address the problem, in the early years of transition some politicians and union leaders issued calls for 'returning' women to the domestic sphere, in part to create work for unemployed men or to provide full-time child-care to mitigate the rapid decrease in public child-care facilities (Graff 2008; Desperak 2009; Kubisa 2009). Some Polish feminists described this process (along with the severe restrictions on abortion enacted by way of a 1993 bill) as the backlash against the People's Republic-era socialist egalitarianism and the backlash against women themselves (Fuszara and Zielińska 2006; Graff 2008; Ksieniewicz Interview, 26 January 2010, Warsaw). Although the process of pushing women out of the labour market was not entirely successful, many women nonetheless found themselves in a much more challenging position under the new conditions (Płomień 2006). Urszula Sztanderska (2006: 4) estimated that after 1992 women's activation and employment rates were consistently lower than men's, if not by much, with the difference in the former ranging between 14.5 and 16 per cent, and the difference in the latter oscillating between 12.6 and 15.9 per cent. While the cycle of the rise and fall of the activation and employment rates varied through the early 1990s, and the overall rates fell for both women and men by about 7 to 9.8 percentage points (Sztanderska 2006: 5; see also Sztanderska and Grotkowska 2009), women's unemployment rates were consistently higher than men's by 1998 reaching nearly 11.2 per cent (Sztanderska 2006: 5). Similarly, women's average earnings during the 1990s were about 24 per cent lower to men's, despite women having higher educational attainment (Balcerzak-Paradowska 2001: 223). Discrimination, which stemmed from the perception that women were expensive workers on the account of their maternity entitlements, combined with the view that women's stronger attachment to the private sphere would make them more capable of dealing with the situation of unemployment, contributed to their deteriorating labour market situation in the early years of transition (Fodor 2005; Glass 2008; Desperak 2009).

Despite these new labour-market conditions, the key features of the Polish working-time regime remained remarkably persistent for those men and women who remained employed (see Appendix B). Most notably, long hours and overtime continued to be widespread post-transition. Indeed, it has been estimated that the percentage of employees working between 40 and 42 hours had actually decreased after 1992, while the proportion of employees working in excess of 48 hours per week had increased (Portet 2005: 293). The latter was a consequence of the rise of self-employment (often disguised employment) on one hand, and the excessive use of overtime on the other (Strzemińska 2002; Portet 2005).

Although some moderate increases in part-time work were reported, they too were insignificant. Between 1992 and 1996, the rates of part-time work oscillated between 10.1 and 10.7 per cent on average, with women's rates varying between 12.8 and 13.3 per cent and the men's between 7.8 and 8.9 per cent (Poliwczak 2003: 18; see Appendix A, Table 4), as compared to the 12 and 7.8 per cent for women and men respectively reported at the end of 1980s. Remarkably, the reasons for such low incidence of part-time work and its lack of popularity amongst Polish workers compared to their western European counterparts remained very similar to what workers had earlier identified as its key drawbacks, including perception of lower social status associated with part-time work, lower earnings, and the habits of full-time work (Poliwczak 2003: 19).

Thus, although the overall labour market situation was generally altered due to the scarcity of jobs and the new rules of labour market engagement, the key characteristics of the working-time regime that existed between 1945 and 1989 were not significantly different after transition (see Appendix B). However, aside from the new insecurity and workers' compromised ability to refuse inferior conditions, these difficult–to-reconcile employment patterns (long hours and overtime) were now also being offered in an entirely transformed institutional context. Their consequences for women and the processes of social reproduction will be considered next.

4.3.3 Shifting the Balance, Keeping the Double Burden – Working-time, Women, and Social Reproduction in Post-transition Poland

Another institutional and ideological shift brought about by the transition process, particularly in its earliest stages (1989–1994), was the near complete re-privatization of the responsibility for individual and family welfare (Rittich 2002b; Konat 2009). Previously centralized at the national level, the responsibility to organize and finance social services, including crèches, kindergartens, grade schools, community centres, and recreational facilities, was shifted to municipalities where a lack of sufficient resources and organizational capacities led to fee increases and consolidation of some public facilities (Balcerzak-Paradowska et al. 2003; Balcerzak-Paradowska 2004; World Bank 2004: 41–43). In the context of rising unemployment and poverty, even moderately higher costs of child-care and after-school programmes placed them out of reach for many parents, which quickly led to a significant drop in child enrolment rates (Balcerzak-Paradowska et al. 2003: 216). Paradoxically, as Bożena Balcerzak-Paradowska (2004) notes, although the drop in enrolment was not a result of decreased demand but rather the inability to pay for the services, it culminated in even further reductions and closures with the consequence that, between 1989 and 2001, the number of daycares dropped from 1,553 to 396, while the number of kindergartens dropped from 12,767 to 8,175 (World Bank 2004: 42; see also Balcerzak-Paradowska et al. 2003: 204). By 2001, 555 municipalities (95 per cent of which were rural) had no care facilities for children under the age of six (Herbst 2004, cited in Sztanderska 2006: 6).

Against this backdrop of shrinking public care infrastructure, the notion that the family constitutes the most appropriate institution for the raising and early education of young children – already very deeply embedded in the Polish society – became further strengthened. The dominant discourse of the family as sovereign – free of state interference and responsible for itself – espoused by the post-transition governments (Balcerzak-Paradowska 2004), gave further credence to state retrenchment and resulting re-privatization of responsibility for personal and family welfare. Bolstered by the revisionist glorification of pre-Second World War Polish traditions, Catholic values, and the firm rejection of the People's Republic era state paternalism, this discourse was pervasive and served to symbolically re-establish the division between the public and the private, a process which was accompanied by the active restructuring of Poland's gender order in accordance with socially conservative values (Graff 2008).

For working mothers, the shrinking access to affordable, good quality child-care ushered in increased difficulties with reconciling their paid work and family obligations. Given the persistence of very traditional attitudes towards gender roles and the appropriate division of responsibilities for unpaid work post-transition (Siemieńska 2011), the working-time regime characterized by excessive hours and the culture of overtime had a particularly negative impact on women workers. Unlike working mothers in the People's Republic, however, Polish women during the transition could no longer count on the public infrastructure to support their efforts. Consequently, the experience of double burden, already common before 1989, was further exacerbated for many. In the face of these difficulties, growing economic insecurity, and the bleak realities of the transition period, many women seemed to have declared a 'womb strike'. The rapid drop in the Polish fertility rate in the years following the beginning of transition, from 2.09 in 1989 to 1.22 in 2003 (Matysiak 2009: 201), was one indication that the tenuous balance between the needs of the economy and the processes of social reproduction that was maintained in the People's Republic, already at the cost of the double burden, has been profoundly upset.

4.4 Into the New Millennium – Political Discourses of the Late 1990s and Beyond

The double bind of economic neo-liberalism and social conservatism that accompanied the early phase of Polish transition continued to shape the country's discursive universe at the end of the 1990s, as Poland prepared for EU accession. Although social conservatism proved an ongoing source of public controversy – polarizing the political arena and the society more broadly – economic neo-liberalism was ultimately a more significant force in shaping Polish policy discourse and adopted measures (Grzymalala-Busse and Innes 2003; Majmurek and Szumlewicz 2009), including labour law and working-time reform. Regardless of official party lines, most Polish parties accepted the primacy of the market (Ost 2005; Majmurek and Szumlewicz 2009) and Poland's ambition to join the OECD and the EU, made it difficult, if not impossible, to shift away from the neo-liberal course (Grzymalala-Busse and Innes 2003; Shields 2008, 2011). Consequently, the emphasis on market building, growth, and competitiveness – all conditions of successful EU accession – became the key objectives for the subsequent Polish governments, with social and employment policies being crafted in ways that would enhance these overarching goals but also providing the arena in which competing parties could differentiate themselves and contest each other (Grzymalala-Busse and Innes 2003;[40] Majmurek and Szumlewicz 2009; Stenning et al. 2010; Shields 2011).

The acquiescence to neo-liberal reforms was particularly costly, in political terms, for the Left. Although the Left Democratic Alliance attempted to forge closer ties with the social partners – particularly to bridge the lack of cooperation between the trade union confederations, Solidarity, and OPZZ – these efforts proved largely futile (Ost 2005). Solidarity remained vehemently opposed to the Left, and, indeed, in the subsequent years, each of the Left Democratic Alliance's losses (in 1997 and 2004) was to parties derived from the Solidarity's political wing. The Electoral Action Solidarity (Akcja Wyborcza Solidarność, AWS) in 1997, and Law and Justice (Prawo i Sprawiedliwość, PiS) in 2005, were two such parties that managed to challenge the Left by running on labour-friendly and 'social-solidaristic' platforms, but also ones that were explicitly anti-communist and socially conservative (Szczerbiak 2005: 204). Both used social and labour policy to distinguish themselves from the neo-liberal others, including the Left's ex-communists, by publically opposing further flexibilization and deregulation. Electoral Action Solidarity, for instance,

[40] See Grzymalala-Busse and Innes (2003), who make a somewhat different argument that the only distinctive feature of various political parties was how they said they would manage the reforms; with the content of the promised reforms being in fact the same. By contrast, my argument is that in the context of labour law reform it was not just the delivery that was different but also the content of reforms differed.

included unfulfilled Solidarity demands from the August 1980 strikes – reduction of the workweek and extension of maternity leaves and benefits – as key elements of their 1997 electoral campaign platform, winning a 33 per cent Parliamentary representation (Ost 2005; Tomaszewska Interview, 25 February 2010, Warsaw). Several years later, in 2005, Law and Justice[41] posed the contest between themselves and the other parties in the running – particularly the economic liberal-social conservative Civic Platform (Platforma Obywatelska, PO),[42] as the Left Democratic Alliance was an unlikely contender due to its very low popularity – as the choice between the and the more egalitarian 'social-solidaristic' and the 'liberal' visions of Poland (Szczerbiak 2005: 204, 211). Characterizing its key opponent, the Civic Platform, as the party that would benefit only the 'winners' of transition, they appealed to those Poles who felt that they 'lost' and who desired a more interventionist, socially redistributive state (Szczerbiak 2005: 211).

Although both the Electoral Action Solidarity and Law and Justice were socially conservative and represented decisively and unapologetically traditional worldviews, as I show in Chapter 5, their appeal to workers' rights and women's need for work–family reconciliation measures and support for social reproduction translated into some legislative proposals aimed at the reduction in working time. This social conservative approach was further reinforced by Law and Justice, which was allied with the clerical-populist League of Polish Families (Liga Polskich Rodzin, LPR): an openly Catholic party, associated with the Radio Maryja[43] radio station run by one of Poland's most notorious public clerics, Father Rydzyk. Explicitly affirming women's 'natural' roles and drawing on the evocative nationalist construct of the Polish Mother, these parties managed to attract

[41] Law and Justice ran along with its allies League of Polish Families and the Self-Defense of the Polish Republic, which also partially derived from the defunct Electoral Action Solidarity. All three presented a similar conservative worldview and opposition to both the ex-Communists and economic neo-liberals. After Law and Justice's electoral victory, these parties formed a coalition government, which remained in power until Law and Justice's loss in the 2007 election.

[42] Many Civic Platform members came from Electoral Action Solidarity, the split within the latter occurring clearly along the official commitment to economic neo-liberalism.

[43] Radio Maryja is Polish for 'Radio Mary' (as in Mary, the Mother of God). Its ultra Christian-Conservative message is often ridiculed in Polish media but the radio has a significant influence on the political discourse, which it actively partakes in shaping through traditionalist, 'family values', and anti-feminist ideas. The station's success exemplifies the way in which the populist Right in Poland has employed the power of public discourse and the media to build 'cultural hegemony'(Majmurek 2009: 141).

significant following among women, with many joining their political ranks. The social conservatism, opposition to abortion, and reification of maternalism that these parties and the 'new feminist' movement (Fuszara and Zielińska 2006) associated with them rallied around fundamentally clashed with the views and interests of more socially liberal Polish women and the feminists, highlighting the ideological split that already existed and further driving a wedge between different women's groups.[44] Paradoxically, because social reproduction and work–family reconciliation were on the conservative Right's agenda, the more socially progressive politicians within these parties, aided by Brussels and EU policy discourse, were able to develop the blueprints for more woman friendly work–family policies in the future. At the same time, as the next chapter will show, the labour-friendly and 'social-solidaristic' rhetoric that Electoral Action Solidarity and Law and Justice utilized so effectively largely failed to translate into very significant policy change.

4.5 Conclusion

As this chapter outlined, the construction of a liberal market economy in Poland began with rapid structural adjustment and significant ideological reorientation along the lines of economic neo-liberalism and social conservatism. The hard-line reforms of the Sachs–Balcerowicz Plan, with their policy-mix of fiscal austerity, rapid privatization, and deregulation, accompanied by the hegemonic discourse of 'country on the make' and 'catching up' left an indelible mark on Poland. As the country's institutional architecture became dismantled and rearranged in accordance with the new political–economic dictates, the notion that people ought to take matters in their own hands legitimized the retrenchment of the state and the re-privatization of responsibility for personal and family welfare. Together, these shifts served to re-establish symbolically and materially the division between the public and the private, thus breaking away from the socialist legacy of state involvement in all aspects of economic and social life. Paradoxically, these post-transition changes were also complemented by the attempt to restructure the People's Republic-inherited

[44] Chapter 5 explains this fragmentation within the labour and women's movements was to some extent overcome in the campaign for supermarket workers, which brought the plight of workers, particularly women workers, into the broad political discourse and Parliamentary debates, resulting in successful legal actions and demonstrating the true power of solidarity (Solik Interview, February 2010, Warsaw).

gender order in accordance with socially conservative values. This intervention was justified on the basis that it meant to 'restore' the more traditional, culturally appropriate, and 'authentic' Polish gender order and thus displace that which was externally imposed (Soviet) and 'unnatural'. While the traditional gender order had been in reality largely untransformed by the socialist egalitarian philosophy of the People's Republic and continued to dominate in the private sphere, and, to an extent, in the public sphere, these post-transition interventions had significant consequences for women; they also caught women's groups off guard. Among others, women's labour market position deteriorated rapidly, with some women being pushed out and others struggling to remain competitive.

The difficult labour market position of women was exacerbated by the fact that the People's Republic culture of long hours and the women's double burden would endure well into the period of transition. Remarkably, despite the magnitude of the ideological and institutional change, the discourse of economic growth surrounding work and employment regulation suggests that the reasons for the persistently long hours in Poland were much the same. Indeed, a striking path-dependence emerges when the persistence of long hours and their justifications are considered. The People's Republic-era 'duty' to assist with rebuilding the country and building a strong socialist economy was, after 1989, replaced with rationales of 'economy on the make' and the notion that Poland had to 'catch up' to the rest of Europe. The methods of 'extensive managing' gave way to managing styles based on notorious overtime abuse and other forms of sidestepping labour regulations (see also Chapter 5). The latter, justified by rationales of labour-cost cutting, business efficiency, and competitiveness, as well as enabled by high rates of unemployment, increased economic insecurity, and a very competitive labour market, put an increasing strain on the working people. As the institutional supports that assisted women with the tenuous balancing act between standard employment based on long hours and the unpaid work of social reproduction became dismantled, work–family reconciliation became increasingly difficult, and the double burden became even heavier than before. Along with the resurgence of socially conservative values, the assumption of women's more limited availability and commitment to paid employment placed them at a much greater risk of labour market discrimination. The rapid drop in fertility rate was partially related to these phenomena, as women postponed procreative decisions in face of new forms of economic and social insecurity.

As Poland prepared for EU accession, social conservatism and economic neo-liberalism continued to dominate the country's discursive universe. While the country's social problems, including the dire situation of women and the difficulties with work–family reconciliation, received increased policy attention as of the mid-1990s, the overarching emphasis on elevating the country's economic position, supporting its new enterprises, and curbing unemployment – all required for successful EU accession – tended to circumscribe the universe of political action. Given the union rate attrition and the fragmentation within the labour movement, Poland's new employers' organizations grew in strength and became an increasingly prominent voice (alone and through their political allies) within the political discourse. As the next chapter will show, these economic rationales and new alliances also had a significant influence on the ongoing re-regulation of the Polish working-time regime.

5

Consolidating Flexibility – Polish Working-time Regime, Gender, and Social Reproduction in the Run-up to and Since the European Union Accession

5.1 Introduction

As Poland entered the new millennium, over a decade had passed since it began its transition to market economy. By then, it was a member of the Organization of Economic Cooperation and Development (OECD), and, having started the accession negotiations in 1998, it was on the way to joining the European Union (EU). However, as I discussed in Chapter 4, Poland's 'return' to capitalism and to Europe had been accompanied by serious costs, including the collapse and instability of its labour markets, a rising unemployment rate, and a resulting increase in social and economic inequalities. A related problem was the fact that the country's fertility rate had dropped so rapidly in the aftermath of transition that it was now below the level required to replace the population. Enhancing the Polish economy and addressing the ailing labour market became the key issues shaping the country's discursive universe, particularly as it prepared for EU accession. While the fiscal austerity and state retrenchment that characterized the early phase of transition gave way to a more active state involvement in social policy, neo-liberal proscriptions of deregulation and removal of rigidities continued to guide policy, reinforced by the influential discourse of 'economy on the make', Poland's ongoing unemployment problem, and the necessity to comply with EU economic conditionalities.

As I will show, the modernization and flexibilization of the Polish *Labour Code*, and the working-time regime, were important elements in the country's economic and unemployment strategies, pre and post the 2004 EU accession. Although compliance with the *acquis communautaire* required Poland to adopt a wide range of EU instruments, including many socially progressive Directives, the focus on economic performance and the necessity to foster the 'right' economic environment for the flourishing of enterprise tended to overshadow other considerations. Following broader European trends, and due to domestic lobbying and pressures, Polish working-time norms became initially reduced and then progressively flexibilized. While local politics and the presence of competing discourses, such as the rise of 'social solidaristic' populism, made the process of flexibilization uneven, the need to comply with EU conditionality in the run-up to the 2004 accession served as an important rationale, adding a sense of inevitability and providing Polish policy-makers with an important source of legitimacy for those changes that were unpopular with political opponents and the labour movement.

Although gender equality and work–family reconciliation concerns were to some extent incorporated into the discussion on working-time reform, they were largely subordinated, typically raised in the context of maternity and parental leaves, and often invoked in response to Brussels-imposed requirements. The ideological orientation of different political parties, particularly the contest between the more 'liberal' or egalitarian (the Left and some Right-wing parties) and the socially conservative or 'social solidaristic' (Right-wing populist) factions played an important role in how the issue was phrased and what measures were promoted. Paradoxically, at least in the context of labour policy and working time, the socially conservative Right appeared more active in championing women's cause than the more egalitarian Left. Despite these differences, however, any focus on flexible working-time solutions as crucial for balancing of work and family obligations, was, along with EU policy trends, largely driven by the objectives of unemployment reduction and women's activation (or their rights as mothers), and the need to address Poland's demographic crisis. The promotion of gender equality *for its own sake* did not feature prominently in the working-time political discourse during this period.

Following on the discussion of the discursive universe and early *Labour Code* amendments in the previous chapter, this chapter describes the process of labour law reform, with the emphasis on the changes in the working-time rules that took place between 1997 and 2004 (see Table 5.1; Appendices B and C). As I show, close reading of the successive amendments reveals how the dominant discourses, and the internal and external pressures evoked to legitimate them, including the 'hard' and 'soft' accession conditionalities, aided the progressive flexibilization of the *Labour Code*'s working-time limits and rules (see Appendix B). I then consider the more recent promotion of work–family reconciliation and 'family-friendly' policies, and the extent to which both have been able to mitigate the overarching trend towards business-friendly flexibilization. I conclude by assessing the contemporary Polish working-time regime and offer some thoughts as to why this regime poses serious problems for workers' ability to balance work and family obligations, the promotion of gender equality, and the broader viability of social reproduction.

5.2 Modernizing the Polish *Labour Code*

While the 1996 *Labour Code* amendment already introduced important changes into the Polish labour-law regime, there was a general consensus among Polish legal experts, politicians, and the social partners that additional adjustments were needed. To support the reform process, on 27 July 1999, the Minister of Labour and Social Policy convened a special Commission on Labour Law Reform composed of several prominent labour law scholars and Ministerial representatives.[1] The Commission was to provide expert opinions on government's and Parliament's reform proposals but also to work on its own draft for an entirely new Code.[2] In the view of the Commission's president, Professor Tadeusz Zieliński, further reform was necessary to address developments related to: (1) Poland's 1997 Constitution;[3] (2) the realities of market economy; and (3) Poland's impending EU accession (M.P. 2000; Florek 2004a; Gienieczko Interview, 22 January 2010, Warsaw). In practice, although compliance with the 1997 Constitution was a consideration,[4] the pressures associated with the country's economic performance and the need to fulfil the EU accession conditionality proved more decisive in the subsequent reforms, including those of working-time rules. Indeed, as I will explain next, regulating working-time *for* the market and *to comply* with Europe were

[1] *Decree of the Minister of Labour and Social Policy of 27 July 1999 concerning the Establishment of the Labour Law Reform Commission*, (1999) Law Monitor, No. 26, item 404 (in force 30 July 1999, repealed on 1 July 2002). Similar Commissions had existed under the auspices of the Ministry of Labour and Social Policy since before the 1976 labour law codification. The 1999 Commission was reconstituted again in 2002 with mostly the same members.

[2] The Reform Commission completed its draft in 2005, proposing two labour codes, one governing individual employment relationships and one addressing collective rights. Both were published on the Ministry of Labour website in 2007 (www.mpips.gov.pl/prawo-pracy/projekty-kodeksow-pracy/) but have not been adopted at the time of writing.

[3] *Constitution of the Polish Republic of 2 April 1997*, Journal of Laws, No. 78, item 483.

[4] The 1997 Constitution, *ibid.*, changed the legal rank of Ministerial executive acts, moving all rights and responsibilities these acts previously regulated to statutes. Since such acts regulated many labour law matters, including working time, the *Labour Code* was given a more prominent role. Some of these changes were already made by 1996, but the 1997 Constitution required a more comprehensive consolidation (Gienieczko Interview, 22 January 2010, Warsaw).

interrelated objectives, which also had specific consequences for the shape of the developing working-time regime.

5.2.1 Regulating for the Market and to Comply with Europe

As Chapter 4 had shown, one goal of the 1996 *Labour Code* amendment was to support – in line with the then prevailing economic strategy (the Left's 1994–1997 *Strategy for Poland*) – the creation of the institutional environment for attracting foreign investment and supporting domestic entrepreneurship. Many of the Code's provisions, including those on working time, were made more flexible to better match the needs of new enterprise; at the same time, however, many obligations previously carried by state-enterprises were downloaded onto private employers. Since the vast majority of Poland's new firms were small, and indeed, 'micro' (nearly 99.8 per cent SMEs, employing nearly 70 per cent of the population) (Eurostat 2008: 3), this approach was criticized for creating prohibitive burdens for small firms and thus, undermining their ability to thrive and create new jobs. This critique became particularly salient as the dynamic growth that Poland experienced between 1994 and 1997 came to a halt in 1998 and was followed by gradual economic downturn and rising unemployment, particularly after 1999. By 2002, unemployment reached the unprecedented 20 per cent (GUS 2005; see Appendix A, Table 2) and the GDP had declined to 1.4 from the 4.3 two years prior (Appendix A, Table 1).

Concerns about high labour costs and excessive administrative requirements as impediments to competitiveness and job growth gave rise to renewed pressure to modernize and streamline employment regulation. While this pressure came mainly from the business lobby, many legal experts, including members of the Reform Commission, agreed that the rigidity of Poland's labour law framework was a problem (M.P. 1999; R.M. 2001; Męcina 2003). Further relaxation of the hiring and firing regulations, diversification of employment contracts, and flexibilization of working-time rules were among the key issues identified as necessary to achieve a more adaptable and flexible legal framework (M.P. 1999; R.M. 2001).

Labour law's potential role in stimulating the economy and supporting enterprise became particularly important with EU accession on the horizon. Having entered into official membership negotiations in March 1998, Poland was now required to take further steps towards fulfilling the Copenhagen criteria, which were substantial and significantly biased towards economic conditionality. Set by the European Council in 1993, these criteria required applicant states to demonstrate that they have: (1) stable institutions guaranteeing democracy, the rule of law, human rights, and respect for and protection of minorities; (2) a functioning market economy and the capacity to cope with competitive pressure and market forces within the Union; and (3) the ability to take on membership obligations, including adherence to the aims of political, economic, and monetary union. This last requirement involved the adoption of the EU *acquis communautaire*, much of which was also economic in nature and related to the functioning of the internal market. As was specified by the Madrid European Council in 1995, transposing the European law was not itself sufficient; the prospective Member States had to demonstrate *effective* implementation of the *acquis* through parallel development of appropriate administrative and judicial structures.

According to *Agenda 2000*, the European Commission's opinion on Poland's EU membership application, prior to the official launch of the enlargement process Poland was already in relatively good standing with respect to the first two criteria.[5] The 1989 democratic reforms, the institution of market economy through the Sachs–Balcerowicz 'shock therapy', and the subsequent, more moderate, yet still market-friendly policies of the Left's *Strategy for Poland*,[6] built sufficient institutional capacities for the accession process to begin. Nonetheless, as of 1998, the country was not only obligated to maintain its course but to increase its efforts. While the Polish market economy was 'well functioning', the Commission's 1998 report, *Poland's Progress towards Accession*,[7] noted the country must 'strengthen the pace of economic restructuring' to safeguard its future competitiveness in the internal market (*Poland's Progress* 1998: 21). Moreover, Poland had only begun the process of achieving compliance with the *acquis communautaire*. While some 'approximation' of labour law had already taken place in 1996 (Sanetra 2004a), many changes were still needed (*Poland's Progress* 1998; Florek 2004b),[8] including the

[5] *Agenda 2000*. Commission Opinion on Poland's Application for Membership in the European Union, DOC/97/16 (15 July 1997) (hereinafter *Agenda 2000*).

[6] The latter was explicitly designed to align Poland's long-term goals with those of the EU (Kołodko 2000). The accompanying 'Euro 2006' was a plan for Poland's Economic and Monetary Union membership.

[7] Regular Report from the Commission of 4 November 1998 (hereinafter *Poland's Progress* 1998).

[8] The 1998 *Poland's Progress* noted that Poland needed further harmonization with EU for equal opportunities, labour, health and safety regulations, strengthening of the administrative competencies, and social dialogue.

adjustment of the weekly working-time norm, incorporation of the mandatory rest periods, and extension of the annual leave entitlement to 4 weeks as required by the EU *Directive concerning certain aspects of the organization of working time* (*Working Time Directive*).[9] Also, provisions on equal treatment of part-time and fixed-term work had to be introduced to conform to the Directives 97/81 and 99/70,[10] while the incorrectly transposed provisions on parental leave introduced in 1996 *Labour Code* amendment had to be revised.

Slow or uneven implementation of labour law Directives and other social *acquis* was partially related to the perception that they would be costly for the employers or the state budget and hence would stall Poland's economic development vis-à-vis the already more prosperous Member States (Sanetra 2004b: 21; Leiber 2005). Consequently, some protective regulations were purposely delayed; they were either 'suspended' until the date of accession or phased in over extended timeframes to accommodate fiscal restraints and address the criticism levied by the business lobby and employers. As I will discuss in more detail further, the reduction of weekly working-time to 40 hours was one example of this strategy. Although originally legislated in 1999, it was not until 2003 that the 40-hour norm was in force. Similarly, the limit on the number of consecutive fixed-term contracts (Article 25 of the *Labour Code*) was suspended until Poland's actual EU accession in 2004. Conversely, various flexibility measures were introduced and justified as temporarily necessary to address unemployment and slow growth problems, and maintain Poland's competitiveness in the run-up to accession. A case in point was the 2002 *Labour Code* amendment, which was explicitly aimed at responding to domestic pressures for more employer-friendly flexibility and was introduced on a temporary basis, with the proviso that its discrepancies with the *acquis* would be addressed by future measures, the specific purpose of which would be to achieve compliance. The amendment introduced the following year did just that; however, some of the

9 *Council Directive 93/104 EC concerning certain aspects of the organization of working time*, [1993] O.J. L 307/18 (23 November 1993), amended by *Council Directive 2000/34/EC of the European Parliament and of the Council of 22 June 2000 amending Council Directive 93/104/EC concerning certain aspects of the organization of working time to cover sectors and activities excluded from that Directive*, [2000] O.J. L 195/41 (1 August 2000).

10 *Council Directive 97/81/EC concerning the Framework Agreement on Part-time Working concluded by UNICE, CEEP and the ETUC*, [1998] O.J. L14/9 (20 January 1998); *Council Directive 99/70/EC of 28 June 1999 Concerning the Framework Agreement on Fixed-term Work concluded by UNICE, CEEP and the ETUC*, [1999] O.J. L 175/43 (10 July 1999).

novel flexibility provisions introduced in 2002 were in fact retained by the follow-up 2003 legislation since they were either permitted by EU law or not explicitly prohibited by any specific Directive (Florek 2004b: 38–39).

Indeed, Polish pursuit of more flexibility found significant support in EU policy discourse and law, which not only enabled working-time flexibility but also increasingly emphasized the need for more flexible reorganization of working time. To begin, the 1993 *Working Time Directive* did not necessarily prescribe the adoption of flexible working-time organization since its key aim was to set minimum standards and protect workers' health and safety. Nonetheless, the Directive's many derogations and exceptions *from* its protective provisions did enable significant employer-friendly flexibility by identifying various possibilities for working-time extensions through, for instance, introduction of longer reference periods for the calculation of rest periods and overtime, or the individual 'opt-out' provision. At the same time, apart from the Article 13 principle of 'adapting work to worker', which obliged Member States to adopt measures to 'humanize' the workplace by, for example, introducing breaks, no explicit provisions encouraged working-time *reductions* below the Directive's minimum standards.

As Chapters 2 and 3 elaborated, by 1997, however, there was a shift in how working-time flexibility was portrayed in the EU policy discourse. Specifically, the EU began to officially promote and mainstream the flexibilization and diversification of work hours and patterns as mutually beneficial for enterprises and for meeting the needs of different groups of actual and potential employees. The Commission's 1997 *Partnership for a New Organization of Work* Green Paper,[11] for instance, urged that more flexible and improved organization of work could stimulate job growth, make a 'valuable contribution' to the 'competitiveness of European firms' and 'to the improvement of the quality of working life and employability of the workforce' (1997: 7). Framework agreements on part-time and fixed-term work negotiated by social partners in 1996 and 1998 respectively, and subsequently adopted as Directives, were also indicative of this approach to flexibility. Both sought to promote and make more secure non-standard (and more flexible) forms of employment and working-time organization, with the view to also accommodating and protecting workers unable to fit the standard patterns of employment *and* responding to employers' needs for flexibility. Flexibility was also incorporated explicitly into the 'adaptability' pillar of the 1997 European Employment Strategy (EES) and the 1998 and 1999 Employment policy guidelines,

[11] COM (97) 128 final (16 April 1997).

making it a common objective for all Member States to consider in drafting their national employment policies, and inviting the social partners to negotiate agreements on modernization of the organization of work, through, for instance, flexible working time arrangements,[12] annualization of working hours, reduction of hours and overtime, development of part-time work, and different forms of career breaks.[13]

While the objectives set by the EES and Employment policy guidelines were not directly binding on the Member States in the traditional sense of having to be transposed in a manner akin to the Directives, this 'soft' coordination measure was designed to influence national employment policy and practice. In 'old' Member States, the effect was that even in areas where relative regulatory diversity remained, coordination led to policy convergence in the field of employment (and others) on the overarching objectives of competitiveness, flexibility, and growth (Ashiagbor 2004). As applicant countries like Poland were also required to engage with the EES guidelines in drafting their own employment policies even before official accession took place (Keune 2008: 12), they were brought into the sphere of EU socialization and exposed to learning from other EU Member States. The close alignment between the EES priorities and the funding criteria for the European Social Fund (ESF) provided further incentives to participate, thereby ensuring EU's influence on future Member States and the local debates in terms of agenda setting, transfer of discourse, and the imposition of framework for national employment policy (Keune 2008: 12).

The EES influence was clear in the Polish context as early as 1999. While the governing Electoral Action Solidarity (Akcja Wyborcza Solidarność, AWS) (1997–2000) that replaced the Left Democratic Alliance (Sojusz Lewicy Demokratycznej, SLD) after 1997 came into office on a 'solidaristic' and explicitly labour-friendly platform, it formed a government with the liberal Freedom Union (Unia Wolności, UW), which was headed by Balcerowicz, the co-author of Poland's 1990 economic reform plan. Consequently, there were some inevitable inconsistencies in the governing party's approach. Its *National Strategy for Employment Growth and Human Resource Development 2000–2006* (*National Strategy*),[14] adopted on 4 January 2000, was closely aligned with European dictates for a

[12] *Council Resolution of 15 December 1997 on the 1998 Employment Guidelines*, [1998] O.J. C 30/01.

[13] *Council Resolution of 22 December 1999 on the 1999 Employment Guidelines*, [1999] O.J. C 96/02.

[14] *National Strategy for Employment Growth and Human Resource Development for the years 2000–2006*. Warsaw: Ministry of Labour and Social Policy, 1999 (hereinafter *National Strategy* 1999).

more active and flexible labour market policy, mirroring the 1997 EES by directly adopting the four-pillar approach and listing labour market and workplace flexibility under the adaptability pillar (*National Strategy* 1999: 26, 39). While the European approach called for the adoption of 'win-win' solutions, however, the *National Strategy* mainly emphasized reorganization of work to promote enterprise-friendly flexibility because its overarching goal was the creation of jobs and reduction of unemployment, and not necessarily the improvement of working conditions. In fact, the *National Strategy* suggested that an overly protective legal framework could be deleterious to workers' interests, as the security it provided was merely illusory in the face of Poland's economic and labour market conditions (*National Strategy* 1999: 40). At the same time, the strategy did point to women's labour market disadvantage and identified promotion of part-time work as a potential solution (*National Strategy* 1999: 44), as did the Electoral Action Solidarity's 1999 *National Pro-Family Policy*[15] programme, which cited part-time work and extended maternity leaves as ways of supporting women's work and family reconciliation.

Both, the 1999 *National Strategy* and *National Pro-Family Policy* echoed the contemporary EU policy consensus that more flexible organization of work was required for enterprise prosperity and job growth and to render work more adaptable for workers (in this case, women). Importantly, the view that the Polish working-time regime needed to be reorganized and flexibilized for enterprise needs was by no means a novel development, as this view was already popular with the employer and business lobby, and shared by many politicians and legal experts. Nonetheless, the fact that the *National Strategy* was drafted by an administration professing to be labour-friendly and committed to the preservation of security and the *status quo* in working conditions was a strong testament to the domestic pressures on the one hand, and the power of EU influence on the other. In the run-up to the EU accession, the disciplinary power of conditionalities and the 'softer' forms of EU policy influence set new frames of reference for the labour law reform. Coupled with the discourses of 'economy on the make' and 'catching up' discussed in the previous chapter, the need to comply with Europe provided Polish policymakers with ample opportunities to make and justify unpopular changes. In effect, working-time norms were reorganized in a way that was more suitable for business

[15] *National Pro-Family Policy*, Document adopted by the Council of Ministers on 3 November 1999, Government Review November–December 1999: 11–12, 101 (hereinafter *National Pro-Family Policy*).

needs than for balancing between the demands of the workplace and the demands of the home.

5.2.2 Labour Code *Amendments between 2000 and 2004*

As I suggested, achieving compliance with the European *acquis* was one of the important drivers of labour law reform, and the change in Polish working-time norms in particular. Nonetheless, the process was relatively uneven due to changes in political administration and Poland's overall economic outlook. The period between the 21 March 1998 launch of negotiations and the 1 May 2004 official EU accession saw two different coalition governments – the first headed by the socially conservative Electoral Action Solidarity, the second by the Left Democratic Alliance – and several *Labour Code* amendments that addressed working-time regulation. The general trajectory of these amendments was to first reduce basic working-time norms (in 2001), and subsequently flexibilize them (2002 and 2003). Not all of these amendments were explicitly aimed at compliance with the EU. The 2002 amendment, for instance, was a temporary measure intended to address domestic (employer) pressures for more flexibility.[16] As I suggested earlier, however, apart from home-grown pressures, the overall conditionality of membership, particularly the requirement of a competitive market economy, necessitated temporary actions that would ensure Poland's 'good standing' in the long term, and its ability to meet the set deadline for accession. For similar reasons, those changes that were required by EU *acquis*, yet deemed to impose additional costs, were 'suspended' or 'phased in' over extended periods of *vacatio legis*. On balance, by 2004 the Polish working-time regime was significantly more flexible than its 1996 predecessor. However, the choice of flexibility measures tended to exacerbate the long hours and the overtime culture that were already prominent in Poland, thereby causing significant problems for the balancing of work–family obligations. Indeed, the issue of work–family reconciliation was only marginally considered in the debate on working-time; instead, the main locus for its consideration remained the context of maternity and parental protections.

[16] Unsurprisingly, this amendment was well received and assessed positively by employers. See: Lewiatan (2002). By contrast, the trade union Solidarity criticized it (NSZZ "Solidarność" 2002a, 2002b).

Phase 1: Working Time Reductions

The first set of changes in working-time regulation was a reduction of the weekly working-time norm, which remained at 42 hours since 1986. The institution of a 40-hour workweek was a campaign promise made by the Electoral Action Solidarity during the 1997 election, as a symbolic nod to one of Solidarity's still unfulfilled August 1980 demands.[17] However, in September 1998, the Parliament considered not one but three proposals for the reduction and reorganization of working time. The first two sought the institution of the 40-hour and 5-day workweek by designating all Saturdays as official days off. One came from the Electoral Action Solidarity-dominated Senate with support of the Solidarity trade unionists,[18] while the other was a Left Democratic Alliance member's bill, officially endorsed by the All-Poland Alliance of Trade Unions (Ogólnopolskie Porozumienie Związków Zawodowych, OPZZ) trade union confederation.[19] The two proposals were unanimous in their key objectives and were justified on a predominately social basis, referring to the Polish labour movement demands, the 1935 ILO convention on the 40-hour workweek,[20] and the legislative or negotiated norms already existing in many European countries (Parliamentary Proceedings, No. 28, 16 September 1998, Stanisław Janas). The key difference was that the member's bill also proposed to increase the permissible annual overtime limit from 150 to 200 hours as a trade-off for employers' flexibility demands.

The third proposal also sought to reduce work hours; however, it proposed to do so as part of a more comprehensive reorganization of the employment and working-time norms. Submitted by the Parliamentary Committee of Small and Medium Enterprises (SME Committee),[21] this proposal had endorsement of all major employers' organizations because its intention was to 'unburden' firms, especially SMEs (Parliamentary Proceedings, No. 28, 16 September 1999, Roman Jagieliński). In terms of reorganizing working-time rules, the proposal envisaged introduction

[17] See Chapter 4 for more on Solidarity's 1980 campaign.

[18] Senate Proposal concerning the amendment of the Labour Code, Doc. No. 490 (7 July 1998). All Parliamentary Documents available online: www.sejm.gov.pl.

[19] Members' Proposal concerning the amendment of the Labour Code, Doc. No. 500 (3 July 1998).

[20] *Convention concerning the Reduction of Hours of Work to Forty a Week*, Geneva, 19th ILC session (22 June 1935), C0 47, 1935 (in force 26 June 1957).

[21] Committee for Small and Medium Enterprises Proposal concerning the amendment of the Labour Code, Doc. No. 560 (27 July 1998).

of additional thirty-nine holidays during the year, the planning of which would be subject to collective agreement, workplace regulation, or agreement between employer and employee (provided that no less than nine were scheduled during a 3-month period). However, this change was to be introduced alongside significant flexibility. Mainly, the SME Committee's proposal sought to increase the permissible overtime ceiling by setting the maximum number of weekly hours, inclusive of overtime, at forty-eight, which in practice would have yielded 416 possible overtime hours per year. Simultaneously, compensation for overtime hours was to be reduced to 25 per cent for the first 2 hours and to 50 per cent for all additional hours (from the 50 and 100 per cent premiums prescribed by Article 134 of the *Labour Code*). Furthermore, unpaid breaks of up to 90 minutes were to be introduced and a broader application of 'interrupted' working-time system, which permitted scheduling breaks of up to 6 hours per working day in circumstances necessitated by the type of work or work organization, allowed. According to the SME Committee's explanatory memo, broad application of the latter system was justified on the basis of recent Polish High Court jurisprudence allowing this type of work organization[22] and the fact that its introduction would not conflict with the provisions of the *Working Time Directive*. Also in the interest of flexibility, the Committee proposed to replace current norms with several provisions of the Directive, particularly the 48-hour weekly norm (inclusive of overtime) already mentioned, and the 11 hours mandatory rest rule.[23]

Radically departing from the existing legal framework, the SME Committee proposal failed to attract broad political support, and with only the Freedom Union liberals willing to back them up (Parliamentary Proceedings, No. 28, 16 September 1999, Adam Szejnfeld), the proposal was voted down in the first reading. As for the other two, following a Parliamentary Commission review, they received assessments from the Ministries of Labour and Social Policy and the Ministry of Finance (Parliamentary Proceedings, No. 28, 16 September 1998). The latter's resistance on the basis

[22] The proposal referred to the 9 October 1997 Polish High Court decision that held that breaks in work (not counted towards working time) introduced by way of a collective agreement, workplace regulation, or employment contract were permissible provided they respected labour law norms (Judgment of 9 October 1997, III ZP 20/99, OSNAPiUS 1998 nr 5, poz. 143).

[23] In addition to these major changes in working time, the proposal suggested a number of other employer-friendly measures, including changes to health and safety regulations, record keeping, hiring and firing, and recognition of collective agreements.

of unfavourable budgetary and economic projections combined with the continued opposition of the business lobby forced the government to introduce yet another proposal on 9 December 1999.[24] Compromise was eventually reached, and in March 2001 the Parliament introduced the new working-time norm of eight daily and 40 weekly hours, to be averaged over a 5-day week and a reference period not exceeding 3 months.[25] However, as a phase-in period was built into the bill to reflect the Ministry of Finance warnings and to give employers time to adjust, the 40-hour workweek did not operate until 2003. The only change actually to take place in 2001 was the introduction of the 5-day workweek (Article 1(2), amending Article 129). Weekly working time was to be reduced to 41 hours in 2002 (Article 2(1)), and further reduced to 40 on January 1, 2003 (Article 2(2)), without reduction in employee compensation (Article 5).

Although the bill provided that the 8-hour norm was absolute and thus any work in excess of 8 hours a day would normally warrant overtime pay, there were exceptions. First, the previously existing 'equivalent' working-time system was to be maintained. This particular system allowed working-time increases to up to 12 hours per day balanced with equivalent time off where the type of work or work organization necessitated daily working-time extensions, as for example in the case of work dependent on seasonal or atmospheric conditions. Second, to accommodate the 5-day workweek, the bill allowed temporary extensions of daily working-time to up to 10 hours, without such extension counting as overtime or attracting overtime pay (Article 2(3) of the amending statute). This last extension, however, was not permitted for some categories of workers, including those exposed to particularly harmful conditions, pregnant women, and workers charged with care of a child under 4 years of age (Article 2(4)). While the exclusion was absolute for the first two categories, employers could require those caring for a child under four to work in excess of 8 hours provided they obtained their express permission (Article 129[5] of the *Labour Code*).

Legislating the 40-hour workweek was a symbolically important nod to labour law's protective functions, even if it were phased in gradually. However, the failure of the 1998 SME Committee's proposal did not stop

[24] Proposal of the Government concerning the amendment of the Labour Code, Doc. No. 1565 (9 December 1999). While in practice the proposal also created a 5-day workweek, it did so by way of retaining the 42-hour workweek and introducing additional holidays (52 days per annum), thereby necessitating work of up to 10 hours on some days.

[25] *Act of 1 March 2001 concerning the Amendment of the Labour Code*, (1999) Journal of Laws 2001, No. 28, item 301, in force 1 May 2001, Article 1 point 2 (amending Article 129 para 1).

the business lobby, which continued to press for more flexibility and liberalization of the working-time regime, and indeed, would eventually manage to secure many of the far-reaching changes included in that proposal. Significantly, the SME's references to the minimum norms prescribed by the *Working Time Directive* heralded that these norms would play an important role in the progressive reform of the Polish working-time regime.

In addition to reducing the overall working time through the 1999 amendment, the Electoral Action Solidarity also envisaged other changes to the working-time regime. As was set out in its 1999 *National Strategy*, the party wanted to promote part-time work as a way of making work more adaptable for women. Likewise, it identified part-time work as a work–family reconciliation instrument in its 1999 *National Pro-Family Policy*, which also proposed to extend maternity leaves and benefits and, to a lesser extent, develop child-care infrastructure (mainly in rural areas). The particular choice of instruments and the latter's emphasis on demographic changes, particularly low birth and marriage rates (Balcerzak-Paradowska 2004: 219–20), suggested, however, that it was less concerned with the facilitation of women's employment through accommodation of caregiving roles, than with the promotion of fertility. The policy was underpinned by a clear preference for women's temporary de-activation after childbirth, followed by reduced labour market participation through part-time work (Racław-Markowska 2008: 76).

In accordance with this work–family reconciliation model, in 1999 the government increased the maternity leave entitlement.[26] The change was phased in; with the duration of the paid leave initially being raised from 16 to 20 weeks for first and subsequent births (on 1 January 2000), and from 26 to 30 weeks for multiple births. As of 1 January 2001, the leave was further extended to 26 and 36 weeks respectively, with a 16-week obligatory portion and the remaining portion elective. To comply with EU equality law, the right to take up the non-obligatory portion of the maternity leave was subsequently extended to fathers.[27] A EU-influenced change was also made to the child-raising leave provisions in August 2001. The right to the child-raising leave – the additional leave of up to 3 years to be taken up before the child's fourth birthday – had been already available to fathers as of 1996, but the leave could

[26] *Act of 19 November 1999 concerning the amendment of the Labour Code*, (1999) Journal of Laws, No. 99, item 1152.

[27] *Act of 25 April 2001 concerning the amendment of the Labour Code*, (2001) Journal of Laws, No. 52, item 538.

be taken only by one parent at the time. Since parents had to choose which one would use their entitlement, its take-up was generally low and particularly unpopular among men (Kotowska et al. 2007; Balcerzak-Paradowska 2008: 20).[28] To encourage fathers, a provision was passed enabling parents to share – and take up simultaneously – up to 3 months of the leave (Article 189^{1}(1)(2)).[29] Intended to also bring Polish law in compliance with the *Parental Leave Directive*,[30] this transposition was not entirely accurate, as the Directive made the entitlement to an *individual* 3-month leave for men and women, meaning that it was non-transferable between parents and each was entitled to it (Leiber 2005: 19–20). Thus, not only was the amendment incorrect, it also was useless in practice since it was unlikely that both parents would stay home to share an unpaid leave.

Although both, the 1999 *National Pro-Family Policy* and the *National Strategy* referred to the promotion of part-time work, no specific actions were taken with regard to its regulation, with the result that part-time work remained a rarely utilized (Eurostat 2007; Głogosz 2007: 96; Gładzicka-Janowska 2009; see Appendix A, Table 4) and unpopular strategy for reconciling of work and family demands, being used instead by pension-age workers or those unable to find any other employment (Poliwczak 2003: 18; Głogosz 2007: 100). Similarly, no efforts were made to support working parents through the provision of institutional care, with the numbers of kindergartens and crèches continuing to decline (Balcerzak-Paradowska et al. 2003: 204; Heinen and Wator 2006: 200–203).

Phase 2: Regulating Flexibility

The political conflicts within the Electoral Action Solidarity–Freedom Union coalition led to its breakdown in 2000. In 2001, Electoral Action Solidarity lost the election to the Left Democratic Alliance, which formed government in coalition with the Peasant Party (Polskie Stronnictwo Ludowe, PSL) and Union of Labour (Unia Pracy, UP). The recession,

[28] Balcerzak-Paradowska (2008: 20) cites figures that show a further drop in the already low number of people taking up the leave: from 336.1 thousand in 1993 to 138.8 thousand in 2000. By 2005, 33 per cent of women entitled to the leave took it up compared to 2 per cent of men (Balcerzak-Paradowska 2008, 20, based on GUS 2006).

[29] *Act of 24 August 2001 concerning the amendment of the Labour Code and certain other Acts*, (2001) Journal of Laws, No. 128, item 1405.

[30] *Council Directive 96/34/EC of 3 June 1996 on the Framework Agreement on Parental Leave concluded by UNICE, CEEP and the ETUC*, [1996] O.J. L 145/4 (19 June 1996), amended by *Council Directive 97/75/EC of 15 December 1997*, [1998] O.J. L 10/24 (16 January 1998).

rapidly escalating unemployment (see Appendix A, Table 2), and high government deficit posed a difficult challenge. One of the new coalition's first orders of business was to cut back on the just introduced maternity leave provisions. In December 2001,[31] the leave was reduced back to 16 weeks for the first, 18 for subsequent, and 26 for multiple births. Effectively, this also cut down on the father's entitlements, since the first 14 weeks were maintained as obligatory for the mother. At the same time, the protection against dismissal, previously only available to pregnant women and women entitled to maternity leave (Article 180), was extended to fathers taking up their portion of maternity leave. Although the change was mainly motivated by budgetary savings (Kotowska et al. 2008: 192), in justifying it some on the Left also argued that long leaves negatively impact women's labour market opportunities (Parliamentary Debate, 13 December 2001, Izabela Jaruga-Nowacka), which was congruent with the party's more egalitarian stance and its promotion of 'interchangeable breadwinning' (Racław-Markowska 2008: 76).

Since the previous government was unable to deliver a comprehensive labour law reform beyond the reduced workweek, the second order of business for the Left was a *Labour Code* amendment proposal. With Poland's EU accession on the horizon, and the European Commission's unsatisfactory 2001 and 2002 pre-accession progress reports,[32] there was pressure to modernize the legal framework. Both reports noted Poland's high unemployment and pointed to the rigid *Labour Code* as a likely culprit. In Poland itself, more flexible legislation was eagerly awaited by employer organizations and supported by the Reform Commission. The worsening economy and the looming EU accession, strengthened the Left's resolve to continue the process of reforming labour law they already began in 1996, as foreseen in its overall strategic *Enterprise-Growth-Work*[33] plan.

Unwilling to act unilaterally, however, the coalition government encouraged social partners to negotiate on the issues concerning them – mainly, the flexibilization of the *Labour Code*, the removal of various

[31] *Act of 21 December 2001 concerning the amendment of the Labour Code*, (2001) Journal of Laws No. 154, item 1805 (Dz.U. Nr 154 poz 1805).

[32] *Poland's Progress towards Accession*. 2000 Regular Report from the Commission (8 November 2000); *Poland's Progress towards Accession*. 2001 Regular Report from the Commission of the European Communities. SEC (2001) 1752 (13 November 2001) (hereinafter *Poland's Progress* 2000; *Poland's Progress* 2001).

[33] Economic Strategy of the SLD-UP-PSL Government adopted by the Council of Ministers, January 2002. (hereinafter *Enterprise-Growth-Work*).

administrative burdens, and lowering labour costs for the SMEs. While social dialogue had been largely ineffective from the moment of its institutionalization in 1994, partly because Solidarity often boycotted talks and refused to cooperate with the Leftist (ex-Communist) government or with the public sector union OPZZ, things deteriorated under the Electoral Action Solidarity administration (Ost 2005: 162). Indeed, Ost recounts that social dialogue was almost entirely stalled during this period (Ost 2000: 515, 2005: 162), presumably because Solidarity's political wing was confident that it could alone speak for labour. The incoming Leftist government had resolved to restore social dialogue, and to give the Tripartite Commission, composed of representatives of unions, employer organizations, and the Ministry of Labour, a more meaningful role in shaping labour regulations once again.[34] Possibly, however, the Left wanted to simply share the responsibility for potentially unpopular changes that were forthcoming, as it had learned from past experience that assuming this burden alone was politically costly. Independent social partner talks on the labour law reform had been indeed underway since February 2001, although they involved only the OPZZ and the Polish Employers' Confederation (Krajowa Konfederacja Pracodawców, KKP) (Stelina 2006: 201) with the Polish Craftsmen Union (Związek Rzemiosła Polskiego) joining the negotiations at the end of 2001 (Błaszczyk 2002: 39; Ost 2005). The talks collapsed in February 2002 because OPZZ members refused to approve the deal made by their negotiating committee. This led the government to present the social partners with its own amendment proposal, but because the labour law group of the Tripartite Commission could not agree on a joint position in response, the government decided to act on its own (Sadłowska 2002).

2002 Labour Code Amendment

By 2002, Poland's growth rate fell to 1.4 from 4.3 in 2000 (see Appendix A, Table 1), its employment rate plunged to 44.5 per cent, and unemployment reached nearly 20 per cent, its highest level since the start of transition (GUS 2005; see Appendix A, Table 2). With the accession deadline approaching and the European Commission's 2001 report pressing

[34] Indeed, the Tripartite Commission was a Left Democratic Alliance innovation, originally proposed by Jacek Kuroń as part of the Pact on State Enterprises negotiated with the trade unions in 1993. Leszek Miller, the Left's Labour Minister (1993–1996), and later Prime Minister (2001–2004), established the commission as a forum for regular exchange between unions and employers, and many labour deals were negotiated therein during the Left's Parliamentary tenure in the 1990s (Ost 2005).

for 'job creation' measures to 'tackle unemployment' and 'improve the functioning of the labour markets' (*Poland's Progress* 2001: 33), complete deregulation of the employment relationship was being advocated in some expert circles aligned with the business lobby. Convinced that restrictive regulations and high labour costs were overburdening Polish firms and preventing job growth, many politicians were prepared to go that far. Indeed, in February 2002, a group of MPs from the business-friendly Civic Platform party introduced a proposal for *Labour Code* amendment that was very much in line with that proposed by the Parliament's SME Committee in 1998.[35] One month later, the coalition government countered with its own, somewhat more moderate position,[36] which formed a part of its *Enterprise-Growth-Work* economic strategy.

While both proposals ultimately sought to make the *Labour Code* more flexible and easier to administer for firms, particularly for SMEs, there were significant differences in how much flexibility each considered acceptable. With respect to working-time reform, the Civic Platform proposed to introduce several of the minimum standards set by the *Working Time Directive*, including the 48 hours weekly maximum and the minimum 11 hours rest break. On the basis of the Directive's norms, the proposal suggested a further revision of the Code's Article 129 to increase the permissible daily working hours from eight to up to 12 hours, and to increase the reference period for averaging the 40-hour workweek from 3 to up to 12 months,[37] without requiring that this latter extension be negotiated or consulted with unions or workers' representatives. In terms of additional overtime, which was already permitted in emergency and rescue operations or special needs of the employer (Article 133(1)), the proposal sought to increase the 150-hour annual limit, to 240 hours. Overtime was to be compensated at the flat rate of 50 per cent; dispensing with the two-tier premium scheme of 50 and 100 per cent depending on the number of excessive work hours and days of the week on which this work took place. Employees would not be entitled to any premium if

[35] *Members' proposal concerning the amendment of the Labour Code*, Doc. No. 334 (12 February 2002) (hereinafter Members' Amendment Proposal 2002).

[36] *Proposal of the Government concerning the amendment of the Labour Code*, Doc. No. 335 (20 March 2002) (hereinafter Government Amendment Proposal 2002).

[37] The exceptions were made only for systems of working-time organization demanding continuous, uninterrupted effort where similar mechanisms were already available but with reference periods set at 1–4 months. Similarly, an exception was to be made for workers in road transport, for whom the permissible daily working time was 10 hours (Articles 129(4), 132 para 2 and 4 of the 1996 *Labour Code*).

they agreed to a retroactive schedule adjustment to reflect any excessive work carried out, provided that this was done within the month in which overtime work occurred (proposed amendment no. 37c). Finally, like the 1998 SME Committee proposal, the Civic Platform also proposed introducing unpaid lunch breaks of up to 90 minutes (regulated by collective agreement or agreement between workers and employers), and the system of 'interrupted' working-time wherein an employer could schedule a single break of up to 5 hours (not 6, as was the case in 1998). In addition to these key changes, the proposal suggested also major changes in the administration of various benefits (certain types of disability insurance or coverage for work-related health assessments) and administrative requirements involved in setting up workplace health and safety boards, among others. Primarily, its aim was to shield SMEs, employing below twenty or, in some cases, fifty workers (previously this was set at five), from the costs involved in their administration.

Compared to the Civic Platform's, the government's proposal was considerably more 'conservative' in that it was not as far reaching, even in face of difficult labour market and economic situation. Nonetheless, it also proposed significant changes. In terms of adjusting the Article 129 working-time norms, the government proposed to retain the 8/40 hours limits, but to increase the basic reference period from 3 to 4 months. In addition, reference periods of up to 6 months were proposed in certain sectors (including agriculture, guarding of persons or property, public works, and essential services), and 12 months in cases where organization of work or technological reasons would justify it, but with the proviso that such extensions be introduced through agreements with unions or workers' representatives, or where no collective agreement or a representative body existed, with prior notification of the health and safety inspector. In terms of overtime and compensation, the proposal retained the 150 hours annual limit already legislated, but, just as the Civic Platform, it proposed to lower compensation to 50 per cent for the first 4 hours. Also, similar to the Civic Platform, the government supported the introduction of the 'interrupted' working-time system, with a single break of up to 5 hours, with the important proviso that such breaks be compensated at the rate of one-half of regular pay. In terms of introducing longer, uncompensated breaks for lunch or personal needs, the government suggested breaks of up to 60 minutes regulated by collective agreement.

Ultimately, both the Civic Platform and the government wanted a more business-friendly and flexible *Labour Code*, even if their justifications were somewhat different. The government's explanatory memo invoked the need to reduce labour costs and flexibilize employment relations as essential to realize its long-term strategy and its *Entrepreneurship First*[38] programme; however, its main goal was to address unemployment: 'The current *Labour Code* is not sufficiently flexible and restricts the contractual freedoms of the parties to the employment relationship, which is particularly detrimental from the standpoint of addressing unemployment' (Government Amendment Proposal 2002: 17). The Civic Platform, also focused on the labour market: 'Modern and flexible labour market cannot be regulated through rigid provisions' (Members' Amendment Proposal 2002: 12) and urged that the current *Labour Code* 'discouraged' employers from creating jobs. However, its key emphasis was on the creation of a business-friendly environment. Specifically, the Civic Platform's explanatory memo suggested that in the course of its various revisions, the *Labour Code* had profoundly upset the balance between employee and employer rights; while it privileged the former, it had become a 'hostile' Act for employers. According to its authors, the proposal was to 're-balance' expectations to make the Code 'safer' for employers (Members' Amendment Proposal 2002: 13).

These differences aside, since there was some overlap between the proposals, the social partners and broader expert community were consulted over both, and a special Parliamentary Commission was established to oversee the reform. In May 2002 the Social Policy and Health Committee, jointly with the Polish Senate, held a conference entitled 'Changes in the *Labour Code* as an Element of Reform and Adjustment of Polish Labour Law to the Law of the European Union' (Senat Rzeczypospolitej Polskiej [Senate of the Polish Republic] 2002). Prominent labour law experts, representatives of all social partner organizations, as well as members of the Parliamentary Work Safety Council attended and commented the proposed changes. Review of the conference proceedings reveals the extent of divergence in the social partner views on what was proposed. It also indicates that while most Polish labour law experts supported the Code's further liberalization (Senat Rzeczypospolitej Polskiej [Senate of the Polish Republic] 2002; Lewandowski 2002: 13–17), some disputed whether the measures proposed would actually address unemployment since they tended to make overtime less expensive and thus unlikely to encourage creation of new jobs (Góral 2002; Kabaj 2002: 23–28).

[38] Programme adopted by the Council of Ministers on 29 January 2002 as part of the Economic Strategy of the SLD-UP-PSL Government 'Enterprise-Growth-Work' (hereinafter *Entrepreneurship First*).

By July 2002, the special Parliamentary Committee drafted the consolidated proposal. In introducing it on 25 July 2002, the Committee Rapporteur, Marek Dyduch, alluded to the tough debate and the significant differences of opinion, but expressed confidence that a fair compromise had been reached and that the proposed changes would have a positive business impact and, hence, prevent further job shedding (Parliamentary proceedings, No. 27, 25 July 2002). During the Parliamentary debate on the consolidated proposal, members of the Leftist coalition government speaking in support of the bill put the value of employment protection on the record but cited the 'desperate' labour market situation, particularly high unemployment, in support of the more flexible framework the bill was ushering in. The overall message was that tough concessions and sacrifices were necessary to turn the economy. In the words of Janusz Lisak of the Union of Labour, his 'workers' party' was willing to accept some of the far-reaching limitations of workers' rights that the bill contained out of solidarity with the '3.5 million people who remain jobless' (Parliamentary proceedings, No. 27, 25 July 2002).

In the end, most MPs were able to converge on the issue of unemployment and the joint proposal was passed. Significantly, the changes were to be temporary only, given that some were in conflict with EU regulations, and a follow-up amendment was to be introduced within a year. Voting against the bill were the members of Law and Justice (Prawo i Sprawiedliwość, PiS) Self Defense (Samoobrona), and the League of Polish Families (Liga Polskich Rodzin), the right-wing conservatives and populist parties that replaced the dissolved Electoral Action Solidarity. While they too agreed that a *Labour Code* amendment was necessary, most of them either opposed the far-reaching deregulation that the bill was proposing (Parliamentary Proceedings, No. 27, 25 July 2002; see Anna Sobecka and Lech Kaczyński), or considered the changes as not going far enough (Parliamentary Proceedings, No. 27, 25 July 2002; see Stanisław Dulias and Tomasz Szczypiński). Although the former's objections mainly centered on the necessity to protect workers, their opposition was also very much a strategic and political one.

The changes introduced by the 2002 bill were indeed business friendly and assessed as such by Polish employers (Lewiatan 2002), although they were more in line with the government's proposal than the Civic Platform's. The bill also made some effort to balance the business-friendly measures with several new protective provisions. In terms of working time, the basic reference period of 4 months was increased, and longer periods of 6 and 12 months in some select cases (i.e. seasonal work, and where required by employers' special needs or technological reasons) were permitted (Article 129). To appease employers, maximum annual overtime hours were set at 416 (previously 150), while overtime costs were lowered through a simultaneous reduction in overtime pay to 50 per cent for all overtime hours (Article 134), albeit not for weekend or statutory holiday overtime, for which the compensation level of 100 per cent was retained. The amendment also gave employers a unilateral right to decide whether to compensate overtime with pay or time off in lieu (Article 143(2)). Another employer-friendly measure adopted was the system of 'interrupted' working time, enabling the scheduling of breaks of up to 5 hours within a 24-hour period during which employees were to retain a right to one-third of their compensation, not one-half as previously proposed. The new law also allowed scheduling 60-minute unpaid breaks not counted as working time. Finally, provisions on holiday entitlements were amended in a way that shifted the responsibility (or right) to draw up holiday schedules from unions or employee organizations to the employers (Article 163(1)), although technically dispensing with the need to draw up such schedules at all.

In addition to the employer-friendly flexibility measures and changes aimed at lowering business-operating costs for SMEs, the 2002 bill introduced several provisions intended to benefit employees. Among others, the requirements and definitions of what constituted the employment contract were tightened to limit the practice of sidestepping the *Labour Code* through civil-contracts.[39] In terms of working time, the bill included a provision allowing employees eligible for child-raising leave to request reduction in working hours for the duration of the leave, with a corresponding employer duty to accommodate such requests (Article 186(3)). The bill also enabled employees to request 4 days of their annual leave 'on demand' (Article 167^{2-3}).

Thus, while the amendment did not go as far as to strip down existing working-time norms to the minimums set by EU law, its overall effect was to permit employers a great deal more flexibility in planning work over longer reference periods and longer breaks, and making overtime hours cheaper. The new freedom to 'interrupt' the workday,

[39] Moreover, the bill introduced a special substitute-worker provision, whereby the employee on leave could be replaced by a substitute contractor whose employment contract would only be signed/valid for the duration of the main employee's leave. This provision was intended to make it easier for employers to temporarily replace workers on leave, without the necessity of dismissing them or replacing them permanently.

previously available only in road transport, had the same intention and in addition was aimed at minimization of passive times during which employees were not 'productively' engaged. All of these forms of flexibility, however, had the potential to conflict with the interests of employees in more predictable working schedules and hours, a problem particularly acute in a context of work culture wherein long work hours were already the norm. According to Eurostat and studies carried out by Warsaw's Institute of Labour and Social Studies (IPISS), in 2000 and 2001, Poles worked some of the longest hours in Europe (reporting 43 and 38.9 hours per week for men and women respectively) and many were reporting hours in excess of the statutory limits (Strzemińska 2002: 123). Over 16 per cent of all workers (17.3 per cent of women) reported hours between 44 and 49, while 13.4 (11.2 of women) per cent worked in excess of 50. In feminized sectors such as retail, the average working time was 43.6 hours (Strzemińska 2002: 116–24).

Given this statistical picture, further working-time extensions, or the introduction of scheduled 'interruptions' of up to 5 hours, could potentially create further burdens for workers with caring obligations. Similarly, interrupted work organization would make it very difficult to plan personal schedules around the more rigidly set times of kindergartens and schools, and could significantly disrupt family time. Granted, the new option to request reduced working time while on child-raising leave was a positive development. The change was intended to accommodate smoother transition between child-care and labour market participation, and to minimize career breaks, which was in line with the Left Democratic Alliances' reduction of maternity leave entitlements earlier that year to shield women from the perception that they were expensive and undesirable employees. However, this provision did not adequately respond to the needs of working parents whose children were older than four or to the needs of people caring for older dependants. Similarly, the right to take-up a portion of annual leave 'on demand' could be used in emergency situations and went some way towards making flexibility work for employees, but on balance the changes introduced by the 2002 amendment were not very 'woman' or 'family friendly'. Given the traditional gender roles and the difficult labour market situation, the take-up of these new forms of 'employee-friendly' flexibility by fathers was unlikely.

Ultimately, the bill's uneven focus reflected Poland's dire labour market conditions. With the EU accession only 2 years away, reducing unemployment, promoting entrepreneurship by lowering labour costs, and the overarching goal of demonstrating that Poland was a stable, well-functioning, and competitive economy topped the policy agenda. As for the needs of workers and women, while the latter's inferior labour market position was acknowledged, the government's key message was that jobs were 'a blessing' and the only secure guarantee that basic subsistence needs would be met; the fact that these jobs may have significantly interfered with private life or people's ability to balance competing demands was not the most significant consideration.

2003 Labour Code Amendment

Several months after the passing of the 2002 statute, the Parliament began working on a further, more comprehensive bill designed to bring the *Labour Code* in full compliance with the *acquis*. Proceeded by several months of parliamentary debate and work in the Special Parliamentary Committee, the statue amending the *Labour Code*[40] was passed on 14 November 2003, just a few months short of the date of accession. Many of the proposed changes were already subject to an earlier bill that had been proposed in 2001 by the Electoral Action Solidarity (Florek 2004a). At the time, the bill was opposed by the Left Democratic Alliance and vetoed by President Aleksander Kwaśniewski because it contained Sunday-rest provisions[41] that he deemed unjustified and ideological. Although the Electoral Action Solidarity's political successors – now dispersed mainly throughout Law and Justice, League of Polish Families, and Self-Defence – were set on political retaliation by way of putting roadblocks in the Left's way, the fact that the EU accession deadline was close made concessions necessary. Similarly, the Civic Platform, again pushing for additional forms of flexibility that they could not achieve in 2002, had only a short timeframe to work with. Thus, despite the discontent among the opposition parties, the necessity to harmonize Polish law with the EU's meant that the bill, with several minor changes, passed in both chambers of the Parliament in the fall and received the Presidential signature by the end

[40] *Act of 14 November 2003 concerning the amendment of the Labour Code*, (2003) Journal of Laws No. 213, item 2081.

[41] The Left and the 'liberal' Right-wing parties, and the 'social solidaristic' Right (Electoral Action Solidarity, League of Polish Families, and Law and Justice) have been divided on Sunday rest, with the former opposing a ban on Sunday work for business or 'freedom to shop' reasons, and the latter fighting, without success, to prohibit Sunday work in the retail sector, where it has been traditionally permitted, on the basis of the right to worship and the need to keep families together and mothers closer to their children. Attempts to institute Sunday rest and additional religious holidays took up a great deal of Parliamentary debate time during the Electoral Action Solidarity and Law and Justice tenures.

of November 2003. The changes the bill introduced were wide in scope as there were many areas in which harmonization with the EU Directives was outstanding.[42] Smaller measures enacted in prior years already addressed select aspects of equality, health and safety, and working time (i.e. the 2002 amendment). However, the purpose of the 2003 amending statute was to bring the *Labour Code* in full compliance with all equality and non-discrimination Directives (2000/78, 2000/43, 76/207),[43] health and safety Directives (89/391, 90/394, 78/610),[44] and, in relation to working time, the *Working Time Directive* (93/104) and the framework agreements and Directives on Part-time work (97/81) and fixed-term work (99/70).

As I will show in more detail further, the overall effect of the 2003 amendment on the working-time regime was to align it closely with the provisions of the *Working Time Directive*: both the protective norms and some of the exclusions and derogations (see Table 5.1). Although some of this was already accomplished in 2002, the changes enacted then were justified as of 'emergency' and 'temporary' nature, and the 2003 amendment made these changes permanent, provided they did not conflict with the provisions of the *Working Time Directive*. Overall, by aligning Polish working-time rules closer with the Directive's provisions, new forms of flexibility to extend work hours were assimilated into the *Labour Code*, so that, on balance, the 2002 and 2003 amendments led to a significant flexibilization of the working-time regime.[45] At the same

[42] The amendment was very wide in scope, and in addition to the changes discussed in this chapter it addressed new provisions on employment contracts, workers' rights to information and consultation, and the protection of young people at work.

[43] *Council Directive 2000/43/EC of 29 June 2000 implementing the principle of equal treatment between persons irrespective of racial or ethnic origin*, [2000] O.J. L 180/22; *Council Directive 2000/78/EC of 27 November 2000, establishing a general framework for equal treatment in employment and occupation*, [2000] O.J. L 303/16; *Council Directive 76/207/EEC of 9 February 1976 on the implementation of the principle of equal treatment for men and women as regards access to employment, vocational training and promotion, and working conditions*, [1976] O.J. L 39/40.

[44] *Council Directive 78/610/EEC of 29 June 1978 on the approximation of laws, regulations and administrative provisions of the Member States on the protection of health of workers exposed to vinyl chloride monomer*, [1978] O.J. L 197/12; *Council Directive 89/391/EEC of 12 June 1989 on the introduction of measures to encourage improvements in the safety and health of workers at work*, [1989] O.J. L 183; *Council Directive 90/394/EEC of 28 June 1990, on the protection of workers from risks related to exposure to carcinogens at work, insofar as it relates to carcinogens other than asbestos*, [1990] O.J. L 196/1.

[45] Note that Leiber (2007: 21) observes that the transposition of the *Working Time Directive* did not lead to the lowering of national standards. Indeed, as I note below the basic *Labour Code* standards remained largely intact, and the main flexibility provisions enacted in 2003 (derogations and exceptions) had already been introduced a year earlier, in 2002, and were merely repeated here.

Table 5.1 Working Time Directive *and corresponding* Labour Code *provisions*

Working Time Directive provisions	*Polish Labour Code provisions*
Art. 3 Daily rest: 11hrs, within 24-hr period	**Art. 132** (2003 Amendment) Daily rest: 11hrs, within 24-hr period
Art. 4 Mandatory break if working-time equals or exceeds 6hrs	**Art. 134** (2003 Amendment) Mandatory break if work-time equals or exceeds 6hrs
Art. 5 Weekly rest: 35 hrs	**Art. 133** (2003 Amendment) Weekly rest: 35 hrs
Art. 6 Weekly working time inclusive of overtime: 48/hrs over 7-day period	**Art. 131(1)** (2003 Amendment) Weekly working time inclusive of overtime: 48/hrs over 7-day period
Art. 7 4 week annual leave (Cannot be replaced by time in lieu)	**Art. 154** (2003 Amendment) 20 days, 26 days (based on 5d average w.w.) Pay in lieu limited to the dissolution of employment
Art. 8–11 Working time of night workers and workers exposed to hazardous conditions: 8 hrs/24 (average) Free confidential health assessment Report to authorities Ensure health and safety needs met	**Art. 151^7 (2)** (2003 Amendment) Definition of “night worker” Set 8hr limit on night work involving dangerous work or work requiring high levels of physical or mental exertion
Art. 13 Patterns of work ‘Adapting work to worker’	**Art. 94 2(a) 2003 Amendment** Employers required to organize work in a manner that minimizes the burden of monotonous work, or work at set rate, by introducing breaks
Art. 16 Basic Reference Periods	**Art. 129(1)** (2002 Amendment) Weekly working time – 4 months
Weekly rest – 14 days Weekly working-time – 4 months Night work – industry agreement	**Art. 333** (2003 Amendment) Weekly rest – 1 week

(*cont.*)

Table 5.1 (*cont.*)

Working Time Directive provisions	*Polish Labour Code provisions*
Derogations, Art. 17(1) Certain categories of workers: • Managing executives or other persons with autonomous decision-making powers • Family workers; • Workers officiating at religious ceremonies in churches and religious communities.	**Arts 132(2), 133(2), 151^7 (5)** (2003 Amendment) Derogation from daily rest rule, weekly rest, night work limits for managerial workers
Derogations, Art. 17 Derogations from overtime limits (reference periods), daily and weekly rest and night work, **Art. 17(3)** • Workers whose **place of work and place of residence are distant** from one another, including offshore work, or where their different places of work are distant from one another; • Workers engaged in **security and surveillance activities**; • Workers involved in activities which require **continuity of service** or production (e.g. hospitals, residential institutions, gas, water and electricity production, industries in which work cannot be interrupted on technical grounds, and research and development activities); • Workers engaged in areas where there is 'a **foreseeable surge of activity**'; • In cases of accident or the **imminent risk of an accident**.	**2002 Amendment**, retained in 2003 **Article 129(2)** Derogation from the basic reference period in some sectors (i.e. seasonal work and workers engaged in security and surveillance activities) 6 months, and 12 months where required by employer's special needs or technological reasons. 'Interrupted working-time' system, breaks of up to 5 hours allowed **Arts 132(2), 133(2), 151^7 (5)** (2003 Amendment) Derogation from daily rest rule, weekly rest, night work limits for 'emergency' workers (risk of accident, risk to life, health and environment)
Derogations from the 11-hour and 35-hour rest rules, **Art. 17(4)** • Shift work; shift change • Where work is split up during the day	**Art. 135–139** (2003 Amendment, Arts. 132–133) Derogations from the daily and weekly rest applied to essential emergency response workers, shift workers, workers employed in system of equivalent working time
Derogations, Art. 18 Legislated or negotiated (by collective agreement) derogations from daily, weekly rest, breaks, night work, weekly working time and reference periods	**Art. 151(4)** (2003 Amendment) Derogations from annual overtime limits (150) by collective agreement, workplace regulation or employment contract (up to 419 annual hours)

Derogations Art. 19 (previously Art. 17(4) Reference Periods • Legislated – up to 6 months • By collective agreement – 12 months (for objective or technical reasons)	***Anti-Crisis Bill, 2009*** (expired 31 Dec 2011, but this provision was included into Code by a 2013 Amendment) **Art. 1** Up to 12 months where required by objective needs of the employer, technological reasons, or requirements stemming from the organization of work time
Derogations, Art. 22(1) (formerly Art. 18(1)(b)(i)) Individual opt-out from Art. 6 (weekly working time)	***Act of 24 August 2007 concerning Health-Care Centers*** Individual opt-out in health-care establishments for doctors and health-care technicians with post-secondary education

Note: Not included here are provisions from the 2000 Horizontal Directive and subsequent Directives and regulations that extended the *Working Time Directive*'s rules to previously excluded sectors. Articles of the *Labour Code* used here and throughout this chapter reflect numbering in the original legislation and may not be consistent with the current numbering in light of subsequent revisions and consolidations.

time, reflecting the EU's broader focus on diversification of working time and adaptability of work, the 2003 amendment also provided for several new employee-friendly forms of flexibility. As I will elaborate in more detail further, however, these new working-time solutions may have been beneficial to some workers, but were not necessarily suitable to better work–family reconciliation.

In terms of changes to working time, the 2003 statute was largely an exercise in 'organizing' the working-time rules (Florek 2004a). Previously dealt with in Chapter Eleven of the *Labour Code*, working-time was shifted to Chapter Six, which restated and reorganized many of the previously enacted provisions (including those from 2002) and introduced further changes designed to adapt them to European norms, and indeed went beyond these norms (Florek 2004a).[46] In compliance with the *Working Time Directive*, the amended Chapter Six maintained the 40-hour weekly norm; however, as per the Directive, it explicitly restated that total weekly working time, inclusive of overtime, was not to exceed 48-hours over a specified reference period no longer than 4 months. The potential extensions of the reference period to 6 (in specified sectors) or 12 months (if required by employer's special needs or for technological reasons), already adopted in 2002, were retained.

Moreover, the Directive's mandatory daily and weekly rest periods of 11 and 35 hours respectively, were introduced (Articles 132 and 133). These minimum mandatory rest periods were novel in Polish labour law, since daily rest had previously been determined only by the number of permissible daily and overtime hours, and by the permissible daily extensions for specific categories of workers. As a result of their implementation, the previously set daily overtime limit of 4 hours (Article 151) was eliminated, effectively increasing permissible daily overtime from 4 to 5 hours because the application of the minimum 11-hour rest rule enabled work for up to 13 hours daily, thus up to 5 hours *over* the basic 8-hour norm.[47]

Also following the Directive, exceptions to the weekly work hours and the daily and weekly rest were applied to managerial staff (Article 132(2)). Similarly, exceptions from the daily and weekly rest were applied to

[46] For instance, the amendment introduced definitions of working day and working week, which are absent in the Directive and which, according to many Polish labour lawyers substantially interfere with more flexible organization of working time: see for instance Rycak (2008a, 2008b); Florek (2004a).

[47] 24 – 11 (daily rest) = 13 permissible hours of work (inclusive of overtime), 13 – 8 = 5 potential legal overtime limit.

essential emergency response workers, shift workers, and workers employed in the system of equivalent working time, with the proviso that these workers had to have at least 24-hours of uninterrupted weekly rest (Articles 132–133). To compensate unused rest periods, workers excluded from the daily rest requirement (but not managerial staff) were entitled to an equivalent time off within the reference period set at 1 week (Article 132(3)). By contrast, the Directive provided that this reference period could be set at 2 weeks, making the Code's norm more favourable for workers. Finally, annual overtime limits – permitted for rescue or lifesaving operations or when justified by employer's special needs – were set at 150 hours (Article 151(3)); however, higher limits were permitted to be set by collective agreement, workplace regulation or employment contract, in practice enabling annual overtime of up to 416 hours (Article 151(4)). Once again, this change was already brought in by the 2002 'temporary' amendment and was now reaffirmed.

Also following the Directive, special rules were applied to the working time of night workers, including a newly specified definition of night worker (Article 151^7 (2)), limit on the working hours of night workers (Article 151^7(3)) and requirement that *if an employee requests*, a workplace inspector should be notified that night work is carried out (Articles 151^7(6)). In the latter case, the Directive's specification on the necessity of notification differed in that its Article 11 provided that the request for information on the performance of night work was to come from the competent national authorities to the employer; the Directive, unlike the 2003 amendment, did not place the burden on the employee to request that such information be forwarded.

In line with the minimum annual leave of 4 weeks mandated by Article 7(2) of the *Working Time Directive*, Article 154 of the 2003 amendment also raised the basic annual leave entitlement to 20 days (from 18) for workers with under 10 years of work tenure, and 26 days for those with work record in excess of 10 years. Finally, the amended Article 171 limited the right to equivalent pay-in-lieu of annual leave to only those situations where the dissolution of the employment relationship conflicted with the employee's leave entitlement. Effectively, it imposed a requirement that the annual leave be taken up in all other circumstances.

In relation to other aspects of working time, the amendment broadened the provisions guaranteeing equal treatment of part-time and temporary workers, stemming from provisions of Directives 97/81 (part-time work) and 99/70 (fixed-term work), by introducing the non-discrimination principle.[48] While no specific provisions for part-time work were made within the chapter dealing with working-time regulation, the amendment imposed an obligation to inform employees of applicable working conditions (Directive 91/533).[49] Specifically, Article 94^2 now required employers to inform workers on part-time or fixed-term contracts of possibilities to 'upgrade' to full-time or permanent positions, or vice versa, to reduce their work hours. Moreover, the amendment 'restored' Article 25(1), which deemed a third successive 'annexation' of a fixed-term contract between the same parties a contract for permanent, open-ended employment. Intended to discourage employers from abusing fixed-term contracts for the sole purpose of limiting costs and sidestepping termination notice provisions, this provision was 'suspended' in 2002 (Gładzicka-Janowska 2009: 166). While the 2003 amendment formally restored it, in practice, the article's operation was 'frozen' until Poland's official EU membership on 1 May 2004. By then, the use of fixed-term work had increased from the negligible 4.8 per cent in 1997 to 22.7 per cent (Eurostat 2006, cited in Gładzicka-Janowska 2009: 169).

One rationale for the amendments related to part-time and fixed-term work was that improving conditions of such work would diversify the Polish working-time regime and make it more employee friendly.[50] The promise of fostering more adaptable organization of work, particularly for those workers for whom the 'standard' schedule was ill-suited, also motivated several new systems of working time, including 'weekend working' (which allowed extended working hours on Fridays, Saturdays, and Sundays) (Article 144), a 'reduced workweek' (Article 143), and the option to set individual schedule (Article 142). However, all of these new

[48] A series of provisions were amended that adjusted the *Labour Code* to EU Directives: 2000/78 (equal treatment) (Articles 9, 11.3, 18, 18.3.a-18.3.e, 94(2b), 94.1), 2000/43 (equal treatment – race and ethnicity) (Article 11.3, 94 (2b), 99/70 (temporary work)(Article 11.3, 25.1, 94.2), 97/81(part-time work)(Article 11.3, 29.2, 92.4).

[49] *Council Directive 91/533/EEC of 14 October 1991 on the employer's obligation to inform employees of the conditions applicable to the contract or employment relationship,* [1991] O.J. L 288/32.

[50] This was particularly so in relation to part-time work, which continued to be unpopular (Poliwczak 2003, 18; Głogosz 2007, 100), having remained relatively stable at about 11 per cent between 1997 and 2004 (GUS 2005; Maytsiak 2007). In reality, as Leiber (2007: 20) notes, the introduction of the protection and information provisions with respect to part-time work was an instance of bare-minimum transposition of EU standards to achieve compliance in time for accession and was not necessarily guided by the belief that part-time work would become more popular.

systems retained the basic standard weekly norm of 40 hours (48 with overtime), which in the first two cases meant significant intensification of work on some days, compensated with rest on others (not unlike in case of equivalent system of working time). While this type of system could be indeed suitable to workers who were studying or retraining, or workers balancing two different jobs, the extent to which it actually facilitated better balancing of work and family obligations was highly questionable. Indeed, the fact that pregnant workers or parents of children under four were explicitly prohibited from these systems was a sufficient indication (Article 148) that these systems were unlikely to assist working parents.

To sum up, the 2003 *Labour Code* amendment introduced new forms of flexibility permitted by the *Working Time Directive* and introduced several new systems of working-time with the purpose of reorganization of work. In reality, many of them – particularly daily and weekly working-time extensions and increases in annual overtime – had already been 'temporarily' introduced in 2002. Here, these provisions were simply restated; with the effect of becoming legitimated as 'in compliance' with the EU law. At the same time, neither the 2002, nor the 2003 amendment went so far as to include all of the *Working Time Directive* exceptions and derogations. For example, while the Directive allowed calculation of the weekly rest (35 hours) on the basis of 14-day reference period, the amendment chose to maintain the reference period at 1 week. Also, the Directive permitted derogations in a range of sectors in which further extensions could be applied (Article 17), many of which the Polish legislators chose not to apply. Finally, the 2003 bill omitted the Directive's Article 18 (later Article 22) 'opt-out' provision applicable in individual employment contracts and the wider use of annual reference periods through collective bargaining or workplace negotiations.

The fact that not all of the Directive's flexibility mechanisms were incorporated into the *Labour Code* was subject to critique, as the Polish business lobby, but also many labour-law specialists, saw it as a missed opportunity to make Polish labour law, and working-time norms in particular, even more flexible (Florek 2004b; Rycak 2008b: 11; Gładzicka-Janowska 2009: 169). At the same time, provisions like the opt-out were still regarded by some commentators as a complete violation of the labour law's protective role, the introduction of which would amount to a return to nineteenth century capitalism (Rycak 2009). Ultimately, however, the government simply decided to act incrementally as additional flexibility was coming in the future.

5.2.3 Developments After Accession – Work–family Reconciliation

Shortly after Poland joined the EU the political landscape changed, as the pendulum swung to the Right once again in the 2004 fall election. Law and Justice formed government in coalition with Self-Defense of the Polish Republic and the League of Polish Families, with Civic Platform in official opposition (Szczerbiak 2005). With this change in administration, priorities had shifted somewhat away from the focus on the economy and competitiveness. The fact that the growth rate began to recover in 2003 and by 2004 it was was back to its pre-recession rate of 5.3 (see Appendix A, Table 1), helped to keep economic rationales from the centre stage. In parallel, unemployment began to decline, although at 17.8 per cent in 2005 it was still among the highest in Europe (see Appendix A, Table 2). With substantial deregulation and flexibilization of labour law carried out prior to Poland's EU accession, the rigidity of the legal framework, albeit still identified as an issue by Polish experts, was no longer singled out as the major reason for the persistence of unemployment by the OECD and the EU (Narożny 2006). In fact, employment protection in Poland was comparable to that in other OECD and EU countries, and even lower than that of both EU-10 and EU-25 (OECD 2004b; OECD 2006 cited in Narożny 2006: 4). What continued to be seen as a problem, however, were the costs resulting from high taxes and low labour mobility (Narożny 2006: 5–6), a conclusion also reached by the outgoing administration's *Unemployment in Poland* report (2005), particularly in relation to low mobility among young and older workers.

While unemployment remained a problem, the new coalition government decided to tackle other major issues: the demographic situation and work–family reconciliation. Both issues had been partially addressed by previous administrations, but the process of EU accession and Poland's economic woes in the early 2000s meant that policy priorities laid elsewhere. Accordingly, adoption of the social *acquis* and the infrastructure for its delivery, while also required and ultimately timely (even if at the lowest common denominator), was at times delayed or subordinated so that Poland's economic progress could be maintained. The frequent political shifts, especially the contest between the more socially egalitarian Left and the socially conservative Right also stood in a way of a more coherent approach. By now, however, Poland was in the EU, where work–family reconciliation had become an important component of the policy discourse. Yet, as was suggested in Chapters 2 and 3, the rise of this issue in the context of EU working-time regulation had been uneven, with only some forms of working-time organization or accommodation – such as part-time work or parental leave – having been gendered and discussed in terms of their impact on and potential role in the balancing of work and family life. In relation to the *Working Time Directive*, the core working-time instrument, the issue of work and family had only come up on the occasion of the instrument's 2003 review – also in response to the broader work–family debate and the mainstreaming of gender in EU policy.

This selective engagement with gender and work–family reconciliation in the EU working-time discourse translated into the Polish context, with most of the local debates on the core working-time norms – and the flexibility to extend them – not paying much consideration to their gendered impacts either. While the Polish politicians paid some lip service to the diversification of working time and promotion of part-time work for the purpose of work–family reconciliation, as guided by the soft dictates of the 1997 EES and the Directive on part-time work, the practical impact of this was much less significant than in the case of standard working-time norms. On balance, despite several provisions introduced to reorganize and reduce working time and to make it more adaptable to people's needs for work–family reconciliation, the main thrust of the changes to the Polish working-time regime was to reinforce the long-hours, overtime culture. Given the traditional gender contracts and enduring unequal division of domestic labour (Saxonberg and Szelewa 2007), this type of regime was not likely to help redistribute men and women's domestic responsibilities and lead to their more equal assumption of care work within the home and risk in the labour market.

Thus, addressing the issue of work–family reconciliation was something that the Law and Justice coalition government set to achieve through its 2007 *Family Policy Project.*[51] Like the approach previously developed by Electoral Action Solidarity in 1999, this programme was similarly concerned with demography and was explicitly pro-natalist; however, there were some marked differences between the two. Notably, unlike its predecessor, the 2007 programme was no longer directed solely at women, but rather aimed to assist *parents* in a variety of family forms. Hence, along measures to support more traditional family arrangements (i.e. the extension of maternity leave and removal of social insurance barriers to temporary or permanent labour market exit), the programme

[51] Government in the Care for Polish Families. Family Policy Project of the Jarosław Kaczyński Goverment. 8 marca 2007 r. Warszawa (hereinafter *Family Policy Project*).

also emphasized measures for better work–family reconciliation, such as better access to quality care and flexible working-time arrangements for working parents. Despite the Law and Justice administration's social conservatism and the influence of the clerical-traditionalist League of Polish Families, according to Racław-Markowska (2008: 76–77), the 2007 *Family Policy Project* represented a definite shift to a more complex model of work–family reconciliation that aimed to promote both employment activation and higher fertility by accounting for diversity of family forms and women's preferences.

There were a number of reasons for this shift. First, the programme was largely developed under the direction of Joanna Kluzik-Rostkowska, a Law and Justice politician who was generally regarded as the progressive voice within her conservative party and was fairly respected by Polish feminists (Heinen and Portet 2009: 16; Ksieniewicz Interview, 26 January 2010, Warsaw). As a Minister of Labour and Social Policy during the Law and Justice government tenure, she prioritized the development of a more family and woman-friendly infrastructure and was keen to promote active focus on redistribution of care work and the promotion of more active fathering (Kluzik-Rostkowska Interview, 25 March 2010, Warsaw). Changes to the structure of maternity leave, and the introduction of the 2-week father's leave was one way of achieving these goals. While respecting a diversity of and preferences about family forms, she nonetheless maintained that women themselves constituted an obstacle to more equal division of labour as they often clutched to their traditional roles (Kluzik-Rostkowska Interview, 25 March 2010, Warsaw). At the same time, she acknowledged that financial disincentives (men's higher earnings) and traditional perception of gender roles was a major obstacle for Polish parents, women and men, who wanted to draw their entitlements (Kluzik-Rostkowska Interview, 25 March 2010, Warsaw).

The second reason was the direct and indirect influence of the EU. The objectives of stimulating women's labour market activation through measures aimed at better work–family reconciliation, including flexible working time, more and better quality child-care, and the promotion of equal sharing of paid and unpaid work between marriage partners had become key components of European policy discourse. Reconciliation of work and family had been included in successive EES Employment guidelines, and the Lisbon Strategy and the Barcelona Council conclusions had set concrete targets for women's employment rates at 60 per cent and child-care coverage at 33 per cent (under 3) and 90 per cent

(3 and up). Poland was lagging behind on all counts. Women's activation rates, at 50.6 in 2007, continued to be far below the set targets (Eurostat 2007). Similarly, the development of child-care facilities was slow and enrolment rates low, with only 2.3 per cent of children under three and 44.6 per cent of children under 5 (55 per cent under 6) being in some form of institutional or private care (GUS 2007b: 109; Balcerzak-Paradowska 2008: 21; Racław-Markowska 2008: 79). Similarly, despite some 'family-friendly' working-time measures having been enacted by the 2003 *Labour Code* amendment, these measures were few (European Foundation 2007) and, in practice, not always available for workers to take up because of barriers in the workplace (Balcerzak-Paradowska 2008: 25–26; Borkowska 2011: 38–39[52]) or lack of information about their availability (Głogosz 2008: 41–43). Indeed, family-friendly flexibility was found to be typically the privilege of own-account or self-employed workers, and significantly more difficult to attain for employees (Matysiak 2007: 357). Nonetheless, participation in the Lisbon Strategy had some effect in recasting the focus on work–family reconciliation (Płomień 2009: 147). In fact, as one Ministry of Labour and Social Policy staffer, Monika Ksieniewicz, a gender expert at the Family Policy Department, remarked, 'the only impetus for action on gender issues stems from the requirements imposed by Brussels' (Ksieniewicz Interview, 26 January 2010, Warsaw). According to Ksieniewicz, so long as there is no EU pressure, nothing happens in Warsaw to meaningfully assist women workers.

Aside from any direct pressures or necessity to adopt EU prescriptions, influence over Polish policy was also exerted through the ESF, which financed an increasing number of projects and programmes addressing gender equality, the use of flexible working-time, and work–family reconciliation or work–life balance,[53] and made possible various NGO and government publications (Kozłowska and Biała-Kalbarczyk (n.d.); Piotrowski 2007), as well as training programmes and awareness-raising

[52] According to Borkowska (2011: 38–40) many firms audited as part of the Leader in Human Resource Management annual competition lacked an official 'work-life balance' policy. In 2003, 54.9 per cent of the audited firms had such a policy, and the numbers for the following years were as follows: 42.9 per cent (2004), 71 per cent (2005), 36.4 per cent (2006), 60 per cent (2007), 43.8 per cent (2008), and 34.8 per cent (2009). According to Borkowska most firms perceived reconciliation of employment and non-employment activities as a private employee matter, not one in which the firm should take an active interest.

[53] See, for example, Racław-Markowska (2008), Sadowska-Snarska (2008), Sochańska-Kawiecka et al. (2009), Borkowska (2011).

campaigns, such as *Reconciliation of Women and Men's Family and Professional Roles 2008–2012*.[54] Projects such as the 'Gender Index' (2007) and the accompanying 'Equal Opportunities Firm' survey and training manual were other examples of initiatives that were spurred by the ESF funding and promoted and spread information about best practices.[55]

Nonetheless, some feminists, including those within the Ministry of Labour and Social Policy, remained very sceptical of the Polish government's sudden embrace of work–family reconciliation. The aforementioned Ksieniewicz, for instance, questioned whether this focus was genuinely motivated by the concern for women's well-being or whether it was in reality driven by other objectives, such as increasing fertility. She was similarly sceptical about the push for working-time flexibility as an activation and reconciliation method. Suggesting that in the Polish context flexibility was a purely employer-friendly strategy, she referred to its promotion as 'the biggest lie that women (and feminists!) bought into' (Ksieniewicz Interview, 26 January 2010, Warsaw). Others, however, did not necessarily share this scepticism. Another staffer within the Ministry's Labour Law Department, Robert Lisicki, expressed the view that Polish regulations in the realm of work–family reconciliation were not only fairly good, but that Poland was actually 'ahead of Europe' on this issue (Lisicki Interview, 22 January 2010, Warsaw). This view was also shared in part by Lisicki's superior, the Director of the Labour Law Department Eugenia Gienieczko (Gienieczko Interview, 22 January 2010, Warsaw) and by the staff lawyer in the public sector union confederation OPZZ (Anonymous, 2 February 2010, Warsaw).

The Law and Justice coalition administration never got to implement its family policy programme as it lost the fall 2007 election to the liberal Civic Platform, which formed a minority government in coalition with the Peasant Party (Polskie Stronnictwo Ludowe, PSL) (Szczerbiak 2007). With Donald Tusk as the Prime Minister, the Civic Platform was generally regarded as one of the most business-friendly parties and

[54] Developed by the Center of Human Resource Development, and co-sponsored by the Human Capital National Cohesion Strategy, the ESF, and the Ministry of Labour and Social Policy, this project included a qualitative and quantitative study (Sochańska-Kawiecka et al. 2009), good practices, conferences, an awareness-raising campaign, including television advertisments, training sessions, and a campaign website (www.rowniwpracy.gov.pl; no longer active).

[55] This project responded to the fact that considerable resistance to the accommodation of working parents and addressing the barriers to work–family reconciliation stems from business practices, not the existing legal framework.

had the backing of the Polish enterprise in prior years. This was the party that, in 2002, authored the radical proposal for labour law reform, which while not introduced, nonetheless managed to influence the 2002 'emergency' amendment. However, the Civic Platform was also a pro-EU party and one that too espoused the family-friendly, 'solidaristic' message. Thus, its first political move was to continue the popular policy direction developed by Kluzik-Rostkowska during the Law and Justice tenure (2005–2007), and, in 2008, the party introduced an extensive bill amending the *Labour Code* and several other statutes which contained a series of provisions aimed at assisting working parents and promoting better work–family reconciliation. Once again, however, the said provisions mainly focused on maternity leaves, including a new, phased-in extension (Article 180(1)), with further paid non-mandatory extensions (Article 181^{1-2}). The leave was also made available to fathers in case of mother's hospitalization (Article $182(6^{1-3})$). A 2-week paid paternity leave was also enacted, with the first week available as of 2010 and the full 2 weeks in 2012 (Article 182^{3}). Job protection was also extended to workers drawing provisions enabling part-time work while on child-raising leave (Article 186^{8}).

While positive, most of the changes were still aimed primarily at accommodating maternity and parenthood in the first years of a child's life, confirming Ksieniewicz's charge that ensuring fertility rates was the likely objective. There was no complementary effort to reorganize working-time or address how work and family demands were to be balanced in the long term, particularly given the continued shortage of child-care facilities, or few provisions for workers managing work with care of older family members.[56] On the contrary, a year later, in July 2009, the Civic Platform introduced another bill amending the *Labour Code*. This one contained new working-time flexibility measures; however, given the fact that the bill's intention was to address the potential consequences of the global financial crisis, there was a significant employer-friendly bias in its approach to flexibility, which was likely to conflict with the 'family friendly' objectives.

[56] The insufficiency of the Polish care infrastructure has been an ongoing problem, attributed to the country's 'implicit familiarist' policy (Szelewa and Polakowski 2008) and, in relation to the care for older dependent adults, to the fact that policymakers often presume that families have endless 'care capacity' (Racław 2012). Importantly, Płomień (2009: 140) reports that by the end of March 2008 nearly 800 new preschools had been set up benefiting more than 10,000 children (and funded mostly from ESF). However, only about 1 per cent of children in the 3–5 age category benefited from this.

5.2.4 *The 2009* Anti-Crisis Bill *as the 'Experimental Field' for Flexibility*

The *Act on Easing of the Effects of the Economic Crisis*, commonly known as the '*Anti-Crisis Bill*'', was passed on 1 July 2009,[57] introducing several important, albeit temporary amendments to various statutes, including the *Labour Code*. Prior to its Parliamentary discussion, the Labour Law Group of the Tripartite Commission was consulted on the bill's labour law-related provisions. As was the case in 2002, outbreak of a 'crisis' provided the perfect opportunity for employers to demand more flexibility. With trade unions by now in a significantly weaker position, compromise on this issue was inevitable, albeit some of the most far reaching management proposals were ultimately rejected. The crucial change in hours of work rules was the introduction of a further extension of the general reference periods for calculating overtime from the 4 months the *Labour Code* permitted, to up to 12 months[58] – a change long on the employer and business lobby 'wish list' and already subject of the 2002 Civic Platform and the 1998 SME Committee proposals (see Table 5.1). Not in the package, however, was another employer-backed proposal seeking the simultaneous introduction of a working-time accounts system, which would enable the full and efficient use of the extended reference periods (Męcina Interview, February 2010, Warsaw; Ambrozik Interview, 26 January 2010, Warsaw).[59] Moreover, as a trade-off for employer-friendly flexibility, the bill also introduced some positive-flexibility measures improving the reconciliation of work and family obligations. Specifically, it created a new right to request reduced working time by employees in standard, full-time positions, who care for a child younger than 14 years or another dependent person, and, importantly, it paired this right with an employer duty to accommodate such requests, except where compelling organizational reasons to refuse accommodation existed.

Given the bill's largely pre-emptive nature in light of Poland's comparatively good economic performance during the early period of the crisis,[60]

[57] (2009) Journal of Laws No. 125, item 1035.

[58] Possible in all sectors with the agreement of a representative trade union or worker representatives. *Ibid.* Article 9.

[59] Working-time accounts enable employees to log shorter or longer hours of work as debits or credits in an individual 'account', which are then compensated with additional time off work. Hours worked in excess of statutory norms are not deemed overtime and do not attract overtime compensation (Schulten 1998).

[60] In fact, Poland was the only country to note economic growth during the 2009–2010 period. In a 2010 speech entitled *After the Global Financial Crisis: the Road Ahead for Europe*,

it is difficult not to see the bill as an opportunity, seized by a willing government, to respond to the employers' enduring calls for more flexibility in labour law. A significant extension of the reference period across all sectors was precisely the sort of change that the Left Democratic Alliance coalition government was not prepared to introduce a few years earlier, but that the enterprise-friendly Civic Platform was eager to implement. Although the bill did not go as far as full deregulation, it introduced yet another *Working Time Directive* provision that the employers were keen to have in the *Labour Code* (see Table 5.1). Granted, the bill was temporary in nature – the provisions being introduced for the duration of 2 years. However, according to the Director of the Labour Law Department of the Ministry of Labour, the Tusk-led Civil Platform government saw the bill as the 'experimental field' for future *Labour Code* amendments designed to further liberalize and flexibilize labour law (Gienieczko Interview, 22 January 2010, Warsaw). Employer organizations were resolved to lobby for the annual reference periods to be moved into the Code on a permanent basis (Męcina Interview, February 2010, Warsaw; Ambrozik Interview, 26 January 2010, Warsaw). Indeed, a year before the bill's expiry, the issue of a permanent inclusion of the annual reference period was already subject to Tripartite Commission negotiations.

While subject to discussions in the Tripartite Commission, the controversial opt-out provision – the most flexible of the *Working Time Directive* mechanisms – remained available solely in the health-care sector, where it was introduced in 2007 in response to the European Court of Justice *SIMAP* and *Jaeger* rulings by the previous Law and Justice coalition government.[61] When questioned about their views on the opt-out, Jacek Męcina and Adam Ambrozik, representatives of the two key employer associations – the private sector Lewiatan and the Polish Employers' Confederation – confirmed that the provision was on their wish list. However, according to Gienieczko, the Ministry of Labour had a policy

the Managing Director of the IMF, Dominique Strauss-Kahn, tied Poland's exceptional economic performance to its sound transition-era macroeconomic policies.

[61] *Act of 24 August 2007 concerning health care centers*, (2007) Journal of Laws No. 176 item 1240. As discussed in Chapter 3, the *SIMAP* and *Jaeger* rulings interpreted working-time to include time spent on-call, causing significant disruptions in national practice in many Member States, including Poland, primarily by necessitating different scheduling of work, and hiring of new staff. Many Member States, which did not apply the opt-out generally, used it in their health-care sectors. In Poland, the opt-out applied to doctors and other health-care technical professionals. Importantly, while the Polish legislation paired the opt-out provision with a 4-month reference period for averaging, there was no explicit limit on the number of hours worked in any given day or week.

of tackling only one controversial issue at the time, and although Poland officially supported the opt-out at the Community-level negotiations on the *Working Time Directive*'s revision, the Ministry was not yet prepared to tackle this issue at home (Gienieczko Interview, 22 January 2010, Warsaw; Lisicki Interview, 22 January 2010, Warsaw). Well aware that the employers were keen on the opt-out, Gienieczko maintained that such an amendment was 'too politically risky' at the moment, and the unions were most certainly going to pull all stops to oppose it: 'The trade unions could still organize a huge manifestation in Warsaw, in front of the Ministry of Labour, and the symbolic power of this act would be great. No government could afford to have this happen' (Gienieczko Interview, 22 January 2010, Warsaw).

Indeed, Solidarity's role in democratization and liberalization of Poland was a historical fact, and this union was very skilled at employing the historical discourse. Moreover, a large nurses' strike that took place in 2007 in relation to the health-care sector wages and work hours was a fairly fresh reminder that workers were quite capable of drawing in significant public support.[62] Likewise, doctors across Poland had a bitter and drawn-out dispute with the Ministry of Health over unpaid wages and overtime (Kozak 2006). As a result, some were withdrawing, in protest, from the opt-out agreements they signed with their employing institutions (Gazeta 2008a, 2012). With the Labour Minister, Izabella Fedak, busy with a controversial pension reform, this one had to wait (Gienieczko Interview, 22 January 2010, Warsaw), although it was likely to eventually come up again. The representatives of employer organizations seemed to be of a similar mindset. The opt-out very much remained on their agenda (Ambrozik Interview, 26 January 2010, Warsaw) and in their view it was only a matter of time before they would be able to secure it.

5.3 Polish Working-time Regime, Gender, and Social Reproduction

Between Poland's first major post-transition *Labour Code* amendment in 1996 and the 2009 *Anti-Crisis Bill*, the shape and content of the Polish working-time regime changed (see Appendix B). Mainly, this regime became much more flexible than it had been as various systems

[62] The conditions in Poland's health-care sector, particularly observance of working-time norms and wage rates, were subject of the successful Białe Miasteczko (White Village) strike/social solidarity protest staged by the Trade Union of Nurses and Midwives, with significant public support, in front of the Premier Jarosław Kaczyński's Warsaw residence (Gazeta 2008b, 2011). On women as a face of new trade union revival in Poland see Hardy et al. (2008) and Mrozowicki and Trawińska (2013).

of working-time organization and possibilities to incorporate breaks that 'interrupt' the working day gave employers more flexibility in deploying workers and managing the production process. Moreover, with reference periods for averaging weekly hours of up to 12 months available in a wider range of sectors in circumstances, and with lower premium rates, overtime became even cheaper and easier to schedule. As a result, although hours of work – already long prior to 1989 – did not increase significantly, Poles continued to work some of the longest hours in Europe, which, apart from health and safety implications also had particular implications for work–family reconciliation. While some forms of working-time flexibility were introduced to accommodate workers' needs, on the balance, the *Labour Code* flexibility provisions tended to be more employer friendly and biased towards flexibility forms resulting in longer work hours and less predictable schedules. Such forms of flexibility have particular gendered consequences as they impact not only on women's ability to combine the competing demands on their time, their well-being, and how they are perceived as labour market players, but also to hamper the likelihood that men will assume a more active role in the provision of care. As a result, the temporal regime which developed tends to maintain and reinforce a particular gender-based division of labour.

What exacerbates this situation is the fact that while overtime is officially considered to be atypical (Golinowska et al. 2008), observance of working-time norms is poor and the availability of 'family-friendly' flexibility at the firm level is still limited (Solik Interview, February 2010, Warsaw); a reality that representatives of both employer organizations and trade unions agreed on (Męcina Interview, February 2010, Warsaw; Anonymous Interview, 2 February 2010, Warsaw). A lawyer for the OPZZ trade union confederation, referred to this state of play as the distinction between 'rules' and 'life' (Anonymous Interview, 2 February 2010, Warsaw). Indeed, despite the fact that the *de jure* working-time rules the *Labour Code* prescribes are still 'decent', examination of the *de facto* workplace practices reveals a more problematic reality. Excessive overtime is the most common violation observed by the National Workplace Inspection (Państwowa Inspekcja Pracy, PIP), although economic necessity, low wages, and increased consumer appetites mean that workers often willingly take on extra hours. Nonetheless several surveys and reports have clearly shown that employers also drive long hours and uncompensated overtime.

In a 2001 survey on working time distribution conducted by Warsaw's Institute of Labour and Social Studies (IPISS), 65 per cent of respondents worked overtime, of which 22.4 per cent worked in excess of the statutory maximum of 150 hours per year and 28.4 per cent exceeded the daily limit of four overtime hours (Strzemińska 2002: 114–22; Strzemińska 2008b: 59). When asked about their motivation for overtime work, 36.2 per cent cited inability to refuse the request for extra hours and 17.9 per cent attributed it to the inability to fulfil the assigned tasks within the allocated time. While 30.1 per cent of these workers received time in lieu of compensation for their overtime work, nearly a third claimed to have not received any compensation (Strzemińska 2008b: 60). Although the 2001 survey reported higher work hours among men, some of the longest work hours were reported in feminized sectors, such as retail and sales (Strzemińska 2002: 122).

Lack of compliance with working-time regulation in the retail sector, including pressure to work without breaks and put in unpaid overtime, was the subject of a highly publicized controversy surrounding workers in a major supermarket chain, 'Biedronka' (Ladybug), a subsidiary of the Portuguese-owned Jeronimo Martins S.A. The Coalition of Persons Harmed by Biedronka,[63] a network of lawyers, trade union organizers, and the chain's former and current employees was formed to support and address the labour grievances of the mostly unorganized Biedronka staff. In addition to raising public awareness, the network also initiated a series of legal suits in Polish courts, many of which were successful. The cases involved, among others, issues of working-time excesses, uncompensated overtime, and mobbing. The first and most significant of the cases was filed with the District Court in Elbląg by Bożena Łopacka, a former manager at a Biedronka store, who claimed that the chain owed her overtime compensation in the amount of 35,000 PLN (about $10,000) for the years 2000–2002. In September 2004, Łopacka won at the first instance.[64] The case was unsuccessfully appealed[65] and after retrial, Łopacka was awarded compensation of 26,000 PLN for 2,500 hours of overtime. Following this first case, a number of other claims were filed with the courts in 2005 (a rejected class action) and 2007 (27 separate claims) with the company found in violation of the *Labour Code* in ten of them (Kowalski and Kopiński 2005; Rewiński 2005). In 2008, eleven individuals were charged for contravening the *Labour Code* in the Lubuski and Wielopolski districts

[63] See www.stowarzyszenie-biedronka.pl/.

[64] *Łopacka v. Jeronimo Martins, S.A.*, [2004] sygn. akt V P 13/03 (Dist. Ct., Elbląg).

[65] *Łopacka v. Jeronimo Martins, S.A.*, [2005] sygn. akt III Apa 125/04 (C.A. III, Dept. Labour and Social Insurance, Gdańsk).

(Gazeta Lubuska 2008; Regional Prosecutions Office Zielona Góra 2008), another twenty-nine in Gliwicki district in 2009 (Gazeta 2009), and further charges were laid against sixty more individuals, primarily managers of Biedronka stores following a country-wide criminal investigation of thirty-nine Biedronka locations on the grounds of alleged violations of health and safety, forced, uncompensated overtime, falsifying of documentation and schedules, and harassment (Ministry of Justice 2009).

The early Biedronka cases and the network's activities precipitated a major socio-legal study of foreign and domestic supermarkets carried out by the NGO Karat Coalition, with the support of the Friedrich Egbert Foundation. The 2008 study report, *Gender Equality Perspective on the Working Conditions and Respect for Worker's Rights in Supermarkets in Poland* (the Karat Report) (Chmielewska et al. 2008), cites employer practices such as preventing workers from taking restroom breaks, forcing workers to work overtime without pay, or keeping two separate work schedules – the 'official' one for the workplace inspectors, and the one according to which employees were expected to report for work, and which often showed work hours breaching the *Labour Code* provisions (Chmielewska et al. 2008: 23–27). Aleksandra Solik, one of Karat's officers involved in the study, recounted extreme situations reported by workers, including being forced to wear diapers during their shifts to eliminate the need for washroom breaks (Solik Interview, February 2010, Warsaw).

The National Workplace Inspection has noted overtime violations similar to those reported by the Karat Coalition for several years prior. Between years 2001 and 2004, violations included poor maintenance of working-time evidence (sometimes double schedules: one for the inspection, one for the employee), unpaid overtime, and failure to provide rest days, and were motivated primarily by cost-saving and insufficient staffing (Państwowa Inspekcja Pracy 2004: 48; Bednarek 2004). They were most common in retail, repair services, and the food-processing industry, particularly in small firms employing fewer than nine people. Similarly, according to the Inspection's 2006 report, in 2005, 50 per cent controlled workplaces in the retail sector (and 60 per cent overall) were found to keep irregular schedules and insufficient evidence of working-time, 42 per cent failed to provide employees with sufficient daily and weekly rest (while 54 per cent failed to award annual leave), 44 per cent were found in violation of overtime compensation, and 27 per cent failed to observe the average 5-day workweek (Państwowa Inspekcja Pracy 2006: 57, 122, Appendix 24). Large and small, foreign and domestic workplaces were found in breach of the rules.

As a result of these findings, in 2006 the National Workplace Inspection initiated a media campaign and significantly stepped up its efforts with the aim to eliminate pathological non-observance of basic employment norms. In 2008, in addition to its regular work, the state agency carried out over 700 inspections of the Biedronka chains on request of the Public Prosecutor's Office. The Inspections' efforts, along with those of Karat and the 'Biedronka' Coalition, appeared to exert some positive influence, as in its annual reports for the years 2007 and 2008, the Inspection noted significant reduction in violations of working-time regulations in large supermarkets (Państwowa Inspekcja Pracy 2008: 73, 82; Państwowa Inspekcja Pracy 2009: 84). At the same time, employment law violations were so considerable in smaller workplaces that the Inspection referred to them as 'endemic'. According to the report for the year 2008, for instance, violations of rest periods – both the 11 daily and 35 weekly hours – had quadrupled, violations of the average 5-day week rule had tripled, and instances of unpaid overtime had more than doubled (Państwowa Inspekcja Pracy 2009: 84–85). While the report attributed some of the irregularities to lack of proper record keeping or insufficient knowledge of regulations, it also cited purposeful ignoring or sidestepping of regulations by responsible personnel and the practice of prioritizing interests of the firm above legal responsibilities vis-à-vis employees as other common reasons for violations (Państwowa Inspekcja Pracy 2009: 84–85). By 2010, the Polish press was again reporting on poor conditions and practices in Polish retail locales of the French chain Carrefour, as well as those of Real, Makro, Kaufland, and others (Lewińska 2010).

As the 2004 and 2009 Workplace Inspection reports suggested, the need to cut costs to remain competitive is a powerful determinant of labour standards violations. Indeed, the discourse of 'economy on the make' and later, the economic crisis, continued to provide employers with rationales for driving down employment conditions by, for instance, increasing overtime without sufficient compensation. The high levels of labour market insecurity and the tendency to view workers as replaceable mean that employees must often comply with employer requests to retain jobs. As the public sector union confederation, OPZZ, staff lawyer observed, such labour market conditions place workers at a significant disadvantage and compromise their ability to seek redress when their rights are violated (Anonymous Interview, 2 February 2010, Warsaw). The activity of the National Workplace Inspection has been an important step in the right direction; however, the scale of the problem is much larger according to the OPZZ staff lawyer. Limited funding, insufficient inspectorate staff, and the strict requirements involved in the carrying out of inspections mean that many employers get away with employment standard violations (Anonymous Interview, 2 February 2010, Warsaw).

Also, while press reports have been important in bringing attention to the most severe cases of violations, such as those reported at the Biedronka supermarket chain or in other supermarkets, the tendency to highlight problems in large, foreign-owned chains detracts attention from problems within home-grown SME sector (Chmielewska et al. 2008; Solik Interview, February 2010, Warsaw). As the 2004 and 2009 Workplace Inspection reports indicated, this is where the problem is most prevalent. Yet despite the fact that working conditions and management–labour relations in Polish SMEs are regularly likened to nineteenth century exploitation, the recognition that these firms are still 'on the make' and thus have a much harder time competing tends to provide excuses for the violations that occur.

Poland's chronic culture of undeclared overtime, lax observance of the law, and the competitive labour market realities makes survival in the labour market very difficult, particularly for lower skilled workers, and make attainment of better balance between work and family obligations particularly hard. With attitudes towards gender roles remaining traditional, and this traditionalism being further reinforced by the strong presence of socially conservative rhetoric in the political discourse, it is Polish women who are most vulnerable to pressures. Given the dearth of public or affordable care facilities on the one hand, and the persistently unequal sharing of responsibility for care and household activities (Saxonberg and Szelewa 2007; Kotowska et al. 2009: 254), women tend to spend more time on caregiving. While this assumption that women are responsible for care and the residual social provisioning makes them appear to be less committed employees, in reality, women's hours of paid work are insignificantly shorter than men's. Forty per cent of mothers of children under three, and fifty per cent of those whose children are between three and six combine child raising with active employment (Kotowska et al. 2009: 254).

Since part-time work is unpopular[66] and women's wages are required to sustain a family, much as in the People's Republic, contemporary

[66] Kotowska et al. (2009: 244) report that 77 per cent of women and men employed full time express no interest in reducing their hours to part-time. Primary reasons cited are low wages (90 per cent of men and 83 per cent of women). Interestingly, as noted by Kulpa-Ogdowska (2006: 50), the hours of work for women working part-time are not significantly lower than those working full-time.

Polish women's total time of work (including unpaid work) exceeds men's, leaving them with less time for leisure, rest, and education (Bobrowicz 2007). While some women who cannot afford or are unable to secure institutional or private child-care decide to withdraw from the labour market, most remain in the labour market[67] but rely on their mothers or other family members for help with child-care. As Irena Wóycicka (2009: 111) observes, such a 'family model' is the most prevalent model of care in Poland, whether it involves household members or the extended kin network. The existence of this model partially reflects cultural preferences and values. However, Wóycicka (2009: 113) notes that structural factors, such as insufficiency of the public care infrastructure, high costs of private facilities, as well as an 'internalization' of the belief that public care is hard to access, are also significant. Given this context, despite women's reported desire to have children and their preference for having more than one, the double burden on the one hand, and the perception and the reality of workplace discrimination on the other, have caused women to postpone procreative decisions (Matysiak 2009). Indeed, Polish sociologists and demographers have observed that low fertility in Poland is a structural issue (Kotowska and Matysiak 2008; Kotowska 2009), and is only marginally related to change in cultural attitudes. According to Anna Matysiak (2009: 218), a Polish demographer specializing in women's employment and fertility, most Polish women adopt a 'work first, child second' strategy when deciding on having a second or third child.

Gradual acknowledgement of the positive correlation between women's employment and parenthood by policymakers has caused a slight shift in the Polish state's approach to its role in supporting social reproduction. More recently, even the socially conservative parties that advocated the discourses of 'family sovereignty' or the 'family on its own' and emphasized women's temporary or permanent labour market withdrawal (deactivation) have moved away from this approach. The traditional rhetoric of 'work–family conflict' has shifted to one of 'work–family reconciliation', with more emphasis on supporting women's lifelong activation. The impact of EU policy, research contributions and policy recommendations of Polish gender scholars, and presence of progressive women like Kluzik-Rostkowska within conservative political parties has exerted some positive influence on the Polish policy.

[67] Despite the backlash and difficult conditions research shows that most Polish women have retained fairly strong labour market attachment: Chinowska (2000), Steinmetz and Matysiak (2008).

The fact that several important 'family friendly' and positive flexibility provisions have been enacted in the Polish *Labour Code* is a positive development, as is the finding that abuses akin to those reported in relation to overtime have not been found in relation to the provisions meant to support working parents (Państwowa Inspekcja Pracy 2008). However, a number of research reports indicate that the legal availability of 'family friendly' provisions has not yet translated into better workplace practices or more availability of positive working-time flexibility to assist working parents (Gender Index 2007; Balcerzak-Paradowska 2008; Głogosz 2008; Borkowska 2011). While the ESF-sponsored research and awareness-raising campaigns will likely contribute to the spread of work–family reconciliation policies in Polish workplaces, the parallel development of negative forms of flexibility, the entrenched long-hours culture, and the practices of overtime work enabled by the legal framework are worrisome. Given that gender contracts continue to be fairly traditional in many Polish households, this approach increases the likelihood that working time will become polarized along gender lines, making a more egalitarian redistribution of paid and unpaid work unlikely.

5.4 Conclusion

This chapter sought to examine in more detail the process of labour law reform, particularly the *Labour Code*'s working-time rules. Focusing on the period since the 1996 *Labour Code* amendment, it encompassed the process of Poland's EU accession and its first decade of EU membership. As I have shown, since the main impetus for this reform came from the related objectives of flexibilization, adjustment to the realities of the market economy, and harmonization of Polish labour law with the *acquis communautaire*, the political discourse surrounding working-time regulation has also been dominated by the push for flexibility and deregulation. The rationales of protecting workers' rights to leisure and a healthy and safe environment have been largely subordinated, though relevant to the extent that they furthered the project of harmonization or helped different political parties distinguish themselves. While the Left and the 'liberal' Right prioritized employment and support for enterprise (and job growth), 'social solidaristic' and populist parties of the far Right invoked the need to protect workers and secure time for families or religious observance.

Overall, however, the embeddedness of neo-liberalism and the notions that Poland's economy was 'on the make' or 'catching up', the pressures from local business and employers' lobby with parallel fragmentation of the labour movement, Poland's economic troubles and particularly high unemployment at the start of the new millennium, as well as the strict conditionalities of EU accession, combined to elevate the discourse of flexibility above all others. The need to harmonize Polish labour law with EU Directives and the 'soft' requirements of the EES influenced local debates, by, among others, further legitimizing the already present discourses of flexibility, competitiveness, and growth, which were, at the time, being discredited and challenged (at least in relation to employment policy) by the 'social solidaristic' and populist political actors. Thus, the need to comply with 'Europe' provided Polish politicians of the Left with the rationale to pass amendments that were not necessarily popular with the electorate but which, they believed, would address local economic problems of high unemployment and slow growth. In the process, they also responded, albeit partially only, to the lobbying efforts of those actors whose involvement was essential to meeting these economic ends (i.e. employers' organizations) and whose interests were represented by Right-wing liberals. The conflict and fragmentation within organized labour meant that trade unions, while vocal, were not as effective in negotiating their best bargains. As a consequence of this interplay between local dynamics on the one hand, and external pressure of conditionality and softer forms of persuasion on the other, many of the derogations and exclusions prescribed by the *Working Time Directive* were implemented into the Polish *Labour Code* with the effect of making the Code's rules much more flexible than before. Particularly, the legislation of longer reference periods and overtime limits ushered in new ways of increasing working time without increasing pay. As Chapter 4 elaborated, this was a 'true-and-tried' way of dealing with time organization and management in Polish firms. Now, however, it was enacted in a more generalized manner and applicable to a broader range of workers.

With the focus on economic growth, unemployment, and the necessity to adapt Polish law to the realities of market economy, the relationship between working time and gender was rarely considered in the mainstream reform debate. When brought up, the accommodation of care and other family responsibilities was treated separately from 'core' discussions on working time – not unlike at the European level, where concerns around gender equality and work–family reconciliation have only recently featured in discussions on the *Working Time Directive.* Ironically, the populist Right was one of the key actors invoking women's rights as mothers but did so through the discourse of traditional 'family-values', thereby causing a cleavage within the Polish women's movement by alienating feminists. In fact, Polish feminists were so occupied with issues of reproductive rights and the relationship between the Polish state and the Church that the issue of women's working conditions only recently emerged as an agenda point for the Polish women's NGOs and the Polish Women's Congress.

Overall, this marginalization of gender contributed to a working-time regime and forms of flexibility that are biased towards those that benefit employers and enable long work hours. In the context of practices of excessive overtime and poor observance of standards, the implications of such a working-time regime are particularly severe for women because long and unpredictable hours make the balancing of work and family life difficult. At the same time, this type of regime also hampers men's ability to contribute to unpaid work of care, thus reproducing unequal division of labour within the home. As researchers highlighted the problem and women's groups like Karat Coalition began to draw attention to the terrible workplace conditions in feminized sectors, the Polish government began to show more interest in supporting working parents and caregivers in their work–family reconciliation efforts. Progressive women within the state administration spearheaded this new attention, but it was also the case of what Ksieniewicz referred to as 'Brussels imposed requirements' and the influence of EU policy discourses. The fact that Poland still lagged behind the Lisbon targets for women's activation and child-care coverage was likely a sore spot with the Civic Platform government, which projected itself as a truly modern 'European' party. While the party's openness to adopting more family-friendly policy was a positive development and gender equality also featured more firmly on the policy agenda, the underlying rationales for reform continued to be those of women's employment activation and Poland's demographic crisis.

6

Social Reproduction, Gender, Working-time Regulation – Change on the Bedrock of Continuity

6.1 Introduction

As suggested in the introduction, the key objectives motivating this study were scholarly as well as political, since the two are often inseparable in feminist work. I began with a premise that placing gender and the process of social reproduction at the centre of labour law analysis, and showing how legal standards are embedded in a social, political, and economic milieu, help to reveal and destabilize the gendered presumptions and biases that underlie these standards, as well as illuminate how law is constitutive of social relations. This approach enabled me to trouble the traditional model of working-time regulation and its two contemporary articulations. It helped me also better understand the regulatory logic behind the European Union's (EU) bifurcated working-time regime, which, in turn, allowed me to assess whether the model that the EU promotes can indeed support the aspiration of helping women and men more equally share the time spent on paid and unpaid work. The case of Poland proved to be a rich testing ground for both of these endeavours.

In this concluding chapter, I wish to recall and elaborate on some of the most significant findings by reconnecting once again the key themes of social reproduction, gender, and working time; the relationship between the discursive and legislative practices; and the interaction between the EU and Poland. Through this I will also return to the key questions posed at the outset of this book in order to suggest some answers, identify new avenues for research and thinking on this topic, and re-emphasize the political importance of lobbying for a more transformative approach to working time as an essential element of gender equality and social sustainability strategies.

6.2 Gender and Working Time – Continuity and Change

As I showed in Chapter 1, the traditional organization and regulation of working time involved a series of gendered assumptions about ideal-typical workers and their lives, which stemmed from what was regarded to be the appropriate relationship between, and allocation of responsibilities for, the processes of production and social reproduction. In effect, while the standardized hours and patterns of work represented historically significant social settlements, and served to protect workers' leisure time and shield them from risks involved in excessive work, the model these hours and patterns of work engendered had an unequal impact on men and women's respective labour market opportunities. In the case of socialist-era Poland, this model negatively affected working women's quality of life, even when institutional supports for their full employment were made. Crucially, as I showed here, this gendered legacy of traditional standards lives on in the contemporary approach to working time – both at the EU level and in Poland. This is so despite the fact that the rise of work–family conflict following women's mass labour market entry in the West, and its escalation due to retreating state institutions during Poland's systemic transition, have posed a clear challenge to the viability of this model. The Polish case particularly vividly illustrates this model's inherent flaw and its gendered consequences.

The historic snapshot of the People's Republic's model of work organization shows that standard organization and regulation of work hours *can* coexist with full employment of all adults where the institutional supports for care and social reproduction are in place. Yet that case also reveals the gendered tensions at the heart of a working-time regime based on long standard hours of work. As I discussed in Chapter 4, even in the context of fairly extensive social provisions, having to work long hours posed a serious problem when the residual unpaid work of care and maintenance had to be carried out within households, and when, according to the traditional gender contract and Poland's cultural specificity, the responsibility for this work fell to women. It was women who paid the highest price for this temporal regime, which came at a cost to their rest and leisure, their health and well-being, and their career prospects.

If the double burden were not enough, the unsustainability of this regime became even more evident with Poland's transition to a market economy. The conditions set by the state's retrenchment and re-privatization of most responsibility for welfare, coupled with high insecurity, rising unemployment, and the emergence of an employer's labour market in which working more, for less, was the daily reality, put this regime to a severe test. Combining full employment with responsibilities involved in having a family and maintaining standards of living became a source of particularly high tension. Women's compromised ability to absorb this tension resulted, on the one hand, in a significant drop in the Polish fertility rate (a prudent way for individuals and households to deal with uncertainty and economic insecurity). On the other hand, women's labour market exit, or the experience of being 'pushed out', was related to either the perception that women must be 'unburdened' to carry on their traditional duties or that they were unreliable employees by virtue of these duties.

I do not suggest that the persistence of long working hours was the sole reason for the strife so many Polish women experienced during the process of transition, or that this case is fully generalizable to other contexts. However, the Polish case is a striking reminder of the close relationship between social reproduction and production, and it clearly shows that working-time regimes that require long work hours without adequately accommodating work within the home are inherently unsustainable, or sustained at major costs of inequality and depressed standards of living. Importantly, this case also illustrates that the subordination of social reproduction to the needs of production and accumulation is not only unique to capitalism but had also taken place in command economies, despite the different institutional and ideological context. The practical outcomes these processes yielded in the People's Republic – women's full employment at the cost of a double burden – confirm both the importance of institutional arrangements, which made it possible for women to participate more or less equally albeit at a cost because these arrangements were not sufficient, but also the power of cultural values that provided a bedrock of continuity for the country's traditional gender order despite the official philosophy of egalitarianism espoused by the party-state leadership.

In this context of long hours of work, insecurity, and pressure to compete against other labour market participants, including men, the potential impact of a more gender-friendly working-time regime could have been significant in Poland. Indeed, one of the early assumptions that I made was that working-time regulation is a good testing ground for some positive EU influence, particularly in light of the emphasis that the Community discourse and policy proscriptions place on supporting work–family reconciliation and gender equality. Nonetheless, as my analysis reveals, the reality has fallen short of the promise. On the contrary, the gradual re-regulation of the Polish *Labour Code*'s working time rules exemplifies that the promulgation of the dominant economic discourses (of flexibility, productivity, efficiency, and growth) at the EU level has had a more significant effect in the domestic arena and in the field of working-time regulation, than the EU's promotion of equality.

This outcome is perhaps unsurprising, given that the EU working-time regime has itself been unevenly gendered, and that despite an increased emphasis on work–family reconciliation, the more traditional rationales for regulation in this area – the protection of health and safety and the demands of the production process – have been much more influential in the context of regular work hours. More so, what I have argued here is that the failure to adopt a more gender-sensitive model of working-time regulation at the EU level in the first place, and to subsequently modify it comprehensively to reflect new social objectives, stems from the historic and ongoing tension between those traditional regulatory rationales. The persistence and strength of the focus on productivity are especially striking, as it is evident in the proposals, recommendations, and negotiations spanning nearly two decades (from the early 1970s) before the adoption of the *Working Time Directive* in 1993. While a range of rationales were invoked in support of a Community-level working-time measure through the 1980s, and the Directive was eventually adopted as a health and safety instrument in 1993, my analysis suggests that the objectives of productivity, efficiency, and the needs of firms were always paramount; the one that was chosen simply provided a traditional reference point and a convenient legal basis for action. The fact that the fundamental conflicts over the original Directive's legitimacy, particularly the UK's opposition to it, had less to do with whether the needs of production and economy were indeed crucial (this was not disputed), and more with how these needs ought to be served (through a regulated flexibility approach or a non-interventionist deregulatory one) tends to support such a reading. Indeed, so does the fact that the finally adopted Directive provides for significant flexibility to extend working hours beyond the set limits – a fairly traditional method of adapting work organization to production needs.

The Polish example demonstrates this high visibility of productivity rationales for working-time regulation in an even more striking manner, because the requirements of production, efficiency of firms (or state enterprises), and economic performance have been dominant in the context of two very different political–economic realities: a socialist command economy and a liberal free market democracy. Indeed, deference to economic objectives during both periods contributed to long work hours, although somewhat differently obtained, being the defining feature of Poland's working-time regime 'then' and 'now'. As we have seen in Chapter 4, the justifications for long hours, overtime, and other types of working-time extensions have morphed from those emphasizing the need to build socialism and meet demands of the Plan, to those of building capitalism, supporting growth, and creating the conditions for the most efficient running of firms. This discursive 'shift' has gone hand in hand with one in management practices: from 'extensive managing' of the People's Republic era characterized by the belief that more hours lead to better productivity, to the contemporary utilization of employer-driven, often uncompensated overtime, largely for the same reasons. The continuity and similarity of these rationales and practices is quite remarkable, particularly in the face of Poland's otherwise profound political–economic and ideological transition.

Again, it may not be in itself surprising that the requirements of the productive process and the needs of firms balanced with the protection of health and safety have been such central rationales in the context of discussions on regulation of work hours. What is significant, however, is that this dual focus has over time subordinated other potential considerations or goals that regulation of working time could serve, particularly in the context of rules related to standard, full-time work, with the result of precluding their more transformative reconceptualization. As I showed in Chapters 2 and 3, the EU-level discursive universe has indeed for some time now contained other social rationales, including those of work–family reconciliation or redistribution of work between marriage partners and hence promotion of equal opportunities. The 1983 *Draft Recommendation* and the Commission's overall approach to working time through the early 1980s show that well. Yet, these rationales were filtered out of the discursive universe surrounding the *Working Time Directive*, instead being deemed as better addressed by instruments providing for the flexibility to reduce hours of work (part-time work) or to accommodate parents (parental leave). To be clear, the development of these other forms of flexibility, while often rationalized as a more adaptable and individualized way to manage work, and ones that are more family friendly, at its core also reflected demands of the new organization of production prompted by technological innovation, competitive pressures of the new economy, and a particular ideology.

The more recent recognition that work–family reconciliation objectives must be mainstreamed in order to promote more gender-equal distribution of work has broadened the universe of political discourse surrounding the *Working Time Directive*. However, this has not translated into policy or regulatory change, as there are still no binding provisions that recognize objectives of work–family reconciliation in the context of full-time work hours. Of course, this point must be qualified with a recognition that the Directive's revision ultimately failed for a number of other reasons. Yet it was evident over the course of the 2004–2009 consultation and review process that the inclusion of such a provision would have been unlikely, particularly since some of the key actors (primarily the employers' organizations) openly contested its addition on the basis that it did not comply with the more narrow legal basis on which the instrument is justified. Moreover, the Council and the employers lobby's insistence on the retention of the controversial opt-out provision made plain that even if a binding provision on work–family reconciliation were incorporated, its effect would have been largely undermined by simultaneous sanctioning of long hours of work.

In effect, as it is currently conceived, the EU approach to working time provides for accommodation of care-giving responsibilities only in those regulations that address what would have once been considered atypical forms of work, while leaving untouched the standards prescribed by the *Working Time Directive.* This means that despite its supposed neutrality, the Directive retains and reproduces the gendered legacy of the traditional employment model because the norms and the derogations it prescribes take for granted workers' availability for full-time or extended work hours. As such, this key instrument and the working-time regime for which it forms a foundation are in conflict with the EU gender-mainstreaming policy and, in practice, are unlikely to provide incentives for a more egalitarian redistribution or re-allocation of work.

6.3 Europeanization of the Polish Working-time Regime

As I outlined in Chapters 4 and 5, the reform of Polish labour law was at the heart of both processes of transition and EU accession, and both proceeded largely along the same trajectory. In face of allegations that high labour costs and rigid regulations are out of step with Poland's new economic realities, working-time reform, particularly in the direction of more flexibility, was deemed to be a top priority. Poland's difficult economic situation, particularly in the years immediately preceding EU accession, only fuelled the process of regulating a more employer-friendly legal framework. While the change was uneven, over the course of Poland's accession preparations the working-time regime became progressively flexibilized and 'Europeanized'. By 2003, the rules of the Polish *Labour Code* governing hours of work had come to contain many of the provisions of the *Working Time Directive* (and some provisions of the Directives governing part-time and fixed term work). Paradoxically, transposition of this 'protective' instrument facilitated enactment of a more employer-friendly working-time regime because Polish legislators elected to apply many of the Directive's exclusions and derogations, enabling new forms of flexibility to extend work hours previously unavailable in Poland. And, as I have argued in Chapter 5, this process continued over the course of the first decade after accession.

While conditionality of accession explains partially the EU influence in Poland's working-time reform, it is also evident that the EU agenda and policy discourses were not 'blindly' adopted but instead utilized by local actors to advance or add clout to their own policy objectives. These economic discourses were already prominent in Poland before the start of the accession process, since the country's structural adjustment in the early 1990s was itself heavily shaped by neo-liberalism and the deregulation ethos. With Polish politicians setting the objective of joining the EU fairly early on, the flexibility discourses operating at the EU level found a fertile ground in Poland and with certain local actors, since they matched and reinforced ideas already shaping Poland's regulatory approach after 1989. Although the politicians of the liberal Right and the employers' lobby (acting largely through the Civic Platform and the Freedom Union parties) pushed for even more far-reaching reforms, it was the governing Left Democratic Alliance – the country's only major social-democratic party – that delivered the most significant labour law reform packages in 2002 and 2003. While referring to itself as a 'workers' party' and attempting to forge better alliances with trade unions (through social dialogue, albeit not with much success), the party nonetheless was both keen to satisfy increasingly well-organized Polish employers and entrepreneurs who were ultimately central to its long-term economic plan and convinced that more flexibility was indeed needed to combat unemployment. Citing the necessity to comply with 'Europe' served to justify changes in labour law that were sufficiently unpopular to have cost the party its 2004 election. Ironically, a striking path dependency emerges as even by the populist Law and Justice, a party with the Solidarity pedigree and a 'social-solidaristic' orientation that replaced the Left, continued the introduction of the Directive's flexibility provisions, implementing the opt-out provision in the health-care sector in 2007. More expectedly perhaps, the same reform trajectory was continued by the business-friendly Civic Platform, which assumed office in 2007 and remained in power until 2015, and which introduced annual reference periods through the emergency 2009 *Anti-Crisis Bill* and subsequently made them a permanent *Labour Code* provision.

All this suggests that local political actors used the process of adopting EU norms, beyond the actual need to comply with the European *acquis*, to 'solve' domestic policy problems and implement their respective versions of neo-liberal labour regulation. The interplay between external pressures of conditionality and opportunism of internal, motivated actors, as conceptualized by the rationalist approaches to Europeanization, was certainly at operation here. By contrast, less organized actors, such as trade unions (because they were so fragmented) or the women's movement (due to fragmentation but also the fact that it was focused on other issues, i.e. reproductive rights) were not able to influence the process in the same way, with the result that their interests were subordinated.

A similar internal–external dynamic is also visible in the context of the more recent attention to work–family reconciliation in working-time policy, which also results from EU pressure, albeit mostly of the 'soft' kind, in combination with local concerns about the need to simultaneously increase employment and fertility rates to improve the still lagging rates of employment and counteract the knock-on effects of Poland's unfavourable demographic profile. Here, EU targets, like those set in Lisbon, and the mechanisms of praise or shaming that are involved in the review of local progress and publication of statistical data, were very effective, particularly with parties like the Civic Platform, which wished to project a 'modern' and 'European' image. More significantly perhaps, these forms of pressure also proved effective even with very conservative and Euro-phobic parties, like Civic Platform's predecessor Law and Justice, although in the latter case the work of feminist activists, progressive woman-friendly politicians, and directed funding was needed to ensure this outcome. Hence, Poland's participation in the Lisbon strategy translated into some positive developments on the work–family reconciliation front, and the importance of assisting families and fostering equal opportunities for women and men to engage in employment and caregiving appeared to have finally started to resonate with Polish politicians. At the same time, it is hard not to be somewhat sceptical about the real motivations that lie under this shift, particularly in light of feminist critiques of EU gender mainstreaming policy, and given my own findings regarding both the shape and the egalitarian potential of the EU working-time regime and the enduring traditionalism of the Polish gender order. This scepticism is particularly reinforced when we remember that implementation of EU norms ultimately facilitated a working-time regime that keeps many Poles working long hours, which in fact conflicts with the objectives of ensuring work–family reconciliation opportunities for everyone.

Overall, the case of working-time reform reveals a complex relationship between Poland and the EU, with both the EU and local actors being crucial in shaping the Polish universe of political discourse and legislative practice. There has been a definite policy convergence around the need for flexibility, which with the EU's 'help' has been reinforced as the key discourse and employment policy objective in Poland. While some positive forms of flexibility have been enacted into the Polish *Labour Code* also because of the EU influence, the practical deployment of flexibility in Polish workplaces has been skewed towards the flexibility to extend work hours, with part-time work remaining unpopular with Poles and other family-friendly forms of flexibility unavailable to most employees in practice. Although most people, women and men, continue to work similar hours, the polarized, bifurcated approach to working-time developed at the EU level threatens to replicate such polarization in Poland should part-time work become more common. Indeed, temporary work, another temporal form of work regulation the EU has promoted, has increased so rapidly in Poland over the last several years that a quarter of all jobs are now temporary, making it the highest proportion in all of the EU. Apart from that development, for the time being, the Polish working-time regime has taken its key cue from the *Working Time Directive* and the long-hours end of the working-time spectrum.

While it may not be entirely appropriate to characterize the EU-Polish relationship as a reflexive or a symbiotic one given that the adoption of EU policies was a legal requirement for Poland's 2004 accession, this relationship will likely change as the position of Poland within the EU stabilizes, its political–economic standing improves, and its ability to influence EU working-time policy increases. Indeed, Poland's alliance with the UK over the course of the *Working Time Directive*'s 2004–2009 unsuccessful revision attempt was already an indication that the country's influence was growing and that its policy preferences might with time be more clearly reflected in the EU policy and regulation (see Szczerbiak 2012). At the same time, the recent victory of Law and Justice, which unseated Civic Platform in the 2015 Parliamentary and Presidential elections, makes it difficult to predict how Poland's role in the EU will continue to evolve.

6.4 Towards a More Egalitarian and Socially Sustainable Model of Working-time Regulation?

As we know from comparative institutional studies, working-time regimes are important predictors of equality because they delimit the range of actual arrangements available for women and men to organize and allocate their time between labour market participation and unpaid work of care and maintenance (Figart and Mutari 1998, 2000, 2001). It is now widely acknowledged that those working-time regimes that enable more equal distribution of hours between men and women, and among different institutions, tend to be more egalitarian, because they are most likely to support models of universal citizen/caregiver (Fraser 1997) or equal worker/equal caregiver. The assumption that underlies this, of course, is that such a more equal redistribution of time will 'free' men to partake in unpaid work in the home, while also creating opportunities for women to engage in paid employment in ways that preserve their chances of advancement, satisfy their career goals, and maximize their financial independence. Even if the precise bargains and arrangements that people strike with each other and within their families should ultimately be a matter of personal preference and choice, policy and law should ensure that all choices and preferences can indeed be exercised and satisfied without detriment to those who make them. This type of policy approach would also entail the recognition that all work is valuable, whether carried out within the context of standard employment, otherwise carried out within the market, or performed out of love and care or obligation, and likely without remuneration. As such, it would challenge the very assumptions underlying standard norms and re-integrate social reproduction into the productive process by erasing the artificial boundaries that have been created between them and by treating both as necessary and interrelated processes. Such a visionary view of working-time regulation and the more general total social organization of work, is precisely the sort that Catélene Passchier, the ETUC's Confederal Secretary, referred to (Chapter 3). Yet, as I have argued here, the regulatory frameworks that exist at the EU level or in Poland do not yet engender the sort of norms that would facilitate this vision in a truly meaningful way. While both regimes have modified the traditional, gendered standards, both still contain norms and forms of temporal adaptation not easily reconcilable with the tasks involved in the process of social reproduction, with the care needed to support one's own well-being and other lives being a key part of this process.

Since 2010, the *Working Time Directive* has been subject to another review and is at the time of writing in the hands of the European Commission. When the current review process began, there was promise that a more progressive recasting of the Directive's approach and its standards might be possible. As noted in Chapter 5, the Commission's *Roadmap to Equality* for the years 2010–2015, which was issued shortly before the Directive's first review Communication,[1] rather explicitly identified the unequal gender division of labour in the home as a key obstacle to achievement of equality, and pointed to regulation of work hours as one element of a potential solution. Similarly, the Commission's consultation documents and the social and economic impact assessments[2] produced prior to their issuing indicated that the matters of work–family reconciliation and gender equality, which had been already included in the 2004–2009 revision process, were still on the agenda. Also significant was the fact that previously uninvolved groups like the European Women's Lobby have now expressed a more active interest in the issue of working time, as regulated by the Directive. The coming into force of the *Charter of Fundamental Rights of the European Union*, which recognizes the right to reconciliation of work and family (Article 33(2)) and the right to the limitation of the maximum work-time (Article 21(2)), was another important development, and one that organized labour strongly emphasized in its responses to the Commission's consultation call (ETUC 2010).

At the same time, however, this latest review process has been taking place in a particularly unfriendly economic and political climate. The EU response to the global financial crisis and its aftermath, for example, left few illusions about the subordinate position of social and employment policy, and raised serious questions about the depth of EU's commitment to social cohesion and gender equality. Following the initial stimulus packages adopted at national levels on the advice of the Commission, since 2010 the EU coordinated response shifted to imposing stringent macroeconomic discipline and forcing some EU members to impose fiscal austerity and adopt further deregulation measures that, among others, left many national working-time regimes (Barnard 2012), including the Polish one, even more deregulated and flexible than before. During the same period, attention to gender and its mainstreaming greatly diminished on the EU policy agenda (Smith and Villa 2010), even though the economic crisis that followed the 2008 financial one disproportionately affected women's labour market standing, while the subsequent policies

1 *Review of the Working Time Directive. First-phase Consultation of the Social Partners at the European Union Level under Article 154 of the TFEU.* Communication from the Commission to the European Parliament, the European Economic and Social Committee and the Committee of Regions. COM (2010) 92 final (24 March 2010).

2 *Study to support an Impact Assessment on Further action at European level regarding Directive 2003/88/EC and the Evolution of Working Time Organization* (21 December 2010) (hereinafter Deloitte Study); *Flexible Working Time Arrangements and Gender Equality: A Comparative Study of 30 European Countries.* EU Expert Group on Gender and Employment Report, Janneke Plantenga and Chantal Remery (eds). European Commission: Directorate General for Employment, Social Affairs and Equal Opportunities, 2009.

of austerity undermined the social support institutions on which women and families often rely (Walby 2009; Bieling 2012; Leschke and Jepsen 2011, 2012).

Against this backdrop, how likely is it that the Directive's revision will be used to champion a more transformative vision of working-time regulation? The legal limitations inherent in the EU's institutional architecture, and in the reach of its competences and the comparative power and influence of its various actors are still present, much as they were in 2009. To address the legal limitations inherent in the health and safety basis for the Directive, the ETUC has suggested updating the Directive's Article 13 principle of 'adaptation' in order to encompass the needs of a feminized and increasingly diversified workforce (ETUC 2010: 7). In the past consultation, the ETUC also proposed to re-characterize work–family reconciliation as a health and safety issue; rejecting the opt-out on these dual basis. Indeed, a broad definition of health and safety could encompass a right to a healthy life; a life that leaves people ample time to partake in their family and community lives, since personal well-being is ultimately connected with one's ability to maintain familial bonds and social relations. The assumption that all working people should be entitled to have this expanded notion of health protected could also in the long term support the goal of diminishing the gender differentials in paid and unpaid work.

As good as this sounds, however, such a view has not found widespread support. The social partners have not been able to – again – come to a consensus on how to revise the Directive. The red lines they drew in their responses to the Commission's consultations largely mirrored those from the previous round, with the result that the instrument is now in the Commission's hands once again, and it remains to be seen what proposals the latter will draw up for the European Parliament and the Council to consider. The Commission's ongoing regulatory fitness exercise (REFIT), which seeks to simplify and streamline EU legislation means that the Directive will be modified to keep it up to date, but it is difficult to anticipate what this modification might entail. Given that most Member States now use the Directive's Article 22 opt-out in one way or another, it is very unlikely that its removal will be an option, as the Commission has acknowledged already. A series of legal challenges involving paid annual leave,[3] sick leave, and most recently, travelling time,

[3] See Commission Staff Working Paper *Detailed Report on the Implementation by Member States of Directive 2003/08/EC concerning certain aspects of the organization of working time ('The Working Time Directive')*, SEC(2010) 1611 final (21 December 2010): 126–135.

also add a new dimension to the current revision. Moreover, the post-crisis regulatory developments, including the 2010 macroeconomic governance reforms, which have empowered EU's finance bodies and national finance ministries (Klatzer and Schlager 2014), suggest that opportunities for transformative social action are probably even more circumscribed now than they had ever been, and that indeed, further erosion of the Directive is a possibility. While the *Charter of Fundamental Rights* may act as the necessary buffer to prevent the curtailment of the rights the Directive currently enshrines, which is why the organized labour's consultation responses so strongly relied on it, improving on them is probably unlikely. Given that the Commission's 2015 Roadmap on work-life balance[4] and the associated first-phase consultation of social partners 'on the possible action addressing the challenges of work-life balance faced by working parents and caregivers'[5] make no reference to the *Working Time Directive*, the likelihood that the latter's revision proposal will seek to incorporate focus on issues concerning accommodation of care and its redistribution between women and men remains rather low.

Thus, in this new, post-crisis environment, the developments surrounding the *Working Time Directive* demand ongoing critical scrutiny. The extent to which this instrument will engender a more holistic approach to working time will reflect on the EU's broader commitments to gender equality but also on its current commitment to building a more socially sustainable and inclusive economic order in the long term. A robust recognition that work–family reconciliation is an issue potentially affecting all workers – those at the 'core', and so covered by the *Working Time Directive*, and those on the 'margins' of the labour market – would be a concrete and a crucial step towards creating regulations and a policy environment that supports these goals. This kind of development would be consistent with the recognition that the time for care is a right (Busby 2011), just as much as it is a responsibility, although this should not preclude development of institutional solutions and good quality care provision to which everyone has access. Given the growing care needs of the aging population, a more robust right to work–family reconciliation combined with supportive institutions is, indeed, a

[4] Roadmap for the initiative "New start to address the challenges of work-life balance faced by working families. (August 2015) http://ec.europa.eu/smart-regulation/roadmaps/docs/2015_just_xxx_maternity_leave.en.pdf.

[5] First Phase Consultation of Social Partners Under Article 154 TFEU on *Possible Action Addressing the Challenges of Work-Life Balance Faced by Working Parents and Caregivers*, C(2015) 7754 final (11 November 2015).

pressing matter. Given that older people are increasingly expected to, or forced to, lead 'active' lives, including through labour market participation into later life, their rights as care providers, not just receivers, should be also paramount, as many of them will inevitably have to combine paid work with care of their aging spouses or grandchildren.

But beyond the urgency to recognize the need to create a more predictable care and family-friendly working-time regime, and the potential long-term social and economic benefits that such a regime might facilitate, policymakers have to also come to terms with broader issues associated with organization of work, whether or not these issues are instrumental to achieving an economic bottom line. A change in our work and economic practices is urgently needed for other reasons as well, and the time to begin the shift is now. In early 2012, the London School of Economics held a conference sponsored by the New Economics Foundation on the latter's proposals for the 21-hour workweek.[6] If working-time reductions have been deemed by some to be a relic of the past, the scholars at this conference foresaw the exact opposite. Juliet Schor, an American economist and sociologist of working time, claimed that periods of financial downturn are precisely the moments when we should work less, not more. She rejected the conventional wisdom that periods such as these necessitate that people 'buckle down' and work harder as a great fallacy. In proposing a 21-hour workweek for all workers, she cited economic, social, and environmental reasons. Indeed, similar calls have been made by other scholars (see Hermann 2014) and policy think tanks, who rationalize the need to reduce work hours as a prudent way to not only improve people's life quality but also to curb consumption and its consequences for ecological sustainability.

These are not easy proposals, as asking people in 'on the make' countries like Poland or in the developing world to accept less income as a trade-off for shorter work hours is unlikely to meet with wide approval, nor will most firms volunteer a bigger share of their profits to keep wages constant should hours be reduced. But, such strategies might not only be effective for rethinking how to best organize the articulation between life and paid work, they might be actually inevitable in the long-term to address the pressing problems associated with climate change. For now, whether or not a 21-hour or even a 30-hour workweek is a feasible

[6] The report that was launched at this event is entitled *21 Hours: Why a Shorter Working Week Can Help Us All Flourish in the 21st Century*. The report is available on the New Economics Foundation website: www.neweconomics.org/publications/entry/21-hours.

proposal remains an open question. It makes perfect sense, however, that a working-time regime that is based on shorter hours of work for all would help to redistribute paid work among people, and in the process free up time for all sorts of other work that is required for the maintenance of lives, or simply for a life beyond work, as Kathi Weeks (2011) provokes us to imagine. Working less might just be one crucial step towards fostering closer human bonds, more equal gender relations, time for what we will, and ultimately, a more economically and ecologically sustainable world.

Appendix A

Statistical Tables

Table A.1 *Poland: Gross Domestic Product, Constant prices (per cent change), 1990–2009*

	1990	1991	1992	1993	1994	1995	1996	1997	1998	1999
GDP	7.171	−7.005	2.033	4.287	5.239	6.728	6.239	7.086	4.982	4.524
	2000	2001	2002	2003	2004	2005	2006	2007	2008	2009
GDP	4.253	1.205	1.443	3.867	5.345	3.617	6.227	6.785	5.127	1.650

Source: International Monetary Fund, World Economic Outlook Database, April 2011

Table A.2 *Poland: unemployment rate (per cent of total labour force), 1990–2009*

	1990	1991	1992	1993	1994	1995	1996	1997	1998	1999
Unemployment Rate	6.3	11.8	13.6	14.0	14.4	13.3	12.4	11.25	10.6	13.9
	2000	2001	2002	2003	2004	2005	2006	2007	2008	2009
Unemployment Rate	16.1	18.3	19.9	19.7	19	17.8	13.9	9.6	7.1	8.2

Sources: GUS Labour Force Survey 2005 (1992–2004); Eurostat Online

Table A.3 *Poland: employment activation (EA), employment rate (ER) as percentage (%), by gender, 15–64 Yrs.*

	1992		1993		1994		1995		1996		1997		1998		1999		2000	
	EA%	ER%																
Total	61.7	53.4	60.9	52.3	60.2	51.5	58.8	50.9	58.2	51.0	57.7	51.2	57.4	51.3	56.7	48.8	56.6	47.5
Men	70.2	61.6	69.2	60.4	68.2	59.3	66.8	58.7	66.2	59.0	65.9	59.6	65.6	59.4	64.4	56.4	64.1	54.9
Women	54.3	46.1	53.3	45.1	53.0	44.5	51.5	43.9	51.0	44.0	50.3	43.7	50.0	43.9	49.7	41.8	49.7	40.7

	2001		2002		2003		2004		2005		2006*	2007		2008*	2009*
Total	56.4	46.1	55.4	44.4	54.8	44	54.7	44.4	55.2	45.9	54.5	53.5	48.4	59.2	59.3
Men	63.8	53.1	62.9	50.9	62.2	50.4	62.4	51	62.9	53.2	60.9	61.9	56.2	66.3	66.1
Women	49.5	39.7	48.6	38.4	47.9	38.2	47.8	38.2	48.1	39.2	48.2	45.9	41.3	52.4	52.8

Sources: GUS 2005 Labour Force Survey (1992–2004), GUS 2008 (2007), Eurostat Online

* Employment Rate only, Eurostat

Table A.4 *Poland: part-time employment as percentage (%) of total employment, by gender, 15–64 Yrs.*

	1992		1993		1994		1995		1996		1997		1998		1999		2000	
Total	10.7		10.7		10.1		10.5		10.7		10.1		10.4		10.5		11.2	
M W	8.9	12.9	8.9	12.8	7.8	12.9	8.2	13.3	8.1	13.8	7.9	12.7	8.1	13.1	8.5	13	8.7	14.2
	2001		2002		2003		2004		2005		2006		2007		2008		2009	
Total	10.8		9.6		9.3		9.6		9.8		8.9		8.5		7.7		7.7	
M W	8.8	13.2	7.3	12.2	6.9	12.1	7.1	12.5	7.0	13.3	6.2	12.2	5.8	11.7	5.1	10.9	5.0	10.5

Sources: GUS Labour Force Surveys (1992–2001), Eurostat Online (2002–2009)

Table A.5 *Poland: hours of paid full-time employment (main job), by gender*

	1992		1997		2002		2004		2007
	M	W	M	W	M	W	M	W	
Ave. work hrs/week	45.7	40.7	44.2	39.2	42.9	38.6	43.7	37.9	42.9*

Sources: GUS 2005 Labour Force Survey (1992–2004), Eurostat Online

* Average only, Eurostat Online

Appendix B

Key Features of the Polish Working-time Regime Over the Years

Table B.1 *Hours of work and overtime limits*

	People's Republic-era 1945–1989	Transition 1990–1997	Accession-era 1998–2004-2009
Weekly/Daily Hours	46/8, 42/8	42/8 up to 9	42, 41, 40/8
Daily Hours Particular Categories	10, 12	10, 12	10,12 (seasonal)
Reference Periods	• 1 wk (basic), 2 wks (drivers) • 4 wks (retail, essential services, continuous work) • 3 wks (security, guarding) • 1 m (seasonal work) • 24 wks (anti-crisis)	• 3 m (basic) • 1 m (essential services) extendable to 3 m by collective agreement • 6 m (specific sectors)	• 3 m increased to 4 m in 2002 (basic) • 6 m (seasonal work) • 12 m (seasonal, technological process and production needs; special needs of employer)
Overtime Limits	48 or 56 per week maximum 120 per year	4 hrs daily 150 per year Requirement to notify of overtime; right to refuse overtime	4 hrs daily; later increased to 5 48 hrs per week 150 per year; with limits up to 416 per year permitted by collective agreement, workplace regulation or employment contract Rest periods: 11 hrs per day and 35 hrs per week

(*cont.*)

Table B.1 (*cont.*)

	People's Republic-era 1945–1989	Transition 1990–1997	Accession-era 1998–2004-2009
Overtime Compensation	50% first 2 hrs above norm 100% for additional hrs above set norm, during night-time, Sundays, and holidays Time in lieu of overtime pay: EE's request	Lump sum payment	50% for all hrs 100% holidays and Sundays Employers decide to pay out overtime or time off in lieu

Table B.2 *Special accommodations and non-standard work arrangements*

	People's Republic-era 1945–1989	Transition 1990–1997	Accession-era 1998–2004-2009
Special accommodations	Mat. Leave: 16, 18, 26 wks; 14 or 4 wks foster mothers. Child-raising Leave: 3 yrs Child-care Leave: 60 d/year Breast-feeding Breaks: 2 × 30 min, or 45 min Leave for Sick Child: 2 days (available to lone fathers)	Mat. Leave: 16, 18, 26 wks. Child-raising Leave: 3 yrs, extended to fathers Child-care Leave: 60 d/year Breast-feeding Breaks: 2 × 30 min, or 45 min Leave for Sick Child: 2 days (available to lone fathers)	Mat. Leave raised in 2001: 20, 30; later 26, 36wks (16 wks obligatory, non-obligatory portion extended to fathers) Mat. Leave reduced in 2002: 16, 18, 26 (14 obligatory) Child-raising Leave: option for both parents to take up at the same time Right to request reduced working time for employees eligible for child-raising leave and corresponding duty to accommodate 4 day annual "on demand" Leave

	People's Republic-era 1945–1989	Transition 1990–1997	Accession-era 1998–2004-2009
			Breast-feeding Breaks: 2 × 30 min, or 45 min Leave for Sick Child: 2 days (available to lone fathers)
Special flexibility measures and non-standard arrangements	No part-time provisions Variable start and end times (experimental) Self or team scheduling/'Own account' (experimental)	No part-time provisions Limit on number of consecutive fixed-term contract Provisions for collective negotiations of working-time reductions	Part-time work promotion; later equal treatment Temporary, fixed-term work equal treatment Interrupted working time, breaks of up to 5 hrs in 24hrs Weekend working, Reduced workweek, Individual working-time schedule

Appendix C

Key *Labour Code* Amendments 2001–2009 Provisions on Working Time and Work–family Reconciliation

Amendment	Working time	EU *acquis*	Work–family reconciliation and equality	EU *acquis*
0.1.03.2001 **Dz.U. Nr 28, poz 301**	Art. 129 **Working-time reduced to 40** (phased in; 01.01.2003)			
24.08.2001 **Dz.U. Nr 123, poz 1354**	*Repealed* Art. 129^6 Working-time in road transport shifted to separate statute; 'interrupted' working-time system deleted from *Labour Code*			
24.08.2001 **Dz.U. Nr 128, poz 1405**			Art. 189^1 (1)(2) Right for **parents to share/take up at the same time child-raising leave**, up to 3 months	96/34
21.12.2001 **Dz.U. Nr 154 poz 1805**			Art. 180, 180^1 **Maternity leave reduced:** 16 wks – first birth 18 wks – subs. birth 26 wks – multiple birth 8 wks – stillbirth Arts. 47, art. 50(5), art. 57(2), art. 163, art. 177(5), art. 180(5–7), art. 183(3) **Parental rights extended to fathers**	
26.07.2002 **Dz.U. Nr 135, poz 1146**	Art. 191(1), $(1^1)(1^2)$ **Ref. period extended**: 4, 6 or 12m Art. 129^{5a} 'Interrupted' work-time extended to all types of work organization	93/104	Art 167^{2-3} Employee entitled to **a portion of annual leave (4 days) 'on demand'**	

Amendment	Working time	EU *acquis*	Work–family reconciliation and equality	*EU acquis*
	Art. 129[11](2) No need to evidence working time in task- or project based work organization Art. 129[10](2)(3) 60 min unpaid break during working day Art. 134 **Reduced overtime compensation**		Art. 186(3) **Right to request reduced working-time** for employees entitled to child-raising leave	
	Art. 133(2) **Increased annual overtime to 416** Art. 143(2) Employer to decide whether overtime compensation paid out or time in lieu Art. 163(1[1]) Employer not required to plan annual leave schedule Art. 167 [1] Employee can be required to take up annual leave during the period of notice to dissolve contract			
14.11.2003 Dz.U. Nr 213			Art. 11[3], 18[3a], 29[2] (1) **Prohibition of discrimination in employment,** including on grounds of part-time and fixed-term work	2000/78 2000/43 99/70 97/81
14.11.2003 Dz.U. Nr 213	Art 129 Principle of averaging" 5-day workweek		Art. 94 point 2a Employer to **organize work in a manner least burdensome to worker**, particularly work that is monotonous or at a set rate	03/88/C
	Art. 131 Maximum weekly time inclusive of overtime is 48 hours, averaged over the accepted reference period (Managerial workers excluded)	03/88/C	Art. 94[2] Employer to **inform** employee about **possibility of full or part-time employment**, and fixed term employees about **permanent vacancies**	99/70 97/81
	Art. 132 Minimum **daily rest** periods: **11** hrs (Managerial and rescue workers excluded; entitled to equivalent rest periods)	03/88/C	Art. 142 **Individual working-time** scheduling possible w/in the adopted working-time system	

(*cont.*)

Amendment	Working time	EU *acquis*	Work–family reconciliation and equality	*EU acquis*
	Art. 133 Minimum **weekly rest** period: **35** hrs, including at least 11 hours uninterrupted daily rest (Managerial, rescue workers, and shift workers entitled to uninterrupted weekly rest of at least 24hrs); Rest day should be Sunday, or another day, if Sunday work permitted in the workplace/system of work organization.	03/88/C	Art. 148 Pregnant women or parents of children under 4 years of age not be employed in the systems of work prescribed by arts. 135–138, 143, 144	
	Art. 135–138 **Various derogations from daily, weekly working time** 'equivalent working time' system, 'supervision or machinery' or where readiness to work required, 'guarding of property, lifesaving, firefighting', 'where technological requirements, reasons related to work-organization or provision of essential services require that work not be interrupted'	03/88/C	Art 154 Annual Leave 20 days – to 10 yrs 26 days – after	03/88/C
	Art. 143, Art. 144 Employee can request to work in system of reduced week and weekend-work (full-time hours)		Art. 292(2) Possibility of reducing working time to part-time	97/81
	Art 151 **Daily limit of possible overtime** set by the 11-hour rest (art. 131) (previously 4 hrs)	03/88/C	Art. 25(1) Limits the number of fixed-term contracts; 3rd equivalent to permanent if break b/w consecutive contracts no longer than 1 month (Suspended until 01.05.04)	99/70
	Art 151^{10} Sunday or weekend work permitted for shift workers			
	Art. 151^{11} Extended period for granting time off in lieu of holiday or Sunday work			
	Art 151^{12} Sunday rest – every 4th Sunday (previously 3rd)			
	Art. 154^{2} Annual leave calculation rules: by hour	03/88C		

Amendment	Working time	EU *acquis*	Work–family reconciliation and equality	*EU acquis*
	Art. 171 Annual leave can only be compensated through "in lieu" "equivalent" on dissolution of employment relationship			
19.12.2006 **Dz.U. Nr 221** **poz 1621 AA**			Art. 180 **Maternity leave extended** 18 weeks 20 weeks 28 weeks (Also to foster and adoptive parents)	
24.08.2007 **Dz.U. Nr. 176,** **poz 1239**	Art. 151^{9-11} Prohibition on work carried out by employees in retail on 12 additional holidays			
06.12.2008 **Dz.U. Nr. 237** **poz 1654**			Art 180 para 1 Maternity leave extended Art. 180 para 6^{1-3} Fathers entitled to portion of maternity leave if mother hospitalized Art. 182^{1-2} Additional, non-mandatory maternity leave (2 weeks, as of 2010; 4 weeks as of 2012; 6 weeks as of 2014) Also available to adoptive parents. Leave can be combined with part-time work Art. 182^{3} Father's leave – 1 week in 2010, 2 weeks as of 2012 Art 184 Right to maternity benefits extended to the non-mandatory leave portion and Father's leave Art. 186^{8} Special protection of workers entitled to child raising leave and taking advantage of reduced working-time arrangements (during 12months) Art. 189^{1} Restrictions on sharing the additional non-mandatory maternity leave by both parents	

REFERENCES

Primary Sources

International Conventions

Convention concerning the Reduction of Hours of Work to Forty a Week, Geneva, 19th ILC session (22 June 1935), C0 47 (in force 23 June 1957).

European Union Materials

Treaties

Treaty Establishing the European Coal and Steel Community, 18 April 1951, 261 U.N.T.S. 140 (expired 23 July 2002).

Treaty Establishing the European Economic Community, 25 March 1957, 298 U.N.T.S. 3.

Merger Treaty, 1965, [1967]O.J. 152 (repealed).

Treaty on European Union (EU), 7 February 1992, [1992]O.J. C 191/1, 31 I.L.M. 253.

Treaty of Amsterdam, 2 October 1997, [1997]O.J. C 340/1, 37 I.L.M. 56.

Treaty of Nice Amending the TEU, the Treaties Establishing the European Communities and Certain Related Acts, 26 February 2001, O.J. C 80/1.

Treaty of Lisbon, Amending the Treaty on European Union and the Treaty Establishing the European Community, Signed at Lisbon, 13 December 2007, O.J. C 306/01.

Single European Act, 17 February 1986, [1987]O.J. L 169/1, 25 I.L.M. 506.

Council of the EU: Directives, Resolutions, Positions, Recommendations, Drafts

Charter of Fundamental Rights of the European Union, [2010]O.J. C 83/389.

Common Position No. 23/2008 of 15 September 2008 adopted by the Council of 15 September 2008, with a view to the adoption of a Directive of the European Parliament and of the Council amending Directive 2003/88/EC concerning certain aspects of the organisation of working time, [2008]O.J. C 254 E/3/18.

Council Directive 75/117/EEC of 10 February 1975 on the approximation of the laws of the Member States relating to the Application of the principle of equal Pay for men and women, [1975]O.J. L 45/19.

Council Directive 76/207/EEC of 9 February 1976 on the implementation of the principle of equal treatment for men and women as regards access to employment, vocational training and promotion, and working conditions, [1976]O.J. L 39/40.

Council Directive 78/610/EEC of 29 June 1978 on the approximation of laws, regulations and administrative provisions of the Member States on the protection of health of workers exposed to vinyl chloride monomer, [1978]O.J. L 197/12.

Council Directive 89/391/EEC of 12 June 1989 on the introduction of measures to encourage improvements in the safety and health of workers at work, [1989]O.J. L 183/ 1.

Council Directive 90/394/EEC of 28 June 1990 on the protection of workers from risks related to exposure to carcinogens at work, insofar as it relates to carcinogens other than asbestos, [1990]O.J. L 196/1.

Council Directive 91/533/EEC of 14 October 1991 on the employer's obligation to inform employees of the conditions applicable to the contract or employment relationship, [1991]O.J. L 288/32.

Council Directive 93/104 EC of 23 November 1993 concerning certain aspects of the organization of working time, [1993]O.J. L 307/18 (repealed).

Council Directive 96/34/EC of 3 June 1996 on the Framework Agreement on Parental Leave concluded by UNICE, CEEP and the ETUC, [1996]O.J. L 145/4.

Council Directive 97/75/EC of 15 December 1997 amending Directive 96/34/EC of 3 June 1996 on the Framework Agreement on Parental Leave, [1998]O.J. L 10/24.

Council Directive 97/81/EC concerning the Framework Agreement on Part-time Working concluded by UNICE, CEEP and the ETUC, [1998]O.J. L14/9.

Council Directive 98/23/EC of 7 April 1998 amending Directive 97/81/EC concerning the Framework Agreement on Part-time Working, [1998]O.J. L 131/10.

Council Directive 99/70/EC of 28 June 1999 concerning the Framework Agreement on Fixed-term Work concluded by UNICE, CEEP and the ETUC, [1999]O.J. L 175/43.

Council Directive 2000/34/EC of the European Parliament and of the Council of 22 June 2000 amending Council Directive 93/104/EC concerning certain aspects of the organization of working time to cover sectors and activities excluded from that Directive, [2000]O.J. L 195/41.

Council Directive 2000/43/EC of 29 June 2000 implementing the principle of equal treatment between persons irrespective of racial or ethnic origin, [2000]O.J. L 180/22.

Council Directive 2000/78/EC of 27 November 2000 establishing a general framework for equal treatment in employment and occupation, [2000]O.J. L 303/16.

Council Directive 2002/15/EC of the European Parliament and of the Council of 1 March 2002 on the organization of the working time of persons performing mobile road transport activities, [2002]O.J. L 80/35.

Council Directive 2003/88 EC of the European Parliament and of the Council of 4 November 2003 concerning certain aspects of the organization of working time, [2003]O.J. L 299/9.

Council Directive 2005/47/EC of 18 July 2005 on the Agreement between the Community of European Railways (CER) and the European Transport Workers' Federation (ETF) on certain aspects of the working conditions of mobile workers engaged in interoperable cross-border services in the railway sector, [2005]O.J. L 195.

Council Directive 2009/13/EC of 16 February 2009 implementing the Agreement concluded by the European Community Shipowners' Associations (ECSA) and the European Transport Workers' Federation (ETF) on the Maritime Labour Convention, 2006, and amending Directive 1999/63/EC, [2009]O.J. L 124/30.

Council Resolution of 21 January 1974 concerning a Social Action Programme, [1974] O.J. C 013/1.

Council Resolution of 18 December 1979 on the adaptation of working time, [1980]O.J. C 2/1.

Council Resolution of 6 December 1994 on certain aspects for a European Union social policy: a contribution to economic and social convergence in the Union, [1994]O.J. C 368/6.

Council Resolution of 15 December 1997 on the 1998 Employment Guidelines, [1998]O.J. C 30/1.

Council Resolution of 22 December 1999 on the 1999 Employment Guidelines, [1999]O.J. C 96/2.

Regulation (EC) No 561/2006 of the European Parliament and of the Council of 15 March 2006 on the harmonisation of certain social legislation relating to road transport and amending Council Regulations (EEC) No 3821/85 and (EC) No 2135/98 and repealing Council Regulation (EEC) No 3820/85 (Text with EEA relevance) – Declaration, [2006]O.J. L 102.

Regulation (EC) No 1899/2006 of the European Parliament and of the Council of 12 December 2006 amending Council Regulation (EEC) No 3922/91 on the harmonisation of technical requirements and administrative procedures in the field of civil aviation (Text with EEA relevance), [2006]O.J. L 377.

Draft Council Recommendation of 23 September 1983 on the reduction and reorganization of working time, COM (83) 543 (final), [1983]O.J. C 290/4.

European Commission: Communications, Green and White Papers, Proposals, Progress Reports, Other Documents

Action for Employment in Europe: A Confidence Pact, CSE (96) 1 final (5 June 1996).

Action Programme relating to the Implementation of the Community Charter of Basic Social Rights for Workers. Communication from the Commission. COM (89) 568 final (29 November 1989).

Agenda 2000. Commission Opinion on Poland's Application for Membership in the European Union, DOC/97/16 (15 July 1997).

Amendment to the Proposal for a Council Directive on the Organization of Working Time, [1991]O.J. C 124/06 (14 May 1991).

Commission of the European Communities. *Community Charter of Fundamental Social Rights for Workers.* Luxembourg: Commission of the European Communities, 1990.

Commission Staff Working Paper *Detailed Report on the Implementation by Member States of Directive 2003/08/EC concerning certain aspects of the organization of working time ("The Working Time Directive")*, SEC (2010) 1611 final (21 December 2010).

Commission Staff Working Document. *Report on Progress on Equality Between Women and Men in 2013.* COM(2014) 224 final, SWD(2014) 141 final (14 April 2014).

Draft Council Recommendation on the Reduction and Reorganization of Working Time. Information Memo. COM (83) 543, P-80/83 (September 1983).

Employment in Europe Report – 2006 (not published in the Official Journal). http://europa.eu/legislation_summaries/employment_and_social_policy/situation_in_europe/c11336_en.htm/.

Europe 2020. A Strategy for Smart, Sustainable, and Inclusive Growth. Communication from the Commission. COM (2010) 2020 final (3 March 2010).

European Social Policy: A Way Forward for the Union. White Paper. COM (94) 333 final (27 July 1994).

European Social Policy: Options for the Union. Green Paper. COM (93) 551 (17 November 1993).

First Phase Consultation of Social Partners Under Article 154 TFEU on *Possible Action Addressing the Challenges of Work-Life Balance Faced by Working Parents and Caregivers*, C(2015) 7754 final (11 November 2015).

Follow-up to the Essen European Council of Employment. Communication from the Commission to the Council. COM (95) 74 final (8 March 1995).

Growth, Competitiveness, Employment: The Challenges and Ways Forward into the 21st Century. White Paper. COM (93) 700 final (5 December 1993).

Memorandum on the Reduction and Reorganization of Working Time. Information Memo, P-77/82 (December 1982).

Partnership for a New Organization of Work. Green Paper. COM (97) 128 final (16 April 1997).

Poland's Progress towards Accession. 1998 Regular Report from the Commission (4 November 1998). http://ec.europa.eu/enlargement/archives/pdf/key_documents/1998/poland_en.pdf

Poland's Progress towards Accession. 1999 Regular Report from the Commission (13 October 1999). http://ec.europa.eu/enlargement/archives/pdf/key_documents/1999/poland_en.pdf

Poland's Progress towards Accession. 2000 Regular Report from the Commission (8 November 2000). http://ec.europa.eu/enlargement/archives/pdf/key_documents/2000/pl_en.pdf

Poland's Progress towards Accession. 2001 Regular Report from the Commission of the European Communities. SEC (2001) 1752 (13 November 2001).

Poland's Progress towards Accession. 2002 Regular Report from the Commission of the European Communities. COM (2002) 700 final (9 October 2002).

Proposal for a Council Directive on voluntary part-time work, [1982]O.J. C 62/7.

Proposal for a Directive of the Council on temporary work, [1982]O.J. C 128/2.

Proposal for a Council Directive Concerning Certain Aspects of the Organization of Working Time. COM (90) 317 final; SYN 295 (20 September 1990).

Proposal for a Council Directive on the Organization of Working Time, [1990]O.J. C 254/4 (9 December 1990).

Proposal for a Directive of the European Parliament and of the Council Amending *Directive 2003/88/EC concerning certain aspects of the organization of working time.* COM (2004) 0607 final, COD (2004) 0209 (n.d.).

Re-examination of *Directive 93/104/EC concerning certain aspects of the organization of working time.* Communication from the Commission to the Council, the European Parliament, the European Economic and Social Committee and the Committee of Regions and the Social Partners at the Community Level. COM (2003) 843 final/2 (15 January 2004).

Report from the Commission to the Council, the European Parliament, the European Economic and Social Committee and the Committee of Regions – Equality between Men and Women – 2010. COM (2009) 0694 final (18 December 2009).

Report from the Commission to the European Parliament, the Council and the European Economic and Social Committee on the implementation by Member States of Directive 2003/88/EC concerning certain aspects of the organization of working time ('The Working Time Directive') COM (2010) 802 final (21 December 2010).

Reviewing the Working Time Directive. First-phase Consultation of the Social Partners at the European Union Level under Article 154 of the TFEU. Communication from the Commission to the European Parliament, the Council, the European Economic and Social Committee, and the Committee of the Regions. COM (2010) 106 final (24 March 2010).

Reviewing the Working Time Directive. Second-phase consultation of the social partners at European level under Article 154 TFEU. Communication from the Commission to the European Parliament, the Council, the European Economic and Social Committee and the Committee of Regions. SEC (2010) 1610 final (21 December 2010).

Roadmap to Equality between Women and Men 2006–2010. Communication from the Commission to the Council, the European Parliament, the European Economic and Social Committee and the Committee of the Regions. COM (2006) 92 final (1 March 2006).

Roadmap for the Initiative "New Start to Address the Challenges of Work-Life Balance Faced by Working Families" (August 2015). http://ec.europa.eu/smart-regulation/roadmaps/docs/2015_just_xxx_maternity_leave.en.pdf.

Second Phase of Consultation of the Social Partners at the Community Level Concerning the Revision of *Directive 93/104/EC concerning certain aspects of the organization of working time* (2004). http://ec.europa.eu/social/main.jsp?catId=706&langId=en&intPageId=205.

Sectors and Activities Excluded from the Working Time Directive. White Paper. COM (97) 334 final (15 July 1997).

State of Implementation of *Directive 93/104/EC of 23 November 1993 concerning certain aspects of the organization of working time.* COM (2000) 787 final (1 December 2000).

Strategy for Equality between Women and Men 2010–2015. Communication from the Commission to the European Parliament, the Council, the European Economic and Social Committee and the Committee of the Regions of 21 September 2010. COM (2010) 491 final (21 September 2010) (not published in the Official Journal).

Strengthened Commitment to Equality between Women and Men. A Women's Charter Declaration by the European Commission on the Occasion of the 2010 International Women's Day in Commemoration of the 15th Anniversary of the Adoption of a Declaration and Platform for Action at the Beijing UN World Conference on Women and of the 30th Anniversary of the UN Convention on the Elimination of All Forms of Discrimination against Women. Communication from the Commission. COM (2010) 0078 final (5 March 2010).

Taking Stock of Five Years of the European Employment Strategy. Communication from the Commission. COM (2002) 416 final (17 July 2002).

Voluntary Part-time Work. Communication from the Commission. COM (80) 405 final (17 July 1980).

European Council Documents

Presidency Conclusions, Lisbon European Council, 23–24 March 2000, Bull EU-3/2000, 7–17.

European Parliament Documents

Committee on Women's Rights and Equal Opportunities. Opinion for the Committee on Employment and Social Affairs on Organization of Working Time (revision of *Directive 93/104/EC*), 2003/2166 INI (20 January 2004).

Codecision News. A Newsletter from the European Parliament Conciliations and Codecision Secretariat. No. 2 (28 April 2009).

Recommendation for Second Reading on the Council Common Position for Adopting a *Directive of the European Parliament and the Council amending Directive 2003/88/EC concerning certain aspects of the organization of working time,* 10597/2/2008, C6-0324/2008, 2004/0209 COD (11 November 2008).

Report on the Organization of Working Time (amendment of *Directive 93/104/EC*), 2003/2165 INI (29 January 2004).

Report on the Proposal for a Directive of the European Parliament and of the Council amending Directive 2003/88/EC concerning aspects of the organization of working time, COM (2004) 0607, C6-0122/2004, 2004/0209 COD (22 September 2004.).

Resolution on the Organization of Working Time (amendment of *Directive 93/104/EC*), 2003/2165 INI (11 February 2004).

Other EU Documents and Records

Deloitte Study 2010. *Study to support an Impact Assessment on Further action at European level regarding Directive 2003/88/EC and the evolution of working time organization* (21 December). http://ec.europa.eu/social/main.jsp?catId=706&langId=en&intPageId=205

Enlarging the European Union: Achievements and Challenges. Report of Wim Kok to European Commission (26 March 2003).

Facing the Challenge: the Lisbon Strategy for Growth and Employment. Report from the High-Level Group Chaired by Wim Kok (November 2004). Luxembourg: Office for Official Publications of the European Communities.

Opinion of the European Economic and Social Committee on the Proposal for a *Directive of the European Parliament and of the Council amending Directive 2003/88/EC concerning certain aspects of the organization of working time,* COM (2004) 607 final, 2004/0209 COD, [2005] O.J. C 267/03 (27 October 2005).

Opinion of the European Economic and Social Committee on the Communication from the Commission to the Council, the European Parliament, the European Economic and Social Committee and the Committee of the Regions and the Social Partners at the Community Level concerning the Re-examination of *Directive 93/104/EC concerning certain aspects of the organization of working time,* [2004] O.J. C 302/6 (7 December 2004).

Social Partners: Documents, Positions, Press Releases

BusinessEurope 2008a. Press Release, "European Parliament Employment Committee Position Endangers Fragile Compromise on Working Time", 5 November.

2008b. Press Release, "Working Time: EP Deprives Companies of Necessary Flexibility", 17 December.

2008c. Working Time Directive – Joint Letter from BusinessEurope, UEAPME, CEEP and Eurochambres to Members of the European Parliament Ahead of their Plenary Vote on 17 December.

2009a. *Go for Growth: An Agenda for the European Union in 2010–2014*. Brussels: BusinessEurope.

2009b. Position Paper: Conciliation Procedure on the Revision of the Working Time Directive, 10 March.

ETUC (European Trade Union Congress) 2004a. ETUC Plan to Revise the Working Time Directive. Adopted by the ETUC Executive Committee, 13–14 October.

2004b. Position in the Second Phase of Consultation of the Social Partners at the Community Level on the Revision of *Directive 93/104/EC concerning certain aspects of the organization of working time*, 9–10 June.

2004c. Position Paper on the Communication from the Commission of 30/12/2003 concerning the Re-examination of *Directive 93/104/EC concerning certain aspects of the organization of working time*, 17–18 March.

2005a. Contribution of the European Trade Union Confederation to the Debate on the Revision of the Working Time Directive. European Parliament Employment and Social Affairs Committee, 17 January.

2005b. Press Release. ETUC is Urgently Calling on the Commission to Support the European Parliament's Amendments on Revision of the Working Time Directive, 25 May.

2005c. Press Release. Revision of the Working Time Directive: The ETUC Calls on the Council and the Commission to Respect European Treaties and Fundamental Rights, 7 December.

2006a. Position on the First Stage Consultation of the Social Partners at the Community Level on the Reconciliation of Professional, Private and Family Life, December.

2006b. "Reconciling Professional, Private and Family life: A Key Objective for the European Trade Union Movement". *Newsletter*. Brussels: European Trade Union Congress.

2009. ETUC Executive Committee 8 July 2009: Declaration on the Working Time Directive, 8 July.

2010. "The Working Time Directive: Limitation of Working Hours and More Influence of Workers, for Healthier Lives". Position of the ETUC on the Communication of the European Commission of 24 March 2010, 3 June.

UNICE 2004a. Position on the Commission Communication Concerning the Re-examination of *Directive 93/104 EC concerning certain aspects of the organisation of working time*, 4 March.

2004b. Position on Re-examination of *Directive concerning certain aspects of the organisation of working time*, 29 July.

2004c. Press Release, UNICE Sees No Prospect of Negotiations on Working Time, 19 May.

2004d. Press Release, Working Time Directive: European Commission Fails to Improve Working Time Flexibility, 22 September.

National Law and Policy Materials Poland

Constitutions

Constitution of the Polish People's Republic of 22 July 1952, (1952) *Journal of Laws*, No. 33, item 232.

Constitution of the Polish Republic of 2 April 2 1997, (1972) *Journal of Laws*, No. 78, item 483.

Legislation, Decrees, and Regulations

Act concerning Protection of Socialist Work Discipline, (1950) *Journal of Laws*, No. 20, item 168.

Act No. 158 of the Council of Ministers of 24 May 1968 concerning Unpaid Leave for Working Mothers Caring for Young Children, (1968) *Law Monitor*, No. 24, item 154.

Act No. 14 of the Council of Ministers of 14 January 1972 concerning Child-care Social Assistance, (1972) *Law Monitor*, No. 5, item 27.

Act of 6 July 1972 on Extension of Maternity Leaves, (1972) *Journal of Laws* No. 27, item 190.

Act No. 41 of the Council of Ministers of 6 February 1974 concerning the Rules and Timelines for Introduction of Additional Holidays in 1974 and 1975, (1972) *Law Monitor*, No. 6, item 43.

Act of 26 June 1974 concerning the Labour Code, (1974) *Journal of Laws*, No. 24, item 141.

Act of 21 July 1983 concerning Special Legal Regulation during Socio-economic Crisis and concerning the Amendment of Certain Acts, (1983) *Journal of Laws*, No. 39, item 176.

Act of 23 May 1991 concerning the Resolution of Collective Disputes, (1991) *Journal of Laws*, No. 55, item 236.

Act of 2 February 1996 concerning the Amendment of the Labour Code and Certain Other Statutes, (1996) *Journal of Laws*, No. 24, item 110.

Act of 19 November 1999 concerning the Amendment of the Labour Code, (1999) *Journal of Laws*, No. 99, item 1152.

Act of 1 March 2001 concerning the Amendment of the Labour Code, (2001) *Journal of Laws*, No. 28, item 301 (in force 1 May 2001).

Act of 25 April 2001 concerning the Amendment of the Labour Code, (2001) *Journal of Laws*, No. 52, item 538.

Act of 24 August 2001 concerning the Amendment of the Labour Code, (2001) *Journal of Laws*, No. 128, item 1405.

Act of 21 December 2001 concerning the Amendment of the Labour Code, (2001) *Journal of Laws*, No. 154, item 1805.

Act of 14 November 2003 concerning the Amendment of the Labour Code, (2003) *Journal of Laws*, No. 213, item 2081.

Act of 24 August 2007 concerning Health Care Centres, (2007) *Journal of Laws*, No. 176 item 1240.

Act of 1 July 2009 concerning Easing the Effects of the Economic Crisis for Employers and Employees, (2009) *Journal of Laws*, No. 125, item 1035.

Decree of the Council of Ministers of 20 July 1972 on Additional Holidays, (1972) Journal of Laws, No. 29, item 203.

Decree of 20 July 1972 on Additional Holidays, (1973) *Journal of Laws* No. 29 item 160.

Decree of the Council of Ministers of 21 February 1986, regarding Increasing Working Time in Some Enterprises during the Period of 1986–1990, (1986) *Journal of Laws*, No. 6, item 34 (repealed).

Decree of the Minister of Labour and Social Policy of 27 July 1999 concerning the Establishment of the Labour Law Reform Commission, (1999) *Law Monitor*, No. 26, item 404 (in force 30 July 1999, repealed on 1 July 2002).

Six-Year Plan of Economic Development and Construction of the Socialist System 1950–1955, Act of 21 July 1950, (1950) *Journal of Laws*, No. 37, item 344.

Three-Year Economic Reconstruction Plan (1947–1949), Act of 2 July 1947, (1947) *Journal of Laws*, No. 53, item 285.

Preparatory Documents*

Committee for Small and Medium Enterprises Proposal concerning the amendment of the Labour Code, Doc. No. 560 (27 July 1998).

Members' Proposal concerning the amendment of the Labour Code, Doc. No. 500 (3 July 1998).

Members' Proposal concerning the amendment of the Labour Code and certain other statutes, Doc. No. 334 (12 February 2002).

Proposal of the Government concerning the amendment of the Labour Code, Doc. No. 1565 (9 December 1999).

Proposal of the Government concerning the amendment of the Labour Code and certain other statutes, Doc. No. 335 (20 March 2002).

Senate Proposal concerning the amendment of the Labour Code, Doc. No. 490 (7 July 1998).

Strategic Documents and Policy Papers

Enterprise-Growth-Work. Economic Strategy of the SLD-UP-PSL Government adopted by the Council of Ministers, January 2002.

* All documents available from the Parliament of Polish Republic Archives. www.sejm.gov.pl/archiwum/arch2.html.

Entrepreneurship First. Program adopted by the Council of Ministers on 29 January 2002 as part of the Economic Strategy of the SLD-UP-PSL: "Government Enterprise-Growth-Work".

Family Policy Program. Warsaw: Inter-departmental Group for the Development of the Government Family Policy Program Headed by the Plenipotentiary for the Affairs of Women and the Family, 1997.

National Pro-Family Policy. Document adopted by the Council of Minsters on 3 November 1999. Government Review, November-December (101).

National Strategy for Employment Growth and Human Resource Development for the Years 2000–2006. Warsaw: Ministry of Labour and Social Policy, 1999.

Strategy for Poland. Mid-term Socio-economic Policy Program adopted by the Parliament of Poland on 20 October 1994. *Law Monitor* No. 57, item 486 (16 November 1994).

Transcripts of Parliamentary Proceedings**

No. 63 (26 October 1995).
No. 65 (23 November 1995).
No.72 (1 February 1996).
No. 91 (24 October 1996).
No. 17 (6 May 1998).
No. 28 (16 September 1998).
No. 31 (13 October 1998).
No. 32 (21 October 1998).
No. 34 (9 November 1998)
No. 53 (2 July 1999).
No. 28 (16 September 1999).
No. 59 (6 October 1999).
No. 94 (15 December 2000).
No. 108 (11 May 2001).
No. 109 (23 May 2001).
No. 112 (4 July 2001).
No. 119 (18 September 2001).
No. 117 (23–24 August 2001).
No. 8 (13 December 2001).
No. 27 (25 July 2002).

Polish Court Decisions

High Court, Judgment of 9 October 1997, III ZP 20/99, OSNAPiUS 1998 nr 5, poz. 143).

Łopacka v. Jeronimo Martins, S.A., [2004]sygn. akt V P 13/03 (Dist. Ct., Elbląg).

** All transcripts available from the Parliament of the Polish Republic Archives. http://orka2.sejm.gov.pl/Debata2.nsf/.

Łopacka v. Jeronimo Martins, S.A., [2005]sygn. akt III Apa 125/04 (C.A. III, Dept. Labour and Social Insurance, Gdańsk).

Social Partner Documents

Lewiatan 2001a. Position of the Polish Confederation of Private Employers concerning the proposal to amend of the Labour Code, undertaken by the Parliament on 23 August 2001.

2001b. Position of the Polish Confederation of Private Employers concerning the Act prepared by the Ministry of the Economy: "Entrepreneurship First" (7 December 2001).

2002. Polish Confederation of Private Employers on the Labour Code Amendment Act adopted by the Parliament and signed by the President on 21 August 2002.

NSZZ "Solidarność" 2002a. Position of the National Committee concerning the amendment of the Labour Code. No. 146/02 (30 July 2002).

2002b. Position of the National Committee concerning the Proposal for the amendment of the Labour Code, No. 209/02 (22 October 002).

United Kingdom

Working Time Regulations 1998, S.I. 1998/1833.

Working Time Regulations 1999, S.I. 1999/3372.

Interviews

Adam Ambrozik, Legal Expert, Employers of Poland (26 January 2010), Warsaw.

Alejandro Cercas, MEP, Group of the Progressive Alliance of Socialists and Democrats, EP Special Rapporteur on Working Time (23 February 2010), Brussels.

Agnieszka Chmielecka, former Activist, Coordinator of NGO Social Dialogue, Department of Women, Family and Anti-Discrimination, Ministry of Labour and Social Policy (11 February 2010), Warsaw.

Anonymous, Policy Officer, European Commission's DG Employment, Social Affairs, Inclusion (17 February 2010), Brussels.

Anonymous, Staff Lawyer, European Commission, DG Employment, Social Affairs, Inclusion (17 February 2010), Brussels.

Anonymous, Staff Lawyer, All-Poland Trade Union Alliance (OPZZ) (02 February 2010), Warsaw.

Eugenia Gienieczko, Director of the Labour Law Department, Ministry of Labour and Social Policy (22 January 2010), Warsaw.

Joanna Kluzik-Rostkowska, Member of the Polish Parliament (Law and Justice), former Minister of Labour and Social Policy (25 March 2010), Warsaw.

Monika Ksieniewicz, Gender Expert, Department of Women, Family and Anti-Discrimination, Ministry of Labour and Social Policy (26 January 2010), Warsaw.

Jean Lambert, Member of the European Parliament, Group of the Greens/European Free Alliance (23 February 2010), Brussels.

Robert Lisicki, Legal Specialist, Labour Law Department, Ministry of Labour and Social Policy (25 January 2010), Warsaw.

Jacek Męcina, Legal Expert, Confederation of Polish Private Employers "Lewiatan" (February 2010), Warsaw.

Catélene Passchier, Confederal Secretary, European Trade Union Congress (16 February 2010), Brussels.

Fernando Pereira, Deputy Head of the Unit for Equality, Action against Discrimination, Legal Questions, European Commission, DG Employment, Social Affairs, Inclusion (17 February 2010), Brussels.

Jørgen Rønnest, Chair of BusinessEurope Social Affairs Committee (16 February 2010), Brussels.

Aleksandra Solik, Women's Rights Program Manager, Karat Coalition (February 2010), Warsaw.

Brian Synnott, former Communications and Campaigns Officer, European Federation of Public Service Unions (18 February 2010), Brussels.

Barbara Surdykowska, Staff Lawyer, Independent Self-Governing Trade Union "Solidarity" (27 January 2010), Warsaw.

Ewa Tomaszewska, Solidarity activist, former Member of Polish Parliament (Electoral Action Solidarity) and MEP (25 February 2010), Warsaw.

Secondary Sources

Abels, Gabriele and Mushaben, Joyce Marie (eds.) 2012. *Gendering the European Union: New Approaches to Old Democratic Deficits.* Basingstoke: Palgrave Macmillan.

Acker, Joan 1988. "Class, Gender and the Relation of Distribution", *Signs* 13: 473–97.

Adam, Barbara 1995. *Timewatch: The Social Analysis of Time.* Cambridge: Polity.

Adnett, Nick and Hardy, Stephen 2001. "Reviewing the Working Time Directive: Rationale, Implementation and Case Law", *Industrial Relations Journal* 32 (2): 114–25.

Ahlberg, Kerstin, Bercusson, Brian, Bruun, Niklas, and Kountouros, Haris 2008. *Transnational Labour Regulation: A Case Study of Temporary Agency Work.* Oxford: Peter Lang.

Albo, Gregory 2010. "The 'New Economy' and Capitalism Today", in Pupo, Norene J. and Thomas, Mark P (eds.). *Interrogating the New Economy: Restructuring Work in the 21st Century*, 3–20. Toronto: University of Toronto Press.

Alter, Karen J 2000. "European Union's Legal System and Domestic Policy: Spillover or Backlash?", *International Organization* 54 (3): 489–518.

Alter, Karen J. and Vargas, Jeannette 2000. "Explaining Variation in the Use of European Litigation Strategies: European Community Law and British Gender Equality Policy", *Comparative Political Studies* 33 (4): 452–82.

Anxo, Dominique 2004. "Working Time Patterns Among Industrialized Countries: A Household Perspective", in Messenger, Jon C. (ed.). *Working Time and Workers' Preferences in Industrialized Countries: Finding a Balance*, 60–107. London: Routledge.

Anxo, Dominique, Fagan, Colette, Lee, Sangheon, McCann, Deirdre, and Messenger, Jon 2004a. "Introduction: Working Time in Industrialized Countries", in Messenger, Jon C. (ed.). *Working Time and Workers' Preferences in Industrialized Countries: Finding a Balance*, 1–9. London: Routledge.

2004b. "Implications for Working Time Policies", in Messenger, Jon C. (ed.). *Working Time and Workers' Preferences in Industrialized Countries: Finding a Balance*, 195–211. London: Routledge.

Arat-Koc, Sedef 2006. "Whose Social Reproduction? Transnational Motherhood and Challenges to Feminist Political Economy", in Bezanson, Kate and Luxton, Meg (eds.). *Social Reproduction: Feminist Challenges to Neo-liberalism*, 75–92. Montreal: McGill-Queens University Press.

Ashiagbor, Diamond 2004. *The European Employment Strategy: Labour Market Regulation and New Governance.* Oxford: Oxford University Press.

2006. "Promoting Precariousness? The Response of EU Employment Policies to Precarious Work", in Fudge, Judy and Owens, Rosemary (eds.). *Precarious Work, Women, and the New Economy: The Challenge to Legal Norms*, 77–97. Oxford: Hart.

Atkinson, John 1984. *Flexibility, Uncertainty and Manpower Management.* IMS Report No. 89. Brighton: Institute of Manpower Studies.

Bakker, Isabella 2003. "Neoliberal Governance and the Reprivatisation of Social Reproduction: Social Provisioning and Shifting Gender Orders", in Bakker, Isabella and Gill, Stephen (eds.). *Power, Production and Social Reproduction*, 66–82. New York: Palgrave Macmillan.

2007. "Review Essay: Social Reproduction and the Constitution of a Gendered Political Economy", *New Political Economy* 12 (4): 541–56.

Bakker, Isabella and Gill, Stephen 2003a. "Global Political Economy and Social Reproduction", in Bakker, Isabella and Gill, Stephen (eds.). *Power, Production and Social Reproduction*, 3–16. New York: Palgrave Macmillan.

(eds.) 2003b. *Power, Production and Social Reproduction.* New York: Palgrave Macmillan.

Bakker, Isabella and Silvey, Rachel (eds.) 2008. *Beyond States and Markets: The Challenges of Social Reproduction.* New York: Routledge.

Balcerzak-Paradowska, Bożena 2003. "Polityka Rodzinna w Perspektywie Integracji Europejskiej" [Family Policy from a European Integration Perspective], in Balcerzak-Paradowska, Bożena (ed.). *Praca i Polityka Społeczna Wobec Wyzwań Integracji*, 323–36. Warszawa: Instytut Pracy i Spraw Socjalnych.

2004. *Rodzina i Polityka Rodzinna na Przełomie Wieków* [Family and Family Policy through the Ages]. Warszawa: Instytut Pracy i Spraw Socjalnych.

2008. "Rozwiązania w Zakresie Ułatwienia Godzenia Życia Zawodowego z Rodzinnym jako Element Polityki Rodzinnej" [Work-family Reconciliation Solutions as an Element of Family Policy], in Sadowska-Snarska, Cecylia (ed.). *Kierunki Działań na Rzecz Równowagi Praca-Życie-Rodzina* [Efforts Concerning the Balancing of Work-Life-Family in Poland], 15–30. Białystok: Wydawnictwo Wyższej Szkoły Ekonomicznej.

Balcerzak-Paradowska, Bożena, Graniewska, Danuta, Kołaczek, Bożena, Głogosz, Dorota, and Hebda-Czaplicka, Izabela 2001. *Kobiety i Mężczyzni na Rynku Pracy. Rzeczywistość lat 1990–1999* [Women and Men in the Labour Market: Realities of the Years 1990–1999]. Warszawa: Instytut Ppracy i Spraw Socjalnych.

Balcerzak-Paradowska, Bożena, Chłoń-Domińczak, Agnieszka, Kotowska, Irena E., Olejniczuk-Merta, Anna, Topińska, Irena, and Wóycicka, Irena 2003. "The Gender Dimension of Social Security Reform in Poland", in Fultz, Elaine, Ruck, Markus, and Steinhilber, Silke (eds.).*The Gender Dimension of Social Security Reform in Central and Eastern Europe: Case Studies of the Czech Republic, Hungary and Poland*, 187–223. Budapest: International Labour Office.

Barnard, Catherine 1997a. "The United Kingdom, the 'Social Chapter' and the Amsterdam Treaty", *Industrial Law Journal* 26 (2): 275–82.

1997b. "The Judgment of the ECJ in United Kingdom vs. Council – The Working Time Directive", in Barnard, Catherine, Dashwood, Alan, and Hepple, Bob (eds.). The ECJ's Working Time Judgment: The Social Market Vindicated, 1–22. Cambridge: Centre for European Legal Studies (CELS).

1999. "Recent Legislation: Working Time Regulations 1998", *Industrial Law Journal* 28 (1): 61–75.

2000. "Recent Legislation: Working Time Regulations 1999", *Industrial Law Journal* 29 (2): 167–71.

2006. *EC Employment Law*, 3rd edn. Oxford: Oxford University Press.

2012. "The Financial Crisis and the Euro Plus Pact: A Labour Lawyer's Perspective", *Industrial Law Journal* 41(1): 98–114.

Barnard, Catherine, Dashwood, Alan A., and Hepple, Bob A. (eds.) 1997. The ECJ's Working Time Judgment: The Social Market Vindicated. Centre for European Legal Studies (CELS) Occasional Paper No. 2.

Barnard, Catherine, Deakin, Simon, and Hobbs, Richard 2002. *The Use and Necessity of Article 18.1(b)(i) of the Working Time Directive in the United Kingdom*. European Commission.

2003a. "'Fog in the Channel, Continent Isolated': Britain as a Model for EU Social and Economic Policy?", *Industrial Relations Journal* 34 (5): 461–76.

2003b. "Opting Out of the 48-hour Week: Employer Necessity or Individual Choice? An Empirical Study of the Operation of Article 18(1)(b) of the Working Time Directive in the UK", *Industrial Law Journal* 32 (4): 231–52.

Bauman, Zygmunt 2000. *Liquid Modernity.* Cambridge: Polity.

Bego, Ingrid 2015. *Gender Equality Policy in the European Union: A Fast Track to Parity for the New Member States.* Basingstoke: Palgrave Macmillan.

Beach, Derek J. 2005. "Why Governments Comply: An Integrative Compliance Model that Bridges the Gap Between Instrumental and Normative Models of Compliance", *Journal of European Public Policy* 12 (1): 113–42.

Bednarek, Magdalena 2004. "Im Mniejszy Pracodawca, Tym Więcej Skarg" [The Smaller the Employer, the More Complaints], *Rzeczpospolita,* June 7. Law.

Bercusson, Brian 1995. "The Conceptualization of European Labour Law", *Industrial Law Journal* 24 (1): 3–18.

Beveridge, Fiona and Velluti, Samantha 2008. *Gender and the Open Method of Coordination: Perspectives on Law, Governance and Equality in the EU.* Dartmouth: Ashgate.

Bezanson, Kate 2006. *Gender, the State, and Social Reproduction: Household Insecurity in Neo-liberal Times.* Toronto: University of Toronto Press.

Bezanson, Kate and Luxton, Meg (eds.) 2006. *Social Reproduction: Feminist Challenges to Neo-liberalism.* Montreal: McGill-Queens University Press.

Bieling, Hans-Jurgen 2012. "EU Facing the Crisis: Social and Employment Policies in Times of Tight Budgets", *Transfer: European Review of Labour and Research* 18: 255.

Blair, Alasdair 2010. "Britain and the Working Time Directive", Paper presented at the Industrial Relations in Europe Conference, Fafo, Oslo, Norway, 8–10 September.

Blair, Alasdair, Karsten, Luchien, and Leopold, John 2001. "Britain and the Working Time Regulations", *Politics* 21 (1): 40–46.

Blanpain, Roger and Köhler, Eberhard (eds.) 1988. *Legal and Contractual Limitations to Working-Time in the European Community Member States.* Deventer: Kluwer.

Blanpain, Robert, Köhler, E., and Rojot, J. (eds.) 1997. *Legal and Contractual Limitations to Working Time in the European Union.* Leuven: Peters Press; Eurofound; Office for Official Publications of the European Communities.

Błaszczyk, Wojciech 2002. "Position of the Vice-President of the Confederation of Polish Private Employers", in Senate of the Polish Republic. Materials from a Conference Organized by the Social Policy and Health Committee under the Sponsorship of the Senate Marshall Longin Pastusiak, 39–42.

Bobrowicz, Barbara 2007. "Praca Zawodowa i Edukacja versus Funkcje Opiekuńcze" [Time Allocation: Occupation and Education versus Care Functions and Household Activities], in Kotowska, Irena E., Sztanderska, Urszula, Wóycicka, Irena (eds.), *Aktywność Zawodowa i Edukacyjna a Obowiązki Rodzinne w Polsce w Świetle Badań Empirycznych* [Professional and Educational Activation and Family Responsibilities in Poland in Light of Empirical Research], 81–134. Warszawa: Scholar.

Borkowska, Stanisława 2011. *Programy Praca-Życie z Teorii i Praktyki* [Work-Family Programs in Theory and Practice]. Warszawa: Instytut Pracy i Spraw Socjalnych.

Bosch, Gerhard 1995. "Synthesis Report", in *Flexible Working Time: Collective Bargaining and Government Intervention*, 17–41. Paris: Organization for Economic Cooperation and Development.

1999. "Working Time: Tendencies and Emerging Issues", *International Labour Review* 138 (2): 131–49.

2004. "Towards a New Standard Employment Relationship in Western Europe", *British Journal of Industrial Relations* 42 (4): 617–36.

Bosch, Gerhard, Dawkins, Peter, and Michon, François 1993. "An Overview", in Bosch, Gerhard, Dawkins, Peter, and Michon, François (eds.). *Times are Changing: Working Time in 14 Industrialized Countries*, 1–45. Geneva: International Institute for Labour Studies.

Boulin, Jean-Yves, Lallement, Michel, Messenger, Jon C., and Michon, François (eds.) 2006. *Decent Working Time: New Trends, New Issues*. Geneva: International Labour Office.

Bourdieu, Pierre 1991. "Political Representation: Elements for a Theory of the Political Field", in *Language and Symbolic Power*, 171–202. Harvard University Press.

Bruun, Niklas and Hepple, Bob 2009. "Economic Policy and Labour Law", in Hepple, Bob and Veneziani, Bruno (eds.). *The Transformation of Labour Law in Europe*, 31–57. Portland, Oregon: Hart.

Burley, Anne M. and Mattli, Walter 1993. "Europe before the Court", *International Organization* 47 (1): 41–76.

Busby, Nicole 2011. *A Right to Care?* Oxford: Oxford University Press.

Busby, Nicole and Grace, James (eds.) 2011. *Families, Care-giving and Paid Work: Challenging Labour Law in the 21st Century*. Cheltenham: Edward Elgar.

Carley, Mark 2005. "Working Time Developments, 2004", European Industrial Relations Observatory (EIRO) (25 April 2005).

Centrum Praw Kobiet [Women's Rights Centre] 2000. *Kobiety w Polsce w latach 90tych: Raport* [Women in Poland in the 1990s: Report]. Warszawa: Fundacja Centrum Praw Kobiet.

Chiappero-Marinetti, Enrica 2008. "Time and Income: Empirical Evidence on Gender Poverty and Inequalities from a Capability Perspective", in Basu K. and Kanbur R. (eds.) *Arguments for a better world. Essays in Honour of Amartya Sen, Vol. 2, Society, Institutions and Development*, 237–58. Oxford: Oxford University Press.

Chung, Heejung, Kerkhofs, Marcel, and Ester, Peter 2007. *Working Time Flexibility in European Companies*. Dublin: Eurofound.

Cichowski, Rachel A. 2004. "Women's Rights, the European Court, and Supranational Constitution", *Law & Society Review* 38 (3): 489–512.

Chinowska, Krystyna 2000. "Czas Pracy Kobiet" [Women's Working Time], *Prawo i Płeć*; (Fall), 15–23.

Chmielewska, Agnieszka, Krzysków, Barbara, and Wojciechowska-Nowak, Anna 2008. *Warunki Pracy i Respektowanie Praw Pracowniczych w Supermarketach w Polsce z Perspektywy Równouprawnienia Płci* [Working Conditions and Respect for Workers' Rights in Supermarkets in Poland from a Gender Equality Perspective]. Warszawa: Koalicja Karat.

Clegg, Hugh A. 1975. "Pluralism in Industrial Relations", *British Journal of Industrial Relations* 12 (3): 309–16.

Clement, Wallace, Mathieu, Sophie, Prus, Steven, and Dahlmann, Simone 2010. "Restructuring Work and Labour Markets in the New Economy: Four Processes", in Pupo, Norene J. and Thomas, Mark P. (eds.). *Interrogating the New Economy: Restructuring Work in the 21st Century*, 43–64. Toronto: University of Toronto Press.

Collins, Hugh 2005. "The Right to Flexibility", in Conaghan, Joanne and Rittich, Kerry (eds.). *Labour Law, Work and Family*, 99–124. Oxford: Oxford University Press.

Conaghan, Joanne 2005. "Work, Family and the Discipline of Labour Law", in Conaghan, Joanne and Rittich, Kerry (eds.). *Labour Law, Work and Family*, 19–42. Oxford: Oxford University Press.

2006. "Time to Dream? Flexibility, Families and Working Time", in Fudge, Judy and Owens, Rosemary (eds.). *Precarious Work, Women, and the New Economy: The Challenge to Legal Norms*, 109–29. Oxford: Hart.

2014. "Gender and the Idea of Labour Law", *feminists@law*4(1).

Conaghan, Joanne and Rittich, Kerry (eds.) 2005. *Labour Law, Work and Family*. Oxford: Oxford University Press.

Connell, Robert W. 1987. *Gender and Power*. Cambridge: Polity.

2005. *Masculinities*, 2nd edn. Berkley: University of California Press.

Craig, Paul and de Búrca, Gráinne 2011. *EU Law: Text, Cases and Materials*. Oxford: Oxford University Press.

Czarnasty, Jan 2009. "Working Time in the European Union: Poland", European Industrial Relations Observatory (EIROnline).

Daniel, William W., Dickerson, Andrew P., Hogarth, Terence, Campbell, D.C., Vivian, D., and Winterbotham, M. 2003. *The Business Context to Long Hours Working*. DTI Employment Relations Research Series No. 23. London: Department of Trade and Industry.

Davies, Karen 1989. *Women and Time: Weaving the Strands of Everyday Life*. Lund: University of Lund, Department of Sociology.

1994. "The Tensions between Process Time and Clock Time in Care-Work: The Example of Day Nurseries", *Time & Society* 3 (3): 277–304.

Deakin, Simon and Wilkinson, Frank 1994. "Rights vs. Efficiency", *Industrial Law Journal* 23 (4): 289–310.

Deakin, Simon and Reed, Hannah 2000. The Contested Meaning of Labour Market Flexibility: Economic Theory and the Discourse of European Integration. ESRC Centre for Business Research Working Paper No. 162. Cambridge: University of Cambridge.

Desperak, Izabella 2009. "Kobiety i Praca. Wielkie Przegrane Polskiej Transformacji" [Women and Work: The Great Losers of Polish Transformation], in Majmurek, Jakub and Szumlewicz, Piotr (eds.). *Stracone Szanse? Bilans Transformacji 1989–2009* [Lost Chances? The Balance Sheet of the Transformation 1989–2009], 51–70. Warszawa: Difin.

Domański, Henryk 1992. *Zadowolony Niewolnik: Studium o Zróżnicowaniu Społecznym między Kobietami i Mężczyznami w Polsce* [A Grateful Slave: Study on the Social Differentiation between Women and Men in Poland]. Warszawa: Wydawnictwo Instytutu Filozofii i Socjologii PAN.

Duncan, Simon 1995. "Theorizing European Gender Systems", *Journal of European Social Policy* 5 (4): 263–84.

2002. "Policy Discourses on 'Reconciling Work and Life' in the EU", *Social Policy & Society* 1 (4): 305–14.

Dunn, Elizabeth 2004. *Privatizing Poland: Baby Food, Big Business, and the Remaking of Labour*. Ithaca, NY: Cornell University Press.

Düvel, Wiebke 2003. "New Times for the Working Time Directive?", *European Trade Union Yearbook* 2003/2004: 177–95.

Ebbinghaus, Bernhard and Visser, Jelle 1998. *When Institutions Matter: Union Growth and Decline in Western Europe, 1950–95*. Arbeitspapiere Arbeitsbereich I/30. Mannheim: Mannheimer Zentrum für Europäische Sozialforschung (MZES).

Einhorn, Barbara 1993. *Cinderella Goes to Market: Citizenship, Gender and Women's Movements in East Central Europe*. London: Verso.

European Industrial Relations Review (EIRR) 1997. "Working Time In Europe: Part One", *European Industrial Relations Review* 278: 14–20.

1999. "Poland: Industrial Relations Background", *European Industrial Relations Review* 307: 22–27.

Esping-Andersen, Gøsta 1992. *Three Worlds of Welfare Capitalism*. Princeton, NJ: Princeton University Press.

1999. *The Social Foundations of Postindustrial Economies*. Oxford: Oxford University Press.

Eurofound Industrial Relations Dictionary 2007. s.v. "flexibility". www.eurofound.europa.eu/observatories/eurwork/industrial-relations-dictionary/flexibility.

European Foundation 2007. *Combining Family and Full-time Work*. Dublin: European Foundation for the Improvement of Living and Working Conditions.

European Trade Union Institute (ETUI) 1986. *Flexibility of Working Time in Western Europe*. Brussels: European Trade Union Institute.

Fagan, Colette 1996. "Gendered Time Schedules: Paid Work in Great Britain", *Social Politics* 3 (1): 72–106.

2001. "Time, Money and the Gender Order: Work Orientations and Working-Time Preferences in Britain", *Gender, Work and Organization* 8 (3): 239–66.

Fagan, Colette, Grimshaw, Damian, and Rubery, Jill 2006. "The Subordination of the Gender Equality Objective: The National Reform Programmes and 'Making Work Pay' Policies", *Industrial Relations Journal* 7 (6): 571–92.

Fajertag, Giuseppe 1998. "Working Time in Europe: Current Trends", in Wheelock, Jane and Vail, John (eds.). *Work and Idleness: The Political Economy of Full Employment*, 219–34. Dordrecht: Kluwer.

1999. "New Paths in Working-time Policies in Europe: The Difficult Challenge of Reconciling Employers' and Employees' Need for Flexibility", *Labour & Industry* 9 (3): 145–160.

Falkner, Gerda and Treib, Oliver 2008. "Three Worlds of Compliance or Four? The EU-15 Compared to New Member States", *Journal of Common Market Studies* 46 (2): 293–313.

Falkner, Gerda, Treib, Oliver, and Holzleithner, Elisabeth (eds.) 2008. *Compliance in the Enlarged European Union: Living Rights or Dead Letters?* Aldershot: Ashgate.

Falkner, Gerda, Hartlapp, Miriam, Leiber, Simone, and Treib, Oliver 2004. "Non-Compliance with EU Directives in the Member States: Opposition through the Backdoor?", *West European Politics* 27 (1): 2–73.

2005. *Complying with Europe: EU Harmonization and the Soft Law in Member States.* New York: Cambridge University Press.

Fidelis, Małgorzata 2004. "Equality through Protection: The Politics of Women's Employment in Postwar Poland, 1945–1956", *Slavic Review* 63 (2): 301–24.

2010. *Women, Communism, and Industrialization in Postwar Poland.* Cambridge: Cambridge University Press.

Figart, Deborah M. and Golden, Lonnie 2000. "Introduction and Overview: Understanding Working Time around the World", in Golden, Lonnie and Figart, Deborah M. (eds.). *Working Time: International Trends, Theory and Policy Perspectives*, 1–17. New York: Routledge.

Figart, Deborah M. and Mutari, Ellen 1998. "Degendering Work Time in Comparative Perspective: Alternative Policy Frameworks", *Review of Social Economy* 56 (4): 460–80.

2000. "Work Time Regimes in Europe: Can Flexibility and Gender Equity Coexist?", *Journal of Economic Issues* 34 (4): 847–71.

2001. "Europe at a Crossroads: Harmonization, Liberalization, and the Gender of Work Time", *Social Politics* 8 (1): 36–64.

Flanders, Allan 1968. "Collective Bargaining: A Theoretical Analysis", *British Journal of Industrial Relations* 6 (1): 1–26.

Florek, Ludwig 2004a. "Dostosowanie Polskiego Prawa Pracy do Prawa Unijnego ze Szczególnym Uwzględnieniem Ostatniej Nowelizacji Kodeksu Pracy" [Adjustment of Polish Labour Law to EU Law with Emphasis on the Latest Labour Code Amendment], *Monitor Prawa Pracy* 1.

2004b. "Zgodność Polskiego Prawa Pracy z Prawem Europejskim" [Compliance of Polish Labour Law with European Law], in Santera, Walerian (ed.). *Europeizacja Polskiego Prawa Pracy*, 31–41. Warszawa: Scholar, Instytut Pracy i Spraw Socjalnych.

Fodor, Eva 2005. *Women at Work: The Status of Women in the Labour Markets of the Czech Republic, Hungary and Poland.* United Nations Research Institute for Social Development (UNRISD), Occasional Paper 3. Geneva: United Nations Research Institute for Social Development.

Fox, Alan 1973. "Industrial Relations: A Social Critique of Pluralist Ideology", in Child, John (ed.). *Man and Organization: The Search for Explanation and Relevance*, 185–233. London: Allen & Unwin.

Fox, Alan and Flanders, Allan 1969. "The Reform of Collective Bargaining: From Donovan to Durkheim", *British Journal of Industrial Relations* 7(2): 151–80.

Fraser, Nancy 1997. *Justice Interruptus: Critical Reflections on the Post-Socialist Condition.* London: Routledge.

Fredman, Sandra 1997a. "Labour Law in Flux: The Changing Composition of the Workforce", *Industrial Law Journal* 26 (4): 337–52.

1997b. *Women and the Law.* Oxford: Oxford University Press.

2004. "Women at Work: The Broken Promise of Flexicurity", *Industrial Law Journal* 33 (4): 299–319.

2005. Control over Time and Work-Life Balance: Comparative/Theoretical Perspective. Report for Labour Standards Review. Government of Canada.

Fudge, Judy 2005. "The New Dual-Earner Gender Contract: Work-life Balance or Working-time Flexibility?", in Conaghan, Joanne and Rittich, Kerry (eds.). *Labour Law, Work and Family*, 261–87. Oxford: Oxford University Press.

2008. "Review of Women, Gender and Work: What is Equality and How Do We Get There?", *Gender, Work & Organization* 15 (2): 3–5.

2013. "From Women and Labour Law to Putting Gender and Law to Work", in Davies, Margaret and Munro, Vanessa (eds.). *A Research Companion to Feminist Legal Theory*, 321–40. Farnham: Ashgate.

Fudge, Judy and Cossman, Brenda 2002. "Introduction", in Cossman, Brenda and Fudge, Judy (eds.). *Privatization, Law and the Challenge to Feminism*, 3–37. Toronto: University of Toronto Press.

Fudge, Judy, and Grabham, Emily 2014. "Introduction: Gendering Labour Law", *feminists@law* 4(1).

Fudge, Judy and Owens, Rosemary (eds.) 2006. *Precarious Work, Women, and the New Economy: The Challenge to Legal Norms.* Oxford: Hart.

Fudge, Judy and Strauss, Kendra (eds.) 2013. *Temporary Work, Agencies and Unfree Labour: Insecurity in the New World of Work.* New York, London: Routledge.

Fudge, Judy and Vosko, Leah 2001a. "By Whose Standards? Re-regulating the Canadian Labour Market", *Economic and Industrial Democracy* 22 (3): 27–56.

2001b. "Gender, Segmentation and the Standard Employment Relationship in Canadian Labour Law and Policy", *Economic and Industrial Democracy* 22 (2): 271–310.

Fuszara, Małgorzata and Zielińska, Eleonora 2006. "Women and the Law in Poland: Towards Active Citizenship", in Lukić, Jasmina, Regulska, Joanna, and Zaviršek, Darja (eds.). *Women and Citizenship in Central and Eastern Europe*, 39–60. Hampshire: Ashgate.

Gajos, Bartłomiej 2009. "Gospodarka Planowa w Dobie PRL. Geneza i Konsekwencje" [Planned Economy in the People's Republic of Poland: Origins and Consequences]. http://historia.org.pl/index.php/publikacje/publikacje/historia-najnowsza/733-gospodarka-planowa-w-dobie-prl-geneza-i-konsekwencje.html/.

Gal, Susan and Kligman, Gail 2000. *Reproducing Gender: Politics, Publics, and Everyday Life after Socialism*. Princeton, NJ: Princeton University Press.

Gardawski, Juliusz 2002. "Declining Trade Union Density Examined", EIROnline (21 August 2002).

Garrett, Geoffrey 1995. "The Politics of Legal Integration in the European Union", *International Organization* 49 (1): 171–81.

Gazeta 2008a. "Lekarze Wypowiadają Klauzulę Opt-out" [Doctors are Withdrawing Opt-out Clauses], 16 April.

2008b. "Szpitale nie Przestrzegają Prawa Lekarzy do Odpoczynku" [Hospitals Fail to Observe Doctors' Right to Rest], 9 July.

2009. "29 Osób Usłyszalo Zarzuty w Śledztwie ws. Sklepów Biedronka" [29 People Charged in the Biedronka Investigation], 18 February.

2011. "Połowa Szpitali nie Przestrzega Przepisów o Czasie Pracy" [Half the Hospitals Fails to Observe Working-time Laws], 13 April.

2012. "Kolejni Lekarze nie Chcą Pracować Ponad 48 Godzin" [More Doctors Refuse to Work over 48 Hours], 8 April.

Gazeta Lubuska 2008. "Koniec Śledztwa ws. Biedronek: 11 Osób Oskarzonych" [End of the Biedronka Investigation: 11 People Charged], 19 September.

Gender Index 2007. *Firma Równych Szans: Przewodnik Dobrych Praktyk* [The Equal Opportunity Firm: Best Practices Guide]. Warszawa.

Gładzicka-Janowska, Alina 2009. *Gospodarowanie Zasobami Czasu w Wybranych Krajach Unii Europejskiej ze Szczególnym Uwzglednieniem Polski* [Time Management in Some EU Member States with Emphasis on Poland]. Szczecin: Wydawnictwo Uczelniane Zachodniopomorskiego Uniwersytetu Technologicznego w Szczecinie.

Glass, Christy M. 2008. "Gender and Work during Transition: Job Loss in Bulgaria, Hungary, Poland, and Russia", *East European Politics and Societies* 22 (4): 757–83.

Glennie, Paul and Thrift, Nigel 1996. "Reworking E.P. Thompson's 'Time, Discipline and Industrial Capitalism'", *Time & Society* 5 (3): 275–99.

Głogosz, Dorota 2007. *Kobiety Zatrudnione w Niepełnym Wymiarze Czasu Pracy: Skutki dla Życia Rodzinnego i Zawodowego* [Women Working Part-Time: Consequences for Family and Professional Life]. Warszawa: Instytut Pracy i Spraw Socjalnych.

2008. "Działania na Rzecz Równowagi Praca-Życie-Rodzina w Polsce" [Balancing Work-Life-Family Measures in Poland], in Sadowska-Snarska, Cecylia (ed.). *Kierunki Działań na Rzecz Równowagi Praca-Życie-Rodzina* [Efforts Concerning the Balancing of Work-Life-Family in Poland], 37–50. Białystok: Wydawnictwo Wyższej Szkoły Ekonomicznej.

Glucksmann, Miriam A. 1995. "Why 'Work'? Gender and the 'Total Social Organization of Labour'", *Gender, Work and Organization* 2 (2): 63–75.

2000. *Cottons and Casuals: The Gendered Organization of Labour in Time and Space.* Durham, NC: Sociology Press.

2005. "Shifting Boundaries and Interconnections: Extending the 'Total Social Organisation of Labour'", *The Sociological Review* 53 (2): 19–36.

Golden, Lonnie and Figart, Deborah (eds.) 2000. *Working Time: International Trends, Theory and Policy Perspectives*, 233–41. New York: Routledge.

Golinowska, Stanisława, Balcerzak-Paradowska, Bożena, Machol-Zajda, Lucyna, and Ruzik, Anna 2008. *Decent Work Country Report – Poland.* Warsaw: Institute of Labour and Social Studies; ILO Regional Office for Europe and Central Asia.

Góral, Zbigniew 2002. "Ocena Projektu zmian w Kodeksie Pracy i Jego Wpływ na Ograniczenie Bezrobocia – Aspekty Prawne" [Appraisal of the Labour Code Amendment Proposal and its Impact on Limiting Unemployment], in Senate of the Polish Republic.

Goudswaard, Anneke and de Nanteuil, Matthieu 2000. *Flexibility and Working Conditions – A Qualitative and Comparative Study in Seven EU Member States: A Summary.* Dublin: Eurofound.

Grabham, Emily 2014. "The Strange Temporalities of Work-life Balance Law", *feminists@law* 4(1).

Graff, Agnieszka 2008. *Świat bez Kobiet: Płeć w Polskim Życiu Publicznym* [World without Women: Gender in Polish Public Life], 2nd edn. Warszawa: Wydawnictwo W.A.B.

Graham, Hilary 1983. "Caring: A Labour of Love", in Finch, Janet and Groves, Dulcie (eds.). *A Labour of Love: Women, Work and Caring*, 13–30. London: Routledge & Kegan Paul.

Grahl, John and Teague, Paul 1989. "Labour Market Flexibility in West Germany, Britain and France", *West European Politics* 12 (2): 91–111.

Grzymalala-Busse, Anna and Innes, Abby 2003. "Great Expectations: The EU and Domestic Political Competition in East Central Europe", *East European Politics & Societies* 17 (1): 64–73.

Guerrina, Roberta 2005. *Mothering the Union: The Politics of Gender, Equality and Maternity Rights in the EU.* Manchester: Manchester University Press.

Haas, Ernst B 1964. *Beyond the Nation-State: Functionalism and International Organization.* Stanford CA: Stanford University Press.

Hall, Mark 1999. "UK Trade Unions and the Euro", *EIRObserver Update.* 4/99: 10.

Hakim, Catherine 1996. *Key Issues in Women's Work: Female Heterogenity and the Polarisation of Women's Employment.* London: Athlone.

2000. *Work-lifestyle Choices in the 21st Century: Preference Theory.* Oxford: Oxford University Press.

Hardy, Jane, Kozek, Wiesława, and Stenning, Alison 2008. "In the Front Line: Women, Work and New Spaces of Labour Politics in Poland", *Gender, Place & Culture* 15 (2): 99–116.

Hardy, Steven 2006. "Harmonising European Working Time in an Enlarged EU: A Case of Failed 'Humanisation'?", *International Journal of Comparative Labour Law & Industrial Relations* 22 (4): 563–601.

Harvey, David 2006. *Spaces of Global Capitalism: Towards a Theory of Uneven Global Development.* Oxford: Oxford University Press.

Heinen, Jacqueline and Portet, Stephan 2009. *Religia, Polityka i Równość Płci w Polsce.* Końcowy Raport Badawczy Podsumowujacy Projekt "Religion, Politics and Gender Equality". [Religion, Politics and Gender Equality in Poland: Final Research Report]. Warszawa: Friedrich Böell Foundation.

Heinen, Jacqueline and Wator, Monika. 2006. "Child Care in Poland Before, During and After the Transition: Still a Woman's Business", *Social Politics* 13 (2): 189–216.

Hepple, Bob 1987. "The Crisis in EEC Labour Law", *Industrial Law Journal* 16 (1): 77–87.

1990. "The Implementation of the Community Charter of Fundamental Social Rights", *Modern Law Review* 53 (5): 643–54.

1997. "Commentary", in Barnard, Catherine, Dashwood, Alan, Hepple, Bob (eds.), The ECJ's Working Time Judgment: The Social Market Vindicated. Centre for European Legal Studies (CELS) Occasional Paper No. 2. 32–34.

2001. "The EU Charter of Fundamental Rights", *Industrial Law Journal* 30 (2): 225–31.

Herbst, Jan 2004. *Uwarunkowania Dostępu do Wychowania Przedszkolnego w Polsce: Analiza Statystyczna na Podstawie Danych BDR GUS, NSP, PKW* [Conditions of Access to Childhood Education in Poland: Statistical Analysis on the Basis of GUS, NSP, PKW Data]. www.frd.org.pl/.

Hermann, Christoph 2014. *Capitalism and the Political Economy of Work Time.* Abingdon; New York: Routledge.

Hervey, Tamara and O'Keefe, David (eds.) 1996. *Sex Equality Law in The European Union.* New York: Wiley.

Hervey, Tamara and Shaw, Jo 1998. "Women, Work and Care: Women's Dual Role and Double Burden in EC Sex Equality Law", *Journal of European Social Policy* 8 (1): 43–63.

Himmelweit, Susan 2000. "The Discovery of 'Unpaid Work'", in Himmelweit, Susan (ed.). *Inside the Household: From Labour to Care*, 102–19. New York: St. Martin's.

Hirdman, Yvonne 1988. "Genussystemet – Reflexioner Kring Kvinnors Sociala Underordning", *Kvinnovetenskapligtidskrift* 3: 49–63.

Hobbs, Richard and Njoya, Wanjiru 2005. "Regulating the European Labour Market: Prospects and Limitations of a Reflexive Governance Approach", *British Journal of Industrial Relations* 43 (2): 297–319.

Hooghe, Lisbet and Marks, Gary 2001. *Multi-Level Governance and European Integration*. Lanham, MD: Rowman & Littlefield.

Hoskyns, Catherine and Rai, Shirin M. 2007. "Recasting the Global Political Economy: Counting Women's Unpaid Work", *New Political Economy* 12 (3): 297–317.

Humphries, Jane and Rubery, Jill 1984. "The Reconstitution of the Supply Side of the Labour Market: The Relative Autonomy of Social Reproduction", *Cambridge Journal of Economics* 8 (4): 331–46.

International Monetary Fund (IMF) 2010. After the Global Financial Crisis: The Road Ahead for Europe. Speech by the Managing Director of the IMF, Dominique Strauss-Kahn, 29 March.

Jeffery, Mark 1998. "Not Really Going to Work? Of the Directive on Part-time Work, 'Atypical Work' and Attempts to Regulate It", *Industrial Law Journal* 27 (3): 193–213.

Jenson, Jane 1986. "Gender and Reproduction: Or, Babies and the State", *Studies in Political Economy* 20: 17–18.

1989. "Paradigms and Political Discourse: Protective Legislation in France and the United States before 1914", *Canadian Journal of Political Science* 22 (2): 235–58.

2009. "Lost in Translation: The Social Investment Perspective and Gender Equality", *Social Politics* 46 (4): 446–83.

Kabaj, Mieczysław 2002. "Ocena Projektu Zmian w Kodeksie Pracy i Jego Wpływ na Ograniczenie Bezrobocia – Aspekty Społeczno-Ekonomiczne" [Appraisal of the Labour Code Amendment Proposal and its Impact on Limiting Unemployment – Socio-Economic Aspects], in Senate of the Polish Republic, 23–28. 14 May 2002.

Kantola, Johanna 2010. *Gender and the European Union*. Basingstoke: Palgrave Macmillan.

2014. "The Paradoxical Gendered Consequences of the EU Policy on Multiple Discrimination: The Nordic Case", Weiner, Eleine and MacRae, Heather (eds.) "The Persistent Invisibility Of Gender in EU Policy", *European Integration Online Papers*, Special Issue 18 (1): 1–19.

Karpinski, Eva C. 1995. "Do Polish Women Need Feminism? Recent Activity of the Parliamentary Women's Group", *Canadian Woman Studies* 16 (1): 91–94.

Kauppi, Niilo 2003. "Bourdieu's Political Sociology and the Politics of European Integration", *Theory and Society* 32 (5–6): 775–789.

Keane, Michael P. and Prasad, Eswar S. 2001. "Poland: Inequality, Transfers, and Growth in Transition", *Finance and Development* 38 (1).

Kenner, Jeffery 2003. *EU Employment Law: From Rome to Amsterdam and Beyond.* Oxford: Hart.

2004. "Re-evaluating the Concept of Working Time: An Analysis of Recent Case Law", *Industrial Relations Journal* 35 (6): 588–602.

Keune, Maarten 2008. "EU Enlargement and Social Standards: Exporting the European Social Model?" Working Paper. Brussels: European Trade Union Institute for Research, Education and Health and Safety.

Kilpatrick, Claire 1998. "Community or Communities of Courts in European Integration? Sex Equality Dialogues Between UK Courts and the ECJ", *European Law Journal* 4 (2): 121–47.

2003. "Has New Labour Reconfigured Employment Legislation?", *Industrial Law Journal* 32 (3): 135–63.

2012. "Internal Market Architecture and the Accommodation of Social Rights: As Good as it Gets?", *European Journal of Social Law* 1: 4–29.

Klatzer, Elizabeth and Schlager, Christa 2014. "Shifts in Direction: Challenges to Gender Equality Achievements in the Context of New Economic Governance Mechanisms of the European Union", Paper presented at the Progressive Economy Forum 2015. Inequality. Consequences for Society, Politics and People. 5–6 March 2014, European Parliament, Brussels.

Knijn, Trudie and Arnoud, Smit 2009. "Investing, Facilitating, or Individualizing the Reconciliation of Work and Family Life: Three Paradigms and Ambivalent Policies", *Social Politics* 16 (4): 484–518.

Kofman, Eleonore and Raghuram, Parvati 2015. *Gendered Migrations and Global Social Reproduction.* Basingstoke: Palgrave Macmillan.

Koldinská, Kristina 2011. "Case Law of the European Court of Justice on Sex Discrimination", *Common Market Law Review* 48 (5): 1599–638.

Kołodko, Grzegorz W. 1996. *Polska 2000: Strategia dla Przyszłości* [Poland 2000: Strategy for the Future]. Warszawa: Poltext.

2009a. "The Great Transformation 1989–2029", *Society & Economy* 31 (2): 175–91.

2009b. "A Two-thirds Rate of Success: Poland's Post-Communist Transformation 1989–2009", *Communist and Post-Communist Studies* 42 (3): 325–51.

Kołodko, Grzegorz W. and Nuti, D. Mario 1997. "The Polish Alternative: Old Myths, Hard Facts and New Strategies in the Successful Transformation of the Polish Economy". WIDER Research for Action 1997/33. Helsinki: UNU-WIDER.

Konat, Grzegorz 2009. "Antypolityka Społeczno-Ekonomiczna, Czyli Niedobór w Gospodarce" [Socio-Economic Anti-Policy, or the Economic Shortage], in

Majmurek, Jakub and Szumlewicz, Piotr (eds.). *Stracone Szanse? Bilans Transformacji 1989–2009* [Lost Chances? The Balance Sheet of the Transformation 1989–2009], 19–50. Warszawa: Difin.

Kotowska, Irena (ed.) 2009. *Strukturalne i Kulturowe Uwarunkowania Aktywności Zawodowej Kobiet w Polsce* [Structural and Cultural Determinants of Women's Professional Activation in Poland]. Warszawa: Scholar.

Kotowska, Irena E. and Matysiak, Anna 2008. "Reconciliation of Work and Family within Different Institutional Settings", *European Studies of Population* 16 (1): 299–318.

Kotowska, Irena E., Sztanderska, Urszula, and Wóycicka, Irena (eds.) 2007. *Aktywność Zawodowa i Edukacyjna a Obowiązki Rodzinne w Polsce w Świetle Badań Empirycznych* [Professional and Educational Activation and Family Responsibilities in Poland in Light of Empirical Research]. Warszawa: Scholar.

2009. "Diagnoza Kulturowych i Strukturalnych Uwarunkowań Łączenia Pracy Zawodowej i Aktywności Rodzinnej przez Kobiety w Polsce" [Diagnosis of the Cultural and Structural Determinants of Combining Employment with Family Activity by Women in Poland], in Kotowska, Irena (ed.). *Strukturalne i Kulturowe Uwarunkowania Aktywności Zawodowej Kobiet w Polsce* [Structural and Cultural Determinants of Women's Professional Activation in Poland], 233–60. Warszawa: Scholar.

Kotowska, Irena E., Józwiak, Janina, Matysiak, Anna, and Baranowska, Anna 2008. "Poland: Fertility Decline As a Response to Profound Societal and Labour Market Changes?", *Demographic Research* 19 (22): 795–854.

Kowalik, Tadeusz 2002. *Economics in Poland: Country Report.* Leibniz: GESIS; Leibniz Institute for the Social Sciences; Knowledge Base Eastern Europe.

2007. "Blaski i Cienie Transformacji Polskiej" [The Highlights and the Shadows of Polish Transformation]. www.ekologiasztuka.pl/txt/tkowalik_blaski_cienie.rtf.

2009. *www.PolskaTransformacja.pl* [www.PolishTransformation.pl]. Warszawa: Warszawskie Wydawnictwo Literackie Muza.

Kowalski, Marcin and Kopiński, Michał 2005. "Stu Byłych Pracowników Pozywa Biedronkę;" [One Hundred Former Employees Sue Biedronka], *Gazeta Wyborcza*, 2 July.

Kozak, Wiesława 2006. Liberalisation, Privatisation and Regulation in the Polish Healthcare Sector/Hospitals. Country Report on Liberalisation and Privatisation Processes and Forms of Regulation. Project Funded by the European Commission's 6th Framework Programme. Warsaw: Instytut Sociologii, Uniwersytet Warszawski.

Kozłowska, Elżbieta and Biała-Kalbarczyk, Alicja (n.d.). Partnerstwo w Rodzinie – Szansą Kobiet na Rynku Pracy: Twój Praktyczny Przewodnik [Partnership within the Family – Women's Employment Opportunities.] Warszawa:

Ministerstwo Pracy i Polityki Społecznej Departament ds. Kobiet, Rodziny i Przeciwdziałania Dyskryminacji.

Kravaritou, Yota 1999. "The Regulation of Working Time in the European Union: Gender Approach." Proceedings of the Conference "The Regulation of Working Time in the European Union – Gender Approach," organized with the European Commission (DG V), as part of the European Forum "Gender and the Use of Time" (1994–1995), Florence, April 27–29. Brussels; Bern; Berlin; Frankfurt; New York; Vienna: PIE Lang.

Kronsell, Annika 2005. "Gender, Power and European Integration Theory", *Journal of European Public Policy* 12 (6): 1022–40.

Ksieniewicz, Monika 2004. "Specyfika Polskiego Feminizmu" [The Particularities of Polish Feminism], *Kultura i Historia* 6: 90–100.

Kubisa, Julia 2009. "Patrząc z Daleka i z Bliska: Kobiety w Polskich Związkach Zawodowych po 1989" [Looking from Near and Far: Women in Polish Trade Unions after 1989], in Kongres Kobiet Polskich (ed.). *Raport Kobiety dla Polski, Polska dla Kobiet: 20-lat Transformacji 1989–2009*, 73–84. Warszawa: Fundacja Feminoteka.

Kulpa-Ogdowska, Anna 2006. *Kobieta Pracująca: Diagnoza Sytuacji Kobiet na Rynku Pracy* [Working Woman: the Diagnosis of the Labour Market Situation of Women]. Kutno: ASM Centrum Badań i Analizy Rynku.

La Faro, Antonio 2000. *Regulating Social Europe: Reality and Myth of Collective Bargaining in the EC Legal Order*. Oxford: Hart.

Lacey, Nicola 1998. *Unspeakable Subjects: Feminist Essays in Legal and Social Theory*. Oxford: Hart.

Laslett, Barbara and Brenner, Johanna 1989. "Gender and Social Reproduction: Historical Perspectives", *Annual Review of Sociology* 15: 381–404.

Leiber, Simone 2005. "Implementation of EU Social Policy in Poland: Is there a Different 'Eastern World of Compliance'?" European Union Studies Association (EUSA) Biennial Conference 2005 (9th), Austin, Texas, March 31-April 2.

2007. "Transposition of EU Social Policy in Poland: Are there Different 'Worlds of Compliance' in East and West?", *Journal of European Social Policy* 17 (4): 349–60.

Lee, Sangheon and McCann, Deirdre 2006. "Working Time Capability: Towards Realizing Individual Choice", in Boulin, Jean-Yves, Lallement, Michel, Messenger, Jon. C., and Michon, François (eds.). *Decent Working Time: New Trends, New Issues*, 65–92. Geneva: ILO.

Lee, Sangheon, McCann, Deirdre, and Messenger, Jon C. 2007. *Working Time around the World: Trends in Working Hours, Laws and Policies in Comparative Perspective*. Geneva: Routledge; International Labour Organization.

Leete, Laura 2000. "History and Housework: Implications for Work Hours and Family Policy in Market Economies", in Golden, Lonnie and Figart, Deborah (eds.). *Working Time: International Trends, Theory and Policy Perspectives*, 233–41. New York: Routledge.

Lehndorff, Stephen 2007. "Flexibility and Control: New Challenges for Working-Time Policy in the European Union", *Labour & Industry* 17 (3): 9–28.

Leschke, Janine and Jepsen, Maria 2011. "The Economic Crisis: Challenge or Opportunity for Gender Equality in Social Policy Outcomes? A Comparison of Denmark, Germany, and the UK". Working Paper: ETUI.

2012. "Introduction: Crisis, Policy Responses and Widening Inequalities in the EU", *International Labour Review* 151 (4): 289.

Lewandowski, Henryk 2002. "Kierunki Reform Prawa Pracy i Ogólna Ocena Rządowego Projektu Zmian w Kodeksie Pracy" [Directions of Labour Law Reform and General Appraisal of the Government's Labour Code Amendment Reform Proposal], in Senate of the Polish Republic, 13–17, 14 May 2002.

Lewińska, Aleksandra 2010. "Pracownicy Dużych Sklepów Mają Dość: Chcą Podwyżek, Wolnych Niedziel . . . " [Employees of Large Shops Have Had Enough: They Want Raises, Free Sundays], *Gazeta Wyborcza*, August 26. Bizness.

Lewis, Jane 1992. "Gender and the Development of Welfare Regimes", *Journal of European Social Policy* 2 (3): 159–73.

2006a. "Care and Gender: Have the Arguments for Recognising Care Work Now Been Won?", in Glendenning, Caroline and Kemp, Peter A (eds.). *Cash and Care: Policy Challenges in the Welfare State*, 11–20. Bristol: Policy Press.

2006b. "Employment and Care: The Policy Problem, Gender Equality and the Issue of Choice", *Journal of Comparative Policy Analysis: Research and Practice* 8 (2): 103–14.

2006c. "Work/Family Reconciliation, Equal Opportunities and Social Policies: The Interpretation of Policy Trajectories at the EU Level and the Meaning of Gender Equality", *Journal of European Public Policy* 13 (3): 420–37.

Lewis, Jane and Giullari, Susanna 2005. "The Adult Worker Model Family – Gender Equality and Care: The Search for New Policy Principles and the Possibilities and Problems of a Capabilities Approach", *Economy & Society* 34 (1): 76–104.

Lewis, Jane and Płomień, Ania 2009. "'Flexicurity' as a Policy Strategy: The Implications for Gender Equality", *Economy & Society* 38 (3): 433–59.

Lewis, Jane, Campbell, Mary, and Huerta, Carmen 2008. "Patterns of Paid and Unpaid Work in Western Europe: Gender, Commodification, Preferences and the Implications for Policy", *Journal of European Social Policy* 18 (1): 21–37.

Lobodzinska, Barbara 1977. "Married Women's Gainful Employment and Housework in Contemporary Poland", *Journal of Marriage & the Family* 39: 405–15.

1978. "The Education and Employment of Women in Contemporary Poland", *Signs – Journal of Women in Culture & Society* 3 (3): 688–97.

1995. *Family, Women and Employment in Central-Eastern Europe*. London: Greenwood.

Locker, Brigid and Prügl, Elisabeth 2008. "Gender and European Integration". Webpapers on Constitutionalism and Governance beyond the State. No. 2.

Luxton, Meg 2006. "Feminist Political Economy and Social Reproduction", in Bezanson, Kate and Luxton, Meg (eds.). *Social Reproduction: Feminist Challenges to Neo-liberalism*, 11–44. Montreal: McGill-Queens University Press.

M.P. 1999. "Najpierw Nowelizacja, Potem Kodyfikacja" [Amendment First, Then Re-codification]. Rozmowa z Prof. dr. hab. Tadeuszem Zielińskim, przewodniczącym Komisji Reformy Prawa Pracy, *Rzeczpospolita*, September 13. Prawo.

2000. "Wstępna Wizja" [Introductory Vision], *Rzeczpospolita*, June 3. Praca.

Machol, Lucyna 1980. "Ekonomiczno-Społeczne Aspekty Elastycznych Form Organizacji Czasu Pracy" [Economic and Social Aspects of Flexible Forms of Working-time Organization]. *Studia i Materiały 2*. [Monograph]. Warszawa: Instytut Pracy i Spraw Socjalnych.

MacRae, Heather 2006. "Rescaling Gender Relations: The Influence of European Directives on the German Gender Regime", *Social Politics* 13 (4): 522–50.

Majmurek, Jakub 2009. "Ideologie Polskiej Transformacji" [The Ideologies of Polish Transformation], in Majmurek, Jakub and Szumlewicz, Piotr (eds.). *Stracone Szanse? Bilans Transformacji 1989–2009* [Lost Chances? The Balance Sheet of the Transformation 1989–2009], 119–46. Warszawa: Difin.

Majmurek, Jakub and Szumlewicz, Piotr 2009. *Stracone Szanse? Bilans Transformacji 1989–2009* [Lost Chances? The Balance Sheet of the Transformation 1989–2009]. Warszawa: Difin.

Masselot, Annick and Caracciolo di Torella, Eugenia 2010. *Reconciling Work and Family Life in EU Law and Policy*. Basingstoke: Palgrave Macmillan.

Matey, Maria (ed.) 1997. *Nowy Ład Pracy w Polsce i w Europie* [New System of Work in Poland and Europe]. Warszawa: Scholar.

Mattli, Walter and Slaughter, Ann 1995. "Law and Politics in the European Union: A Reply to Garrett", *International Organization* 49 (1): 183–90.

1998. "Revisiting the European Court of Justice", *International Organization* 52 (1): 177–209.

Matysiak, Anna 2007. "Organizacja Czasu Pracy i Opieki" [Organization of Work-time and Care], in Kotowska, Irena E., Sztanderska, Urszula, and Wóycicka, Irena (eds.), *Aktywność Zawodowa i Edukacyjna a Obowiązki Rodzinne w Polsce w Świetle Badań Empirycznych* [Professional and Educational Activity and Family Responsibilities in Poland], 345–82. Warszawa: Scholar.

2009. "Zatrudnienie Kobiet w Polsce a Posiadanie Dzieci: Bariera czy Warunek?" [Women's Employment in Poland: A Barrier or a Precondition to Childbearing?], in Kotowska, Irena (ed.). *Strukturalne i Kulturowe Uwarunkowania Aktywności Zawodowej Kobiet w Polsce* [Structural and Cultural Conditions and Women's Labour Force Participation in Poland], 197–232. Warszawa: Scholar.

Matysiak, Anna and Steinmetz, Stephanie 2006. "Who Follows Whom? Female Employment Patterns in West Germany, East Germany and Poland". Working Paper No. 94. Mannheim: Mannheimer Zentrum für Europäische Sozialforschung.

2008. "Finding Their Way? Female Employment Patterns in West Germany, East Germany, and Poland", *European Sociological Review* 24 (3): 331–45.

Mazey, Sonia 2001. *Gender Mainstreaming in the EU: Principles and Practices.* London: Kogan Page.

2002. "Gender Mainstreaming Strategies in the EU: Delivering on an Agenda?", *Feminist Legal Studies* 10 (3): 227–40.

McCann, Deirdre 2004. "Regulating Working Time Needs and Preferences", in Messenger, Jon C. (ed.). *Working Time and Workers' Preferences in Industrialized Countries: Finding a Balance*, 10–28. London: Routledge.

2005. "The Role of Work/Family Discourse in Strengthening Traditional Working Time Laws: Some Lessons from the On-Call Work Debate", in Murray, Jill (ed.). *Work, Family and the Law, Law in Context* 23 (1), 127–47. Annandale: The Federation Press.

McGlynn, Clare 2001. "Reclaiming a Feminist Vision: The Reconciliation of Paid Work and Family Life in European Union Law and Policy", *Columbia Journal of European Law* 7 (2): 241–72.

2005. "Work, Family, and Parenthood: The European Union Agenda", in Conaghan, Joanne and Rittich, Kerry (eds.). *Labour Law, Work and Family*, 217–35. Oxford: Oxford University Press.

2006. "Families, Partnerships and Law Reform in the European Union: Balancing Disciplinarity and Liberalisation", *Modern Law Review* 69 (1): 92–107.

Męcina, Jacek 2003. "Znowelizowany Kodeks Pracy: Szansa na Większą Elastyczność;" [The Amended Labour Code: An Opportunity for Greater Flexibility], *Zarządzanie Zasobami Ludzkimi* 3 (4): 9–27.

Messenger, Jon C. (ed.) 2004. *Working Time and Workers' Preferences in Industrialized Countries: Finding a Balance.* London: Routledge.

Michalik, Sebastian 2003. "Nowa Formula Umowy Społecznej" [New Social Contract], *Bez Dogmatu* 55.

Mills, Shaun 1996. "The EC Legal Base Debate: Working Time and Workers Protections: A Matter of Health and Safety or the Rights of Employed Persons?", *European Business Law Review* 7 (6): 137–40.

Ministry of Justice 2009. Letter of 7 January 2009 concerning the Progress of the Poland-wide Investigation on the Exploitation in the Chain "Biedronka". Warszawa: Ministerstwo Sprawiedliwości.

Moffat, Graham 1997. "Competition, Competitiveness and Re-Regulating the Labour Market: The Working Time Directive", *Nottingham Law Journal* 6 (1): 46–68.

Molyneux, Maxine 1990. "The 'Woman Question' in the Age of Perestroika", *New Left Review* 183: 23–59.

Monks, John 2007. Speech to Danish Confederation of Trade Unions. www.etuc.org/a/4183/.

Moravcsik, Andrew 1993. "Preferences and Power in the European Community: A Liberal Intergovernmentalist Approach", *Journal of Common Market Studies* 31 (4): 473–524.

Morgan, Kimberley J. 2009. "Caring Time Policies in Western Europe: Trends and Implications", *Comparative European Politics* 7 (1): 37–55.

Mosher, James S. and Trubeck, David. M. 2003. "Alternative Approaches to Governance in the EU: EU Social Policy and the European Employment Strategy", *Journal of Common Market Studies* 41 (1): 63–88.

Mrozowicki, Adam and Trawińska, Marta 2013. "Women's Union Activism and Trade Union Revitalization: The Polish Experience", *Economic and Industrial Democracy*. 34 (2): 269–89.

Murray, Jill 1999. "European Developments. Normalising Temporary Work. The Proposed Directive on Fixed-term Work", *Industrial Law Journal* 28 (3): 269–275.

Narożny, Michał 2006. "High Unemployment in Poland – Not Only a Labour Market Problem", *ECFIN Country Focus* 3 (6).

Nussbaum, Marta 2003. "Capabilities as Fundamental Entitlements: Sen and Social Justice", *Feminist Economics* 9 (2–3): 33–59.

Ojeda Avilés, Antonio and Garcia Viña, Jordi 2009. "Regulation of the Labour Market", in Hepple, Bob and Veneziani, Bruno (eds.). *The Transformation of Labour Law in Europe*, 59–98. Portland, Oregon: Hart.

Organization for Economic Cooperation and Development (OECD) 1973a. *Flexibility in Working Life*. Paris: OECD.

1973b. *New Patterns for Working Time: International Conference, Final Report*. Paris: OECD.

1976. *Lifelong Allocation of Time*. Paris: OECD.

1986. *Labour Market Flexibility: Report by a High-Level Group of Experts to the Secretary-General*. Washington: OECD Publications and Information Center.

1994. *Jobs Study: Facts, Analysis, Strategies*. Paris: OECD.

1995. *Flexible Working Time*. Paris: OECD.

2001a. *Governance in the 21st Century*. Paris: OECD.

2001b. *Work and Family Life: How Do They Balance Out?* Paris: OECD Employment Outlook.

2002. *Babies and Bosses: Reconciling Work and Family Life, Vol. 1: Australia, Denmark, the Netherlands*. Paris: OECD.

2003. *Babies and Bosses: Reconciling Work and Family Life, Vol. 2: Austria, Ireland and Japan*. Paris: OECD.

2004a. *Babies and Bosses: Reconciling Work and Family Life, Vol. 3: New Zealand, Portugal, Switzerland*. OECD.

2004b. *Employment Outlook*. Paris: OECD.

2005. *Babies and Bosses: Reconciling Work and Family Life, Vol. 4: Canada, Finland, Sweden and the United Kingdom*. OECD.

2006. *Employment Outlook: Boosting Jobs and Incomes*. Paris: OECD.

2007. *Babies and Bosses: Reconciling Work and Family Life – A Synthesis of Findings for OECD Countries*. Paris: OECD.

Ost, David 2000. "Illusory Corporatism in Eastern Europe: Neoliberal Tripartism and Postcommunist Class Identities", *Politics and Society* 28 (4): 508–30.

2005. *The Defeat of Solidarity: Anger and Politics in Postcommunist Europe*. Ithaca, NY: Cornell University Press.

Pacewicz, Piotr 2011. "Środa, Szczuka, Bratkowska: Trzy Siostry" [Środa, Szczuka, Bratkowska: Three Sisters], *Gazeta*. Wysokie Obcasy. 1 August.

Parent-Thirion, Agnès, Fernández Macías, Enrique, Hurley, John, and Vermeylen, Greet 2007. *Fourth European Working Conditions Survey: Report*. Dublin: European Foundation for the Improvement of Living and Working Conditions.

Pascall, Gillian and Manning, Nick 2000. "Gender and Social Policy: Comparing Welfare States in Central and Eastern Europe and the Former Soviet Union", *Journal of European Social Policy* 10 (3): 240–66.

Pearson, Ruth 1997. "Renegotiating the Reproductive Bargain: Gender Analysis of Economic Transition in Cuba in the 1990s", *Development and Change* 28 (4): 671–705.

1998. "The Political Economy of Social Reproduction: The Case of Cuba in the 1990s", *New Political Economy* 3 (2): 241–59.

Perrons, Diane 1998. "Flexible Working and the Reconciliation of Work and Family Life – or a New Form of Precariousness. Medium Term Community Action Programme on Equal Opportunities for Women and Men, Action Opportunities", *Final Report, Directorate General for Employment, Industrial Relations and Social Affairs*. Brussels: European Commission.

1999. "Flexible Working Patterns and Equal Opportunities in the European Union: Conflict and Compatibility?", *European Journal of Women's Studies* 6 (4): 391–418.

2000. "Living with Risk: Labour Market Transformation, Employment Policies and Social Reproduction in the UK", *Economic and Industrial Democracy* 21 (3): 283–310.

2005. "Gender Mainstreaming and Gender Equality in the New (Market) Economy: An Analysis of Contradictions", *Social Politics* 12 (3): 389–411.

Perrons, Diane, Płomień, Ania, and Kilkey, Majella 2010. "Migration and Uneven Development within an Enlarged European Union: Fathering, Gender Divisions and Male Migrant Domestic Services", *European Urban & Regional Studies* 17 (2): 197–215.

Perrons, Diane, Fagan, Colette, McDowell, Linda, Ray, Kath, and Ward, Kevin 2005. "Work, Life and Time in the New Economy", *Time & Society* 14 (1): 51–64.

Pfau-Effinger, Brigit 1994. "The Gender Contract and Part-time Paid Work by Women: A Comparative Perspective", in Duncan, Simon (ed.) *Spatial Divisions of Patriarchy in Western Europe. Environment and Planning A* (Special Issue) 26 (2): 1355–76.

1998. "Gender Cultures and the Gender Arrangement: A Theoretical Framework for Cross-National Gender Research, Innovation", *European Journal of Social Sciences* 11 (2): 147–66.

Picchio, Antonella 1992. *Social Reproduction: The Political Economy of the Labour Market.* Cambridge: Cambridge University Press.

(ed.) 2003. *Unpaid Work and the Economy: A Gender Analysis of the Standards of Living.* London: Routledge.

Pierson, Paul 1996. "The Path to European Integration: A Historical-Institutional Analysis", *Comparative Political Studies* 29 (2): 123–63.

Pillinger, Jane 2006. *Challenging Times: Innovative Ways of Organizing Working Time – The Role of Trade Unions.* Brussels: ETUC.

Piotrowski, Bartłomiej 2007. *Elastyczna Praca, czyli Jak Pogodzić Aktywność Zawodową z Obąwizkami Macierzyńskimi* [Flexible Employment, or How to Reconcile Professional Life with Motherhood]. Warszawa: Ministerstwo Pracy i Polityki Społecznej Departament ds. Kobiet, Rodziny i Przeciwdziałania Dyskryminacji.

Plantenga, Janneke and Remery, Chantal (eds.) 2010. *Flexible Working Time Arrangements and Gender Equality: A Comparative Review of 30 European Countries.* EU Expert Group on Gender and Employment Report. Luxembourg: Publications Office of the European Union.

Płomień, Ania 2006. "Women and the Labour Market in Poland: From Socialism to Capitalism," in Blossfeld, Hans-Peter and Hofmeister, Heather (eds.). *Globalization, Uncertainty and Women's Careers: An International Comparison,* 247–74. Cheltenham, UK: Edward Elgar.

2009. "Welfare State, Gender, and Reconciliation of Work and Family in Poland: Policy Developments and Practice in a New EU Member", *Social Policy & Administration* 43 (2): 136–51.

Poliwczak, Iwona 2003. "Zatrudnienie w Niepełnym Wymiarze Czasu Pracy" [Part-time Employment], *Polityka Społeczna* 7: 17–20.

Pollert, Anna 1988. "The 'Flexible Firm': Fixation or Fact", *Work, Employment and Society* 2 (3): 281–316.

2003. "Women, Work and Equal Opportunities in Post-communist Transition", *Work, Employment & Society* 17 (2): 331–57.

2005. "Gender, Transformation and Employment in Central Eastern Europe", *European Journal of Industrial Relations* 11 (2): 213–30.

Portet, Stephan 2005. "Poland: Circumventing the Law or Fully Deregulating?" in Vaughan-Whitehead, David (ed.). *Working and Employment Conditions in New EU Member States: Convergence or Diversity?*, 273–337. Geneva; Brussels: ILO; European Commission.

Racław, Mariola 2012. "Opiekunowie Nieformalni: Krótkookresowa Funkcjonalność Nieopłacanej Pracy" [Informal Carers: Short-Term Functionality of Unpaid Work], in Hryniewicz, J. (ed.). *O Sytuacji Ludzi Starszych* [The Situation of Older People in Poland], 71–81. Warszawa: Zakład Wydawnictw Statystycznych.

Racław-Markowska, Mariola 2008. "'Między Domem a Etatem': Instrumenty Polityki Rodzinnej Ułatwiające Godzenie Obowiązków Rodzinnych i Zawodowych" ['Between the Home and Job Tenure': Family Policy Instruments Assisting in the Reconciliation of Family and Professional Responsibilities], in Piątek, Krzysztof and Karwacki, Arkadiusz (eds.). *Partnerstwo, Rodzina, Równość, Praca*, 71–89. Toruń: Wydawnictwo Naukowe Uniwersytetu Mikołaja Kopernika.

Radaelli, Claudio 2001. "The Domestic Impact of European Union Public Policy: Notes on Concepts, Methods, and the Challenge of Empirical Research", *Politique Européenne* 5 (Autumn): 105–136.

Rai, Shirin M., Hoskyns, Catherine, and Thomas, Dania 2014. "Depletion. The Cost of Social Reproduction", *International Feminist Journal of Politics* 16 (1): 86-105.

Regional Prosecutions Office, Zielona Góra 2008. "Naruszenia Praw Pracowniczych w Sklepach Sieci Biedronka" [Worker's Rights Violations in the Supermarket Chain 'Biedronka']. September 19. www.zielona-gora.po.gov.pl/index.php?id=51&ida=3480.

Rewiński, Robert 2005. "Z Biedronką Osobne Procesy" [Separate Suits in the Biedronka Case], *Gazeta Wyborcza*, November 17. Kraj.

Rittich, Kerry 2002a. "Feminization and Contingency," in Conaghan, Joanne, Fischl Richard M., and Klare, Karl (eds.), *Labour Law in an Era of Globalization: Transformative Practices and Possibilities*, 117–36. Oxford: Oxford University Press.

2002b. *Recharacterizing Restructuring: Law, Distribution and Gender in Market Reform.* New York: Kluwer.

2005. "Equity or Efficiency: International Institutions and the Work/Family Nexus," in Conaghan, Joanne and Rittich, Kerry (eds.). *Labour Law, Work and Family*, 43–78. Oxford: Oxford University Press.

2006a. "Rights, Risk and Reward: Governance Norms in the International Order and the Problem of Precarious Work", in Fudge, Judy and Owens, Rosemary (eds.). *Precarious Work, Women, and the New Economy: The Challenge to Legal Norms.* Oxford: Hart.

2006b. "The Future of Law and Development: Second Generation Reforms and the Incorporation of the Social," in Trubek, David M. and Santos, Alvaro (eds.). *The New Law and Economic Development: A Critical Appraisal*, 203–52. Cambridge: Cambridge University Press.

2010a. "Families on the Edge: Governing Home and Work in a Globalized Economy", *North Carolina Law Review* 88: 1527–57.

R.M. 2001. "Funkcja Ochronna" [The Law's Protective Function], *Rzeczpospolita*, April 6. Prawo.

Rogowski, Ralf 2013. *Reflexive Labour Law in the World Society*. Cheltenham: Edgar Elgar.

Rogowski, Ralf and Deakin, Simon F. 2011. "Reflexive Labour Law, Capabilities and the Future of Social Europe," in Rogowski, Ralf, Salais, Robert, and Whiteside, Noel (eds.). *Transforming European Employment Policy: Labour Market Transitions and the Promotion of Capability*, Research Paper No. 2011/04. Cheltenham, UK: Edward Elgar; Warwick School of Law.

Rönnmar, Mia (ed.) 2008. *EU Industrial Relations v National Industrial Relations. Comparative and Interdisciplinary Perspectives*. Alphen aan den Rijn: Kluwer Law International.

Rosamond, Ben 2002. "Imagining the European Economy: 'Competitiveness' and the Social Construction of 'Europe' as an Economic Space", *New Political Economy* 7 (2): 157–77.

Roth, Silke (ed.) 2008. *Gender Politics in the Expanding European Union: Mobilization, Inclusion, Exclusion*. Oxford: Berghahn Books.

Rubery, Jill 2005. "Reflections on Gender Mainstreaming: An Example of Feminist Economics in Action?", *Feminist Economics* 11 (3): 1–26.

Rubery, Jill, Deakin, Simon, and Horrel, Sara 1994. "United Kingdom", in Bosch, Gerhard, Dawkins, Peter and Michon, François (eds.), *Times are Changing: Working Time in 14 Industrialized Countries*, 261–87. Geneva: International Institute for Labour Studies.

Rubery, Jill, Smith, Mark, and Fagan, Colette 1998. "National Working Time Regimes and Equal Opportunities", *Feminist Economics* 4 (1): 71–101.

1999. *Women's Employment in Europe: Trends and Prospects*. London: Routledge.

Rubery, Jill, Ward, Kevin, and Grimshaw, David 2006. "Time, Work and Pay: Understanding the New Relationships", in Boulin, Jean-Yves, Lallement, Michel, Messenger, Jon C., and Michon, François (eds.). *Decent Working Time: New Trends, New Issues*, 123–52. Geneva: ILO.

Rycak, Magdalena 2008a. "Prawne Uwarunkowania Elastycznego Kształtowania Czasu Pracy w Polsce: Propozycje Zmian" [Legal Determinants of Flexible Management of Working Time in Poland: Recommendations for Change], *Monitor Prawa Pracy* 5 (1): 10–17.

2008b. *Wymiar i Rozkład Czasu Pracy* [The Measure and the Schedule of Working Time]. Warszawa: Wolters Kluwer Polska.

2009. "Instytucja Opt-out: Próba Powrotu do XIX-wiecznego Postrzegania Czasu Pracy" [Institution of the Opt-out: An Attempt to Return to the 19th Century Approach to Working Time], *Monitor Prawa Pracy* 6 (1): 510–12.

Sachs, Jeffrey 1994. "Shock Therapy in Poland: Perspectives of Five Years." Lecture delivered as part of the Tanner Lectures on Human Values, the University of Utah, Salt Lake City, Utah, April 6–7.

Sadłowska, Katarzyna 2002. "Rządowy Projekt Zmian w Prawie Pracy Trafi do Semju bez Akceptacji Związkow Zawodowych" [The Government's Proposal for Changes in Labour Law Will be Considered in the Parliament without the Acceptance of Trade Unions], *Rzeczpospolita*, March 20. Kraj.

Sadowska-Snarska, Cecylia (ed.) 2008. *Kierunki Działań na Rzecz Równowagi Praca-Życie-Rodzina* [Efforts Concerning the Balancing of Work-Life-Family in Poland]. Białystok: Wydawnictwo Wyższej Szkoły Ekonomicznej.

Sanetra, Walerian 2004a. "Polskie Prawo Pracy pod Wpływem Prawa Wspólnotowego – Ogólne Uwarunkowania i Dylematy" [Polish Labour Law under the Influence of the Community Law – General Conditionalities and Dilemmas], in Sanetra, Walerian (ed.). *Europeizacja Polskiego Prawa Pracy*, 14–30. Warszawa: Scholar; Instytut Pracy i Spraw Socjalnych.

2004b. "Wprowadzenie" [Introduction], in Sanetra, Walerian (ed.). *Europeizacja Polskiego Prawa Pracy*, 1–13. Warszawa: Scholar; Instytut Pracy i Spraw Socjalnych.

Saxonberg, Steven and Szelewa, Dorota. 2007. "The Continuing Legacy of the Communist Legacy? The Development of Family Policies in Poland and the Czech Republic", *Social Politics* 14 (3): 351–79.

Schimmelfennig, Frank and Sedelmeier, Ulrich 2005a. "Conclusions: The Impact of the EU on the Accession Countries", in Schimmelfennig, Frank and Sedelmeier, Ulrich (eds.). *The Europeanization of Central and Eastern Europe*, 210–28. Ithaca, NY: Cornell University Press.

2005b. "Introduction: Conceptualizing the Europeanization of Central and Eastern Europe," in Schimmelfennig, Frank and Sedelmeier, Ulrich (eds.). *The Europeanization of Central and Eastern Europe*, 1–28. Ithaca, NY: Cornell University Press.

Schor, Juliet 1991. *The Overworked American*. New York: Basic Books.

Schulten, Thorsten 1998. "Provisions on Working Time Accounts in Collective Agreements", European Industrial Relations Observatory (EIRO), March 23.

Sciarra, Silvana, Davies, Paul, and Freedland, Mark (eds.) 2004. *Employment Policy and the Regulation of Part-time Work in the European Union: A Comparative Analysis*. Cambridge: Cambridge University Press.

Seccombe, Wally 1973. "The Housewife and Her Labour under Capitalism", *New Left Review* 83: 3–24.

Sedelmeier, Ulrich 2009. "Post-accession Compliance with EU Gender Equality Legislation in Post-Communist New Member States", in Schimmelfennig, Frank and Trauner, Florian (eds.) Post-accession Compliance in the EU's New Member States, *European Integration Online Papers*, Special Issue 13(2). Available at SSRN: www.ssrn.com/abstract=1562670.

2011. "Europeanisation in New Member and Candidate States", *Living Reviews in European Governance* 6(1). http://eprints.lse.ac.uk/38293/.

Senat Rzeczypospolitej Polskiej (Senate of the Polish Republic) 2002. *Zmiany w Kodeksie pracy jako element reformy i dostosowania polskiego prawa pracy do prawa Unii Europejskiej* [Changes in the Labour Code as an Element of Adjustment of Labour Law to the Law of the European Union. Senate of the Polish Republic]. Materials from a Conference Organized by the Social Policy and Health Committee under the Sponsorship of the Senate Marshall Longin Pastusiak, 14 May 2002. Warszawa: Dział Wydawniczy Kancelarii Senat.

Sennet, Richard 1998. *The Corrosion of Character: Personal Consequences of Work in the New Capitalism.* Warsaw: Muza.

Seweryński, Michał 1995. *Polish Labour Law and Collective Labour Relations in the Period of Transformation.* Warsaw: Ministry of Labour and Social Policy, Social Dialogue Library.

1999. *Polish Labour Law from Communism to Democracy.* Warszawa: Dom Wydawniczy ABC.

Shaw, Jo 1996. "European Union Legal Studies in Crisis? Towards a New Dynamic", *Oxford Journal of Legal Studies* 16 (2): 231–53.

2000. "Importing Gender: The Challenge of Feminism and the Analysis of the EU Legal Order", *Journal of European Public Policy* 7 (3): 406–31.

2001. "Gender and the Court of Justice", in de Búrca, Gráinne (ed.). *The European Court of Justice*, 87–142. Oxford: Oxford University Press.

Shields, Stuart 2001. "Transnational Social Forces and the Configuration of Polish Transition: Neo-Liberalism Revisited", *Irish Studies in International Affairs* 12: 21–37.

2008. "How the East Was Won: Transnational Social Forces and the Neoliberalisation of Poland's Post-Communist Transition", *Global Society* 22 (4): 445–68.

2011. "From the Washington Consensus to the Brussels Consensus: Neoliberalisation by Depoliticisation in Post-Communist Poland", *Socialism & Democracy* 25 (2): 81–103.

Siemieńska, Renata 2011. "Kontrakt Płci: Między Sferą Prywatną i Publiczną;" [The Gender Contract: Between the Public and the Private Spheres], in Słana, Krystyna, Struzik, Justyna, and Wojniacka, Katarzyna (eds.). *Gender w Społeczeństwie Polskim*, 196–224. Kraków: Nomos.

Smith, Mark 2009. Analysis Note: Gender Equality and Recession. Commissioned by DG Employment, Social Affairs, and Equal Opportunities of the European Commission. www.epp-women.org/media/documents/2009/Equality-crisis-final[1]_copy_1.pdf.

Smith, Mark and Villa, Paola. 2010. "The Ever-declining Role of Gender Equality in the European Employment Strategy", *Industrial Relations Journal* 41 (6): 526–43.

Snyder, Francis 1987. "New Directions in European Community Law", *Journal of Law & Society* 14 (1): 167–82.

Sochańska-Kawiecka, M., Kołakowska-Seroczyńska, Z., and Morysińska, A. 2009, *Badanie I lościowe i Jakościowe Pracodawców i Pracobiorców w Ramach Projektu Systemowego: Godzenie Ról Rodzinnych i Zawodowych Kobiet i Mężczyzn*, Białystok: PAG Uniconsult, Laboratorium Badań Społecznych.

Sokołowska, Magdalena 1978. "Poland", in Kamerman, Sheila B. and Khan, Alfred. J. (eds.). *Family Policy: Government and Families in Fourteen Countries*, 239–69. New York: Columbia University Press.

Spike Peterson, V. 2003a. "Analytical Advances to Address New Dynamics", in Tétreault, MA et al. (eds.). *Rethinking Global Political Economy: Emerging Issues, Unfolding Odysseys*, 23–45. London: Routledge.

2003b. *A Critical Rewriting of Global Political Economy: Integrating Reproductive, Productive and Virtual Economies*. London: Routledge.

Standing, Guy 1986. "Meshing Labour Flexibility with Security: An Answer to British Unemployment?", *International Labour Review* 125 (1): 87–106.

2009. *Work after Globalization*. Cheltenham, UK: Edward Elgar.

Stelina, Jakub 2006. "Working Time Regulation in Poland – Recent Trends", in Keune, Maarten and Galgóczi, Béla (eds.). *Collective Bargaining on Working Time: Recent European Experiences*. Brussels: European Trade Union Institute for Research, Education and Health and Society.

Stenning, Alison, Smith, Adrian, Rochovská, Alena, and Świątek, Dariusz 2010. *Domesticating Neo-Liberalism: Spaces of Economic Practice and Social Reproduction in Post-Socialist Cities*. Oxford: Wiley-Blackwell.

Stewart, Ann 2011. *Gender, Law and Justice in a Global Market*. Cambridge: Cambridge University Press.

Stratigaki, Maria 2004. "The Cooptation of Gender Concepts in EU Policies: The Case of 'Reconciliation of Work and Family'", *Social Politics: International Studies in Gender, State & Society* 11 (1): 30–56.

Strzemińska, Helena 1964. *Wyniki Badania Budżetu Czasu Kobiet Pracujących i Niktóre Problemy Ich Pracy Zawodowej* [Results of the Employed Women's Time-use Research and Certain Problems of Women's Professional Work]. Warszawa: Instytut Pracy.

1970. *Praca Zawodowa Kobiet i Ich Budżet Czasu* [Women's Professional Work and their Time-use]. Warszawa: Państwowe Wydawnictwo Ekonomiczne.

1988. *Czas Pracy i Czas Wolny w Polityce Społecznej* [Work Time and Leisure Time in Social Policy]. Warszawa: Państwowe Wydawnictwo Ekonomiczne.

2002. *Czas Pracy w Przedsiębiorstwie: Wyniki Badań nad Rozkładami Czasu Pracy i Zdrowiem Pracowników* [Working Time in a Firm: Results from the Research on Working-time Schedules and the Health of Employees]. Warszawa: Instytut Pracy i Spraw Socjalnych.

2008a. *Working Time and Its Organization in New Member States of the EU: Economic, Legal and Social Aspects*. Warsaw: Instytut Pracy i Spraw Socjalnych.

2008b. *Czas Pracy w Nowych Krajach Członkowskich Unii Europejskiej: Aspekty Ekonomiczne, Prawne i Społeczne* [Working Time in New Member States of the EU: Economic, Legal and Social Aspects]. Warszawa: Instytut Pracy i Spraw Socjalnych.

Strzemińska, Helena and Sobótka, Elżbieta 1984. *Polityka w Zakresie Czasu Pracy* [Working-time Policy]. Warszawa: Instytut Pracy i Spraw Socjalnych.

Supiot, Alain 1999. "The Transformation of Work and the Future of Labour Law in Europe: A Multidisciplinary Perspective", *International Labour Review* 138 (1): 31–46.

(ed.) 2001. *Beyond Employment: Changes in Work and the Future of Labour Law in Europe.* Oxford: Oxford University Press.

Syrpis, Phil and Novitz, Tonia. 2015. "The EU Internal Market and Domestic Labour Law: Looking Beyond Autonomy," in Bogg, Alan, Costello, Cathryn, Davies, Anne, and Prassl, Jeremias (eds.). *The Autonomy of Labour Law*, 291–308. Oxford: Hart.

Szczerbiak, Alex 2005. "'Social Poland' Defeats 'Liberal Poland'? The September-October 2005 Polish Parliamentary and Presidential Elections", *Journal of Communist Studies & Transition Politics* 23 (2): 203–32.

2007. "The Birth of a Bipolar Party System or a Referendum on a Polarizing Government? The October 2007 Polish Parliamentary Election", *Journal of Communist Studies & Transition Politics* 24 (3): 415–43.

2012. *Poland within the European Union: New Awkward Partner or New Heart of Europe?* London: Routledge Taylor; Francis Group.

Szelewa, Dorota and Polakowski, Michał P. 2008. "Who Cares? Changing Patterns of Childcare in Central and Eastern Europe", *Journal of European Social Policy* 18 (2): 115–31.

Szkorzyński, Z. 1965. *Między Pracą a Wypoczynkiem* [Between Work and Rest]. Warsaw: Ossolineum.

Sztanderska, Urszula 2006. *Działalność Organizacji Pozarządowych Świadczących Usługi na Rynku Pracy Skierowane do Kobiet* [Activities of NGOs Providing Labour Market Services Targeting Women]. Warszawa: Polsko-Amerykańska Fundacja Wolności; Fundacja Inicjatyw Społeczno-Ekonomicznych.

Sztanderska, Urszula and Grotowska, Gabriela 2009. "Rynek Pracy Kobiet w Polsce w latach 1992–2007" [Women's Labour Market in Poland from 1992–2009], in Kotowska, Irena (ed.). *Strukturalne i Kulturowe Uwarunkowania Aktywności Zawodowej Kobiet w Polsce* [Structural and Cultural Determinants of Women's Professional Activation in Poland], 57–98. Warszawa: Scholar.

Szubert, Wacław 1976. *Zarys Prawa Pracy* [An Outline of Labour Law]. Warszawa: PWN.

Szyszczak, Eryka 2006. "Experimental Governance: The Open Method of Coordination", *European Law Journal* 12 (4): 486–502.

Tang, Ning and Cousins, Christine 2005. "Working Time, Gender and Family: An East-West European Comparison", *Gender, Work & Organization* 12 (6): 527–50.

Tarkowska, Elżbieta 2002. "Intra-household Gender Inequality: Hidden Dimensions of Poverty among Polish Women", *Communist & Post-Communist Studies* 35 (4): 411–32.

2011. "Ubóstwo Dzieci w Polsce" [Child Poverty in Poland], in Szafenberg, Ryszard (ed.). *Ubóstwo i Wykluczenie Społeczne w Polsce: Raport Krajowy Polskiej Koalicji Social Watch i Polskiego Komitetu European Anti-Poverty Network*, 57–62. Warszawa: Social Watch; Kampania Przeciw Homofobii.

Taylor, Rebecca F. 2004. "Extending Conceptual Boundaries: Work, Voluntary Work and Employment", *Work, Employment & Society* 18 (1): 29–49.

Tergeist, Peter 1995. "Introduction", in *Flexible Working Time: Collective Bargaining and Government Intervention*, 9–16. Paris: Organization for Economic Cooperation and Development.

Teubner, Günter 1983. "Substantive and Reflexive Elements in Modern Law", *Law & Society Review* 17: 239–85.

Thompson, Edward P. 2001. "Time, Work Discipline and Industrial Capitalism", *Past & Present* 38: 59–97. First published 1967.

Titkow, Anna 1995. "Kobiety Pod Presją? Proces Kształtowania się Tożsamości" [Women under Pressure? The Process of Identity Formation], in Titkow, Anna and Domański, Henryk (eds.). *Co to Znaczy Być Kobietą w Polsce?*, 9–39. Warszawa: Insytut Polityki Społecznej PAN.

Toshkov, Dimiter 2008. "Embracing European Law: Compliance with EU Directives in Central and Eastern Europe", *European Union Politics* 9 (3): 379–402.

Trieb, Oliver 2008. "Implementing and Complying with EU Governance Outputs", *Living Reviews in European Governance* 3 (5). http://europeangovernance-livingreviews.org/Articles/lreg-2008-5/.

Trieb, Oliver and Falkner, Gerda 2008. "Conclusion: The State of EU Social Compliance in Central and Eastern European Practices", in Falkner, Gerda, Treib, Oliver, and Holzleithner, Elisabeth (eds.). *Compliance in the Enlarged European Union: Living Rights or Dead Letters?*, 157–82. Aldershot: Ashgate.

Trubek, David M. and Trubek, L.G. 2005. "Hard and Soft Law in the Construction of Social Europe: The Role of the Open Method of Co-ordination", *European Law Journal* 11 (3): 343–64.

True, Jacqui 2003. *Gender, Globalization and Postsocialism: The Czech Republic After Communism*. New York: Columbia University Press.

True, Jacqui and Mintrom, Michael 2001. "Transnational Networks and Policy Diffusion: The Case of Gender Mainstreaming", *International Studies Quarterly* 45 (1): 27–57.

Vaughan-Whitehead, Daniel 2003. *EU Enlargement versus Social Europe? The Uncertain Future of the European Social Model*. Cheltenham, UK: Edward Elgar.

Velluti, Samantha 2010. *New Governance and the European Employment Strategy*. New York: Routledge.

2014. "Gender Regimes and Gender Equality Measures in Central Eastern European Countries post-Accession: The Case of Hungary and Poland", *Journal of Comparative and International Social Policy* 30 (1): 79–91.

Velluti, Samantha and Beveridge, Fiona 2008. *Gender and the Open Method of Coordination: Perspectives on Law, Governance and Equality in the EU*. Dartmouth: Ashgate.

Viebrock, Elke and Clasen, Jochen 2009. *Flexibility – A State-of-the-Art Review. Working Papers on the Reconciliation of Work and Welfare in Europe*. Edinburgh: RECWOWE Publication, Dissemination and Dialogue Centre.

Vielle, Pascal and Walthery, Pierre 2003. *Flexibility and Social Protection*. Dublin: European Foundation for the Improvement of the Living and Working Conditions.

Von Prondzynski, Ferdinand 1994. "Council Directive 93/104 EC Concerning Certain Aspects of the Organization of Working Time", *Industrial Law Journal* 23 (1): 92–95.

Vosko, Leah 2007. "Precarious Part-Time Work in Australia and in Transnational Labour Regulation: The Gendered Limits of SER-centrism", *Labour & Industry* 17 (3): 45–70.

2010. *Managing the Margins: Gender, Citizenship, and the International Regulation of Precarious Employment*. Oxford: Oxford University Press.

Walby, Sylvia 2003. Gender Mainstreaming: Productive Tensions in Theory and Practice. Contribution to ESRC Gender Mainstreaming Seminars, 2003–2004.

2004. "The European Union and Gender Equality: Emergent Varieties of Gender Regime", *Social Politics* 11 (1): 4–29.

2009. Gender and the Financial Crisis. Paper for UNESCO Project on Gender and the Financial Crisis.

Ward, Ian 1996. "Beyond Sex Equality: The Limits of Sex Equality in the New Europe", in Hervey, Tamara and O'Keefe, David (eds.). *Sex Equality Law in the European Union*, 369–82. Chichester: John Wiley & Sons.

Warren, Tracy 2000. "Diverse Breadwinner Models: A Couple-Based Analysis of Gendered Working Time in Britain and Denmark", *Journal of European Social Policy* 10 (4): 349–71.

Weeks, Kathi 2011. *The Problem with Work: Feminism, Marxism, Antiwork Politics, and Postwork Imaginaries*. Durham and London: Duke University Press.

Wierzbińska, Halina 1978. "Labour Law in Relation to Working Women in Poland", *Bulletin of Comparative Labour Relations: Women & Labour* 9: 313.

Woehl, Stephanie 2008. "Global Governance as Neo-liberal Governmentality: Gender Mainstreaming in the European Employment Strategy", in Rai, Shirin M. and Waylen, Georgina (eds.). *Global Governance: Feminist Perspectives*, 64–83. Basingstoke: Palgrave Macmillan.

Wolkowitz, Carol 2002. "The Social Relations of Body Work", *Work, Employment and Society* 16 (3): 497–510.

World Bank 2001. *Engendering Development: Through Gender Equality in Rights, Resources and Voice.* Washington: The International Bank for Reconstruction and Development/the World Bank. New York: Oxford University Press.

2004. *Polska: Płeć a Możliwości Ekonomiczne w Polsce – Czy Kobiety Straciły na Transformacji* [Gender and Economic Opportunities in Poland: Has Transition Left Women Behind?]. Report No. 29205-POL. Warszawa: BBŚ.

Wóycicka, Irena 2009. "Model opieki w Polsce" [Model of Care in Poland], in Kotowska, Irena (ed.). *Strukturalne i Kulturowe Uwarunkowania Aktywności Zawodowej Kobiet w Polsce* [Structural and Cultural Determinants of Women's Professional Activation in Poland], 99–118. Warszawa: Scholar.

Zajicek, Anna M. and Calasanti, Toni M. 1995. "The Impact of Socioeconomic Restructuring on Polish Women", in Lobodzinska, Barbara (ed.). *Family, Women and Employment in Central-Eastern Europe*, 179–91. Westport, CT: Greenwood.

Zeniewski, Peter 2011. "Neoliberalism, Exogenous Elites and the Transformation of Solidarity", *Europe-Asia Studies* 63 (6): 977–94.

Zieliński, Tadeusz 1986. *Prawo Pracy: Zarys systemu, Cześć II – Prawo Stosunku Pracy* [Labour Law: Outline of a System, Part II – Law of the Employment Relationship]. Warszawa: Państwowe Wydawnictwo Naukowe.

1997. "Nowy Ład Pracy: Rzeczywistość i Wizja Przyszłości" [The New System of Work: The Reality and the Vision of the Future], in Matey, Maria (ed.). *Nowy Ład Pracy w Polsce i w Europie* [New System of Work in Poland and Europe], 9–50. Warszawa: Scholar.

Statistics and Reports

Centrum Badania Opinii Społecznej (CBOS). 2002. *Opinie o Związkach Zawodowych: Komunikat z Badań* [Opinions on the Labour Unions: Research Report]. No. 2274. 03 September. Warszawa: CBOS.

2004. *Polacy o Swoim Zatrudnieniu: Komunikat z Badań* [Poles on Their Employment: Research Report]. No. 3124. 29 April. Warszawa: CBOS.

2006. *Opinie o Pracy Zawodowej Kobiet: Komunikat z Badań* [Opinions on Women's Employment: Research Report]. No. 3642. 12 December. Warszawa: CBOS.

2008. *Sposoby Poprawy Sytuacji Materialnej: Komunikat z Badań "Warunki Życiowe Społeczeństwa Polskiego: Problemy i Strategie"* [Ways of Improving One's Material Situation: Research Report from the Study "Living Conditions in Poland: Problems and Strategies"]. No. 3888. 3 March. Warszawa.

Eurostat. 2005. *Labour Force Survey: Ad hoc Module on Reconciliation between Work and Family Life.* http://ec.europa.eu/eurostat/.

2007. *Europe in Figures: Eurostat Yearbook 2006–2007.* Luxembourg: Office for Official Publications of the European Communities.

2008. "Enterprises by Size Class: Overview of SMEs in the EU." Eurostat: Statistics in Focus 31. http://epp.eurostat.ec.europa.eu/cache/ITY_OFFPUB/KS-SF-08-031/EN/KS-SF-08-031-EN.PDF/.

2010. *Europe in Figures: Eurostat Yearbook 2010.* Luxembourg: Office for Official Publications of the European Communities.

Główny Urząd Statystyczny (GUS) [Central Statistical Office]. 2005. *Badanie Aktywności Ekonomicznej Ludności w Latach 1992–2004* [Labour Force Survey in Poland in the Years 1992–2004]. Warszawa: GUS.

2006. *Rocznik Statystyczny Rzeczypospolitej Polski* [Statistical Yearbook of the Republic of Poland]. Warszawa: GUS.

2007a. *Rocznik Statystyczny Rzeczypospolitej Polski* [Statistical Yearbook of the Republic of Poland]. Warszawa: GUS.

2007b. *Kobiety w Polsce* [Women in Poland]. Warszawa: GUS.

Państwowa Inspekcja Pracy (PIP) [National Workplace Inspection]. 2004. *Sprawozdania Głównego Inspektora Pracy z Działalności Państwowej Inspekcji Pracy w 2003 r.* [Report of the Central Work Inspector on the Activities of the National Workplace Inspection in 2003]. Warszawa.

2005. *Przestrzeganie Przepisów Prawa Pracy w Supermarketach, Hipermarketach i Sklepach Dyskontowych w Latach 1999–2005* [Observance of Labour Laws in Supermarkets, Hypermarkets and Discount Shops in the Years 1999–2005]. Warszawa.

2006. *Sprawozdania Głównego Inspektora Pracy z Działalności Państwowej Inspekcji Pracy w 2005 r.* [Report of the Central Work Inspector on the Activities of the National Workplace Inspection in 2005]. Warszawa.

2007. *Przestrzeganie Przepisów Prawa Pracy w tym Bezpieczeństwa i Higieny Pracy w Placówkach Handlowych* [Observance of Labour Laws, Including Health and Safety Regulations in Commercial Outposts]. Warszawa.

2008. *Sprawozdanie Głównego Inspektora Pracy z Działalności Państwowej Inspekcji Pracy w 2007 roku* [Report of the Central Work Inspector on the Activities of the National Workplace Inspection in 2007]. Warszawa.

2009. *Sprawozdanie Głównego Inspektora Pracy z Działalności Państwowej Inspekcji Pracy w 2008 roku* [Report of the Central Work Inspector on the Activities of the National Workplace Inspection in 2008]. Warszawa.

Other

Coalition of Persons Harmed by the Supermarket Chains "Biedronka" www.stowarzyszenie-biedronka.pl/.

INDEX

Books in the series

EU Enlargement and the Constitutions of Central and Eastern Europe
Anneli Albi

The European Civil Code: The Way Forward
Hugh Collins

The Limits of Legal Reasoning and the European Court of Justice
Gerard Conway

New Governance and the Transformation of European Law: Coordinating EU Social Law and Policy
Mark Dawson

Social Rights and Market Freedom in the European Constitution: A Labour Law Perspective
Stefano Giubboni

The European Convention on Human Rights: Achievements, Problems and Prospects
Steven Greer

European Broadcasting Law and Policy
Jackie Harrison and Lorna Woods

Ethical Dimensions of the Foreign Policy of the European Union: A Legal Appraisal
Urfan Khaliq

Services Liberalization in the EU and the WTO
Marcus Klamert

The Evolving European Union: Migration Law and Policy
Dora Kostakopoulou

Implementing EU Pollution Control: Law and Integration
Bettina Lange

EU Renewable Electricity Law and Policy: From National Targets to a Common Market
Tim Maxian Rusche

Referendums and the European Union: A Comparative Enquiry
Fernando Mendez, Mario Mendez, Vasiliki Triga

The Constitution for Europe: A Legal Analysis
Jean-Claude Piris

The Lisbon Treaty: A Legal and Political Analysis
Jean-Claude Piris

State and Market in European Union Law
Wolf Sauter and Harm Schepel

The Transformation of Citizenship in the European Union: Electoral Rights and the Restructuring of Political Space
Jo Shaw

The European Union's Fight Against Corruption: The Evolving Policy Towards Member States and Candidate Countries
Patrycja Szarek-Mason

International Trade Disputes and EU Liability
Anne Thies

European Constitution
Kaarlo Tuori

The Eurozone Crisis
Kaarlo Tuori and Klaus Tuori

Brokering Europe
Antoine Vauchez

The Allocation of Regulatory Competence in the EU Emissions Trading Scheme
Jospehine Van Zeben

The Ethos of Europe: Values, Law and Justice in the EU
Andrew Williams

Gendering European Working Time Regimes: The Working Time Directive and the Case of Poland
Ania Zbyszewska

Printed in the United States
By Bookmasters